ENG:

TELEVISION NEWS AND THE NEW TECHNOLOGY

SECOND EDITION

RICHARD D. YOAKAM
INDIANA UNIVERSITY

CHARLES F. CREMER
WEST VIRGINIA UNIVERSITY

RANDOM HOUSE  *NEW YORK*

For those peerless unit managers:
Mary Bob, and Frances

Second Edition
987654321
Copyright © 1985, 1989 by Random House, Inc.

All rights reserved under International and Pan-American Copyright Conventions. No part of this book may be reproduced in any form or by any means, electronic or mechanical, including photocopying, without permission in writing from the publisher. All inquiries should be addressed to Random House, Inc., 201 East 50th Street, New York, N.Y. 10022. Published in the United States by Random House, Inc., and simultaneously in Canada by Random House of Canada Limited, Toronto.

Library of Congress Cataloging in Publication Data

Yoakam, Richard D.
  ENG, television news and the new technology / Richard D. Yoakam,
Charles F. Cremer.—2nd ed.
        p.   cm.
  Bibliography: p.
  Includes index.
  ISBN 0-394-37102-X
  1. Electronic news gathering.   I. Cremer, Charles F.   II. Title.
PN4784.E53Y6   1989
070.1'9—dc19
                                                    88-24024
                                                        CIP

Cover and Text Design: Lisa Polenberg

Manufactured in the United States of America

A STATEMENT OF ENDORSEMENT BY RTNDA PRESIDENT ERNIE SCHULTZ

Speaking for the Radio-Television News Directors Association in this space in the first edition of ENG, I made reference to the value of good relationships between professional broadcasters and communicators, and professors and their students.

The RTNDA continues to value that goal and to work to improve those relationships.

The program of scholarships and fellowships administered by our foundation, RTNDF, has been increasing. We maintain our participation in the work of the Accrediting Council for Education in Journalism and Mass Communications (ACEJMC) and our status as a professional member of the Association for Education in Journalism and Mass Communications (AEJMC). Our program of student affiliates has been established and is expanding. Broadcaster campus visitations by way of a broadcaster-in-residence program is in motion and has our support. We value our roster of professor and student members, a roster that continues its steady growth.

Our endorsement of this second edition of ENG provides a most appropriate occasion to reaffirm our belief that where professional communicators and educators work cooperatively and in a spirit of mutual concern and respect, society will be the ultimate beneficiary.

FOREWORD

Tom Pettit*

Technology came in with the first wire-recorders in the late 1940s. That is when the broadcaster's perception and ability to transmit reality were first distorted.

As recording technology improved, it became increasingly difficult to distinguish live from tape. There had been a time when radio networks refused to carry anything but live programs. In the 1940s, Bing Crosby finally broke the barrier into a recorded presentation.

But when recorded sound sounded live, the corrosion of reality began. Live was live. It was real time. What you heard was occurring as you heard it on radio. Or saw it on television.

Today, technology permits producers to speed up or slow down actual events, actual voices. This is alteration of reality akin to forging a check.

But in the beginning, when it became possible to edit paper audio tape, we were freed of the old restrictions—with only a vague understanding of the responsibility for honest handling of the editing process. With tape we could do all kinds of tricks, and now with highly sophisticated editing of videotape, we can reshape reality with great ease.

To be sure, the days of 16mm film produced some geniuses who could rearrange the world. But film had scratches and dirt. Film could not be endlessly reedited and still look live. Film never did look real.

But back to radio for the pioneers in manipulation of fact. When it became possible to put phone calls on the air, we knew we had something big. It was less that someone had something to say than that we had the technology to have them say it to our listening audience.

You could interview the mayor of the city, or the police chief, or a child of ten—all without leaving the newsroom. Projected into the future, it was the technological equivalent of a network anchorperson interviewing a Soviet official in Moscow, all by long distance, and mainly for no solid reason.

Television has matured from the grainy kinescope recording to flawless tape of a frequently flawed subject. We used to shoot pictures right off the TV tube. Now we shoot pictures into the satellites, up link and down, to a TV station and then into your home. Television networks spend more on satellites, more on editing machines, camera machines, recording machines and operators than on reporters. Facts are less important than pictures.

Television has become the ultimate Polaroid™ Land Camera—(which at the be-

*Authors' Note: Tom Pettit is a National Correspondent for NBC News. His career as one of America's most distinguished political reporters has brought him virtually every major award including three Emmys, a Peabody, a DuPont, and the George Polk Memorial Award.

ginning was a prime source of pictures for TV); we take sophisticated cameras, editing machines, and operators, and freeze frames of action-packed stuff into single still pictures that can be used over and over and over.

The use of file pictures is akin to a small station in Iowa in the 1950s that had access to the carefully indexed photographs from somebody's lifelong collection of *Life* magazine. In that newsroom, with that system, whatever happened, we had a picture of it. That is, we had a picture something like it.

Do viewers have a right to know what they are looking at?

That is one question.

Another is: Do they have a right to have meaning with the pictures?

I am not against pictures, by Picasso or by TK-76 or Ikegami. There are certain single moments of truth that only television can transmit to so many people so effectively.

But: Are we to carry only the pictures we can obtain and transmit so easily if not carelessly? Well, there is the day's news to cover. But the war we never saw, the Falklands (or Malvinas) War eluded our satellites and groundstations.

Speed is not the only factor in reality. Speed keeps out the hard-to-get stuff. It is like a chromakey that keeps out the colors associated with history or art. Technology works fast. Very fast. I am tired of technology. I want a machine to write, to think, to speak, to feel, to express outrage. I want a machine that cries, instead of making me cry.

The truth is machines have advanced beyond the people.

PREFACE

Shortly after the publication of the first edition of *ENG* in 1985, the book was reviewed by a professional television news producer, Rob Puglisi, who concluded his critique with the following observation:

> Just as these books were rolling off the presses, mobile satellite uplink trucks were rolling into station parking lots across the country. They bring with them new technology, new potential and new material for the authors.
>
> And now we know why God created second editions.

Puglisi's observation about the impact of technical change was right on the mark, especially considering the fact that satellite news gathering (SNG) is a good example of how change in electronic news technology immediately begins to affect TV news profoundly. The changes have an impact not only on how, when, where, and why television news functions, but even on who the players are.

Like the first edition, this second edition of *ENG* results from a need to understand and get control of a technological revolution that has caused far-reaching changes in television journalism. Electronic news gathering—using sophisticated electronic equipment to record, report, write, edit, package, and produce television news stories and news programs—is a concept as well as a method. Journalists who use ENG technology must develop policies, procedures, applications, innovations, and controls to ensure that stories and programs produced with the technology are journalistically sound and communicate their messages clearly.

Assumptions that served as a theoretical base for the first edition are no less important for the second edition of this television writing, reporting, and production text as well.

1. Broadcast journalists must know the limits of the technology so that they can understand how to use the technology to communicate as clearly as possible.
2. The content of the message is always more important than the technology used to create it.

Therefore, from the very beginning we have said the technology and the journalism are intimately interconnected. Just as film technology had an impact on storytelling in the days when film was the visual medium, so too does electronic technology affect the way TV news tells stories today.

And so too does the way television journalists work affect the end product—the newscast, the live special, live spot news. Therefore, we insist that television news ''writing'' and ''reporting'' are more than just digging out facts and putting words on paper. They are an amalgamation of motion pictures, words, graphics, and on-air reporting, visually structured to make the most of the twin channels of sight and sound and the linear nature of the delivery of the message.

That is why the reader will find not only that this book discusses what ENG technology is, but that the book's main thrust is to show how to use ENG to report in the field, how to shoot and edit videotape, how to create text that works with the visuals, and how to produce both scheduled and live television news using the tools of the technology. We also deal with the impact of the technology on: legal and ethical issues that relate specifically to television news; newsroom management and operations; and careers. To conclude, we take a look into the future for the young professional and preprofessional electronic journalist.

PLAN OF THE BOOK

In Chapter 1 we examine the immediate and lasting effects of ENG on television news and the people who create it.

Chapter 2 is devoted entirely to explaining the technology and equipment in clear, nontechnical language. Here and throughout the book, our goal is to provide the broadcast journalism student and professional with what they need to know about the *characteristics* of typical ENG equipment, its strengths and weaknesses, and how to use this equipment to produce electronic journalism.

In Chapter 3 we concentrate on how television news is communicated to the audience, the structural elements of that communication, and how that structure can be used to make the content of the news clearer, more interesting, and more understandable to the audience.

Chapter 4 takes the student through a step-by-step process for shooting videotape in the field.

Chapter 5 follows logically with editing the visual story.

Chapter 6 is devoted solely to reporting, and Chapter 7 solely to writing—with many examples in both chapters ranging from the simple standup to the edited package with graphic enhancements.

Chapter 8 takes the student into the workings of the TV newsroom and the world of the producer, with extensive examples explaining how newscasts and news programs of all kinds are put together and presented on the air.

Chapter 9 discusses at length and with unique, real-world examples, the techniques, problems, strengths, and weaknesses of the most exciting and demanding capability of ENG technology—live news reporting.

Chapter 10, contributed by Dwight Teeter and David Anderson, deals with the legal pitfalls and implications of ENG/SNG.

And for those who aspire to a career in television news, we have looked into the future in Chapter 11 to see the implications of the technology for newsroom organization, news management, and news policy.

Finally, to provide unique views of this journalistic and technological mix, we have called on four of the nation's top professionals to update their splendid essays, which look at the ethical, organizational, and operational problems that came with the technology and how to cope with them. Their essays follow Chapters 1, 4, 6, and 9.

FEATURES OF THE SECOND EDITION

In this second edition of *ENG* we and our guest essayists have created, edited, and revised text to take account of even newer technology such as satellite news gathering (SNG), including changes in the structure of television news that have rippled outward as a result of these technical advances. For instance: We have selected fresh examples and minute-by-minute chronologies of the coverage of major news events in which newer technical capabilities were crucial to the techniques used to gather the story, to distribute the coverage, and to broadcast the results. John Premack has even provided a "survival kit" for photographers and reporters using SNG.

We have freshened *ENG* in other ways as well. For one thing, there are always places where one might have done something differently, and this revision has given us a chance to make changes. For another, we have received reactions from readers, students, colleagues, and professionals: constructive criticisms and valuable reader feedback, suggestions that we have found most helpful and have put to good use. Some of the text has been rearranged. For example, material covering on-camera delivery was moved into the reporting chapter, where it fits more logically with other field reporting elements.

The chapters on reporting and writing have been completely rewritten and expanded significantly to include more and better examples of stronger and weaker techniques. The section on interviewing is also greatly enlarged and now includes commentary and examples showing the crucial role that listening plays in the craft of reporting and interviewing.

The law chapter has been revised to fold in legal developments that have occurred since the publication of the first edition, including very recent changes in the FCC's Fairness Doctrine.

The chapter on future developments has also been expanded to include an extensive review of the basics and the latest on mobile satellite news gathering—something that didn't even exist when we started the original manuscript.

What we have not altered from the first edition to the second is our basic purpose in creating this book, the basic plan of the material, or the basic philosophy that energizes the commentary.

ACKNOWLEDGMENTS

As was the case in the preparation of the first edition, in getting this revised manuscript together we have had wonderful help from TV news directors, technology managers, technicians, and the reporters, editors, desk managers, and legal experts who deal with ENG/SNG every day.

Another round of cheers for our guest essayists: Tom Wolzien, Vice President for News Production and Program Development at NBC News; Larry Hatteberg, Executive News Director (and now anchor) at KAKE-TV, Wichita, Kansas, former President of NPPA and twice NPPA News Cameraman of the Year; veteran staff reporter Lynn Cullen, WTAE-TV, Pittsburgh; and John Premack, Chief Photographer, WCVB-TV, Boston. Applause, as well, for Dwight Teeter and David Anderson, the authors of the law chapter.

Many thanks to Bob Campbell, WTHR, Lee Giles, WISH-TV, and Steve Hinkle, WRTV-TV, all in Indianapolis—all of whom responded with great patience to showers of phone calls day and night.

Terry Oprea of WDIV-TV, Detroit opened his files and planning books to show how the station's six months of planning for the pope's visit was carried out. David Howell at KTSP-TV Phoenix was equally helpful regarding that station's extensive papal coverage.

Regarding SNG and newsroom computerization, many thanks to John Spain and Skip Haley at WBRZ-TV, Baton Rouge; Marty Haag and John Miller at WFAA-TV, Dallas; Stephen Smith and Bob Crawford at WXIA-TV, Atlanta; Ed Turner and Earl Casey at CNN, Atlanta; Mel Martin and Mike Hurt at WJXT-TV, Jacksonville; and Spencer Kinard and Greg James at KSL, Mike Youngren and Tom Mitchell at KUTV, and John Edwards and Bob Sullivan at KTVX-TV—all in Salt Lake City, fighting the battle to cover the largest ADI in the nation.

Skip Hapner and Dick Bieser of WHIO-TV, Dayton, were most gracious with time and facilities to permit the preparation of the diary of that station's award-winning coverage of "The Cloud."

We have been cheered by the enthusiasm of broadcast and journalism educators, who have adopted this book as their television news text in colleges and universities everywhere and have made excellent suggestions for this revision.

Thanks to the reviewers, bless them: Doug Allaire, University of Iowa; Tony Atwater, Michigan State University; Mark J. Banks, Marquette University; Larry Burris, Middle Tennessee State University; Barthy Byrd, University of Texas at El Paso; Milan D. Meeske, University of Central Florida; Adrienne Rivers-Waribagha, University of Kansas; and John P. Walsh, Colorado State University.

Al Anderson of the University of Texas at Austin, and James Hoyt, University of Wisconsin at Madison, both of whom were mentioned in the first edition preface, have stayed with us to review this edition. And another bow to Caroline Beebe, whose enhanced and redrawn computer-created illustrations look better than ever.

Dan Drew of the Indiana University School of Journalism was most helpful in suggesting revisions for the reporting and writing chapters. Thanks too to G. Nick Smith, production manager of West Virginia University's office of radio and television services for his careful and thorough review of the glossary of acronyms and terms.

At Random House, Roth Wilkofsky reacted with positive enthusiasm at the idea of bringing out a revision so quickly, and Brian Henry nursed us along through the labors of throwing it out, keeping it in, and making sure it is new. Good help too from Barbara Gerr and Jeannine Ciliotta.

Lastly, we want to make special mention of a category of help that was completely new to us in our work as authors, and to give special thanks to a group of professionals without whom we simply would not have made it through the labyrinthine paths of computer networking. We are referring to the user-service consultants at the Indiana University Bloomington Academic Computer Services and at the West Virginia University Computing Services. We are deeply in debt to Don Baker at the IU School of Journalism and someone known only as INFOCTR:GOLD at

IUBACS, and at West Virginia University to Michael Cremer and Cris Fuhrman. Without them we never would have gotten an IBM/XT at Yoakam's home in Bloomington, Indiana, to communicate over the phone with an Apple Macintosh-512 at Cremer's domicile in Morgantown, West Virginia. With the help of mysterious forces called 3Generic.PRN, Kermit, and Bitnet and the two universities' giant academic computer facilities, they talked, and talked, and talked. There were lots of "it never showed up here" messages in the beginning, and we may have been using an elephant to step on a flea, but the system worked through thunderstorms, power outages, and author ineptitude . . . and it sure beat the U.S. mail or any of the overnight services.

We are eternally grateful that this technological application came along just in time for the second edition of *ENG*. For us it was a technological advance not even the prescient Mr. Puglisi anticipated.

CONTENTS

FIGURE 1-4. A cam-corder, a one-half-inch videotape recorder that will hold a cassette capable of recording up to twenty minutes, is built right into the camera body. This arrangement has become very popular because it eliminates the separate videotape recorder altogether. *(Courtesy of Sony Corporation of America.)*

ing functions can be performed by the transfer of selected scenes and sounds from one tape to another merely by pushing a few buttons. In the simplest technique, selected scenes from the raw tape made in the field are transferred to another tape with no pictures on it, one at a time.

More sophisticated equipment allows for the recording of a time code—a visual number that appears in each frame of picture—during the original shooting or later. This code can be used with editing equipment which has a computer memory to program edits. The operator types the beginning and ending time codes for a series of scenes into the editing controller. It then searches out those "edit points" and makes a series of edits to assemble a whole story, or even a whole program. Very advanced systems can take pictures, sound, and electronic effects from a wide array of sources and put them all onto one finished videotape in a very short period of time.

Beyond these central units there is the fourth dimension of ENG—that whole range of mobile equipment, microwave sending and receiving units, satellite dishes, control room digital switching consoles, and electronic special effects that television journalists use to get their raw material and process it to put it on the air. Looking into the future only conjures up images of more machines, more technology, and more opportunities and challenges.

FROM ISOLATION TO INVOLVEMENT

It is almost impossible to overemphasize the profound effect ENG and SNG have had on television news. These new electronic reporting systems changed the way television stations organized themselves, the role of the news department in station management and operation, and even the roles of a wide variety of people within the station. And, of course, they changed the content of the news.

Let's look at some before and after still frames.

The Studio

Before ENG/SNG: Almost every news program came from a studio. From the first days of radio, there were specially constructed rooms—soundproofed, acoustically treated, carpeted sanctuaries as small as a toll booth or as large as a concert hall. When television started up, the studios became sound stages big enough to house a small circus, all the sets for a play, or a full symphony orchestra. They had hundreds of lighting instruments that could create almost any lighting effect. Connected directly to these studios were control rooms where the heart of the technology waited to send the studio broadcast over the air.

"The studio" was both a place and a concept. Programs came from studios, reporters went and covered the news and brought it back to the studio, and those who broadcast it went to "the studio" to do it.

Live remote TV broadcasts were a rarity because they involved moving virtually all that space and equipment to the remote site and then renting expensive video circuits from the telephone company.

After ENG/SNG: The news can come from almost anywhere, but especially from where it is happening or has just happened. Reporters routinely report from the scene. The newscast can move to the scene of a major event, or portions of it can come from different venues. Though the studio remains a home base much of the time, the new technology gives stations much more flexibility.

Engineers and Unions

Before: A wide gulf stretched between the station's engineers and journalists that involved both attitudes and territorial claims. Engineers ran the studio/control room sanctums; journalists ran the newsroom. Sometimes the barriers were almost cultural.

Many television journalists looked upon engineers as truly foreign people with different views on life, different priorities, and different ways of doing things. One veteran news director said, "They even did different things on their days off." Reporters would get all excited about dramatic scenes from a fire—engineers would criticize the technical quality of the pictures. Engineers understood all of the buttons and switches—reporters barely could find the on-off control.

Some of the problems had to do with the fact that most station engineers were union members, while unions in the newsroom were slow to develop and confined to larger markets. The unions, like all craft unions, tended to put the jobs to be done and the work force to do these jobs into small and specific compartments. A film crew required a camera operator, an audio engineer, and a lighting technician. Some studios could not operate without stagehands. Audio engineers did one thing for one rate of pay, video engineers did another thing for another rate. Hours worked, coffee breaks, callback restrictions (a required minimum number of hours between shifts), and overtime were all governed by strict rules for union members.

Yet nonunion reporters worked until the story was finished. Most frustrating, a nonunion assignment desk editor often was expected to keep track of all the rules. If he or she did not ''lunch'' a crew on time, it was called a ''blown lunch.''

After: ENG has made everyone, especially the journalists, much more aware of technology. And because the newsroom uses so much technology and is responsible for almost all the local programming a station does, journalists and engineers are immersed in the technology together. The unions are still in place, and jurisdictional squabbles persist. Automation will eliminate some jobs. Yet the news staff now includes people whose job it is to coordinate coverage and technology. These people are called ENG/SNG coordinators, or production systems specialists; they start with a program or audience goal and then design the facility and the team to do the job.

Film

Before: Sixteen-millimeter film was the medium for visual reporting. Its traditions and genesis were from the motion picture industry and the movie theater newsreel. TV news adopted those same traditions, and it took time for the television news-people to realize that TV news was not radio with pictures or the theater newsreel. It was, they found, a close-up and personal medium where visual images were often more powerful than the words that went with them.

Immediacy was the key word, but it was hard to come by because the film had to be physically delivered to a processing lab before it could be edited into stories— so there was a built-in delay in getting breaking news on the air. Moving film across land or oceans also required hand delivery or expensive and rare video circuits.

Television did adopt the visual and structural conventions of film storytelling. And it did work hard to mold people who came from a film background into motion picture photojournalists—creating a hybrid of film-making creativity and journalistic ethical considerations.

After: ENG made videotape the medium of visual reporting, while the visual and structural conventions of film carried over. Not only did ENG speed up the editing process, but microwave and satellite technology delivered the visual material wherever it needed to go faster than you can read this sentence. Also, since the whole news-gathering system was now electronic, graphics of all kinds could be added.

News Immediacy

Before: ''We'll have film at eleven.'' That phrase was heard too often during the film days. Even if the film was ready for the late news, the major problem was that between the time the film was shot and the time it got on the air later developments often changed the nature of the story dramatically. Even if the news staff turned itself inside out, what the audience saw was pictures and sound made at *the time the film was shot*. On that day for that event, the viewer got only one version, one slice of time.

After: Live news. With ENG and microwave or satellite signals, it is possible to take the audience to the scene of the event and to update on a minute-by-minute basis.

Management Philosophy

Before: Since the news department spent more money than the station made from newscast advertising, news was not a profit center. Further, journalistic traditions which carried over from newspapers dictated that there should be a clear separation between the business functions and the journalistic functions.

After: The separation is still there, but the news department is a profit center and the main focus of the station's image. ENG is not the total reason for this, but there is no doubt that the technology has contributed much to the fact that news programs attract much bigger audiences than before and therefore more sponsor interest. Also, since local and network TV news is the most competititive of all journalism, investments in technology, as large as they are, are looked at as part of the cost of doing business.

"ENG"-ING THE NEWS

Television News Today

ENG is now a lot of things to television news: a technology, a concept, even a philosophy of how to go about covering the news and delivering it to the audience. The basic ENG benefits are deceptively simple.

1. Speed: Film had to be delivered and processed before editing. Videotape from ENG equipment is ready to edit immediately after it is shot.
2. Editing flexibility: The technology allows for quick construction of a basic story *and* the addition of audio and visual effects to that story for emphasis, clarity, and depth.
3. Mobility: With added helicopter, microwave, and satellite technology, ENG allows stations to reach out faster and farther to provide more breadth and depth to their coverage. It also allows them to go live to the scene of major stories.
4. Quality: Videotape has a richness and depth to it that film does not. It is crisper and brighter. Related equipment gives it more visual range and definition and provides better quality control.

ENG As a Unifying Force

ENG has had a broad impact on local television news. It has caused changes in station organization, operation, and management. Most of this impact has been unifying.

1. New tasks, jobs, and skill requirements have evolved that have mixed technology and journalism in the editorial process.
2. The escape from the confines of the studio and control room to the place where the news is being gathered brings journalists and technicians closer together in situations where the need for "team spirit" is crucial.

FIGURE 1-5. Newsroom and technology move together. At WCCO-TV, Minneapolis, Minnesota, the station's news studio and control room are integrated into the newsroom. The desks for the anchors, interviews, sports, and weather are arranged in a circle. Wall areas behind the desks contain key windows, and projection and video screens to display weather graphics, satellite pictures, live reports, or any other video source. *(Courtesy of WCCO-TV, Minneapolis.)*

3. Taking the entire newscast ''on the road'' can involve station personnel (such as sales, programming, and promotion people) who never before had any direct contact with the news effort.
4. As the technology becomes more complex, more engineers who work very closely with the news operation on both minute-by-minute and long-range planning are needed. Greater appreciation of editorial and technical problems evolves.
5. The news director and his/her job have moved much closer to top station management. As manager of a huge budget, an enlarged staff, and the station's major daily broadcast programs, the news director is now intimately involved with the competition for ratings and with overall station strategies and long-range planning.

PEOPLE

ENG also makes a difference in the way people who hold the key newsroom jobs do their work. Writers, reporters, photojournalists, editors, assignment managers, and producers all work with the technology almost every moment of the day and night. If a station's priorities are ''Get it first, but first get it right,'' the technology can help get it very fast—getting it right requires reporters and editors to have their news-judgment and editing skills working in highest gear. If the priorities require depth, investigation, and amassing vast amounts of visual evidence and illustration—the technology provides the kinds of tools people only dreamed of a decade ago. Here and in Chapter 8 we look at how ENG and people are linked together in newsrooms all over the United States.

The Reporter

Television news reporters have always had to work with two channels of information: words and pictures. They've had to be attuned to the strengths and weaknesses of each, and they've especially had to learn how to make words and pictures work together to tell a story.

In its simplest form the TV story shows the reporter at the scene, standing in front of a camera and telling the audience what has happened. This is called a **standup**. Add some videotaped scenes that illustrate what the reporter is talking about and show them synchronized with the reporter's voice narration. Then the reporter appears again at the end to wrap up and conclude—another standup. For more impact, interview a news maker at the scene and edit some of those remarks into a short take or two to add some of the whys and hows to the story. These are called **sound bites.** It is the judicious mixture of showing the reporter, scenes that illustrate what the reporter is talking about, and sound bites to help explain what happened that makes a visual story successful with any technology.

ENG lets reporters work closer to the program deadlines, and the deadlines are right up to and into the newscasts themselves. Chances are good that a report will be done live from the scene or source. That means reporters must be very selective about the informational value and timeliness of the visual material and very conscientious about developing the latest angles to the story.

For example, the governor holds a morning news conference and gives out some important information. Before ENG that might have been all that could be shown. But with ENG's speed the reporter can continue to pursue other angles and reactions to that story throughout the day. Research—check the governor's facts, previous position, political or self-interest. Get reaction—how this will go over with voters, politicians, experts. Then put the story together.

This method, of course, requires more effort and more imagination. But more important, such in-depth reporting requires the reporter to understand the technology that can be used to do these things.

A Midwest news director said of reporters and their new responsibilities: "Action news formats, those little packages that purport to tell the whole story in one minute and twenty seconds, are a quick and dirty way of telling the news. They all look the same: Reporter standing before the courthouse telling about a new tax cut announced today; sound bite of the assessor saying a few words while his hand rests on a stack of tax assessment forms; back to the reporter saying something like, 'And so, at least today, your pocketbook got a break; how long it will last only time can tell.'"

"That," he said, "won't do any more. That's because the reporter can get the sound and pictures at the courthouse, and then go on to interview people about the impact of the cut on the individual taxpayer and on the institutions the higher taxes previously supported. He or she can get to the experts so that at 6 P.M. the story can include some indication of whether the tax cut is a good or bad idea."

Live Reporting   Live reporting is the ENG benefit that involves the most difficulties for reporters. It is easy to say, as many do, that it means reporters must be able to think and talk at the same time.

Live reports are far more complicated than that. The news is breaking on the air. The reporter at the end of that microwave or satellite link has to make split-second decisions—reporting what is happening, explaining it, and putting it into some perspective.

A Boston news director said, "One of my reporters, coming back after doing her first live report, said, 'That's like patting your head and rubbing your tummy at the same time.' What scares them—and me—is that they are out there running the television station at the end of a high-technology system. What they are saying is going directly to the audience; it's a tremendous responsibility and only some can carry it off."

Any reporter who has to do a lot of live reports must have a strong sense of time and timing. Even though ENG makes live reporting a relatively simple news activity, that doesn't mean the reporters aren't bound by deadlines. In fact deadlines become even more stringent.

Unless it is the first report from a major breaking story, any live report has time limits. Within newscasts the live reports are scheduled to fit into a certain spot. Even if the live reports are segments within a live special, producers give them a length assignment and expect reporters to conform.

Satellite live reports are even more strictly timed since satellite time is bought by the minute and often other stations are waiting to use the satellite immediately after the first report is off the air. A major axiom of SNG: "Don't miss your uplink!"

Another major skill requirement—being at ease (or seeming to be at ease) out there in front of God, the camera, and everyone else—is a natural one. Some have it. Some don't.

The Boston news director: "They've got to blot out the distractions, think about what the camera is showing, and work with it. They have to explain to the audience what they are seeing and try to explain what it means."

Another dimension of ease is being careful.

A Milwaukee news director: "Every word is important. The reporter has to think about what he or she is saying and what that has to do with the story . . . and about what the people being interviewed are saying, and what that means. They've got to come up with the pertinent information quickly and then deliver it, ad lib, in a focused way . . . clean, spare . . . stick to what they know . . . don't speculate."

A Washington, D.C., news vice president thinks speculation is the most dangerous thing to do. During a hostage situation a live reporter noticed the police moving in a large quantity of boxes. He speculated the boxes contained arms for a SWAT team assault. Actually, the police were delivering food demanded by the hostage takers.

Other attributes: Know the territory. Be a psychic. Be an instant psychologist. Above all, keep editorial control. The first three are elements of the last, editorial control, which is another name for news judgment.

News directors everywhere said they were extremely leery of live interviews because of the lack of editorial control inherent in the situation. They try to direct reporters regarding whom to talk to and what to talk about. They almost seem to be saying that reporters have to have a psychic sense of what someone is going to say before he or she says it.

A San Francisco news director was blunt: "People can give out wrong information accidentally, or they can do it on purpose. All the reporter can do is try to avoid demagogic material.''

"I tell my reporters," she said, "Don't interview kooks. You know who they are because they show up at everything ready to talk. Why should we let them run on, live? If you could edit it, you'd cut them out; reporters have got to have their news judgment working in high gear when they're out on a live shot.''

Learning the territory is something most news directors wish their reporters would spend more time doing. In a business where there is a lot of moving around from city to city by young reporters on their way up, the nomadic career seeker doesn't put down many roots.

A Detroit news supervisor told the story of a young woman from the West Coast who moved to a network-owned station in Chicago.

"To me what she did is *the* way to get yourself ready for the new world of local TV news: the live remote," he said. "On her days off she spent a lot of time going around government offices and neighborhoods talking to the people in these places: 'What goes on here? What do you do here? Who are the people who live in this area?' She did this because she has the kind of curiosity you want in a reporter, and because she was getting ready for that next live broadcast. She might end up someplace she had been before, and thus have a little edge because she already knew something about it. You can't ever do enough preparation or talk to enough people to be ready for everything, but you sure can improve the odds.''

How about instant psychology?

A live broadcast attracts a crowd. Sometimes they are quiet and friendly and just want to watch. More often they want to get into the picture—these are known as **hi moms.** Sometimes the hi moms make rude gestures or want to play tricks on the reporter after they get on the air.

A Milwaukee reporter with a lot of field experience said reporters should take their psychologist hats along with them on a live shot. She was confronted by a group of twelve-year-old boys holding soft-drink cups and making motions that clearly indicated they planned to give her an ice shower once she began her broadcast.

"It wasn't a serious story," she said, "just a feature on the day's events at Summerfest. But I knew what they had in mind. So I went over to one of the kids and said, 'What's your name, haven't I interviewed you before?' The kid gave me his name and that took care of any plan to let me have it.''

Sometimes the crowd members don't appreciate the efforts of the TV station at all. They can turn surly, especially if they don't like what the reporter is saying or if the spotlight of the news is coming down hard on them, their neighbors, or friends. Here the reporter must have more judgment: The standing rule for most stations is for the reporters and their crews to leave a hostile situation immediately.

Over and over again the people who are running the nation's newsrooms talked about the need for a reporter to be "a higher-quality" person.

In Columbus, Ohio, a news director said, "Old-time, hard-nosed police reporters have a place in any news operation. But they tend to be narrow and parochial in interest. I'm looking for the college-educated, professional person who can handle the tough stories but still represent you in the board rooms.''

Renaissance men and women—that's what a Chicago news producer thinks

ENG reporters have to be. "I mean by that," he said, 'that they've got to be more curious and socially and politically conscious than ever before. They've got to go beyond covering the breaking elements of the story and to begin to think immediately about the impact of that story. That means they've got to be people who read widely about urban government, and economics, and even about the art, culture, and history of the area where they work. If you are going to get reaction to develop the well-rounded story, you've got to know where and how to find the reactors, *and* what to ask them when you find them.

The Photojournalist

ENG has made a major difference for the motion picture photographer working in the television newsroom. With electronic field equipment, microwave vans, mobile satellite uplinks, and helicopters, the photographer is a member of a powerful team and the key figure in visual news gathering. The visual facts and impressions he or she collects complement the words and information the reporters dig up. Perhaps even more than the reporter, the photographer in the field is the leader of that team, combining photo professionalism with much involvement in the electronics that gets the pictures and delivers them where they're needed.

ENG has accelerated and made complete a move to find a more appropriate—and significant—title for the photographer. Elsewhere in this book Larry Hatteberg rejects the word *shooter*, saying, "Shooters kill things." Film camera operators of great skill were called cinematographers. Not all people who shot film deserved so grand a title. "Cinematographer" meant that the person was an artist with a camera and on the editing table. A cameraman was someone who ran the camera—in the film pecking order, there was a big difference between a technician and an artist.

But *cinema*tographer connotes the cinema. Some have tried "videographer," but that hasn't caught on, either.

Most professional news photographers in all media have been using the term *photojournalist* for some time. Given the new journalistic responsibilities they've gained with the adoption of ENG, that term makes sense. So "photojournalist" it is—and may they wear the badge with honor.

The ENG Photojournalist   What does it take to be a photojournalist in ENG today?

As with reporters, ENG has changed the "kinds" of people television stations are looking for to handle the photojournalism.

A Detroit producer: "I've found that those who have made the transition to tape are younger, more imaginative, better educated people who like to get outside the station and into the middle of the news."

An echo from a San Francisco ENG coordinator: "The big change is that the people who are [photojournalists] with the new technology are younger, more aggressive, and get their thrills out of getting the story. . . . We expect our crews to keep us informed as the story develops. They must be photojournalists."

An ENG coordinator in Los Angeles said there are three qualifications for photojournalists using ENG: ''They've got to have photo skill, but they also have to have news appreciation.''

He also said that some electronic training would be a plus, but that if a person doesn't have that he or she should at least have a sympathy for it. And he said the ''types'' are changing: ''In the old days the crews sat around with their shoes off talking about when the surf would be up. . . . The new ENG types are liberal arts, or law, or electrical engineering combinations . . . bright . . . motivated by being in the news.''

It is clear from this that the emphasis on journalism has completed its penetration into the making and editing of television's visual material. For those interested in that part of the business the title *photojournalist* is apt. The journalism is more important; the technology is an aid.

The Assignment Desk

ENG technology quickly starts a large flow of raw material back to the television newsroom. Out in the field, reporters and photojournalists are doing their end of the news coverage. Inside the newsroom the assignment desk is supposed to manage their movements, and with the aid of writers, editors, and coordinators, process the raw material. ENG has made this more complicated and caused news directors to look for more efficient ways to operate.

The desk is supposed to know where everyone is and what they are doing. When there is breaking news the desk moves equipment and personnel to respond. When there is a need for more information about a story for those in the field, the desk gets it and passes it on. The system works only as well as the mobile radio communications linking it with the field and the ability of the desk crew to plan and react. It is a fragile system that often puts a premium on a few people's ability to make snap decisions that are practical and wise. Practical is much easier to achieve than wise.

Basic news gathering is simple. A crew and reporter go to a story, shoot some videotape, and return to the station with it for editing.

The order of difficulty in managing the coverage increases if the idea is to feed the tape back by microwave—a faster delivery system since the crews don't have to deadhead back in city traffic.

Then there is the live shot. This takes two forms: live-tape coverage and live-live coverage.

With live-tape, the crew sets up the cameras and microwave and sends the pictures and sound back as the story unfolds. In the station, the pictures and sound are videotaped as they come in and each scene is logged for later editing.

Finally, there is the live shot with the reporter and crew at the scene, broadcasting directly.

While any or all of these things are going on, the assignment desk continues to supervise all the other news coverage and to plan ahead.

At least two major problems can arise. First, the desk is expected to have logistic, strategic and tactical roles. That is: The desk is to arrange for the coverage, design how it will be carried out, and follow it as it develops.

The second problem is that with more volume and longer newscasts, planning coverage and supervising it are now much bigger responsibilities. In too many newsrooms too few people are involved in this.

Solutions to these problems are evolving, and the good news is they all mean more editorial people will be introduced into the system. Also, the organization of the system has become more horizontal—a line of responsibilities that is clearer and more precise.

The ENG Coordinator

Another answer has been the development of a whole new set of personnel roughly called ENG coordinators. Their jobs are to work with the reporters, editors, and technicians in liaison with the assignment desk and program producers.

When these jobs were evolving, they seemed to be more technical than journalistic; they required people who spoke the language of the technicians and who would represent the news interests in the organization and operation of equipment. The first ENG coordinator may have been installed in the control room where the video material came in, to report back to the newsroom on its content and length. Or the first ENG coordinator may have been appointed as a referee, to arbitrate the arguments that begin when too many people try to do too many things with too little equipment, all at the same time.

Now the jobs fall into two general areas: inside and outside. No matter where they spend most of their time, ENG coordinators must be people who know technology and journalism. And their jobs are becoming more and more editorial as the need for tighter control over editorial content has become crucial.

In many stations the acquisition of the "outside stuff"—vans, helicopters, bureaus in remote locations—has led to creation of an "inside stuff" area that looks like the control deck of a nuclear submarine. It is space-age stuff. Here technicians supervise and operate the machines that receive and record the pictures and sound from remote locations. There are walls filled with racks of equipment. Colored

FIGURE 1-6. The WCCO-TV video editing area. Here technicians, directors, and producers can monitor and process all video and audio from videotapes, satellite signals, microwave transmissions from the station's news vans and helicopter, and combine them with any special effects desired using computer-driven editing equipment. (*Courtesy of WCCO-TV, Minneapolis.*)

lights blink to indicate what is functioning and how it is performing. Scopes glow green and flicker as they report on the technical quality of the signal, the pictures, and the sound. There are dozens of television monitors which show scenes from the remotes. There are panels of lighted buttons which can route pictures and sounds to other control rooms, editing rooms, on the air—wherever they are supposed to go or are wanted.

Always there is a continuous chatter from the communications system. The technicians in the field and those in the station talk to each other by two-way mobile radio, lining up antennae, microwave relays, satellite feeds, sending and receiving pictures and sound on cue.

On another set of radio channels, editors, the desk, and producers are talking to the journalists in the field, evaluating the story, relaying and updating supporting information.

If those discussions lead to a decision to go live, the activity may shift to a studio and control room, or a production area in the newsroom itself. Wherever that activity is, the live broadcast is produced and directed just as if it were a regular program. Anchors are brought in to introduce it and to provide the basic information and bridges to and from the reporters in the field. Producers join the control room people to supervise and coach. ENG coordinators provide the liaison between the technicians and the news staff.

In the field, ENG coordinators keep an eye on the crews and on how efficient they are, solve technical and editorial problems, help with production, and generally keep things moving like a staff sergeant on a forced march. They are traffic cop, electronic wizard, coach, cheerleader, and intelligence network all rolled into one.

Systems Managers

A brand-new professional specialty has come to television news because of the advances of technology. More and more news staffs are beginning to include someone whose title hasn't really been clearly established but who is essential.

MICROWAVING THE NEWS

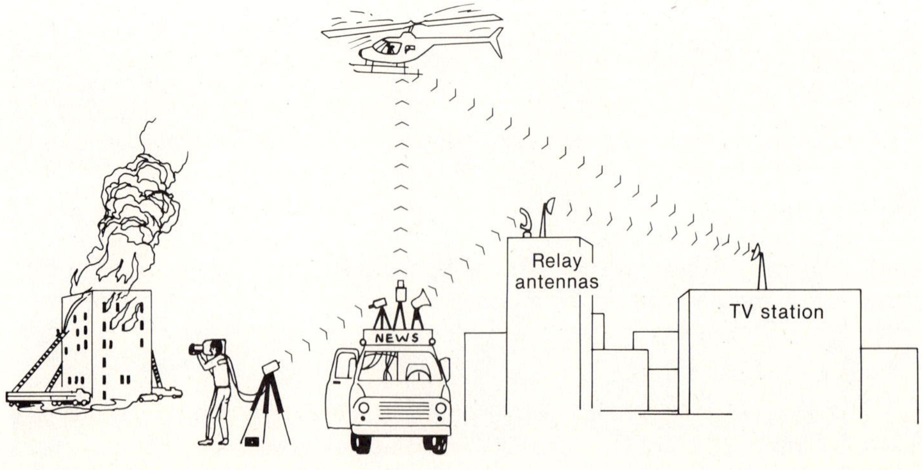

FIGURE 1-7. Microwave units relay the news. A small microwave unit near the photojournalist sends pictures of the fire to the news van. From there, other microwave units can relay those pictures back to the TV station through antennas in the helicopter or on top of tall buildings or natural terrain.

Tom Wolzien, NBC News Vice President for Special Production and Design, whose essay follows this chapter, was the first to spot this trend. He calls these people production systems specialists.

The root of the specialty grew out of pressure from producers, directors, and nontechnical managers for more bridges between the engineer and the producer. Like the ENG/SNG coordinators, the people who hold these posts started from a variety of beginnings. One may have first worked between a news director and chief engineer involved in purchase of millions of dollars' worth of equipment. Another may have started out as a producer who got very involved in applying technology to solve coverage problems on a news special, such as election night.

However they got started, the thing they have in common, Wolzien says, is their approach. They start with the audience or program, not with the hardware. The idea is to decide first what to put on the air, and then figure out what technology, hardware, and people will be needed to make it work.

Around the nation a few score people are now playing this role, and they are more and more powerful. They advise networks, syndication companies, and their own stations and groups, and help each other as each new technical phase comes along. The key to success in the field is keeping it uppermost in mind that no matter how fancy the gear becomes, the message is still what counts.

The Producer

At one time the job of news **producer** didn't exist in local television news. News directors, anchors, and the assignment desk got the program elements together and on the air. If there were people called producers, they were low on the totem pole, with little decision-making power and no news judgment power. They were clerks who timed the stories, assembled the script, and got copies of it to anyone who needed one. Today producers are newsroom nobility. Executive producers are the most royal.

ENG has changed the producer's job in two important ways. First, the speed it provides puts a premium on the ability to make fast news and production judgments. Those decisions also affect the way almost everyone else in the newsroom does his or her work, as well as its cost. So the producer enforces the deadlines and serves as a career advisor, cheerleader, disciplinarian, teacher, and psychiatrist to the staff after the dust of the dinner hour or late news has settled.

Second, the producer is at the center of adaptation of the new technology. It is the producer who must control how this technology affects news coverage and content. By inventive and creative use of the new technology the producer can push for that extra step, direct that extra effort that makes the finished story and newscast more interesting, more complete, and more satisfying to the viewer.

Then there are the show-business angles. ENG and the related digital technology provide the producer with a wide array of effects that can be shown on a three-to-four ratio television screen.

These effects bring with them a new language:

Squeeze Zoom™—place any kind of picture into any portion of the screen; move it to any other part of the screen; bring it to full screen or make it disappear entirely.

Multiple Split—a number of pictures put on the screen at the same time in almost any pattern.

Rotary Wipes—an effect that looks like pages are being turned in a book, or pictures rotate or tumble from the sides, top, bottom, background to foreground or vice versa.

Keying—using the color spectrum to insert pictures on top of other pictures electronically.

Unrestricted Keying—multiple layers of pictures placed on top of each other.

Frame Store—graphics, designs, words, and still pictures stored in a memory one frame at a time for instant recall.

Computer Graphics—graphics created entirely by a computer, or existing graphics modified by a computer, using electronic ''pens,'' ''pencils,'' and ''painting palette.'' Can appear to be three dimensional. Can be animated. Can be stored for reuse.

PUP—portable uplink. A small, portable satellite uplink that can be transported almost anywhere to feed a signal to a satellite transponder.

Window—the time when a satellite transponder becomes available, thus: The window will open at 01:45:30 and will close at 05:45:30.

The producer can order up any or all of this gadgetry, or anything else that comes along in the future. A far cry from an anchor reading words with accompanying pictures, or a reporter in the field talking into a camera? Yes—but. The important point is that the decision to use these ''bells and whistles'' is a journalistic one: Their use must be aimed at making the story in which they are used more complete and clearer to the audience.

News directors view the producers who work for them as the key people who make ENG and related technology work for the journalism.

SOME CONCLUSIONS

In our look at the impact of ENG on the way television journalists do their jobs and its impact on the jobs themselves, we have tried to point to a most important relationship—the impact of ENG on the content of television news.

Our premise is that technology is something to be learned and mastered. But that is no more important than learning any other skill or craft. Artists adopt new media, new tools, new techniques to help them become more creative. Athletes find new ways to train their bodies to gain a split second, more height, more strength. Doctors and scientists use technology to find new ways to heal or unlock the mysteries of the atom.

Journalists must look at a new technology in the same way. It is a means toward a goal. For the journalist that goal is to create messages that are clearer, easier to understand, and more useful to the audience.

A man who is the production manager of a Louisville television station said it best: ''The technology is like the covers of a book; the important stuff—the content—is on the inside.''

PROFILE

*T*om Wolzien is the vice president of NBC News in charge of worldwide news production operations and editorial support. Among his responsibilities are satellite news gathering, ENG operations, graphics, production computers, and the new area of production robotics.

Wolzien has been with NBC since 1976, when he was first assigned as White House field producer, and handled coverage of President Gerald Ford's campaign. The 1976 Ford-Carter campaign was the first national race to be covered with ENG technology. After President Carter's election, Wolzien field-produced the NBC coverage of the first months of the Carter presidency and produced "A Day in the Life of President Carter," the network's first ENG documentary. He has worked as an executive and senior producer of NBC Nightly News, and has been the executive in charge of major specials, remotes, and election broadcasts.

Wolzien began his career as a reporter-photographer at KMGH-TV while a junior at the University of Denver. On graduation he joined the United States Army, went through Officers Candidate School, and was assigned to run the photo branch of the Army's Southeast Asia Pictorial Center in Vietnam. His orders: "Take your forty photographers and cover the war."

Most important for this study, from 1973 to 1975 Wolzien was news producer for KMOX-TV (now KMOV), then the CBS-owned station in St. Louis. He was there at the time KMOX-TV became the first station in the United States to switch completely to ENG technology.

TAMING THE TECHNOLOGY: A MAN WHO WAS THERE

TOM WOLZIEN
NBC NEWS

Outside it was a normal spring afternoon in St. Louis: sunny and muggy with thunderheads forming down to the southwest. But inside Channel 4's newsroom, things were moving. The boss was in town. Not just KMOX-TV's general manager, Tom Battista, but the boss—then CBS President Arthur Taylor.

It was 1974. Taylor had ventured from CBS headquarters in New York to the smallest of the CBS-owned stations to see our one minicamera and to learn of plans to make KMOX the first all-**minicam** station. The forward-looking genius of CBS Engineering, Joseph Flaherty, wanted to eliminate film and substitute small TV cameras and videotape. But like any new idea, electronic news gathering needed a place for experiments. KMOX was the ideal guinea pig. It was the smallest of the CBS O&Os (affiliate owned and operated by CBS). Not much would be lost if CBS blew it.

So that spring day Taylor had come to check out KMOX. Battista guided him through the newsroom, describing his dreams for editors' "decision booths," a huge central assignment desk, and the technical area glassed in at the back of the newsroom. Battista was the rising star of the CBS stations then. He was determined that ENG would make his star rise even faster.

We producers watched the tour and tried to find some news for our one minicam to cover. We wanted to put on a show for Taylor, but we couldn't find anything. The news day was dull, and Taylor appeared to be losing interest. What good's a live minicam, we wondered, if there's no action?

But then news happened. The gods heard us. The gods heard Battista. A tornado hit a Catholic school—a tornado, thunderstorms, flooding, and spot news. The minicam rolled.

The school was on high ground. The microwave could hit our receiving dish. Pictures started to come in. Bleeding kids, dozens of them, and their nuns, all slightly cut by flying glass—great pictures. We switched live.

Taylor ate it up. He and Battista sat on top of the assignment desk, blocking the phones and radios as they watched those pictures come in. We did bulletin after bulletin, one live shot after another. It was the best-covered storm in St. Louis history. And the show inside Channel 4's newsroom was the best show in town.

It worked. Taylor was sold. Thanks to Flaherty's engineering, Battista's brashness, a tornado, and several dozen of us who shot and put the stuff on the air, the first all-ENG newscasts started six months later.

Television news technology hasn't stopped changing since: Terrestrial microwave has been supplemented by satellite microwave, tape formats have improved in quality while getting smaller in size, and camera tubes have given way to chips. There have been thousands of corollary changes, but nearly all are derivatives of that big leap to ENG in 1974.

It didn't take long to realize that all the changes, all the hardware improvements were worthless unless they had a positive impact on news program content. When you get by the glamor of the expensive hardware, all we are dealing with are the tools of reporting the news. ENG technology is a tool of content just as pencils and paper are tools of content.

So with content in mind now, let's go back to 1974. As the minicams matured, so did minicam journalism. Like growing children, we went through phases at KNOX.

Euphoria lasted until the second day, when we lost all color. Terror set in a few days later when we lost most of a newscast. Nothing worked. Flames didn't show in pictures at night fires. A four alarmer showed up as a black screen. Fire trucks dropped hoses over camera cables. (There was no portable tape at first—we recorded in the trucks.) Our bright red minicam trucks drew throngs of slum kids. Riots were only moments away.

We went through the "live is good" phase: If the minicams can go live, we should go live. That resulted in lots of shots of reporters in empty ballrooms saying, "Here we are live at the Chase Park Plaza where just a few hours ago Henry Kissinger. . . ." It didn't take long to realize that live didn't necessarily equal good.

Next came the "bloody sidewalk" phase as we learned that ENG had much more visual impact than film. KMOX reporter Sandy Gilmour was doing a live report on a boy killed by a guard after a robbery. Halfway through the report, the camera zoomed in on the sidewalk where the kid had fallen. The body was gone, but the blood was still wet and glistening. It was a shot that might have been included in a film report, but this time it was live, fresh, and real. Viewers had never seen such vivid pictures. They were outraged, and the phones rang all night.

After a while the novelty wore off, ENG was accepted as a tool, and producers became gamblers. Where you once could have relied on the station's film projectors to run stories without fail, now the stories were in minicam trucks scattered across the station's thousand-square-mile coverage area. When you wanted to take a story, you didn't know whether it would be there. The show that aired didn't resemble the show that was planned. Either the stories would be changing or the equipment wouldn't be working.

We producers were forced to change our ways of thinking. News judgments became snap judgments. "Do you go live now or wait for a better shot?" "Is the jury really leaving the courthouse, or if we go live will we die trying to fill the time?" "If we take those shots will we start a riot? Is that like saying 'We're having a riot, so come on down'?" "Do we take political candidates live or tape them so we can check their claims?"

Local station producers began to make serious journalistic decisions in a new place—the control room. Until then only network producers at political conventions or space shots had to make control-room editorial calls.

Reporters learned they had to change, too. The minicams required a new, much sharper breed of reporter who could think on his or her feet, knew the history of a story, and could challenge interview subjects who were trying to stretch the truth. Before live minicams stupid reporters could get by. They were protected by producers and editors who forced them to rewrite and retrack until they got the story right. Live minicams guaranteed that stupid reporters would look stupid.

The switch to minicameras was like moving from a manual typewriter to an electric. You can type faster on an electric, but you can make mistakes a lot faster, too. Survival with this new technology required faster thinking, more flexibility, and more accurate decision making.

We realized that we had to find ways to tame the technology because we were spending more time and effort dealing with ENG than we were putting into the content. Quiet news days became technological terrors in seconds as stories got away from producers and reporters. So much tape would come in at the last minute that editors couldn't handle it all. You might know what you wanted to say on the air, but the mechanics just kept getting in the way.

The nature of television is to keep going, to fill the show no matter how rugged the going may be. "Anything is better than black," was the "first law" of NBC Nightly News tape producer Bill Boyle in those days.

We all worried that the product was suffering. The audience wasn't being given its due because the quality was not what it could be. So producers began to develop contingency plans for a quality program despite tape overloads, last-minute feeds, and technical disasters.

"Assume nothing—always have a place to go" became the rule for successful producers. We learned that technology drives the art. We can use it as a tool, or we can let it force us into corners. If we don't understand it and make it work for us, we'll spend our time reacting to the problems it causes.

By 1976 the minicams had changed the nature of presidential campaign reporting. Freed from film processors, projectors, and transmission facilities of the big cities, the networks started feeding stories from anywhere the phone company could get a circuit.

Political coverage was transformed. Edit packs were set up at candidates' last stops before news time—sometimes in airports or railroad stations. Storerooms became control rooms. Toilet stalls doubled as announce booths. All this so the candidates' last speeches of the day could be covered. The early afternoon deadlines of film days were gone. Now the only true deadline was when the show went off the air.

This extra time gave correspondents and producers more opportunity to report, to review the tape, to edit, and to prepare higher-quality stories than with film. It also got the candidates thinking about how the technology could be used for their benefit as well.

The 1976 campaign changed midway. Candidates Gerald Ford and Jimmy Carter made major policy statements later and later in the day. They realized that later deadlines left less time for reporting and criticism. Speeches at 5:30 or 6:00 P.M. made the 6:30 Nightly News with little or no analysis by correspondents.

Then came Ping-Pong politics. In earlier years candidates might have one back-and-forth exchange over a day or two. The GOP candidate would say one thing, and the Democrat would respond with his own proposal. Now the minicams extended the opportunity for debates that Ping-Ponged across the country; idea and response, response to the response, and the last word.

It went like this. The Democratic candidate got off the plane and said something. The correspondent radioed what the candidate said to his producer, who was talking on the phone with the network newsdesk. The netdesk relayed the information to the producer with the other candidate. The producer radioed his correspondent, who asked for a response from the GOP candidate. Back and forth, several times each day.

Since tape was cheap and assassination attempts were frequent in 1976, crews started rolling on everything. For the first time everything the candidate did or said in public was recorded—everything including the mistakes. Constant taping caught every inconsistency, flub, and error. Things said months earlier came back to haunt the candidates. Nineteen seventy-six was the year of the gaffe.

New story-telling techniques started to evolve with ENG. During the 1976 campaign, for example, NBC correspondent Tom Pettit developed a new— and what has become standard—method of combining the very latest news with background material gathered over several days. Pettit and his team would pre-cut a "core" that contained everything available up to an hour before air. Then he'd go live with the latest news on the top and bottom of the "core."

Pettit had found a way to add depth and perspective to late-breaking stories in remote locations. He'd also done it in a way that cost no more than regular coverage. The minicam was already there, and the expensive AT&T line had to be ordered anyway, so both background report and breaking story could be fed at the same time.

Just as minicams brought changes on the road, they also forced institutions to change the way they dealt with television. At the White House, for example, "photo opportunities" had been controlled in film days by simply turning out the lights. An electrician would hold two giant reflector floodlights on the president and his guests while crews filmed for a minute or so. Then a press aide would call, "Lights," and the lights would go off. Without lights the film crews would leave.

That changed with minicams. Even though the lights would go out, the more sensitive cameras would keep recording. By the Reagan presidency, the cameras were so sensitive that the White House press staff found it hard to get crews out of the room, and that encouraged reporters to hang around and ask questions during the "no-question" photo ops.

ENG brought competitive changes to television across the country. In the late 1970s, "minicam wars" were fought in every major city. The station that had the fastest systems, tallest antennas, quickest edit packs, and helicopter relays would try to beat the competition. They hoped it would lead to bigger audiences, higher ratings, more revenues. Sometimes it did. Other times the technology just cost a lot of money, and other stations with better content kept the lead in the local ratings race. The most successful stations maintained a combination of solid reporting and content while adding the new technology.

Minicams were firmly established and debugged by the 1980 campaign, which brought the application of new transmission and production systems compatible with ENG. Domestic satellites were tied to local station minicams for the first time, raising a possible challenge to network dominance of national news.

If stations could get the news of their area on faster with minicams, why couldn't they go across the country to do stories and feed them back live or on tape? The communications satellite became the corollary to the local minicam microwave system. At that point the differences between local station and network technology evaporated.

Just about every major television station fed its own live stories from the 1980 political conventions. The stories were geared to the specific needs of the local audiences, while the networks—with their huge staffs and resources—covered the main event. The local-network coverage split at the 1980 conventions set a pattern for the decade—a pattern that became more important as satellite news collection took hold of local stations in the mid-eighties.

Two groups took a major gamble with satellites at that time. One was led by broadcast entrepreneur Stanley Hubbard. The other was NBC. Both acquired space on a new type of satellite in the **Ku-band** frequency range. Hubbard saw Ku as a way to let local stations gather and exchange news material. At NBC we needed a satellite system to replace AT&T lines. We were concerned about rising costs of the land lines and the effect of the breaking up of AT&T. The NBC satellite would be used for two purposes: network distribution and news collection from bureaus and affiliates. Both Hubbard and NBC acquired space on RCA satellite K-2.

Ku wasn't supposed to work—that was the common wisdom. Engineers from AT&T and the other networks said the Ku signal would be wiped out by rain because it was at a higher frequency than C-band satellites. CBS and ABC established C-band distribution systems to replace land lines. But C-band had a drawback, as well. There is so much interference on C-band frequencies that to get a clean feed the dishes often have to be located many miles from a station. That means expensive microwave links between the dish site and the station.

NBC and its affiliates decided Ku would let us co-locate receive dishes at the stations. And that not only would let the station receive the network signal without additional microwave, it would also let the station's regional minicam microwave system be tied to the rest of the country through an inexpensive satellite transmitter hung on the station's receive dish. We called the transmitter package a PUP, or portable uplink, because the package could be moved from one dish to another. With the PUPs we'd have the first truly national news collection system.

Meanwhile in Minneapolis, Hubbard was going at it from a different direction. Not having a network, he didn't have a reason to install PUPs on station downlink dishes. However he did see a market in satellite trucks for local stations so they could feed stories from remote distances back to their stations without ground microwave. Just as the communications satellite was the corollary for a minicam microwave relay on a building, Hubbard's satellite truck became the corollary for the minicam microwave van.

Then Hubbard, through his CONUS news cooperative, gave stations a means to use their trucks to exchange material. Other ad-hoc news cooperatives followed with a mixture of affiliates from all networks.

At NBC we were concerned that this exchange of material between affiliates and nonaffiliates could jeopardize the flow of video to NBC News. We worried that NBC would have about as much access to station news video as merchants in a dusty downtown have to travelers when the new interstate highway is built twenty-five miles outside town.

Some stations didn't think the NBC PUP concept would work and wanted the network's help in buying the expensive satellite trucks.

A huge debate raged over the summer of 1985—trucks or PUPs. Should NBC establish a news cooperative with its affiliates? Should NBC help stations purchase satellite trucks (often from Hubbard), or should they be able to get most of their material from the PUPs across the country? This wasn't a debate over hardware, but rather over the nature and content of local news programs. Were stations more interested in having their own trucks and people at remote locations or in acquiring material from as many other stations as possible across the country?

In the end NBC and its affiliates realized there was too much at stake, and they had to do everything. NBC established the Skycom affiliate news cooperative, helped those stations that wished to purchase trucks, and installed the PUPs. The stories started flowing—thousands a month—from one affiliate to another on transponders owned by NBC and coordinated by a special NBC News unit. The trucks handled live remotes, and the PUPs moved most of the material between stations, regardless of where they were located. And NBC News had access to it all.

Without a Ku system, ABC and CBS could not have a truly national news exchange. They were technologically limited to subsidizing affiliate truck purchases, acquiring some Ku transponder time, and trying to market "regional feeds."

In those discussions of 1985 are questions that will haunt the industry well into the 1990s. There are no technological limits anymore. The local station can do anything it wants to pay for. Money, not technology, is the limiting factor now.

Everything is international today. There are no local, regional, or national boundaries for news. There is only one distance in the world today—the distance to the satellites—22,300 miles.

ENG and satellite technology have made local news coverage of just about anything possible. And that means broadcast journalists will have to make conscious choices about the role of their organizations. In the early days, we asked "do we go live, just because we can?" Now the question is "do we go there, just because we can?"

Recent NBC research indicates that people want more news about their local areas from local stations. This conflict between what the technology allows and how it should be used by local stations will be one of the most difficult issues of the 1990s.

On an international basis, the big questions will come from combining minicam technology with the new very small satellite transmit dishes. The dishes fit into a handful of shipping cases, which can easily be carried as baggage. They were successfully used for major scheduled news stories starting in 1986 and have the potential for use from any remote locations where they can "see" the equatorial satellites. That raises many questions for national governments and military organizations, for now there is no technical limitation to prevent live broadcasts from revolutionary groups or during military activities, even war.

The decisions will be difficult but may be easier if we look at ENG along these four parallel paths:

1. The Audience. This is the reason television news exists. Forget your commitment to the audience, and it will forget you.
2. The Content. The ideas and information communicated are more important than the tools used to communicate them.
3. The Technology. Understand the technology so you can control it. If you don't, you'll be worrying about the mechanics when you should be worrying about what's being said on the air.
4. The Responsibility. ENG is fast. It's easy to shoot from the hip. Think twice about how, where, when, and whether you're going live. Remember, live doesn't necessarily equal good.

It has not been an easy evolution for ENG, with the many difficult editorial decisions and technical problems over the years. The technology will get simpler in the future; the editorial decisions more complex. But the rules learned in the early days of ENG will continue to apply. Don't assume that things will always work. Protect your audience and the program quality by always having a place to go while you take time to think out editorial issues or fix a technical problem.

And there's one more thing you need in the ENG business: luck. But a lot of that you make yourself.

ENG Technology: A Nontechnical Guide

2

No matter what part of the news-gathering field they work in, broadcast journalists today will be dealing with cameras, recorders, microphones, and lights in the field—and perhaps a lot of complex electronic equipment to get the pictures and sound from the scene of an event to the television station's news and control rooms. And they will be working with other machines to edit the pictures and sound into coherent stories. Still other machines will provide graphics, words on the screen, and a large variety of other production elements.

It is not necessary to know the technical *details* of the new technology to be a broadcast journalist using it. If it were, the journalist might be called upon to understand paragraphs like this:

> The original and still only FCC specification for creating a chrominance signal from three R, G, and B signals is represented in the fig. 4.5 matrix unit and modular sections. It stipulates that they shall be combined in separate matrices to form ''I'' (In Phase) and ''Q'' (Quadrature) signals, each of which is then separately amplitude-modulated on commonly generated 3.58 subcarriers which are 90 degrees apart in phase.*

If the broadcast journalist needed to know what that means, journalism program requirements would include courses in physics, and there would be fewer students enrolled in the program.

But electronic journalists using electronic news-gathering equipment to report the news do need to know something about how it all works. More important, they need to understand the capabilities and limitations of the equipment because those are parameters for what the journalist can or cannot do.

---

*G. Robert Paulson et al., *ENG/EFP/EPP Handbook* (New York: Broadband Information Services, 1981), p. 97.

This chapter provides you with the necessary technical information to understand better the operational details that come later in the book. We will speak of the characteristics of the various units used for making pictures in the field, for editing them later, and in the production of television news programs on the air.

We have avoided mentioning specific equipment makes or model numbers as much as possible. By the time this book gets into your hands, models that were current will have disappeared and new ones with different numbers (and probably different specific characteristics) will be on the market and in use. As in other segments of the electronics industry, obsolescence is very rapid.

CAMERA-VTR ENSEMBLES

Color pictures and sound are recorded on videotape in the field by the use of the portable camera-videotape recorder ensemble or with a camera which has a video-tape recorder built into the camera housing. The camera "sees" the picture it is aimed at through a lens that transmits the picture onto the face of one or more electronic picture tubes or **solid-state** image sensing devices. The former—picture tubes—have been around for as long as there has been television, since they are what makes the pictures. The solid-state image sensing devices are relative new-comers.

These devices are a member of the ubiquitous "chip" family—silicon chips imprinted with the ability to register a visual image. In the camera application they are called CCDs—charge-coupled devices—and they do the same thing as the tubes they replace: translate the light intensities into electronic signals. CCDs have become quite popular for ENG, since they don't retain an image memory as tubes do and thus avoid the "comet-tail" effect in low-light situations and "burn-in" when aimed at bright lights. The chips also last much longer than tubes, are lighter, and use less power.

Think for a moment about something you may have learned in an art class. Or if you've never taken an art class, you probably spent some time in primary school messing with paints and brushes. You discovered that if you mixed all of the colors together you got brown. And you may have experienced a thrill when you mixed yellow and blue to get green.

What you learned there was that any shade (hue) and intensity (saturation) of color could be made by mixing various amounts of three primary colors: red, blue, and yellow.

Marshall McLuhan gave us many special words to use when talking about the various media. Besides calling them "cool" or "hot," he called media that reflect light, such as a newspaper or magazine page, "light on" media. He called television a "light through" medium because it projects light through a picture tube toward the eye of the viewer. Others have called them, respectively, *subtractive* and *additive*.

In television the primary colors are red, green, and blue. The tube you look at when you are viewing color television contains "guns" that send beams of electrons to activate red, green, and blue dots on the face of the tube from behind. The brightness of those dots is controlled by another signal. Your eyes and brain take over then and mix (integrate) the primary colors to reproduce the actual shades of the scene on the television screen.

The standard for the color television system in the United States was established by a group of engineers in the mid-1950s at the same time the industry was rushing to get more black-and-white stations on the air. The group was known as the National Television Systems Committee; therefore the U.S. standard is known as the NTSC standard.

In simple terms what the NTSC did was to decide that the light coming through the lens of the camera would be split—or filtered—through prism-housed **dichroic filters** into its red, green, and blue components. (A dichroic filter is a piece of optical glass that has been coated with chemical film that lets through all colors except the one which it was created to reflect.) This was a dramatic decision with a lot riding on it. CBS and NBC-RCA were locked in a battle of giants to get approval of their own systems for color signal production and color set manufacture. The CBS design called for a color filter wheel that would rotate in front of the color tubes to do the splitting; NBC-RCA favored the prism-filter system that was later adopted as the common standard by the Federal Communications Commission.

The NTSC standard therefore is the one U.S. broadcasters must adhere to when they broadcast their signals under their FCC license.

Until recently, most ENG cameras have produced what is called a composite video signal that meets NTSC requirements. In this system color and brightness are mixed, in the camera, with all of the other signals needed to produce a picture. The camera then delivers the composite video signal to a recorder, or any other place it is needed. But, when that signal is recorded and played back there is always some loss of picture quality.

Coming into use, especially with the newer one-half-inch videotape formats, is component video. In this system the color and brightness information is recorded separately, which provides better band width, less interference in the picture, and therefore better fidelity and detail. However, the two systems thus far are incompatible.

ENG cameras, as they control and process the various electronic signals, also

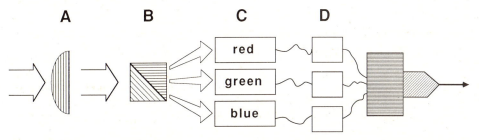

A   **B**   **C**   **D**

FIGURE 2-1. A simplified diagram of the inside of a video camera shows how the images come through the lens and are converted into a composite video signal. The light passes through the lens (A) and strikes the beam splitter (B). The prism and dichroic filters in the beam splitter break the light into red, green, and blue components and direct them to the red, green, and blue pickup tubes or the CCD chips (C) that are rapidly replacing tubes. The tubes or chips convert the light waves into electronic signals that are then fed through a series of amplifiers (D) and combined with other electronic signals to form the composite video signal. *(Courtesy of C. J. Beebe.)*

control the color balance so that, given the lighting conditions that exist, the image that the camera produces is as truly representative as possible of the scene being shot.

White Balancing

This is done by what is called **white balancing,** white being a mixture of all the colors. The idea is to adjust the red, blue, and green signals so that they are exactly equidistant from each other. Actually, only the red and blue signals are adjusted, with green being used as a constant reference. By adjusting the red and blue signals against the green constant the ''whitest'' white is established, or ''balanced.'' When that is achieved, all of the other colors will be rendered accurately.

In the earliest portable color cameras the red and blue adjustments were done manually. Now most cameras have an automated white-balancing system that is activated at the touch of a button, and many of them have memory circuits that remember the white balance and maintain it throughout the shooting done under a particular light condition. Nevertheless, it must be adjusted each time the camera location, and thus the light condition, changes. That is why you see ENG crews holding a sheet of white paper or a white target in front of the camera before they start recording. If this is not done, the colors in the pictures are not true.

The portable ENG camera has many other automated features. Such automation has been added with the idea of making the camera easier to use under the different conditions found in news gathering. With memory circuits and microprocessors the camera can be ''set up'' to be ready to make good pictures in a few seconds. If all the systems are working properly—if the beam splitting is properly aligned, if the electronic impulses are correct, if the digital and analog monitoring systems are properly monitoring all functions—then the camera will make pictures that are very close to what the human eye can see.

Exposure

Most portable TV cameras today provide for automatic exposure control with an auto iris. The **iris** in a lens is like the pupil in your eye; it can be opened or closed to allow more or less light to go through the lens. When you look at something that is very bright, the pupil in your eye contracts to reduce the amount of light going to your optic nerve. An auto iris works the same way. A light sensor reads the amount of light coming through the lens and causes a tiny motor to rotate the iris in the lens to the proper setting.

A general characteristic of all cameras with automatic exposure controls is that the sensors that read the light and adjust the lens opening concentrate on the brightest spots in the picture the camera is seeing. If you have a very bright spot in the picture—a ray of sun reflecting from a piece of jewelry, a white plastic coffee cup in the hand of a person wearing dark clothing, the rotating beacon on top of a police car—then the automatic exposure controls adjust the iris to compensate for the bright spot and the rest of the picture goes dark. This can create many problems on a news assignment, so most cameras have more switches to allow for *manual* operation of the iris. That, in turn, calls for the photographic skills of the camera operator to adjust the f-stop by hand so that there is detail (**definition**) in both the brightest and darkest parts of the picture seen in the viewfinder.

The viewfinder, in which the camera operator composes the shots, is a tiny TV monitor that shows a black-and-white picture. As on many single-lens reflex 35mm still cameras, there are indicator lights—light-emitting diodes (LEDs)—around the edge of the viewfinder. They tell the operator whether there is enough light to make pictures and, if the tape recorder is running, when the battery or tape supply is getting low.

Many cameras also have controls to enhance the picture at low light levels, giving the whole system a boost in sensitivity. Some of the most expensive cameras have sophisticated exposure adjustment systems that may include such features as a fleshtone indicator, with a switch to be thrown so that skin tones are properly rendered when lighting conditions are difficult.

Lenses

The lens on an ENG camera is very similar to that on any still camera you have ever used. This lens controls the amount of light coming to the camera picture tube or tubes, and the sharpness (focus) of the picture. There is a whole field of advanced study having to do with the properties of lenses that predates ENG by as far back as the origin of photography. It is not our intention to go into that in detail here, but there are some characteristics of lenses that a broadcast journalist needs to understand.

Focal Length   Virtually all ENG cameras use a zoom lens. This is a lens that is built so that its elements can be moved closer to or farther away from each other inside the lens, thus providing everything from a telephoto shot to a wide-angle closeup—and everything in between. Zoom lenses are very convenient, yet they have the same characteristics as all lenses, properties that affect the pictures you are going to record. These have to do with four things:

1. Focal length
2. Lens speed
3. Depth of field
4. Magnification

When you **zoom** a zoom lens you are actually changing its focal length from a wide angle of viewing for subjects close to the camera all the way "out" to a closeup of subjects or objects some distance away. When you change the focal length you run into Rule 1:

RULE 1. **Different focal lengths produce different effects that actually change the nature of the picture being made.**

Zooming to a long focal length tends to distort or foreshorten the depth in the scene. Subjects or objects that are really far away seem to be closer, and items in the background seem to be almost as close as items in the foreground.

One of the most famous scenes in a popular 1960s movie, *The Graduate,* shows the hero running to the church to prevent his love from marrying another man. He starts running toward the camera from a great distance away. And he runs, and runs, and runs . . . but he never seems to get any closer or to be making any progress toward the church. The tension builds; it is excruciating as time passes.

That scene was shot with an extremely long focal-length lens, so the depth—the distance our hero is from the movie audience—never seems to change. Years later the same technique was used to present the dramatic running scenes in the Oscar-winning *Chariots of Fire.*

In a news story about heavy traffic on a freeway, pictures shot at a long focal length will make the cars seem very close together, and their relative motion toward the camera will seem slow.

Pictures made at shorter focal lengths restore more normal depth relationships in the picture. The standard lens focal length for ENG cameras is 25mm, which provides a horizontal viewing angle of about 50 degrees.

Pictures shot at even shorter focal lengths can take in a much wider view of the scene, one which is sometimes even wider than the normal human eye can span.

Lens Speed
The speed of a lens—the amount of light it will let through—is determined by the diameter and focal length of that lens. Here we are talking about f-stops. The larger the diameter of the lens, the lower its f-stop. The lower the f-stop—f/1.4 for example—the more light it will transmit. The iris diaphragm inside the lens, as we have already noted, can be opened or closed to control the amount of light being transmitted. Therefore all lenses are calibrated with f-stops: f/1.4 is ''wide open''; at f/16 or f/22 the lens is closed down to a very small aperture.

Depth of Field
TV photojournalists want almost everything in their pictures to be in focus. So when they are working with a zoom lens they have to be conscious of **depth of field**—the area in the picture from the closest object to the farthest object that is in focus. Two characteristics of lenses affect depth of field: f-stop setting and focal length. They are interrelated.

RULE 2. **Depth of Field: The area in focus, from the closest object to the farthest object, changes when the f-stop and the focal length being used are changed.**

Regarding f-stop: The *lower* the f-stop, the *shorter* the depth of field. If the light conditions are poor, the auto iris will open up the lens to let in more light. When that happens, the depth of field is made shorter. Further, at any given f-stop, one-third of the area in sharp focus will be in front of the point where the lens is focused, and two-thirds of the area in sharp focus will be behind that point. Finally, the better the light conditions, resulting in closing down the lens, the longer the depth of field.

Regarding focal length: The *longer* the focal length used, the *shorter* the depth of field at any f-stop. So when the zoom lens is zoomed all the way in—to its longest focal length—the depth of field is shortest. When the lens is pulled back to make a wider shot, the focal length is deeper.

Zoom and Focus   Experienced photojournalists using zoom lenses always make one move before doing anything else—they zoom to the tightest shot and then focus on the main subjects in that shot. Since depth of field diminishes with focal length, the corollary is also true: All shots wider than the tightest shot will be in focus if the tightest shot is in focus. Yet as the auto iris changes with the amount of light coming through the lens, so does the depth of field. The camera operator thus must be alert to refocus as the depth of the area in focus changes.

A zoom lens is easy to use. You can make any size shot by rotating a ring on the lens, or by pushing a button to activate a motor that moves the lens elements with a gear drive.

The lenses come from various manufacturers in "families" with zoom ranges from about 6 to 1 to 42 to 1—the kind of zoom lens used for sports coverage. Range extenders can be attached to the back of most zoom lenses to increase their magnifying power. Some lenses have separate elements that can be added to the front of the lens body to provide extreme wide-angle and close-to-the-camera focusing. Most also have built-in back focus adjustments so they can be matched precisely to the camera they are installed on. Those zoom lenses used for ENG work are specially made for TV cameras so that their resolution and contrast characteristics match the relatively narrow band width of the TV spectrum.

You have one more thing to worry about. That is Rule 3:

RULE 3.   **The magnifying elements of the zoom lens or any long lens also magnify all other shooting conditions.**

Any unsteadiness of the camera will be magnified and a jiggly picture will result. Camera operators using long focal lengths must use a tripod or steady themselves carefully. Pans and quick movements of the camera are also magnified, as are heat waves, insects at the ballpark, water droplets, or smoke particles in the air.

The Videotape Recorder

One of the most dangerous phrases in television news is "Let's assume that. . . ." But let's assume for a moment that all of the automatic camera systems are working and that we have a good steady picture of the size and composition we want. The picture we are making goes from the camera through a coaxial cable to a videotape recorder.

Videotape recorders come in a variety of configurations and formats. Their manufacturers give them a bewildering array of letter and number designations that make ENG users at a cocktail party sound like a bunch of airplane manufacturers: "AU 400," "BETA SP," "BVW 21," "M-II," "D-1 DVR-1000."

The videotape recorder connected to the camera in the field is relatively light in weight, about twelve pounds. If the recorder is built right into the camera itself, it's much lighter than that. Three-quarter-inch video cassette recorders have been standard for some time. The combination cam-corders using one-half-inch video cassettes have become very popular. With some new technical formats that use metal-particle tapes the cam-corders produce pictures that are superior to anything seen to date. Some one-inch **reel-to-reel** recorders are portable enough to be used in the field. All of them operate either on battery power or on alternate current (AC) converted to 12-volt direct current (DC).

If the machine is a video cassette recorder (VCR), the video cassette is inserted through a slot or drawer in the recorder's case. Inside the recorder, the tape is "loaded" by a series of mechanical actions: The cassette door is opened, then the tape is pulled out in a loop and wound around the recording heads.

If it is a reel-to-reel recorder, the tape is threaded around the recording heads manually, or with an automatic threading device that uses a stiff leader to pull the tape through the tape path to the other reel.

The controls on most VCRs are quite similar to those on an audio tape recorder. Levers or switches provide forward, stop, fast forward, rewind, record, pause, and

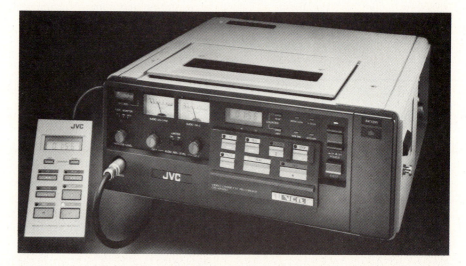

FIGURE 2-2. The workhorse of ENG, a three-quarter-inch videotape recorder. The videotape cassette is inserted in a drawer on the top of the machine. Controls on the front provide for forward, record, fast-forward, rewind, and eject functions. Meters, knobs, and diodes indicate whether the various functions are working properly and allow for control and monitoring of audio levels. Microphone and camera cable connections go in the receptacles on the end. *(Courtesy of JVC.)*

eject functions. As on most audio tape recorders, both the forward and record levers must be pressed at the same time to make a recording. The controls on cam-corders are integrated with the camera-operating controls.

Other characteristic features are a volume control (VU) meter, a battery strength meter, and a display of warning lights that indicate which function the machine is performing, whether the battery is working normally or running low, status of tape supply, and so on.

Although most cameras have microphones incorporated in the camera housing to pick up sound along with the pictures, these mics don't work very well. The microphone on the camera housing has somewhat the same characteristics as the condenser microphone built into audio tape recorders—good microphone technique for optimum sound quality is difficult to obtain. For better audio quality, other microphones may be plugged into the VCR, with the sound being monitored through earphones worn by the camera operator or by a sound technician. Most VCRs operate with either **automatic gain control** (AGC) settings or allow you to switch to manual control of the levels on the two or more audio channels provided. This makes it possible to set the channel levels individually or to ride **gain** (control loudness levels) on them. But if serious sound mixing is desired, a separate mixer must be inserted between the microphones and the VCR audio inputs.

Most VCRs—but not all—provide playback picture and sound monitoring of the recording through the camera viewfinder and the headphones respectively. It is important to check the recorded results in the field so that if there are problems additional material can be shot. And by monitoring pictures and sound on the ride back to the newsroom, you can make some preliminary editorial decisions.

What's Going On in There?   When you are recording on a video cassette or one-inch tape, four separate signals are being put on the tape: picture and synchronization **(sync),** two separate sound channels, and a **control track.** The last item—the control track—is the most important. You may have the most beautifully posed, composed pictures ever made—you may have the makings of a twenty-first-century Francis Ford Coppola—but if you haven't got a control track you haven't got anything.

Why is this? Tracking consists of pulses recorded on the tape, one for each field of the television picture. These tracking pulses are analogous to the sprocket holes on motion picture film. They are absolutely essential to the editing process because they insure that the picture will be stable—in sync—on playback. Some VCRs now have tracking indicator meters to tell you tracking is occurring; some do not.

Most editing control units work by counting the tracking pulses recorded on the tape. If these tracking pulses are not there the editing control units will not operate properly because there is nothing for them to lock to. In addition, the pulses are used by the editing control units to time the preroll and rehearse-edit functions, and, of course, to insure that the edits themselves are made at the correct point. Chapter 4 will fully explain the rehearse-edit functions and will provide additional information to help you make certain the pulses are there.

The Mysteries of Helical Scanning   Whether the recording is being done on a VCR or on a one-inch open-reel machine, it is being done *helically*. That is,

FIGURE 2-3. How control, video, and audio tracks are laid down on the videotape by the recorder. In assemble mode editing, the control track is laid down as the edit is made. In insert mode, editing tracking is placed along the entire length of the videotape prior to editing. Since this track is already there the machines are locked to it even before the edit begins, and the edit will be more stable. *(Courtesy of C. J. Beebe.)*

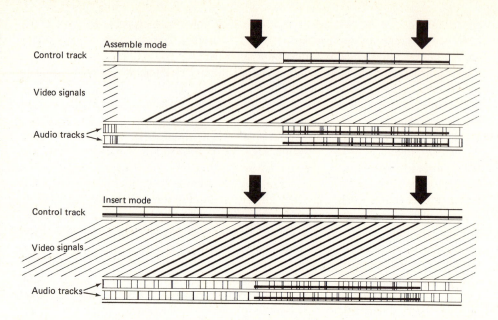

the tape is being transported past the record heads in a helix—a spiral. Two motions are involved: The tape is moving forward past the recording heads, which are located on a spinning drum.

The frequency of these video signals is so high and at the same time covers such a wide range that a high relative head-to-tape speed is needed to record (and reproduce) them. As the head drum spins and the tape passes by it, the video signals are put on the tape in slanted tracks (see Fig. 2–3). Because the control track and the audio tracks are lower in frequency, they are laid down horizontally.

Part of the composite video signal coming from the camera to the recorder is a sync (synchronize) signal that goes on the slanted tracks along with the picture and color burst. All this happens simultaneously. During a recording, the machine is constantly comparing the pulse signal with the sync signal so that the timing of the sync signal corresponds to the start of each slant video track on the tape.

The Servo System

The quality of the performance of any videotape recorder (VTR) and editing system depends mostly on its ability to reproduce exactly the video signal recorded on the tape. The video heads of the playback machines must make a precise tracing of the video signals placed on the tape during recording. This requires what are called **servo systems**—a drum servo and a capstan servo. The **drum servo** controls the speed of the rotation of the head drum. The **capstan servo** controls the speed of the tape passing the head drum. During playback the machine again constantly compares the sync signal with the pulse signal and feeds this information to the servo systems controlling head drum rotation and tape speed. Such precision controls are essential for editing the recorded tape.

Videotape

Of all the things we use in ENG coverage, the basic medium we record on—videotape—is the most taken for granted, and therefore the most abused, bent, stapled, and folded by those who ought to know better. Perhaps this is because the tape is concealed inside a plastic box, or perhaps because it is so useful: It can be used over and over again, stored temporarily almost anywhere, sent through the mails. Maybe it's because the tape is relatively cheap and considered to be relatively expendable.

The truth is that videotape should be handled carefully. It should always be kept in its protective box. It should be stored in a cool, dry place, on end like a book. It should not be spliced, in fact, should never be touched. The cassette itself should be handled gently: The door that closes over the tape when it is outside a VCR can be bent, and the cassette case itself can be cracked.

Videotape and cassettes have certain characteristics that you need to know about. Videotape is plastic, coated on one side with a metallic layer of material which is bonded onto a polyester backing. This metallic layer captures and holds the electronic signals from the recording and tracking heads. Since the tape moves past the recording heads at a constant speed, the smoothness of the tape surface is an important factor in fidelity of reproduction.

Several things besides human carelessness can damage videotape. Improper functions in the VTR—particularly poor alignment of the tape guides within the recorder and playback machines—can cause the tape to be folded along an edge. Since those essential control track signals are on one edge, this can be disastrous to proper editing.

Improper use of the portable VCR is another danger. If the battery is removed or the power turned off before the recorder is stopped, serious tape damage can occur. This is because when the recorder is stopped in the normal manner, the tape is unwound from the record heads. If power is interrupted with the tape partially or fully loaded, the recorder will hold on to the tape with a death grip. When the eject button is pushed, curls of creased and folded tape come out along with the cassette.

Since the tape itself is wound onto two wheels inside the cassette, make sure

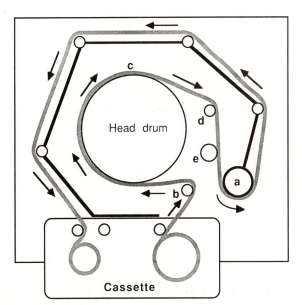

FIGURE 2-4. The path of the tape from a video cassette inside the videotape recorder. The tape is in a loop that is pulled out of the cassette and carried around the head drum by the threading arm (a). The video erase head (b) removes previous signals from the tape before it comes to the video (c) and tracking signal head (d). The audio erase and record heads (e) are located nearby. The recorded portion of the videotape then continues along the path and is returned to the take-up reel in the cassette. *(Courtesy of C. J. Beebe.)*

the tape is wound firmly on the wheels before it is inserted into the machine. Arrows on the cassette indicate the direction of the tape wind. It is a good precaution to tighten the wind slightly so there are no loose loops inside. But do this gently, since tape can be stretched if too much force is applied. Before using a new cassette, you should run it to its end on the fast forward setting, and then rewind it at fast rewind. This will correct any improper winding or crimping that might have occurred during manufacture and shipping.

Weather conditions can affect tape and tape recorders. The hot, humid, dirty trunk of a car is not a good place to carry either one. Moving from cold to hot conditions does the same thing to the head drum of a tape recorder that it does to your eyeglasses—steam up. The tape is very susceptible to moisture; moisture on the head drum can cause the tape to plaster itself to the drum so that both the magnetic coating and the entire plastic backing will "melt" right onto the drum. Drastic temperature changes can also cause the tape to change physical dimension; going from cool to hot conditions will make it swell and stretch.

Each time a videotape is run past the record or playback heads of a tape recorder, it comes into contact with those heads, and a tiny amount of the magnetic recording material is worn off. At the networks and at major-market stations, each cassette is used only once and is then stored in the station's archives. Other stations use the tapes more than once. But the microscopic bits of tape surface that have been worn off repeatedly used tapes will show up in the picture as dropouts in the video signal. Tapes that are being held in pause—a frozen frame on the picture screen—are still in contact with the whirling heads, so leaving the tape in pause-freeze for lengthy periods of time will result in tiny pits being dug out of the recording material. Dust and dirt are perhaps even bigger factors in tape damage. Particles of dust or dirt can get ground into the recording surface and will cause more wear than head contact.

Creased or folded tape cannot be used again. You will never forget the sound a creased tape makes when it runs past the record heads—it is an awful buzzing, hissing sound. The next event will probably be a jamming of the recorder mechanism. And it will happen in a flash. When you hear that sound, stop the machine quickly! A jammed videotape can damage the guide path and the heads and render the recorder useless.

In the event a tape is creased in the field *and* it is absolutely necessary to use that cassette—and if the machine is not jammed—you can try an emergency remedy. It is possible to advance the tape beyond the creased portion and record on the undamaged portion of the tape. But don't try to rewind back over the creased part.

LIGHTING

Now you know more than you thought you wanted to know about cameras, lenses, and tape recorders. If your own "head drum" is spinning, remember that key word: *parameters,* the electronic limits that help or hinder the things you can do to cover the news visually. Let's move on to lighting, one of the most poorly done things in all of TV news.

Color

Since we are working in color, we have to be concerned with and know something about the natural properties of light in the scenes we want to shoot. These qualities may adversely affect the color in the pictures we are making unless we do something to control them. Light sources may be a mixture of natural and artificial light; there may be too much contrast, or too little. Saturation (intensity) and hues (shades) can be drastically changed by the quality of the light we have, and to make things even more exciting, the lighting conditions may change constantly—especially on spot news stories.

Scientists define light as visible electromagnetic radiation. The human eye is sensitive to only a small part of the entire electromagnetic spectrum; therefore ''light'' is that part that can be seen. The wavelengths of visible light range from about 3,500 to about 8,000 angstroms (one angstrom equals one ten-millionth of a millimeter). When light is separated or diffracted by a prism, each wavelength is seen to correspond to a different color.

Color Temperature

The balance of colors in light can be measured in terms of temperature. For this we use the **Kelvin** scale. In the late nineteenth century, William Thompson Kelvin established it as an absolute measure of temperature related to the temperature of a standard ''black body'' of specified density.

As Kelvin heated this black body, he noted that it changed color from black to red, then blue, then white. He recorded the temperatures at which these changes occurred and thus developed his scale. For our purposes the Kelvin scale can be considered to measure wavelengths of light in terms of temperature, and therefore is a standard comparative measure of colors in light.

But warmer and cooler colors don't work the way we are accustomed to consider them. Red, which we think of as warm, has a lower Kelvin temperature than blue, which we think of as cool. This is because red light has a lower wavelength than blue light. A look at Figure 2-5 shows the temperatures of various sources of light commonly used by ENG crews at news events. All this has a kind of unity: Remember that we adjust the red and blue portions of the video signal (with green as a constant) to reproduce the white parts of the scene as white, and therefore balance all of the other colors. In Chapter 4 you will learn how to manipulate and control the light at a news event to achieve the most natural reproduction possible. For now, let's look at some other characteristics of light from the point of view of news coverage.

Natural Light

The sun is a wonderful source of light, but sunlight creates serious problems for the ENG photojournalist. It is overhead. It changes color temperature dramatically as it

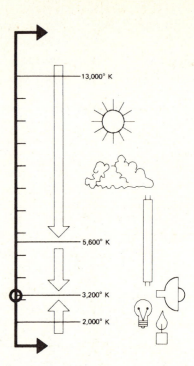

FIGURE 2-5. The Kelvin scale and the color temperatures associated with the various lighting instruments and lighting conditions found at news stories. At the low end of the scale are ordinary (incandescent) lights and candlelight, which will produce red light waves. Quartz lights provide the 3200° K standard lighting for indoor ENG shooting. Fluorescent lights provide a wide range of color temperatures. Outdoor light (no sun) and direct sunlight provide increasingly higher Kelvin temperatures and blue light waves and therefore must be filtered. *(Courtesy of C. J. Beebe.)*

travels through the atmosphere; it is more blue in the middle of the day, more orange or red in the late afternoon. The intensity of sunlight is the same over all of a given scene. Sunlight casts only one sharp-edged shadow, approximately the same width as the subject. The contrast ratios are very high: as much as 7 to 1 between direct sunlight and shadowed areas or the clear sky light above the subject compared to the horizon. Furthermore, people standing in direct sunlight tend to squint; if they are wearing sunglasses, you can't see their eyes, or the glasses reflect.

Artificial Light

As Figure 2-5 shows, various kinds of **artificial light** give off different color temperatures and therefore create color balance problems for the ENG photojournalist.

Artificial light is usually dimmer than natural light, even though it may not appear to be.

Neon or **fluorescent lights** give off different color temperatures than either natural light or the quartz lights normally used for ENG.

Normal light bulbs—**incandescent light**—give off another, and different, color temperature than natural light, quartz, neon, or fluorescent.

Mercury-vapor lights (used to light some sports arenas, highways, and parking lots), produce still another different color temperature.

Mixing Natural and Artificial Light

It is difficult to get good overall lighting and color values when you have to mix natural light with artificial light, but since television news camerapersons usually shoot video stories where people live, work, and play, these conditions must be coped with on a daily basis.

Fortunately cameras have been improved very rapidly in a very short time, particularly those cameras in the middle and higher price ranges. With white balancing and a careful use of filters, many on-the-scene lighting problems can be solved—as long as the photojournalist is conscientious.

Most ENG cameras contain a filter wheel mounted inside the camera behind the lens. Some lower cost cameras require that filters be manually installed on the lens. In general the filters are designed to do two things: knock down the intensity of direct sunlight and correct the excessive blueness of daylight (no sun) on a cloudy day.

Generally the cameras contain:

1. A clear filter for use indoors with quartz lights (3200° K)
2. A magenta (85B) filter for use in daylight (no sun) (5600° K) to correct excessive blueness
3. Some combination of magenta and neutral density filters to give an overall reduction of the intensity of full sunlight (as high as 11,000° K to 13,000° K) and correct for blueness

The trick is to use the camera's white-balancing system plus the required filters. In operation indoors, with a mix of fluorescent and incandescent light, the normal thing to do is to place the clear filter in position and then carefully white-balance on faces in the picture to get the best possible flesh tones.

Outdoors the thing to do is to place the proper blueness/intensity filter in position, and then white balance—again on the flesh-tone area. When the shooting moves from indoors to outdoors or vice versa, the most important thing to remember is to change to the appropriate filter. Failure to do so will result in people in the pictures looking like the Green Monster or the Terror from the Blue Lagoon or a landscape that looks more like a moonscape. You cannot change the color balance on a recorded tape; you just have to go back and shoot the scenes again with the correct filter in place.

Lighting Ratios

Television itself and the cameras it uses cannot handle sharp differences in lighting contrasts as well as film can. Film systems can handle ratios of as high as 100:1, whereas television systems cannot handle ratios higher than 20:1 to 30:1. Besides this technical limitation, the contrast ratio problem is complicated by the way we view films and television. We see the films in darkened theaters, whereas we view television under all kinds of conditions. We are all familiar with the spooky detective thriller on the late movie in which the scenes are so dark and dingy it is hard to tell what is going on. In the theater the dark areas show up in sharper contrast to the bright areas, but on the TV screen they all blend together because room light is reflected off the screen, and the TV set itself provides some illumination.

The dark areas on the TV screen fill up with specks and wiggly things that are called **noise.** It is a good idea to try to minimize noise in the pictures made for news coverage by aiming for setups with overall flat lighting rather than setups with very bright and very dark areas. In other words, keep the bright-to-dark ratios low; try to avoid high-contrast ratios in the pictures.

Color Reflects

One final characteristic of light: It reflects from all surfaces within the picture area, and in color. A green wall will reflect green light onto the face and clothing of a subject. A bright red blouse will reflect red on the neck, and under the chin—even on the tip of the nose. Flooding light onto a colored background may reflect an overall hue to the entire picture. Shadows may take on the color reflected into them.

Lighting Equipment

News seldom happens in a studio; more likely it happens where there is a lighting problem. In a Hollywood studio, or on a TV commercial setup, the problems of color temperature and its effect on the colors reflected back to the camera can be carefully controlled. In a television station studio all of the lighting instruments are quartz lights, all of which give off the same 3,200 degrees Kelvin. If we wanted to duplicate daylight—5,600 degrees Kelvin—we would have to buy or rent huge high-intensity carbon-arc lights and a huge DC generator to drive them. It is very difficult to sneak up on a news story with a U-Haul van full of lighting equipment and the lighting crew needed to run it.

ENG crews carry portable lighting equipment with them at all times and use it extensively. There are times when picture quality must be sacrificed in order to get the story on tape, but these occasions are much rarer than most people think.

The lighting kits used today supply adequate lighting conditions under most circumstances. The kits include lighting instruments, tripod stands on which to mount them, power cords, battery belts to provide power for portable lights, and accessories to help put the light where it is needed and screen it from where it isn't. All units supply a constant source of light at proper color temperatures. Chapter 4 includes the details about lighting in the field.

Various companies manufacture different kinds of lights for ENG use. The units themselves are quite similar, but they are used in at least four important ways:

1. **Key Lights:** Here "key" means "main." They light the general area.
2. **Fill Lights:** They "fill in" the shadows created by the key lights.
3. **Back Lights:** They light the back of the *subject* to outline head, hair, and shoulders, and provide separation from the background.
4. **Wash Lights:** They light the background to help reduce high contrast ratios.

FIGURE 2-6. Typical lights found in an ENG field lighting kit. The two lower lights are floodlights, usually used as fill lights, designed to throw a wide-angle beam of light over a large area. The two lights above are spot lights, usually used as key or back lights, which can be aimed in a narrower beam. *(Courtesy of Will Counts.)*

Many news events require much more lighting than can be provided with a portable light kit or two. This in turn requires careful planning. Almost any scene can be properly lit for television pictures, but a proper lighting setup for large-scale shooting requires considerable time. A famous cinematographer once lit the inside of St. Peter's Basilica in Rome. He was given permission to do so on one condition: The pope himself would come in to approve the setup before shooting could start, and if the pope was able to see even one lighting instrument, permission would be revoked. The scores of lights were so carefully placed and hidden that the pope did not see any of them, and the shooting went ahead.

Battery-Powered Lights ENG crews carry battery-powered lights for situations where a reliable AC source is not available. Such lights can be mounted directly on the camera or hand held by another person. They can be adjusted to provide either a narrow focus—a **spotlight**—or a somewhat wider pattern—a **floodlight.**

Battery-powered lights require a large amount of power. Thus the length of time they can be used continuously is limited to perhaps thirty minutes before the batteries are completely drained. Other problems with these lights are:

1. When mounted on the camera itself they provide a very high-contrast picture, make sharp-edged shadows, and create shadow problems on the background.

2. They tend to blind people facing them. These lights should be first turned on as they are pointed upward, then tilted down onto the subject. This will give him or her (and your competitors) at least a short period of time to adjust to the glare.

Batteries   Some of the most colorful language ever heard in broadcast journalism has been prompted by and directed at the batteries used to power ENG equipment in the field. Batteries are, however, the lifeblood that keeps the equipment fueled and running, and they should be given careful treatment and care.

ENG equipment (other than lighting) draws very little power—less than two amps an hour for recorders and cameras. The rechargeable batteries used to run it are given ratings that relate to the number of hours they will deliver a specific amount of direct-current power. For example, a 30-amp-hour battery will deliver fifteen hours of 2-amp current, or three hours of 10-amp current, and so on. Generally, the larger a battery is, the more power it can sustain.

But like your car battery, the batteries used to run ENG equipment respond to the temperature. The colder it is, the less output they will give, and the shorter the life of the charge they contain. On cold days in the field the only answer is to try to keep the equipment as warm as possible and change the batteries frequently.

Batteries are mounted on or housed in the equipment, or are worn on a belt by the camera operator. The most usual charge-holding material inside the battery is an alloy of **nickel and cadmium—Ni-Cad** for short. More recently some manufacturers have come out with silver-zinc batteries, which are more efficient and require less space. The trade-off is that they are very expensive and more difficult to charge.

ENG batteries are rechargeable. In the field they can be recharged on portable recharge units or from an AC power converter. After use they are usually recharged in the news department. Normally this takes about three hours, although high-speed battery chargers can cut that time in half, or to as little as twenty minutes.

The process is relatively simple: The batteries are plugged into a recharger with a built-in protective system to prevent overcharging and LEDs that indicate the status of the charge. Almost all battery belts have rechargers built into them.

How the battery is used and how it is recharged are very important to battery life. Batteries should be discharged as completely as possible before they are changed—most cameras and recorders shut themselves off when the battery gets low, and warning lights tell the operator when that is about to occur. All batteries hold a charge better, and last longer, if they are completely discharged before recharging. They do lose a little of their charge as they are stored. But ''topping off'' with a short charge period actually reduces their charge-holding qualities.

Batteries look rugged, but they are not. They do not react well to harsh treatment—dropping them may make them short out or fail completely.

MICROPHONES

Perhaps you have already had a course in **audio** production or radio news, where a good bit of attention is paid to the technical properties of microphones and the kinds of sound they will reproduce. At that time you may have wondered why, as a broadcast journalist, you needed to know something so arcane. The answer is that you need to know what the microphones you use can or cannot do.

Microphones contain metal diaphragms that vibrate when sound waves strike them. Those vibrations are converted into electric impulses by backplates or coils. Those impulses can then be amplified and recorded on the videotape audio tracks and stored there for editing along with the pictures. Finally, the impulses are converted back into sound by similar vibrating diaphragms in the television set's loudspeakers.

Two kinds of mics are common for TV news use: **dynamic microphones** and **condenser microphones.** Each has somewhat different characteristics.

Dynamic mics are rugged. They are less sensitive, and therefore can be used in noisy places. Even so, unless dynamic mics are used carefully, "p" and "s" sounds tend to pop and hiss.

Condenser mics have been developing rapidly. They are becoming more and more sensitive. They need their own power supply, so most of them contain tiny batteries like those used in hearing aids. The amount of power needed to run a condenser mic is very small, so these batteries last a long time. But a dead battery can be a hazard in field reporting. You will find a number of very good books about microphones and their uses in all kinds of situations in the bibliography.

Television field reporting uses four kinds of microphones as basic equipment: the hand-held omnidirectional, the tiny lavalier mic, which can be clipped to the clothing or worn on a neck strap, the transmitter (wireless) mic, and the shotgun mic. Each has particular characteristics that dictate its particular use.

Hand-Held Omnidirectional Microphones

Omni means "all," and these microphones pick up the sound from all around (see Fig. 2-7). They come in many different shapes and sizes and are adequate for situations where the background sound is low or normal. They work best when pointed directly at and close to the sound source. In situations where the background sound is very loud, an omnidirectional microphone may not discriminate between sounds, and this in turn creates problems in sound recording.

Because most portable ENG equipment has automatic gain control regulating the sound levels, loud background sound will be "pumped up" when there is little foreground sound—as when the reporter or news source stops speaking. When the speaker starts up again, the background sound will be pumped back down. On the recording it sounds like ocean waves are crashing on a beach.

Another disadvantage of hand-held omnidirectional mics is that they are usually connected by a cable to the recorder and thus the maneuverability of the person using them is limited. Then, too, they often are seen in the picture, which complicates editing.

Lavalier Microphones

These very small mics have a more unidirectional pick up pattern and thus a more limited reception range. Therefore they are attached to the reporter's or subject's clothing with clips at or near the lapel level or are worn around the neck on a cord. When they are used that way, they provide very good sound quality for interviews, especially where the background sound is high.

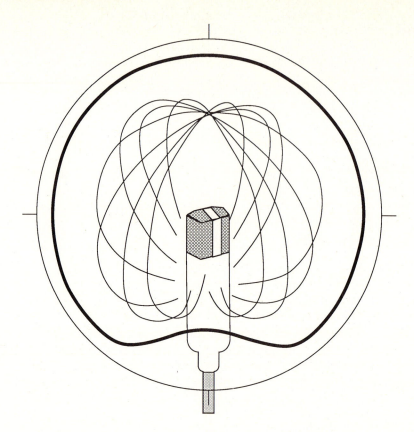

FIGURE 2-7. The sound receiving pattern of an omnidirectional microphone. This microphone picks up sound waves from all directions and therefore might pick up unwanted noise at a news event. *(Courtesy of C. J. Beebe.)*

Because they are quite directional, they must be aimed carefully at the sound source they are expected to pick up.

Wireless Microphones   A **wireless microphone** contains a tiny transmitter that can send the audio signal to a receiver attached to the tape recorder or elsewhere. They are very handy for close-in situations, as Larry Hatteberg explains in the essay after Chapter 4. They are also useful when the reporter doesn't want to be (or can't be) attached to the tape recorder by a cable. The range of a transmitter mic varies according to the power of its transmitter.

A disadvantage is that transmitter mics use radio frequencies that are also used by others, so their receivers often pick up such distracting things as cab calls, or other transmitter mics being used in the same area. Wireless microphones require battery power to operate, and since they use quite a lot of power, batteries need to be changed frequently.

Shotgun Microphones   These mics (see Fig. 2-9) pick up sound at a considerable distance from the source. They are very directional and must be aimed right at the sound source. When that is done, however, good sound quality can be obtained from many feet away. They are excellent for getting the questions from the floor at a public meeting or the words of a subject who is surrounded by a crowd.

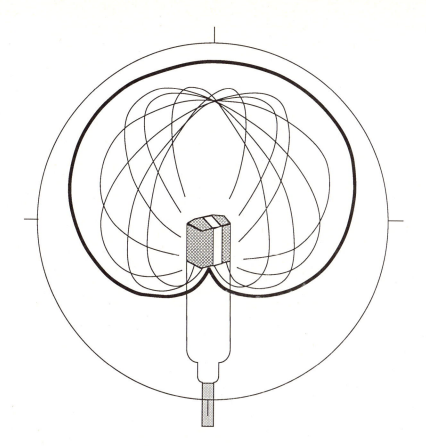

FIGURE 2-8. The sound receiving pattern of a unidirectional microphone. This mic picks up sound only from in front of the mic. Unidirectional microphones are used to eliminate unwanted background noise. *(Courtesy of C. J. Beebe.)*

Larger models can be mounted on tripods and can pick up sound from a remarkable distance away. They can also be used to pick up certain parts of ambient sound, or to shield out portions of background sound that are not wanted. A small shotgun mic can be mounted on top of a camera to pick up the sound in the area directly in front of the camera lens.

Camera-mounted shotgun mics should not be used for interviews. The best use of a shotgun is to get specific sound from about three to six feet away. Shotgun mics look very awkward when they are hand held by a reporter during an interview. And they bear a startling resemblance to the barrel of a gun. Network crews working in El Salvador with a newly developed shotgun mic found this out the hard way. A sound crewman cautiously pointed the mic over a wall. The crew drew rifle fire from somewhere nearby within a few seconds.

Microphone Cords

We cannot leave this subject without a mention of mic cords. They are, of course, the much-ignored, much-abused but essential link between most microphones and the amplifiers and recorders that process and store sound. They have connectors at

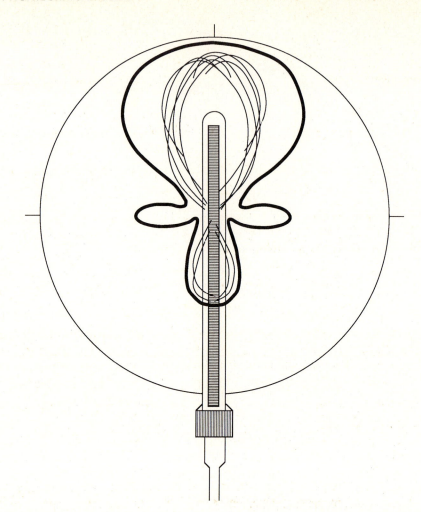

FIGURE 2-9. The sound receiving pattern of a shotgun microphone. This mic picks up sound in a very narrow angle directly in front of it. Shotgun microphones are used to pick up specific sound from a distance, such as questions from the audience in crowded, informal news conferences or to isolate the speech of one person in a group. *(Courtesy of C. J. Beebe.)*

each end that come in the form of single or double jacks, multiple-pronged plugs, or locking plugs.

There are two things to understand about these connectors. First, they should be treated with care. A majority of sound problems in the field are a result of broken or damaged connectors. If dirt gets into the connector it will not connect. If a trunk lid or car door is slammed on it, it can be crushed or broken off.

Second, since the connectors come in different shapes and sizes, you can find yourself with a connector that won't plug into a socket, or a mic cord extension that won't plug into a mic. The only solution is to make sure you have compatible equipment before you take off for the news site.

The mic cords themselves are easily damaged. If they are, they can short out, producing either a bad buzz or hum or no sound at all. They should be coiled carefully after use and stored in a safe place.

One final warning: Power cables and mic cords don't mix. A mic cord draped over or placed under a power cable will conduct electricity from the power cable. This will result in a bad hum that will accompany the sound you wanted onto the recording.

Audio experts consider the sound work done by TV crews to be quite primitive, and they are right. But using the proper microphones, a news crew can obtain good sound quality. Using them improperly can produce sound that is not clear, not understandable, or so mixed up with the other sounds at the event that no one can really hear what the principal subjects had to say.

So far we have dealt with the equipment used in the field to record the raw material that will be made into news stories. The content elements of videotape editing will be presented in Chapter 5. This section deals with how the editing equipment works and its capabilities and limitations.

Audio and Video

A big advantage of videotape over its ancestor, 16mm motion picture film, is that the pictures and two channels of sound are placed on the tape at exactly the same moment during the recording. Even in the most simple video edits, the editing controllers can do a number of things at the same time. They will edit video and sound together, or video or sound separately. With them you can add other sound to either of the **audio tracks,** or (using a sound mixer) combine additional sound with the sound already on one or both of the audio tracks.

The following options are possible.

1. The story can be edited with the sound on tape just by transferring scenes from the original tape to the edited tape.
2. Or the story can start out with a reporter narrating over scenes, then sound bites from interviews can be added.
3. Or the reporter can be seen starting the story from the scene of the action, then illustrative scenes can be edited into the tape while the reporter continues with narration.
4. Or music and other sound elements can be edited into and mixed with the natural sound.

Most important, whatever is created comes out on one tape cassette, ready to be played back into the news program with the touch of one button.

The Editor Package

Equipment packages can be simple or complex. The basics are two servo-controlled videotape recorders (VTRs) connected together by an editing controller. Remember the control track we emphasized earlier? That track—that is, the pulses on it—is what locks the two machines together so that precise edits are possible. What happens is that the picture, and perhaps also the sound, from the VTR (source) containing the original recorded material is being electronically transferred to a video cassette in the other machine (record) one scene at a time to build the edited story.

It is a ''cuts only'' system. Some cameras will perform fade-in and fade-out functions with the auto-iris, but without other equipment it does not allow **dissolves,** wipes, or any other visual effects. The number of things that can be done with the audio or video is relatively primitive compared to the elaborate things that can be done in post-production using an entire control room full of sophisticated mixers, switchers, and effects generators. But it is fast and efficient, and for news work that is important. Furthermore, more complex production equipment is just a step away in most television stations, and portable production switchers and effects generators are becoming standard in field-editing packages.

How the Systems Work

The specific tasks that are performed before and during an edit are not difficult to understand.

1. The original material is played back, and each scene is located and timed. This is called "logging."
2. Scene selection and order are determined. This is called making a "scene list" or **cut sheet.**
3. Edit points are established by moving the tape backward and forward to find the desired start and end of each scene.
4. The machines preroll: Together they back up from the precise edit point on both the source and record machines as they count the pulses together.
5. The machines stop together at the preroll point.
6. The machines roll forward together down to the edit point, and the recording on the record machine begins at that precise point.

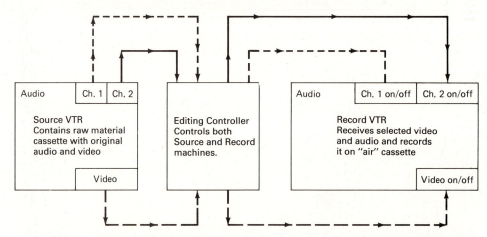

FIGURE 2-10. The basic functions of an ENG editing station. It contains two videotape (VTR) machines—the source machine on the left, the record machine on the right. They are connected to and controlled by an editing controller. Audio and video signals are fed from the source to the record machines through the controller, which is used to select edit points, preroll both machines, and perform the edits. Switches on the record machine control whether the edits contain video and audio, video only, or audio only, and which audio channel will be used.

7. *Note that steps 4, 5, and 6 happen as one continuous movement.*
8. The operator ends the edit by the touch of a button, or the machines stop and wait for the next command.
9. Subsequent edits are made the same way by establishing an edit point on each machine, and then commanding them to perform again, one scene at a time, until the story is finished.

Finding the Edit Point

All VTR–editing-controller combinations allow for manual movement of the tape forward or backward at a variety of speeds from fast to one frame at a time. Thus, the operator can search for the exact frame desired by listening to the sound and watching the video monitor as the tape moves. When that frame is found, different machines handle it in different ways. The simpler editing controllers freeze the frame and use it as a reference point. More sophisticated controllers display the exact frame count on a screen or on a read-out counter, and a memory keeps track of it. Editing controllers with such memory units and keyboards will perform search functions and can be programmed to perform a series of edits.

Rehearsing the Edit

One of the nicest things about video editing is that all modern VTR-editing-controller systems provide for a rehearsal of the edit before it is actually made. Buttons or switches command the machines to back up, pause, go forward, and complete the edit—except that the actual edit is not performed. The

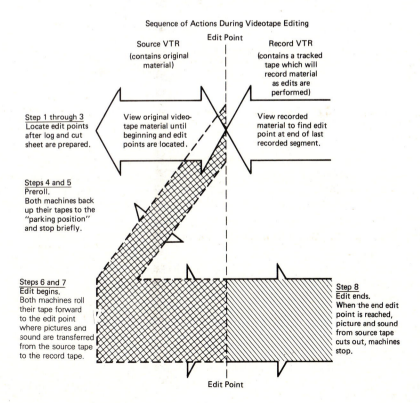

Sequence of Actions During Videotape Editing

Edit Point

Source VTR (contains original material)

Record VTR (contains a tracked tape which will record material as edits are performed)

Step 1 through 3
Locate edit points after log and cut sheet are prepared.

View original videotape material until beginning and edit points are located.

View recorded material to find edit point at end of last recorded segment.

Steps 4 and 5
Preroll. Both machines back up their tapes to the "parking position" and stop briefly.

Steps 6 and 7
Edit begins. Both machines roll their tape forward to the edit point where pictures and sound are transferred from the source tape to the record tape.

Step 8
Edit ends. When the end edit point is reached, picture and sound from source tape cuts out, machines stop.

Edit Point

FIGURE *2-11.* What happens when a videotape edit is made. The editor selects the edit points on each VTR by moving their tapes backward and forward to the appropriate video frame on those tapes. Then the edit controller takes over to back up both tapes, stop at the parking position, and then roll both tapes forward through the edit point and to the end of the edit.

machines then return to the edit point. The editor can then decide whether to perform that edit or to make changes in it by moving the edit point backward or forward. Some controllers have keypads that permit the editor to add or subtract individual frames of picture and sound by typing this information into the digital memory. When the edit is performed, the alterations are made automatically.

Insert and Assemble Functions   You can edit material from one VTR to another in two ways: **assemble mode editing** and **insert mode editing.** The difference has to do with the way the control tracks are used.

In assemble mode editing, the source machine sends all the elements of the picture to the record machine. The record machine erases all other material on its tape while laying down the new material coming from the source machine—including a new control track.

Today, almost all edits are made in insert mode. Using insert mode to edit requires that the tape in the record machine be "tracked" in advance of its use. Sync pulse and black video or color bars are fed to the record machine and are recorded over the full length of the tape needed for the edit. There are two reasons for this:

1. In insert mode, the new track put on the record tape in advance will be used to control the capstan servo—the mechanism that controls tape speed exactly on both machines, thus making a very precise edit.
2. Putting new video and tracking signals onto the record tape avoids the possibility that there were dropouts or holes in the tracking in the material that was already on the tape. The tape is given a clean coating of tracking and video signals, and old audio signals are erased.

A brand-new video cassette cannot be used to do insert mode edits until tracking and video signals are laid down on it. (In the field the portable VCRs will put tracking and video signal on a new blank tape as the recording is being made. But even so, it is standard practice to track any tape before using it in the field.) Assemble mode edits may not be as clean and precise as insert mode edits because the way the control pulse and video signals are recorded on the videotape makes assemble-mode edits less smooth. Look again at Figure 2-3 to see the difference between the track patterns in assemble and insert mode edits. Note that important gap between the control track and video track at the beginning and end of the assemble edit. That represents a "hole" in the track where the machines will temporarily not be locked together. Assemble mode edits are used mainly to do what the word implies, *assemble* material from the source tape or tapes onto the record tape, or to dub material from one machine to the other.

Audio Only/Video Only   Even the simplest editing setups have the ability to separate the audio and video editing functions. It is possible to edit only the pictures, or only the sound, or only one of the two sound channels. It is also possible to lay down sound on either or both of the sound channels from another audio source. When you do this you flip switches to tell the machines which channels you want new material put on. Thus the original video or audio remains on the source tape. Only the new video or audio is added to the record tape.

This is another significant characteristic of these video editing systems. The original video and audio material is always available on the source tape. Unless by some freak accident someone has managed to erase the original material, you can always go back to it if you want to re-edit your story.

Time Code, Time Base   Most video editing bays in TV station news departments will contain two VTRs, a controller, an audio mixer, and a time base corrector. Many editing machines also have components that allow the use of time code in locating taped material and in editing.

Time coding is a simple idea that grew out of the space age. The idea is to have a machine that generates a continuous standard code—in most cases the exact hour, minute, second, and video frame at the time the tape was being recorded. It shows up at some location in the picture when that material is played back on video screens (see Fig. 2-12). The National Aeronautics and Space Administration began putting time code on all of its video and data tapes during the Apollo and Gemini space programs. Thousands of miles of various kinds of video and data tape are made during every space mission. In order to be able to find a batch of pictures and data relating to a single event, NASA inserted Greenwich Mean Time (GMT in hours, minutes, seconds, and frame) on all the tapes. Then if something broke down at 14:22:05:16, all of the material on tape—telemetry, computer data, video, audio, data streams, and so on—that was recorded at that time could be located quickly by using the code. NASA uses it as a filing system with time as a universal index.

Small time code generators were developed so that they could be attached to or

FIGURE 2-12. Time code on a video frame. The numbers indicate the hour, minute, second, and frame number at the time that frame was recorded. Time code is used in videotape editing to locate edit points, to program a series of edits, or to program the editing of an entire story. *(Courtesy of Will Counts.)*

built into cameras and recorders. These then put time code on video tape as it is being recorded.

Time code is seen on video monitors because time code readers pick it up off the videotape and insert it separately into the monitor picture. It is not seen by the viewer at home because it is not inserted into the video signal at any time during the recording or editing process.

Editing with time code is even easier than normal editing. Scenes can be selected by marking down the time code as the logging procedure is carried out. Editing controllers with microprocessors that read the code can then be used in the editing process to locate edit points quickly. And since microprocessing involves memory units, once again the editing controllers with these features can be programmed to perform a series of edits or even an entire story.

Time code can also be used as a standard reference point for all hands. Most stations use the precise local time as their time standard. Those reporters in the field and those in the newsroom can simply note the exact time something important happened during coverage of a story and then use that time to locate the important material quickly during the editing.

More important to news operations, time code can be used to lock together the various units of the editing system more precisely than pulse count. Therefore edits are cleaner and tapes more stable on the air.

The Vertical Interval

The Vertical Interval   The most useful place to put time code is in the vertical interval in the video picture. Without getting too technical about it, the vertical interval is that area of the television picture between the frames that normally is not seen at all on a television set. Lines of information are put there as the picture is being made to stabilize the horizontal and vertical timing of the picture, among other things, in order to bring it up to FCC standards. But that unseen segment contains unused lines, so it is possible to put the time code signal into those lines and therefore *include* it in the video signal but not in that part the viewer sees. Time code inserted this way is much more dependable, and can be used in various ways to add stability to other functions such as switching and programmable editing from a variety of video sources.

Time Base Correcting

Time Base Correcting   A frame of television picture is much like a frame of film: one complete picture. But two television **fields** make up that one complete frame containing (in the U.S.) 525 scanning lines of resolution. Each recording head on the spinning head drum puts one field on the tape, therefore, each head lays down 262.5 lines alternately on odd and even lines.

Obviously it is important to get those lines exactly where they ought to be for stable broadcast performance. Since helical scan recording equipment has not always performed as precisely as desired, another operation—time base correcting (TBC)—was developed to bring the pictures up to FCC standards.

Going into detail about how TBCs work is beyond the scope of this book but briefly: A TBC is a "black box" that converts the video signal coming to it into digital information. Once the information has been digitized all sorts of signal processing can be done using standard computer circuitry. In essence what the TBC does is make sure that each line of the picture occurs at a uniform interval. As each line of picture comes to the TBC from the tape being played back, the TBC corrects its timing, stores it, and then retrieves it and sends it on its way at a uniform interval. This not only straightens up the picture, but it also corrects all timing elements using sync as a standard referent. Of course, this happens in microseconds.

The result is a picture that meets standards and is stable when seen on the home receiver. A patient engineer friend once told one of the authors who was struggling to understand the TBC: "These pictures jiggle, so the TBC gets them and everything else to jiggle all together."

The TBC has a second function that allows use of more sophisticated production elements in ENG editing. We have already said that most standard ENG editing functions are "cuts only." Adding fades or dissolves and inserting words or graphics during the editing process can be done with the use of a TBC and a switcher. The TBC serves to stabilize and lock the signals coming through it from the source machine to the switcher. It will also process material from any other video source coming through the switcher, such as a character generator putting name identifications on the bottom of the screen. The TBC is used to help combine the video effects from various sources together onto the recorded tape in the record unit.

When pictures coming from the field on helical scan machines are being played over a microwave or satellite relay system, TBCs are used to lock them to the other in-station signals so that they can be broadcast.

In addition to the TBC a station's control room contains a lot of other electronic wonders that are designed to improve picture stability: field and frame synchronizers and picture enhancers, to name just two. When digital video takes over—and it soon will—things like these will probably disappear because that digital technology won't need them any more. One thing is certain: The broadcast journalist will always find strangely named gadgets are a part of the jargon of the job and the workplace.

"AND NOW—LIVE FROM THE SCENE. . . ."

An Indianapolis television station used to refer to the reporter who did most of the live remote inserts into the station's newscasts as "our live anchor." They changed that to "field anchor" after it was pointed out to them that it sounded as though the anchors in the studio were "dead" anchors.

Live news broadcasts are in many ways the heart of ENG. Let's look at the technology involved, its problems, and its strengths.

Two important developments—lightweight, self-contained camera-recorder and switching units, and miniaturized microwave equipment—are responsible for the growth of local live news coverage. The equipment is expensive; it is easy to spend $200,000 or more for a fully equipped remote van including microwaving capability.

Live remote units need trained crews to run them; the reporter you see doing a live story on the 6 P.M. news has not just raced out there and plugged him/herself in. It takes engineers at the TV station to handle the signals coming back from the remote site and to get them on the air. ENG crews can work quickly, and station installations are designed to pull everything together in a few minutes. Yet it does take time to set things up. Travel time is always a factor—it takes so many minutes to reach the scene of the news story. Once there, just how fast the van can be activated depends on how easily the microwave system can be linked to the station.

Microwave

The microwave being discussed here is essentially a wireless transmission system. The basics are simple: High-frequency radio signals carrying the video and audio information are transmitted from one point to another using antennae to send them and "dishes" to catch them. The antennae may be omnidirectional (sending signals in a broadly scattered pattern) or directional (sending signals in a narrowly focused beam). There are no wires or cables connecting the remote site with the TV station.

Gigahertz   Now you learn a wonderful-sounding word: *gigahertz*. It means thousands of millions of **hertz,** just as megahertz means millions of hertz. Each of those words denotes a segment of the radio frequency spectrum.

The microwave transmitters in news vans use the 2-, 7-, 13-, and 40-gigahertz bands for their relatively short-range transmissions. These bands are designated for use by the FCC, and therefore each transmitter must be licensed. Within these bands are a number of separate channels, each of which is wide enough to carry both video and audio signals. Generally speaking, the lower the gigahertz band the less power is needed to transmit signals on it. This is an important consideration in ENG field production since portability of the equipment and the power supply to run it are significant factors. But the less power available, the shorter the distance the signal will travel.

The manufacturers therefore have produced microwave transmitting equipment with as many as ten separate channels available. This equipment allows for switching from channel to channel, or band to band, so that the best signal can be achieved rapidly.

The equipment comes in a variety of packages. Some transmitters can be attached to the side of a portable camera so it can go almost anywhere without having to be attached to the van by cable. Somewhat larger units can be mounted on tripods or attached to any stable upright with clamps. If these small units are omnidirectional, the distance they can "throw" the signal may be limited to a couple of hundred feet. If they are undirectional, their range may be longer.

Covering the News with Microwave

Many of you will be familiar with what a news van looks like. It has a dish or a rodlike antenna on top that can be raised, tilted, or panned to aim the signal from the van. The microwave transmitter uses these antennas to send the signals to the station.

Because of the very high frequencies used, these transmitters usually require a *line of sight* between the transmitter antenna and the receiving dish at the other end of the link. In many cities line of sight between the van and the station's receiving antenna is not possible, so more than one link is required. Therefore many stations mount higher-powered receivers and transmitters atop the tallest building or nearby natural terrain. The signals can go from the van to the high receiver-transmitter, and from there to the receivers at the station.

However, the microwave signals can also be bounced off the side of a tall building or a natural obstacle, so crews get very adept at making these "carom shots." Newsroom walls and engineering complexes contain maps showing the locations for the best bounces.

In Chicago, enterprising crews from one TV station actually painted unobtrusive marks on the street near Daley Plaza so they would know exactly where to put the wheels of their microwave van for the best bounce shot to the receiving antennas atop the Sears Tower. In Saint Louis one station regularly uses the city's famous arch to bounce signals from its vans down to its station antennas located nearby.

Depending on the terrain and the height of the receiving antenna, the vans sometimes can send signals over quite long distances: fifty- to sixty-mile links have been made in very flat country. The ultimate limit is dictated by the amount of sending power and the distance to the horizon: Microwave signals do not bend around the earth.

Besides these major transmission problems having to do with line-of-sight characteristics, there are similar smaller-scale problems at the scene of the news event. For example: An interview must be done in an office on the tenth floor of a building. The camera there is connected to a small microwave transmitter—often called a "two-gig"—that is aimed out the window at the news van parked in the street below. Everything will work well until something like a big truck gets between the transmitter and the receiving antenna on the van. Then, suddenly, the picture disappears. Answer: Move the van, move the transmitter, get the big truck to move, or all of the above. All you can do is hope that the news story remains where it is. If it doesn't, you will have to do the whole thing all over again.

If the news story moves then the answer may be a small microwave transmitter attached to the camera. But it can't move very far away, and suffers even more from being blocked by intervening solid obstacles.

In the fall of 1981, a San Francisco television station, KRON-TV, claimed the world's record by setting up an eight-hop, 232-mile set of microwave links. The signal went from the KRON-TV news van at the Diablo Canyon nuclear plant demonstration to the station by way of microwave receivers and transmitters set on top of six consecutive mountain peaks.

The more usual microwave-ENG setup is much less complicated, but a lot of technology is involved in even a simple live broadcast. The news van, carrying cameras, tape recorders, perhaps a small switcher and audio mixer, a power generator and the microwave antenna, goes to the news event and is met by reporters, field producers, and photojournalists. The reporters and some of the photojournalists go off to cover the news with portable tape recorders and cameras, while the van crew sets up another camera or cameras for the field anchors to use. They also set up a television monitor so the anchors and reporters can see what is on the air. Using their radio equipment they establish one or more radio links to provide intercommunication between the station news editors and the field anchors and between the station engineers and the van crew.

For a successful live broadcast the aural communications are as important as the video links, since the field anchors must be able to hear what is on the air and receive instructions and cues. Often the anchors in the studio will want to ask questions of those reporters in the field, and news editors will want to make suggestions about further coverage or provide additional story information they have received from other sources.

The same news van that provides live coverage can also feed pretaped material back to the station for use later, or to be edited and rolled back into the live report to illustrate what had happened earlier. Or tape made on other portable units at the scene can be edited in the news van for similar insertion into the live report.

Another way to get the signals back is to use a helicopter. If it is properly equipped, it can receive microwave signals from the ground and retransmit them to the TV station. Thus the chopper acts as a floating antenna that can send signals over great distances, depending on how high it is. Such ground-to-air-to-ground links are used frequently when line-of-sight transmission is blocked.

Covering the News by Satellite

The ultimate microwave unit is the one that uses communications satellites in space to deliver television signals from one point to another. Instead of bouncing signals off tall buildings or relaying them from hilltops, the satellite news gathering (SNG) vehicles send signals from the ground to transponders on a satellite 22,300 miles in space. The satellite then sends the signal back to a receiver on earth, and the link is completed. Technological breakthroughs have made the equipment necessary to

FIGURE 2-13. A helicopter equipped with ENG and microwave equipment. The helicopter can be used to transport ENG crews to and from a news event or for aerial photography. Its microwave receivers and transmitters also can be used as a way to originate live broadcasts or to relay video and sound signals from units on the ground to the broadcast station. *(Courtesy of Bell Helicopter.)*

do this small enough to be mounted on a truck about the same size as a microwave van. Because of the height of the satellite these trucks can send signals back to their stations from anywhere in the United States in one hop. We will deal with the significance of SNG in detail in Chapter 11.

"ONE MORE TAKE, PLEASE"

In the early 1950s, a group of resolute but nontechnical folks were starting up a TV station in Cedar Rapids, Iowa. Throughout this process there was a lot of determination, and a lot of doubt. Near the date when the station was to make its first broadcast, some wag put up a sign in the control room. It read: GOD NEVER MEANT FOR PICTURES TO GO THROUGH THE AIR. A lot of those folks half believed that. But, the pictures did go through the air all right, and everywhere they still do.

In the more simple days of broadcast journalism, it was considered smart to say: "I don't want to know about the technology, because if I do someone will ask me to fix it." Now it is essential that the broadcast journalist understand at least the outlines of the technology. You may never get a chance to touch many of the buttons we've talked about because others may be assigned to do that, and because many technicians are quite jealous of their prerogatives. But if you know enough about what that other person does, and what the equipment contributes to making the information you are passing on better and clearer, then you have an advantage. You are controlling the machines rather than letting the machines control you. And you can do a better job of communicating to your viewers.

The Structure of Television News

3

B efore we begin with the application of the new technology to the daily work of reporters, photojournalists, editors, producers, and those on the air, let us look at one overriding concept: structure.

All kinds of communication have structure: poetry, prose, and spoken language. Music—even the most radically modern or primitive—has structure. All art, painting, ceramics, sculpture, furniture making, stained glass, basket weaving, whatever form it takes, has structure.

Structure is involved in the way individual television news stories are shot, edited, produced, and aired within the larger structure of the newscast itself. This is the single most important idea you will need to grasp because it is central to how journalists communicate with their audiences. For television journalists, structure is even more important because of the *way* they communicate with the viewers.

Some people believe that what television news should do is present a whole event without narration, analysis, or commentary. Some say, for example, that the national political conventions should be telecast gavel to gavel, with the cameras fixed on the rostrum and delegates. There would be no floor reporters or anchorpersons in their skybooths explaining and interpreting what is going on. Those who hold this view say that then the audience could make up its mind as to what was important, could decide for itself the meaning of the event.

The new electronic technology already provides such a service during some sessions of the House of Representatives and the Senate, as well as committee hearings, deliberations by the United Nations, meetings of state legislatures, local city councils, and court sessions.

But the task of journalism is also to help explain and interpret the importance and significance of news events. There are reasons why the rhetoric and actions of one person are more important than those of another, why strategies and ideas expressed will or will not work.

These reasons are revealed by interviewing, digging for facts, taping, editing, and writing stories about the reasoning, the motives and the strategies of those involved. These elements are processed into news accounts and provide structure—the "how" and the "why" of the news as well as the "who," "what," "when," and "where." If we left the "how" and "why" out of our reports, the audience would be less well informed. Editing is, in fact, the work of the journalist. To avoid editing would be to burden the audience with a huge mass of information without fulfilling our obligation to make it clear and understandable.

With the concept of structure in mind, we will look now at some of the ingredients of the structure of television news communication. It has five distinct parts: showing and telling, the relationship between the people on the air and the viewers watching their television sets, storytelling, linear clarity, and visual structure.

SHOWING AND TELLING

As television news has expanded and all-news channels develop, the common dialogue today is:

Did you hear about . . .?
Yes, I saw it. . . .

The important word here is *saw*, and by using it people seem to mean they either "saw" a newscaster telling them about it or, because the technology makes it possible to bring pictures of the news to people very rapidly, it is also more and more likely that they really did "see" at least some of it. Instant replay and other production techniques also make it possible for the audience to "see it" again and again, to analyze it in slow motion or frame by frame. *Life* magazine used to show people the visual details once a week. Now television does it instantly, and it is not unusual to see frames from television pictures included in the photo coverage of newspapers and news magazines.

Pictures and Words

But television news is more than just pictorial coverage. It also "tells" the news with words spoken by anchorpersons, reporters, and news makers. The link between the pictures and the words is crucial. At the basic level that wedding of the right words with the right pictures is the greatest strength and greatest weakness of television news. When the pictures and words don't work together, when the screen is showing one thing and the words are telling something else, confusion quickly results.

THE ANCHOR INGREDIENT

Now add in the second unique ingredient: the fact that the audience is watching anchorpersons and reporters tell them the news.

When NBC's Reuven Frank said, "Television news is at its best when it provides an experience for the audience," he seemed to be saying that television allows the audience to *go along* with the **anchors** and reporters to the scene of a news story, either with live coverage or visual coverage on film or tape, and *be there* with them as the action unfolds.

Longtime NBC News anchorman John Chancellor, asked what he thought his role in the television news process was, said, "I think of myself as a guide, someone who is viewing the news along with the audience, and helping them understand it."

Although anchorpersons are not supposed to become emotionally involved in the news they are telling the audience about, they are human. Occasionally they break out of their shells and indicate what they think about what they have just watched with the audience.

Few will forget Walter Cronkite's close identification with United States space exploration, or the words he spoke immediately after the first landing on the moon.

He said, "Oh boy, oh boy. . . ."

The anchor ingredient is worth closer examination because it is an integral part of the television news communication process.

Anchors earn huge salaries and are promoted with the ruffles and flourishes befitting heads of state. They are true national or local celebrities. TV reporters also get more recognition than their print colleagues. People wave at them and call them by their first names as they walk down the street. Tourists are as likely to report they saw a network news correspondent getting out of a cab in New York or Washington as they are to talk about any other historic event or place they saw on their trip. There are anchor groupies just as there are rock star groupies. But the important fact is that viewers develop a personal relationship—an empathy—with the anchors and reporters who are there in their living rooms every day.

Hundreds of research studies have tried to define just how this relationship works. Consultants who advise TV stations on how to increase the size of the news audience have earned millions of dollars in part because they have concentrated on the viewer-anchor relationship. In general a few things stand out:

1. The audience and the anchorperson are involved in an empathic relationship—the audience has personal feelings about the anchor.
2. The audience respects the anchors because they deliver an important commodity—the news.
3. The audience attributes human characteristics to the anchors; it looks at them closely and reacts to any change in their appearance, dress, or on-air conduct.
4. The audience is forgiving about personal frailties—an occasional flub or a bad performance.
5. The audience is not very forgiving about professional failures—repeated mistakes, repeated poor performance, lack of clarity or precision.
6. The audience likes to get the news from people it likes more than it likes getting the news from people it dislikes.
7. The audience feels that it gets the news more clearly from anchorpersons it likes.

8. When things go wrong, the audience is often more likely to blame the news organization the anchor works for than to blame an anchor it likes.
9. The audience develops a very strong loyalty and viewing habit because of the continued presence of a likable anchor.

There are as many stories that illustrate this important personal relationship between the viewers and anchorpersons as there are successful (and unsuccessful) anchors. Cronkite always was rated number one in polls asking questions about who is the most believable person in the nation. People called him ''Uncle Walter.'' He was there almost every night for more than eighteen years . . . and almost every time there was a major story or a major national catastrophe. CBS's news ratings went down when Cronkite went on vacation, and back up again when he returned.

Cronkite is the only person who has ever motioned 18 million people to be quiet. When word of former President Lyndon Johnson's death came, Cronkite was on the air. The newscast had just shown a report from Tom Fenton in Paris on the progress of the Vietnam peace talks. The camera switched to Cronkite, who was talking on the phone with Johnson's former press aide. Cronkite raised a finger towards the audience in a ''wait a minute'' gesture. Cronkite then told them that Johnson was dead, listened to the phone a bit more, then added some more information. He thanked the press aide, and reported what he had learned a second time. A prerecorded obituary on Johnson was worked into the end of the newscast. It is easy to imagine what happened when Cronkite raised his finger towards the audience. People grabbed the dog, told the kids to shut up, and leaned forward with full attention. Cronkite's action was a simple, human one, something anyone would do when talking to someone else face to face.

In Chicago WLS-TV had a famous anchor of its own. The late Fahey Flynn presided at the anchor desk, wearing his distinctive bow tie, for over fifteen years. New management came to the station and decided to make Flynn look younger by having him switch from a bow tie to a four-in-hand. The audience rebelled vigorously. Flynn went back to his bow tie, and peace between the audience and WLS's top-rated newscast was restored.

When Dan Rather replaced Walter Cronkite, CBS's news management experimented with all kinds of production details to try to make Rather's presentation and appearance attractive to the audience. One night in the winter of 1982 Rather showed up wearing a sweater under his jacket. Whether that was accidental or planned is not clear, but *everyone* talked about it for days.

''Today'' show correspondent Jane Pauley received more mail and comment about her hairstyle—which she changed from time to time—than she did about almost anything else she did on the program during the first years she was there.

STORYTELLING—A DIALOGUE WITH THE VIEWERS

We have seen that there is a strong audience identification with the personality, the looks, the style of the anchorpersons who tell the audience the news each night. There is also strong evidence that *how* they tell and show the news is also important.

The authors believe what takes place is a dialogue between the anchors and reporters and the audience.

Consider how you would tell the news of a plane crash in a nearby city to a friend.

Friend: Well, you've been in the newsroom all day. Tell me what's been going on.

You: There was a terrible plane crash.

Friend: Oh, what happened?

You: A small plane crashed into a passenger plane as it was making an approach to the airport.

Friend: Which airport?

You: The Indianapolis airport. It was an Allegheny flight and the small plane hit it near the tail, and both went down southwest of Greenfield.

Friend: When?

You: About 3:30.

Friend: How many were hurt?

You: They say that all of the people, about 83 on the Allegheny flight are dead, and so is the pilot of the small plane.

Friend: How could that happen?

You: They don't know yet. The Allegheny plane was on final approach, and the other plane either came from the side, or was under the Allegheny plane, and none of the controllers saw it until it was too late.

Friend: Don't they have radar?

You: Of course, but they say only the Allegheny plane showed on the screen, and then it disappeared. The small plane pilot was a student making a solo. He'd taken lessons for three years, and would have got his license next week.

Friend: What did it look like at the crash?

You: It was grim, wreckage and bodies all over the place. The wreckage almost landed in a trailer court . . . made a ten-foot hole in the ground.

Friend: What's going on now?

You: Well, they've set up a morgue and are bringing the bodies there, and there will be an investigation about how the planes got so close; they're bringing the inspectors out from Washington, and they've found the flight recorder. . . .

The telling and showing of that story on television would involve, of course, pictures—probably live pictures—from the scene of the crash, interviews with airline officials, airport officials, police, fire fighters, rescue workers. Perhaps you would see interviews with relatives of the victims—who, one would hope, had been asked for permission before being interviewed. The station might develop some graphics to try to show the flight paths of the planes. It might even have eyewitness reports from people who had seen the crash.

The anchors and reporters telling the story would put in a lot more facts, identify sources more precisely, give a list of the names of the dead (if it was available), interview experts who might speculate on how and why the crash occurred. The station would put together a package of information it hoped would be as complete and clear as possible, a package based on up-to-the-minute information.

Regardless of the visual and word content of the story, there would be a dialogue going on between the reporters or anchors and the viewers. Those viewers have tuned in asking to be shown and told about the events of the day. The news staff at the television station has chosen the plane crash as its lead story because of its importance. For Indiana viewers, the event happened nearby, and for that reason—proximity—is more important than a similar story farther away. Barring war or atomic disaster, for those viewers the story was also more important than any other. Viewers count on the broadcast journalist to make that selection—they expect the important news to come first.

But the viewers also are participating in the process. Just as your friend asked you questions, the viewer is posing questions to the television set.

Who was involved?
When did it happen? and *where*?
How and *why* did it happen?

The above listing is, of course, nothing more than the classic outline of a news story: the hallowed five Ws and H. But because the viewer is being told the news by someone on the screen who is "familiar," and because the information includes pictures from the scene of the event, the report has become a visual and personal experience. It is more involving than reading the story in a newspaper, or listening to the voices of reporters and others involved coming over a radio. In fact, the dialogue, or conversation, is similar to the face-to-face report between you and one of your friends.

Yet the situations are different. The viewer cannot interrupt the flow of the story. The story must be written and structured so that the important points (answers to the classic news questions) are made clear. Further, these details need to be in the order in which the viewer is asking the questions.

How on earth, you say, is a writer or reporter supposed to know what those viewers out there are asking? If we had interactive television news, the stories might be put out in a much different form. Companies that have installed interactive cable systems have done a great deal of research trying to find out what kinds of questions the users will ask, and what those questions mean to the way information can be communicated on those systems.

So far the viewers of over-the-air television news can't talk back to the anchorpersons. However, with the viewers in mind we can imagine how a conversation might go, and then structure news stories to match that kind of experience.

LINEAR NEWS

A fourth structural consideration: Broadcast news is linear.

It took the industry a long time to realize this. Most experimentation with developing what is called "broadcast news style" grew out of physical problems. For

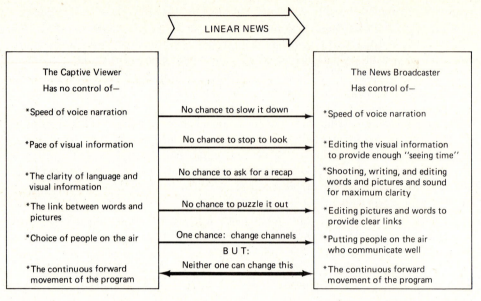

FIGURE 3-1. The linear structure of broadcast news.

example, cues indicating where audio or video material was to be inserted into the broadcast must be on the same page with the narration in the script.

For those trying to read the conventional wire service reports on the air, breathing space was lacking. Delivering the long sentences and convoluted paragraphs without taking a breath led to oxygen deprivation. The wire services, particularly United Press International, came up with "broadcast wires" in which the writing was simpler—short sentences, conversational words. It turned out that such a writing style was not only easier to read out loud but also easier for the audience to understand.

Forward Motion

What we now know is that listeners get the news in a flow of information that is constantly moving forward. The first story is immediately followed by the second, and so on through the entire newscast. A listener cannot stop the flow to go back and pick up missed points the way a newspaper reader can stop and return to an earlier element or slow down to ponder a confusing paragraph. The listener cannot speed ahead, or skim, and cannot slow down the newscaster if he or she is talking too fast.

Even within a story the structure is linear. The structure contains:

The beginning—the **lead**
The middle—the development of facts and details
The end—the conclusion

It is natural to want to finish all the parts of Story Element A before moving on to Story Element B. We also know that there is a linear logic to the arrangement of those story elements. What is needed is a logical progression of both aural and visual facts. The audience quickly becomes confused and irritated if we jump back and forth from one element to another in the narration or visual segment. We also know we should keep subjects and verbs close together, avoid too many dependent clauses, and make sure the referents of pronouns are clear, all because the audience can't stop and go back to puzzle it out.

Just as an individual story has linear structure, linear structure runs throughout the newscast. Television news producers spend a large amount of time figuring out where to place stories and how to group stories together in the newscast to ensure:

A logical arrangement

A logical progression

Forward movement

This is because the producer wants to try to maintain the highest level of interest and attention throughout the newscast. A great deal of time is spent determining what the lead story will be, but perhaps as much time is also spent arranging the order of the entire news program.

No one would want to arrange the stories in descending order of importance or significance. To do so would be to set up a newscast which loses half of the audience's attention and interest halfway through the newscast.

Total newscast strategies concerning the forward flow are developed. A station that has a sixty-minute newscast in competition with another station that changes program or joins the network news after thirty minutes works very hard to be sure there is something very interesting on the screen at the thirty-minute point to keep the audience from dialing away. Stations that program large blocks of news—the two-and-a-half and three-hour news programs in major markets—use elaborate strategies to keep the audience. These include frequent updates of top stories and a great deal of internal program promotion of items coming later in the program. Some plan the format so that regular departments within the news occur at the same time every day. The audience will, they hope, learn when the features they are most interested in come on.

Even commercials affect the linear strategy by which the newscast is organized. It is common practice to allow news producers to decide the precise location of commercial breaks. How many there will be is decided by commercial considerations and station policy. But the producer knows that the commercials represent a break in the news action, that whether or not the viewers watch the commercials, the forward motion of the newscast continues since there will be more news after the spots are played.

Therefore, producers do a great deal of planning and structuring the news segments between the commercials. The story order within a segment should follow both logical arrangement and logical progression rules.

Purists complain about the loss of news time resulting from the heavy use of **bumpers, teasers,** and promotional graphics. But the need for these comes as much from the basic linear nature of the way people receive broadcast news as it does from the station's promotion department.

VISUAL STRUCTURE

The fifth major element of the structure of television news concerns the linear nature of the way the audience receives the news pictures themselves. The scenes of the news event must move forward in an orderly fashion, or randomness will defeat clear communication.

Visual structure in television news is everyone's responsibility. The photojournalist and reporter covering a story must be aware that unless they provide the elements for visual structure in the raw videotape it will be impossible to achieve when the story is edited. Editors and writers must be aware of the rules of visual structure and apply them carefully during the editing and visual-word matching process.

In fact, what the writer does in selecting and arranging the elements of a word story into an orderly sequence strongly parallels what the photojournalist and video editor do in selecting and arranging the elements of a visual story. The material they gather and process must have the same linear structure as a written story. Compression is essential with both words and pictures. You've heard the expression: "Well, to make a long story short. . . ." Broadcast news stories are that way. A story that may take ninety minutes to unfold may have to be reduced to ninety seconds for a newscast. To do that for television news the key is to have the scenes necessary to compress the action into a smoothly flowing whole. It is writing with words *and* pictures.

Composition

GENERAL RULE 1. **Good visual composition is essential to good visual communication.**

In visual reporting, shot composition is an art. Some people just plain have the "eye" to see good visual composition. Some people learn it. Others never do. Composition is much more abstract than some of the other elements of visual structure that we will discuss later. We are talking here about the "feel" and the "look" of the shots as they are produced in the field and edited in the newsroom.

Framing   For the photojournalist this involves proper framing of the picture. Attention must be paid to the use of the space within the frame, the spatial relationships of subjects or objects in the frame, and the spatial relationships of subjects or objects across a sequence of scenes. For the video editor it involves the same sensitivity to those elements while the raw material is being edited. For both it requires understanding that the elements of visual composition are also journalistic elements that affect the way the pictures will communicate to the audience.

Some pictures are comfortable, some are uncomfortable. When a picture is framed properly, the important visual information is comfortably within it. Heads that are cut off or that are so low in the frame that it looks like the subject is trying to climb back into the frame, and heads or objects that are cut off on one side or the other are unusable shots. Even if you do not realize how uncomfortable these shots are, many members of the audience do, and they are distracted by them.

Shots that are composed with exact symmetry, that is, with the center of interest in the exact center, are visually less pleasing than shots that are asymmetrical, or slightly off center. Imagine that a TV picture frame is divided into thirds across its horizontal axis. A head shot that places the head exactly equidistant from the sides of the frame is less visually interesting than one that places the head in either the left or right two-thirds of the frame.

Looking Room   Using the thirds also gives you a chance to provide looking room. For example, an interview always has a line of action. In a **two shot** the reporter may be on the right side of the frame, while the subject is on the left. Once established, that spatial relationship remains in the viewer's mind even when only one or the other person is on the screen.

Now, dividing the frame into thirds to provide "looking room," the shot of the reporter should put him or her in the right two-thirds of the screen looking into the frame. And the shot of the person being interviewed should put him or her in the left two-thirds of screen, looking into the frame.

When these shots are edited together, the two people are looking toward each other, and both shots leave space on the side where the other person is sitting. By using the thirds, space has been created for the other person to move into when the edit is made.

Natural framing opportunities are everywhere. Examples of some of the more obvious ones are:

An arch that can be used to shoot through to the object of interest, say a park fountain in the distance shooting water plumes into the air.

FIGURE 3-2. Two scenes from an interview shot to allow "looking room." The interviewer is located in the left two-thirds of the screen, the subject in the right two-thirds. When the scenes cut from him to her and back again, there is enough space; they are still facing each other although each is alone in the scene. *(Courtesy of Will Counts.)*

A traffic control highway sign in the foreground, looking off to the wreckage of a vehicle in the background.

Overhanging branches of a tree through which the shot looks out onto the site of a proposed new industrial park.

Such compositional elements are all around us. Photojournalists and editors must raise their visual consciousness levels to see and use them, and to avoid making and using shots that contain distracting compositional elements.

Backgrounds Backgrounds and surroundings can be distracting. The experts say, for example, to watch out for horizontal lines running through the background. It is visually distracting to have a telephone wire seemingly entering a newsmaker's ear on one side and exiting on the other. Similarly, a tower of a building that seems to be resting on top of the head of a newsmaker, thus forming a "hat," is a visual gaffe, and someone in the viewing audience is bound to see it even if you don't.

How Long? Students of the art of telling a story with motion pictures will ask sooner or later—usually sooner—about the length of things: how long a story should be, how long a sequence should be, how long an individual shot should be. These are good questions and should not be fobbed off with the quick answer: "As long as necessary, as short as possible." Too many variables affect the question to answer it with precision. These include such things as the news value of the story, the quality of the raw materials (pictures and sound), the amount of time available for the entire newscast, and the number and newsworthiness of other stories competing for that time.

A professor of cinematography, himself a student of those early movie house newsreels from which our shooting and editing conventions developed, did a study. With stopwatch and steno pad he timed individual scenes from some *March of Time* newsreels. This was, he admitted, an unscientific approach, but it nonetheless produced some interesting data. He found that the average running time of a *March of Time* scene was seven seconds.

He was careful to note that he was reporting an *average* running time per scene, which of course meant that some scenes were longer than seven seconds, some shorter. Some other data show that it takes a viewer about five seconds to receive and understand the visual information in a single scene.

How does one gauge seven seconds? A simple yet remarkably accurate way to measure seconds is by counting "one thousand, two thousand, three thousand, four thousand. . . ." and so forth as you shoot. When you are editing, you can time the scenes with a stopwatch or counter.

Visual Continuity

The heart of visual structure lies within the rules of visual continuity. Visual continuity is necessary to compress the action of a story into a smoothly flowing whole. The word *continuity* means uninterrupted connection, succession, union, or duration over time. The idea of continuity over time makes the word an especially useful one in any discussion of the techniques of telling a story by using motion pictures.

A story occurs over time. It is a narrative with a beginning, a middle, and an end. Just as there are any number of verbal techniques for telling a story with words, so also there are numerous visual techniques for telling a story with motion pictures.

Visual continuity started long before ENG developed. Most of the visual techniques used by television photojournalists are very much like those used in the now largely outmoded news film technology. These conventions, in turn, had been copied from the earlier newsreels that became a staple of motion picture theater fare in the 1920s and the 1930s. Going back even further, the newsreels got their storytelling structure from motion picture production itself.

Long Shot, Medium Shot, Closeup   The newsreel narrative story began by visually establishing the story line in the mind's eye of the viewer. Photographers called this part of the story the **establishing shot.** On seeing this shot first, the viewer was ready to receive the details: a **long shot** (LS), a **medium shot** (MS), and a **closeup** (CU). This trio of shots, first photographed and then edited in a way that achieved a fluidity of continuous motion (and avoided interruption) formed the basic structure of the motion picture story. Each time a new idea or fact was introduced into the story line, it was first established and then narrated by using some combination of the now familiar LS-MS-CU approach. Each such combination was called a **sequence**. Sequences were joined together to make the story move from the beginning through the middle to the end.

This fundamental approach worked then, and it continues to be the most satisfactory way to tell a television news story using videotape. All of the other visual devices and motion picture skills applied to make the visual part of the story more unified, more coherent, and more emphatic to the viewing audience have as their starting point one of these three basic elements of visual continuity: the long shot, the medium shot, and the closeup.

You cannot successfully identify any of these shots when they stand alone. This is because each of the terms gets its meaning by comparison with the two other terms as they are used in a particular story. Thus, what is correctly labeled a long shot in one LS-MS-CU sequence may correctly be called a medium shot in a different sequence.

As a rule, the long shot shows the object of interest in its surroundings or setting. It doesn't clearly distinguish between the object of interest and its setting because it gives roughly equal space, and consequently equal emphasis, to both.

Scene 1	Scene 2	Scene 3	Scene 4	Scene 5	Scene 6
LS Establishes location and general area of story	MS Moves closer to focal point of the story	CU Gets very close to subjects or objects that are the focal point of the story	Cutaway Avoids jump cut, shows reaction	CU Again, close up on main subjects or objects	MLS Reestablishes locale of story, indicates ending, or beginning of new sequence

FIGURE 3-3. A typical sequence using visual continuity concepts. There is a LS-MS-CU series at the beginning, then a cutaway to bridge the two closeup scenes, and a medium long shot for an ending. This sequence carries the viewer to closeup scenes of the main subjects or objects, and ends with the medium long shot. At that point the story could end, or additional sequences could be added on to continue it.

a   *b*   *c*

FIGURE 3-4. One set of scenes shot with the traditional LS-MS-CU sequence in mind. The long shot (LS) establishes the locale of the story *(a)*, the medium shot (MS) moves the audience closer to it *(b)*, and the closeup (CU) picks up the central figure in the story as he moves toward the door *(c)*. *(Courtesy of James Gustke.)*

Although it looks like there are a lot of details or a lot of elements of the story in a long shot, they are not easily absorbed in the relatively short time the scene is on the air. Conversely, the closeup shot greatly reduces or eliminates the surroundings and shifts nearly all the visual space, and thus all the attention, to the object of interest. To return to the analogy of the written mode, the long shot might be compared to a verbal generalization, and the closeup shot to the example or words that provide supporting argument and details about the generalization.

The medium shot falls somewhere between the long shot and the closeup and visually bridges the gap between the two. The point where a long shot ends and a medium shot begins is arbitrary. One idea that you might find helpful in looking for some kind of standard for recognizing a medium shot is the notion of the "full figure" shot. It shows just what the term implies, the complete object of interest from top to bottom and from side to side. However, the assumption is that the size and shape of the object of interest have a "normal" spatial relationship with the other shots in the sequence. If the object of interest is a person, a medium shot shows the person's head and shoulders. (A long shot of a person shows that person full figure in the environment of the story; a closeup of a person shows just the face.)

Extreme long shots (ELS) are sometimes called "panoramic" shots and they are an extension of the LS. A shot of the Grand Canyon from a mile-high airplane is an ELS. The ELS suggests the idea of grandeur, magnificence, sweep.

At the opposite end of the scale, extreme closeup shots (ECU), which are sometimes also called **inserts,** are suggestive of the notion of narrow perspective, very specific example, or detailed illustration. Such shots are, of course, extensions of the CU. If a shot of the entire head of a subject is a CU, a shot of just the eyes, nose and mouth—cutting off the hair and the chin—is an ECU.

Sequencing

You now have the three fundamental units of a motion picture sequence: LS-MS-CU, with the ELS the expansion of the LS, and the ECU the compression of the

a   *b*   *c*

FIGURE 3-5. The relative nature of the terms long shot, medium shot, and closeup. The long shot (LS) begins at a point much closer to the building, but still establishes the locale *(a)*. The medium shot (MS) resembles the closeup in the previous sequence *(b)*, and the closeup (CU) moves the central figure right to the door *(c)*. *(Courtesy of James Gustke.)*

CU. In combination, and almost always in that order, they form a sequence, the basic component of motion picture visual continuity. Sequences are joined together to move the story along smoothly from beginning through climax to conclusion.

The sequence also serves another important function. It moves the viewer closer to the center of action. Think for a moment of what you do when you enter a room full of people. You take a general look (LS), then you pick out the point where the major action is (MS), then you move toward that point and look more closely at it (CU). If that point is very interesting you may walk up even closer and lean over to take a very close look (ECU). The LS-MS-CU-ECU sequence does exactly the same thing for the viewer that your legs do for you.

Taken together, these three basic shots do not seem at first glance to be enough to form the foundation of the mechanics, or grammar and syntax, of motion picture stories. But there are many possibilities for individual variations of their combina-

a   *b*

FIGURE 3-6. The extensions of scenes that can be made on either end of a sequence. An extreme long shot (ELS) takes in not only the building but part of its environment *(a)*. An extreme closeup (ECU) allows the audience to travel right along with the central figure up to and through the door *(b)*. *(Courtesy of James Gustke.)*

tion and sequencing and many innovations of technique for each basic shot. The possibilities for variety seem to be limited only by the number of people going into the field to record the pictures and the imagination of the people using the raw material to construct the finished story. Nevertheless, because the shooting and editing processes of the videotaped raw material are so intertwined, everyone involved in the process must understand and use the same set of basic rules. The rules begin, of course, in the field when the scenes are being shot. You need to master them as concepts long before you actually get to the mechanics of shooting and editing.

GENERAL RULE 2. **Avoid jump cuts: After each shot, change the size of the image or the angle of view, or both.**

If you follow this rule you will greatly increase your chances of getting shots that satisfy two needs:

1. You will have shots that will help the editor achieve smoothness, fluidity of motion, that sense of continuity in the progression of scenes and sequences which makes the visual story absorbing and viewable.
2. Following the rule is an absolutely foolproof way to avoid shooting what is called a "jump cut."

Jump Cuts A **jump cut** is a visual interruption in the flow of the picture when two scenes in a sequence do not match or fit together. The idea is difficult to express. A student once said, "A jump cut is a lot easier to shoot than it is to describe." The surest way to get a jump cut is to record two or more shots of some

a   *b*

FIGURE 3-7. A baseline description to help achieve consistency in the designation of a shot in the LS-MS-CU sequence is the "medium-medium," which shows the object of interest "top to bottom," or in "full figure." Thus a building would be shown from ground level to the roofline (*a*), a person from head to foot (*b*). (*Courtesy of James Gustke.*)

continuing action from the exact same position without changing the size or angle of the shot. When they are edited together, the action will appear to jump at each point where the scenes join.

For example: The governor is making a speech. You have him framed in the viewfinder head and shoulders. In shot 1 the governor's head is tilted to the right. In shot 2 his head is tilted to the left. If those two scenes are edited together, the governor's head will jump from one side to the other.

Another: You are shooting an interview of a man whose dog has just won best-in-show. In your first shot the man and the dog are shown together, the man talking, the dog drooling happily. Then between shots the dog gets down and goes to investigate some fascinating scent. If you make your second shot the same size and with the same framing, and the two shots are edited together, the dog will have magically disappeared.

In both instances an interval of time has elapsed (and thus the content of the action has changed) between the shots. A jump cut calls visual attention to itself—"Does the governor's head wobble uncontrollably?" "Where did the dog go?"—thus distracting viewer attention from the story content. Among professionals the jump cut is to visual communications what the non sequitur is to verbal communications. Various editing techniques have been devised to cope with the jump cut, but you will avoid shooting one in the first place if you follow General Rule 2.

If you move either closer to or farther from the object of interest between shots, the size of the image will, of course, change. With a zoom lens, changing shot size is very simple: Just move the lens to get a closer or wider image. Either way, it should be clear to you that by recording combinations of LS, MS, and CU shots you accomplish the first half of the rule.

Another Angle

The use of different **angles** opens the way to following the other half of the rule. One way to approach the idea of angle in shooting motion pictures is to look at it as representing a point of view. Let's go back into that room full of people. You look at some things head-on and at eye level. To see other things you must look up or down. To see still other things you must turn sideways, and occasionally you turn all the way around and look behind you. You use a camera the same way: You choose the point of view by choosing where to aim it.

Flat-Angle, High-Angle, and Low-Angle Shots
The eye-level shot is called a **flat-angle shot**. These are the kinds of shots which, when viewed in succession, seem routine, dull, boring, visually unimaginative, and uninteresting. Several flat-angle shots in a row tend to become visually tedious. Scenes shot head-on at eye level certainly have their place in the visual story, but different shots from a variety of angles are more interesting and also help move the story along.

As its name indicates, the **high-angle shot** is made by placing the camera above the object of interest and taking the shot looking down at it. If this shot is selected during the editing it tends to create the visual effect of subordinating the object, making it recede, minimizing, or deemphasizing it. It also has the effect of slowing down the action.

a   *b*   *c*

FIGURE 3-8. Visual information as well as visual interest may be increased by a careful use of angles. The low-angle shot (looking up at the center of interest) tends to emphasize the figure *(a);* the high-angle shot (looking down at the center of interest) tends to deemphasize it *(b).* Shots taken head-on at eye level (the flat-angle shot) may be used for visual contrast *(c). (Courtesy of James Gustke.)*

Conversely, the **low-angle shot** is made by placing the camera below the object of interest and taking the shot looking up at it. The visual effect of looking up at an object is the opposite of looking down at it. The low-angle shot tends to magnify the object of interest, to make it dominate the shot, and generally to heighten or intensify the feeling and the pace of the action.

Whereas flat-angle and high-angle shots tend to create the visual effect of slowing the pace of the action, the **side-angle shot** has the opposite effect, that of quickening the pace. If you want a graphic demonstration of these contrasting visual effects, try this experiment. Using the same size shot, record some scenes from a moving vehicle, first shooting forward through the front windshield, and then sideways through a side window. You'll notice on playback how leisurely the forward shots seem when compared with the side-angle shots, in which the motion appears accelerated and even exaggerated.

Reverse Angle   Another kind of shot that has its special uses for television news is the **reverse angle**. For example, take a story about a homecoming parade with its floats, marching bands, and homecoming queen and other celebrities. The object of interest is the parade and its participants. Reverse angles will show the spectators, the background of the line of march, what the participants see as they look out from their positions in the parade. Reverse angles help the editor give the audience both points of view.

The reverse-angle shot is also frequently used in television news reporting in the interview situation. The subject of interest is the person being interviewed, of course, and the main shots focus on him or her as the center of visual attention.

An interview technique that provides viewer satisfaction and at the same time achieves visual unity and editorial clarity is one in which the picture sequence shows the subject speaking, followed by a CU shot of the reporter asking a question, then cutting back to the subject for the answer. This technique provides pace and visual interest, makes for a smooth flow, and allows for fluid continuity and time compression. All are achieved by the careful use of reverse-angle shots that have been

a   *b*

FIGURE 3-9. The primary shot in an interview situation is the shot of the subject *(a)*. The reverse-angle shot—showing the reporter as the center of interest—is especially useful in these situations, as it allows for visual variety, time compression, and smoothness of editing *(b)*. Also, by reshooting the reporter questions in reverse angle, with the subject still present, the reporter gains an additional check on the accuracy of the respoken questions. *(Courtesy of James Gustke.)*

skillfully composed and framed. The idea of reverse angles brings up the next general rule.

GENERAL RULE 3. **Observe screen direction.**

Line of Action This rule is sometimes called the rule of 180 degrees, or the rule of the *line of action*. It applies to any situation where the central action moves along a line, or axis.

The most easily understood application of the rule is exemplified by a parade, or a basketball game, or an aircraft moving along a runway. In all of these situations the action goes along an axis or line of action. The parade line of march is, say, left to right across the screen. The airplane might be moving right to left. The home team is moving left to right during the first half, in the opposite direction in the second. The screen direction rule recommends that you not cross the center line of the action. If you do so in either the shooting or the editing, you will have sequences of pictures in which the line of action is going in one direction mixed with pictures in which it is going in the other direction.

Let's go back to the parade. Shots of the various units as they move past you convey the visual effect that the parade is moving in a certain direction, either screen right to left, or screen left to right depending on your point of view. Cross the street (thus crossing the center line of action) and shoot from the other side. Now, everything that has been moving from right to left suddenly appears to be moving from left to right, back in the direction the parade came from.

You must observe the screen direction rule in all situations from the simplest interview to the most action-filled sequence. If you cross the line, you must also shoot (and use) transitional scenes which will bring the audience across the line with you and establish a new point of view. The important thing is to establish the center line of action in your own mind as you are shooting and editing. Then when you make the straight-on shots, the reverse angles will conform to that center line of action.

GENERAL RULE 4. You must have cut-ins and cutaways.

Two of the most important shots used to provide visual continuity are the **cut-in** and the **cutaway**. Both can be quite brief, and both are essential to achieving smoothness and flow in the finished product. Editorially, however, the two shots are quite dissimilar.

Cut-Ins and Cutaways   As the name implies, the cut-in is used to cut in to the central action. The cut-in is also called an *insert*. Consider again the homecoming parade. The central action is the royal float with the homecoming queen waving and smiling to the crowds as the parade moves by. The most logical cut-in would be a full-screen shot of the queen's smiling face.

Or the central action is the varsity marching band stepping smartly down the line of march. In one possibility for a cut-in, the point of view might be down at the pavement level. The camera would be aimed straight across the street, and at right angles to the line of march. What you'll get is a shot of a line of marching feet stepping by in unison, left, right, left. When that shot is edited in between two

a   *b*   *c*

FIGURE 3-10.   These three shots illustrate a main difference between the ''cut-in'' shot and the ''cutaway'' shot. In photograph *a* the center of interest is the dancing bear and other ballet performers. The cut-in (*b*) looks closer in to the central action; the cutaway (*c*) looks away from the central action at the audience watching the ballet. (*Courtesy of James Gustke.*)

wider shots of the band marching, it gives a visual accent and allows for compression of time.

Cut-ins are usually closeups. The cutaway, on the other hand, is made by turning away from the central action to something that is not part of it although it is directly related. At the parade, a cutaway might be a shot of spectators, a parent with a small child perched on his or her shoulders, a police officer directing the crowd, an elderly man with a ''Class of '04'' button on his lapel.

Cutaways can also be thought of as reaction shots. In crowds, people look around at other people to see how they are reacting to what is going on. If you are attending a play and something shocking happens, you will very likely look at other people in the audience to see how they are affected by it. If you are listening to a politician making a campaign speech, you might look around to see whether others in the audience are agreeing or disagreeing with what the politician is saying. Television news should provide the audience with as accurate a representation as possible of the human reactions to the news event as well as the action itself. Cutaways will do that if they are shot during (not before or after) the event.

Expert opinion differs as to whether the cut-in or the cutaway is more useful, more logical, more consistent. The real question is whether the cut-in is editorially more consistent and thus preferable. Some believe it is because it stays with the central action, is part of that action, adds detail, and thus is a unifying factor in the sequence. Those who hold this view also argue that the cutaway, no matter how much it is in character with the thrust of the story being developed, looks *away* from the central action. It interrupts the continuous flow of the story. Those who disagree say that cutaways provide the reaction to the central focus of the story, giving the viewer a broader look at what happened.

The primary requirement for both cut-ins and cutaways is that they be appropriate to the story. They must be as ''true'' as possible. The cut-in of a subject's fingers pulling at his mustache may depict nervousness. If the subject was nervous, then the cut-in depicts reality.

A cutaway at the political rally of a person sleeping under a newspaper while the politician is orating at the rostrum may be appropriate. But if that person is the only one asleep and the rest of the audience is cheering wildly, including that shot in the speech sequence would be an editorial comment, and therefore inappropriate. Both cut-ins and cutaways must be *related* to the action.

Even with the editorial problems these shots present, there is general agreement that both the cut-in and the cutaway serve a number of very valuable functions. They convey information about an event to the viewing audience. They are visually interesting and add excitement and pace to the story. Most important, they are convenient—and indispensable—editing material for the compression of action.

Take a simple sequence of a school bus coming to a bus stop, loading and unloading passengers, and then continuing on its route. The entire action, from when the bus first comes into view, until it disappears from view down the street after having made the stop, will take five minutes. You want to compress five minutes of action into a twenty-eight-second version. Here is one way to do it using cut-ins and cutaways.

FIGURE 3-11. This seven-shot sequence illustrates the basic grammar of visual continuity, editing techniques of time compression, and the forward movement of story line. The sequence is established with the bus approaching the bus stop *(a)*. The group of waiting passengers in the foreground sets up the continuity of the cutaway, that is, having the group in the opening scene establishes the logic for the cutaway *(b)*. The pair of reverse angle shots speeds up and condenses the business of getting off and getting on *(c and d)*; and the insert *(e)* allows the editor to move the story from the off-and-on action smoothly to the concluding scenes, with bus doors closed *(f)* and bus moving away *(g)*. *(Courtesy of James Gustke.)*

Scene 1   LS, school bus coming into view some distance from bus (4 sec.)   stop.

Scene 2   *Cutaway, MS*, four people standing near sign that says BUS (2 sec.)   STOP.

Scene 3   CU, bus bounces to a stop, doors full frame, they swing (8 sec.)   open, a passenger steps down.

Scene 4   CU, reverse angle, group in Scene Two climb on. (5 sec.)

Scene 5   *Cut-in, CU*, first person of group shows his bus pass. (3 sec.)

Scene 6   MCU, bus doors close, full frame, bus pulls away, slow pan (6 sec.)   right to follow shot as bus disappears screen right.

Notice that the cutaway compresses time by getting to the people at the bus stop quickly. The cut-in speeds things up by condensing the business of climbing on and paying a fare into one quick shot. By making these shots at the scene the photojournalist has provided the ingredients with which the twenty-eight-second sequence is accomplished in the editing bay.

Into Frame, Out of Frame   Another pair of shots that are simple to shoot and visually effective in the appropriate circumstances are called *into-frame* and *out-of-frame*. The into-frame shot first shows the general location of the subject of interest but without that subject in view. While the tape is rolling the subject of interest comes into frame and is centered to become the visual center of attention. The out-of-frame technique simply reverses this order, so that the subject is centered up and is the center of attention as the shot begins. As the shot proceeds, the subject moves out of the frame. Note that in both kinds of shots, the camera is held steady in one position while the action and motion are provided by the object of attention.

GENERAL RULE 5.   **Action must match direction of action.**

When shooting into-frame and out-of-frame the photojournalist must be careful to make the action in related scenes match the into-frame and out-of-frame scenes so that the viewers don't become confused.

For example: A free tuberculosis patch-test clinic is being offered by a local hospital. The first four shots may show (1) the outside of the hospital (establisher); (2) the front door; (3) a sign, with an arrow, saying CLINIC (cut-in); and (4) the waiting room full of people (reestablisher). Editing those together creates the effect of moving the audience to the center of action.

Now comes the time for patients to go into the doctor's office. Instead of providing one lengthy medium-shot scene in which a nurse comes into the waiting room with a list on a clipboard and calls out names, the photojournalist has shot a sequence about one person's being called in.

    Shot 5   MS, nurse comes out of door at the back of the waiting room, moving *right to left,* and calls out a name.

    Shot 6   MCU, seated person looks up, nurse enters frame from *right* side

    Shot 7   MS, seated person stands, nurse and patient exit screen *right*.

    Shot 8   Cutaway LS, waiting room.

    Shot 9   MS, door to doctor's office. Patient in Shots 6 and 7 comes out the door, thanks nurse, turns, and exits screen *left*.

By carefully observing the line and direction of the action, the photojournalist has provided a sequence in which the nurse's and patient's directions of movement relate to each other, to the door of the doctor's office, and to the outside. When the patient leaves screen left, the audience is shown that the action is over—the patient is not going back into the doctor's office.

The purpose of the story is to inform people of the free clinic and to try to encourage them to come in to get the tests by showing them how simple it is. By using the into-frame, out-of-frame technique it is possible to compress spread-out action and time and focus on the center of interest.

Tilts and Pans   So far our discussion of shots and their uses in visual continuity and story structure has allowed the subjects or objects of interest to provide the motion.

By purposely moving the camera while the tape is rolling, you can produce other kinds of shots. If the camera is moved horizontally, the motion is called a **pan**. If the camera is moved vertically, the motion is called a **tilt**.

Some beginners—maybe most—seem to have a compulsion to pan. Perhaps that's because we pan and tilt our heads and bodies to look at various objects in sight. On the beginners' tape the pans go left, the pans go right, the pans start left and go right, and then come back left again. The camera is always in motion. It is time to invoke:

GENERAL RULE 6.   Pans, tilts, and zooms must be motivated.

The fact is that a pan is a very useful shot—sometimes. But it often can make things difficult for the editor. The trick is to learn how to pan and when to pan.

The most important reason to pan is, of course, to follow action. In addition, you *may* use the pan to show the spatial relationship between any two related subjects, objects, or pieces of information. Both reasons have a logical motivation. For example, you might make a shot that starts with the beginning point of black skid marks on a street and at right angles to them (high angle, looking down at the pavement). Then you pan in the direction of the skid marks, centering up, ending with a vehicle crumpled against a tree.

The pan is also a useful technique in physically confined spaces, enclosed areas, or places where movement to get another shot is inhibited. A pan may be just the shot needed to show the spatial relationship of various objects of interest in that area.

But photojournalists must keep in mind the main reasons editors so dislike pans in the first place. For one thing, pans are time consuming; once a pan is started it must run its course. Editors hate to interrupt a pan before it ends. For another, panning is hard on the eyes, and it doesn't take very long for some people watching them to reach for the seasick pills. Usually it is better to cut from one scene to another during the editing process, but some pans—those which are motivated—are useful and necessary.

You won't run into so many rules about tilts. The slow tilt up or down to relate two objects of interest to each other is often quite useful, particularly in combination with high-angle or low-angle camera placement. But they, too, must be motivated; you must have a storytelling reason for making them and using them.

With both pans and tilts, always hold the beginnings and endings of the shots for at least five to ten seconds so that the stationary portions of the shots are usable even if the editor decides to eliminate the pan or tilt movement.

Zooms Zooming is like panning and tilting in that the motion of the camera becomes a part of the shot. As you will recall, the major purpose of a zoom lens is to provide an infinite number of focal lengths in one lens. With the zoom lens, the size of any shot can be changed at will. This should be the primary use of a zoom lens: to establish the size of the shot, to trim that shot size for more comfortable composition, and to change the size of the shot between takes.

But you might have a good reason for making shots that include a zoom. If you want to show the spatial relationship between a subject or object in the foreground to something else in the background, a zoom will sometimes accomplish that. It is useful for following action that moves toward or away from the camera position since the size of the center of attention in the shot can be maintained as the distance changes.

On a spot news story where the action is uncontrolled and fast moving, the zoom is used regularly to frame up the next shot while the tape is rolling. Doing this gives the editor a well-framed shot with tracking on it to cut to *after the zoom is finished*.

Beginners seem to like to zoom almost as much as they like to pan. Their tapes are full of shots which move closer to or farther away from the subject while the shot progresses. These scenes are difficult to edit for the same reason pans are difficult to edit (the zoom must be completed before the shot can be cut) and difficult to watch because the motion can distract.

A famous cinematographer at a television news workshop told the students that if they didn't stop zooming, he was going to remove the zoom cranks from their cameras. He said: "Your tape is full of MSTTP shots—My Son the Trombone Player."

COMMITMENT

We began this chapter by discussing structure for a very good reason: It is an essential to one more concept, what the professionals call "commitment." They have a special meaning in mind when they use this fundamental—you might even say philosophical—word to describe how they go about their work.

The process of commitment begins with the news assignment. Experience is the television journalist's guide just as imagination is his or her tool.

For the photojournalist and reporter the basic questions are: How am I going to cover and shoot this story? What will its outstanding ingredients be? What photographic opportunities might this story present? What hazards or obstacles is it likely to impose? How will I overcome these obstacles, and how will I take advantage of the opportunities? How can I get the maximum there is out of this story? What is this story *really* about?

For the writer, the editor, and the producer the basic questions are: How can I put this story together so it will flow in a logical way? How can I tell it so the audience will understand it? How can I be sure that the important and significant information is there? How will it work with the rest of the stories in today's news?

Finding the answers to those and other questions is part of the everyday business of television journalism. When the answers come, the professionals make their commitment and get to work. But they will do a better job in all of their reporting, shooting, editing, and writing activities if the commitment is made against a background of understanding how television news is structured and delivered to the audience, and how that audience receives and uses it.

Making Pictures and Sound

4

True or False. Each correct answer is worth two points.

1. Television is a visual medium. *(Boy, is this easy.)*
2. The trouble with TV news is that pictures affect news judgments. *(Yeesss, but . . . .)*
3. Graphics and production effects are better than pictures. *(Watch it!)*
4. Television news is too visual. *(Ah, I knew it, right away a trick question.)*

Tests like this one remind you of those surveys in which the questions are worded in such a way that you have to agree with no chance to argue. Only question 1 is true; the next two must be qualified; and the last one is a non sequitur—a conclusion that does not follow from the premise.

Television *is* a visual medium; television news must have pictures or it wouldn't be television news. Graphics and production effects *can add* information. But the charge that television news is *too* visual doesn't make any sense. What those who make that charge really mean is that some of the visual material presented on television news doesn't inform or illuminate or illustrate effectively.

That charge is often a valid one, and in this chapter we will focus on how material can be shot and edited into an orderly presentation of words, pictures, and sounds that can show and tell the news in the most effective way.

MAKING PICTURES

The photojournalist involved in making motion pictures and sound for television news is an artist, a journalist, and a technician all rolled into one.

Photojournalists must know their equipment intimately. They also need to know how to apply the art of composition, visual continuity, and the uses of lighting and sound; how to find the best location for shooting; how to shoot each scene so that it relates to all the other scenes.

In sum, they must know how to use the technology to get to the art. This should be the goal of anyone seeking to become a television photojournalist. To get there they must learn to operate at practical and abstract levels at the same time. This chapter deals with the practical: those skills of operation which, once they become automatic, open the door to abstraction.

Equipment

The essays by Larry Hatteberg and John Premack in this book have one common theme about the technology: You must learn to operate it automatically. The camera must become a part of your body, the recorder controls an extension of your fingertips.

It all starts even before you leave for the assignment. Since your operational success depends to a large degree on how the equipment functions, making sure that all of the equipment you will take to the story is assembled and in good working order is essential. So first you will have made sure that all cables, connectors, microphones, lighting units, accessories, and other parts are with you, and where you can find them quickly.

In military basic training much time is spent on what they call "familiarization": getting to know your equipment and taking care of it. A constant phrase is: "Your life depends upon it." It may be stretching it a point or two to say that about a camera and tape recorder, but there is a lot of truth in it. And because your equipment is sensitive, giving it tender loving care is just plain smart. If you have to go back to get a missing piece of equipment or replace a broken part you may miss the story or make someone waiting to be taped very angry. It is too easy to blame the equipment for things that are really errors of commission or omission. Many things that result in failure to get necessary scenes or even a whole story are caused by "pilot errors," not mechanical or electronic failures.

Let's start with the physical elements and the problems involved in setting up for operation in the field.

Camera, Lighting, and Sound Setups

In most TV stations around the country the photojournalist is expected to know the proper techniques of camera operation, lighting, and sound recording. Furthermore, the photojournalist usually is the boss of the audio-video end of news gathering in the field. Only in the larger markets (where union contracts may still call for workers to handle lights and operate the video and audio recording equipment) will individual crew members perform those functions.

You will have three separate elements to set up and worry about: camera placement and operation, lighting, and the installation of sound equipment.

For the photojournalist working alone (or perhaps aided by a cooperative reporter) it may seem like a great many things to think about. Which comes first depends on the situation. If you are on a spot news story you must start shooting as soon as possible. Get out the tape recorder and camera or, cam-corder, make some quick decisions about lighting conditions, plug in the microphones, do the electronic adjustments, and roll.

If the story is an interview shot out of doors with good light, then the setup procedures will be simpler. If you are doing a feature or an interview indoors it becomes more complicated. Every photojournalist has personal ways of going about it, but usually on anything except the spot news story camera and lighting setup come first, with the sound installation close behind.

Of course, where you place the camera—the point of view—affects both the lighting and sound setups. Good camera placement involves many elements: the comfort of your subject, lighting conditions, environmental and background problems, and the aesthetics of good photography. All of these things will be discussed later. For now let's assume you have made a decision that will work.

Preflight Checklist

The following list should become engraved in your mind as soon as possible so that you can perform all the items on it automatically. We will point out the places where sound and lighting setups cross over as we go along.

✔ 1. Get the camera and tape recorder out of storage, put them where you are going to shoot, and connect batteries or power supplies. If you are working on battery power, check the battery status indicators briefly, then turn the power off.

If it's a spot news story, you will have to start shooting immediately.

But if you are setting up lights and other equipment for an interview, you can lose a significant amount of battery charge if you keep the camera on and the tape recorder in pause while you do all of those other things.

Cameras and tape recorders can use separate batteries or can be run from the recorder batteries alone.

Recorders use more power than cameras, so operating solely on the recorder battery shortens shooting time.

Camera viewfinders display a battery status light next to the picture. Depending on the camera model being used, that light will blink or give some other indication when power is running low. If you see that signal, change the battery as soon as possible since the first thing you will lose is color—the final scenes made with that battery may be in black and white.

Tape recorders won't even start if the batteries are low and will stop before they run completely out of power. That allows time to get the tape cassette out of the recorder.

If you are operating on AC power, you will need an AC converter because the power for both the camera and tape recorder must be converted to 12 volt DC. For long shooting sessions it is important to use an AC converter.

✔ 2. Connect and check all cables between the camera and the tape recorder, and connect the microphones to the tape recorder.

The cable from the camera to the tape recorder carries the combined video signal and the sound from the camera microphone.

The camera mic sound will go onto audio channel 2 unless you plug another mic into channel 2 or put a blank plug in the channel 2 receptacle on the tape recorder.

✔ 3. Check the audio from the microphones by plugging headphones into the audio monitor receptacles on the tape recorder or by listening to the audio monitor system if one is contained in the camera.

Some portable VTR audio systems have automatic gain control to set and maintain audio levels. Others have volume control knobs and meters that allow you to set audio levels before recording while the automatic gain control takes over during recording.

(Note: Cam-corders are cameras with the tape recorder built into the camera body. This eliminates a lot of cables and cords. The recorder and audio controls and the mic connectors are located on a panel, also on the camera.)

At this point your preflight checklist should tell you whether the camera and recorder are getting proper power to make pictures and sound and whether the microphones are working. The next step is to deal with the lighting situation. If you are out of doors and the lighting conditions are good, you can begin the next steps immediately. If you are indoors or need additional lighting, you should light the scene now (see pp. 90–92).

✔ 4. Set the camera video level. Almost all cameras have an automatic video control or auto iris feature that sets the proper video level—exposure—for you. Therefore, under most conditions the exposure will be determined by the auto iris. However:

Most cameras can be adjusted to manual exposure by the flip of a switch. If lighting conditions are difficult, you may have to do this. Furthermore, if you are in a situation where the amount of natural light is going to vary widely, you will have to rely on manual exposure settings.

To control exposure manually, look into the viewfinder and adjust the lens diaphragm (f-stop) until clear definition (details) are visible in both the highlights and shadows. Look for washed-out bright spots and shadows with no details, then adjust the f-stop until you see details in both.

✔ 5. White balance the camera. Most modern cameras have an automated white-balance system. But, white balancing must be done *before* any shooting is done, and must be done *each time* the shooting location or lighting conditions change.

Be sure you have chosen the *correct filter* for the lighting conditions you are operating with *before* you white balance.

Take a white target, or a piece of white paper you have with you and put it *directly in front of and close to the subject* you are going to shoot.

Make sure the target is straight up and down. If you tilt it upward or downward, or angle it to either side it may not accurately reflect the light back to the camera; thus the white balance will be faulty.

Zoom or otherwise adjust the lens so that the white target *completely* fills the viewfinder screen.

Most modern cameras allow you to set the white balance by flipping a switch. Some cameras have a memory circuit that will maintain the white-balance setting for any one shooting location.

6. Insert a video cassette into the tape recorder, and push down *both* the forward and record buttons or levers.

The tape recorder will load the tape around the record heads and wait in pause until you are ready to begin recording.

If you have a new tape you should track it before leaving the office or put color bars on it in the field if the camera you are using provides a color bar signal.

Be sure your tape is where you want it—at the beginning if it's a new shooting, after the previously recorded material if you have already shot some scenes on it.

Be sure the *red button* or *knockout tab* is in your cassette. These buttons or tabs can be removed to prevent recording over something you want to save.

7. Start the tape recorder and record a brief take. Then play it back and check the picture and sound by switching the camera ensemble to playback. You should see the picture in the camera viewfinder and hear the sound through the audio monitor system. *Remember to switch back to record mode after checking picture and sound.*

Lighting

Lighting is one of the photojournalist's chores that often gets too little attention. This causes the pictures made to be of poor quality both technically and artistically. Sometimes the shooting has to be done so quickly that the lighting setup can be only rudimentary. On breaking stories the pressure to record the events may force you to turn on a battery-powered light, hit the white balance button, and roll the tape with the hope that the auto iris will take care of the problems. In low light conditions many cameras have a "boost" feature to increase the sensitivity of the picture tube or tubes.

The basic camera placement and lighting setup for an interview, or any shooting in which the subject or object will not move around, is shown in Figure 4-1. Figures 4-2 and 4-3 show standard lighting setups for a news conference or speech and for shooting reverse-angle questions.

The portable lights and light stands that are part of the standard ENG field kit are quartz lights that provide 600 to 1,000 watts of artificial light at exactly 3,200 degrees Kelvin. Some of them are floodlights, some can be adjusted to be either

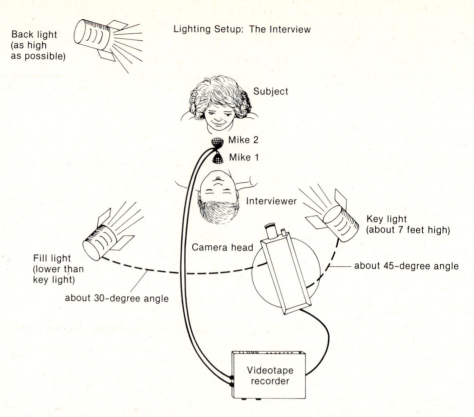

Lighting Setup: The Interview

Back light
(as high
as possible)

Subject

Mike 2

Mike 1

Interviewer

Key light
(about 7 feet high)

about 45-degree angle

Camera head

Fill light
(lower than
key light)

about 30-degree angle

Videotape
recorder

FIGURE 4-1. The proper way to set up the lights and the camera for an interview. The reporter and the subject are facing each other, and the camera is shooting over the reporter's shoulder. Key, fill, and back lights are aimed at the subject. The camera zoom lens can get any size shot—from one including the reporter to a tight closeup of the subject. The subject can relate to the reporter and will seem to be talking to the audience.

floods or spots. The stands they are attached to can be raised or lowered as necessary. The lights can also be attached to a spring-jawed clamp that can be clipped to almost any sturdy upright such as a door or window frame. But don't clip them to someone's antique highboy or enameled wood trim without first padding the jaws; you can lose your welcome in a hurry.

A Lighting Formula
The way you position these lights is critically important. The most important of them is the **key light**.

The key light is the main light. It lights the general area and should be placed near the camera, about 45 degrees to one side or the other and aimed at the subject area. It should be *well above* camera level—at least seven feet from ground level if you can get it that high.

Height is particularly important if you are going to photograph a person wearing eyeglasses. You don't want the key light to bounce off those glasses and right back into the camera lens. The key light should also be close enough to the subject to provide the main light source, but not so close as to blind the subject. This is another reason for getting the light up high.

The **fill light** (or lights) fill in the shadows caused by the key light. They should be placed lower and at about 30 degrees to the side of the camera opposite the key light. They should also be placed somewhat closer to the subject because their second function is to light the background.

Lighting the background is *very* important and a little bit tricky. What you want

Lighting Setup: Speeches and News Conferences

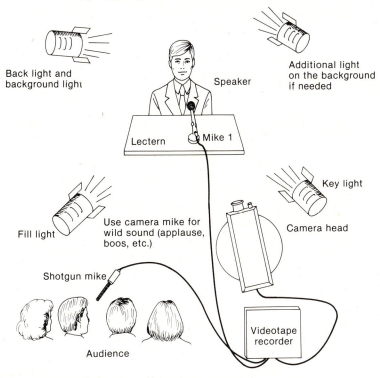

Back light and background light

Additional light on the background if needed

Speaker

Lectern   Mike 1

Key light

Fill light

Use camera mike for wild sound (applause, boos, etc.)

Camera head

Shotgun mike

Audience

Videotape recorder

FIGURE 4-2. The proper lighting setup for coverage of speeches and news conferences. The key and fill lights usually must be augmented with back and background lights to get enough light on the speakers. Also the key and fill lights must be placed so that they provide some lighting on the audience. That way, you can shoot questions from that audience. A shotgun microphone, rather than the camera microphone, should be used to pick up those questions.

the fill light to do is eliminate the shadows caused by the key light on the subject and on the background. Another function of the fill light is to provide good separation between the subject and the background.

Too many photojournalists neglect the **back light**. This lights the back of the subject, and is used especially to outline the head, hair, and shoulders of the subject so that he/she (or it) is clearly separated from the background. The back light is placed behind and to the side of the subject or object and as high as you can get it. It should shine down on the subject or object to give a halo effect. Be very careful about the placement. If you place the back light too low and too close, the halo effect is overpowering, and the back light may shine directly into the lens of the camera. This will create flare on the camera lens or wash out portions of the picture.

Note in Figure 4-4 *a* and *b* how the key light casts strong shadows under the chin and beside the nose and how adding the fill light reduces those shadows. Figure 4-4 *c* shows how adding the back light separates the subject from the background. Back lighting can do more to improve the quality of the picture than any other move you make, and it only takes a few more minutes to do it.

One more light may be useful to overcome problems with the background. A **wash light** (or lights) may be added on the opposite side of the backlights and aimed entirely at the background. They should "wash across" that background adding more light than it is getting from the fill lights. This is particularly important if you have dark backgrounds such as wood paneling or draperies, or if you are lighting a dark-skinned person against a dark background.

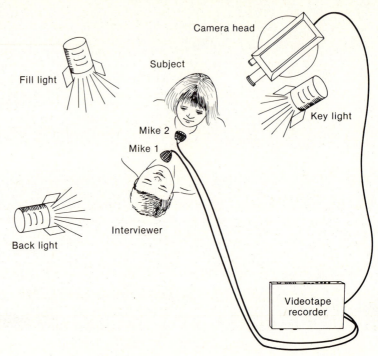

Lighting Setup: Reverse-Angle Questions

FIGURE 4-3. How to change the standard interview lighting setup to shoot the reverse-angle questions by the reporter (see pp. 105–106). Only the key light has to be moved. The other two lights are simply rotated on their stands to fill and back light on the reporter. The camera position is moved to get face-on shots of the reporter over the shoulder of the subject.

This lighting plot sounds complicated. But it isn't, and it takes a surprisingly short time to set up. Once it is established you can make small adjustments to fit a particular situation. Very blond persons with very light skin will reflect more light than persons with darker complexions, so you may want to move the lights farther away to compensate. Because the auto iris will adjust for the brightest spot in the picture, you will want to check to make sure no "hot spots" like glittering jewelry, the face of a clock, or a metal picture frame bounce light back toward the camera. Figure 4-5 shows the effect of a hot spot on the auto iris and the overall exposure of the picture.

Lighting Ratios   You will also want to check on lighting ratios. In a studio such ratios can be checked carefully with a light meter. But there is no such thing as a light meter for ENG, and usually no time to turn the lights on and off and check their footcandle output.

What you can do more quickly is look at the scene and try to determine that you have achieved *overall flat lighting* by using the key and fill lights. They normally should supply about twice as much light as the back and wash lights, and a 3-to-1 ratio is about as high as you should ever go. The rule always is that there should be *more light on the subject than on the background*. You can learn to see that with your eye and by looking through the viewfinder. Nothing can replace a good, close look at the lighting by the photojournalist.

Power Supply Problems   There you are, all set up. The subject is ready and eager to tell the world how she won the Nobel Prize in literature. She has agreed to

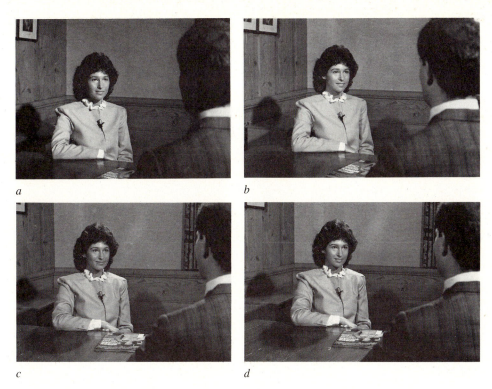

a   *b*

c   *d*

FIGURE 4-4. The effects of each of the lights used in the standard light plot (Fig. 4-1). The subject has just the key light on her in *a*. Note the heavy shadows on the right side of her face and under her nose. Those shadows are softened when the fill light is added *(b)*. When the back light is added *(c)*, her hair and shoulders are outlined, and she is separated from the background. In *d* the subject is ready to answer the first question; the low shadows on the table and background can be further softened by moving the fill light closer, or adding scrims, and will not show at all in medium shots or closeups. *(Courtesy of Will Counts.)*

do an exclusive interview for your station because she "just loves" your anchorperson. Then the lights go out. You have blown the fuses. Embarrassed, you grope around trying to find the fuse box in her home or get the building supervisor to reset the circuit breakers.

In applying the lighting formula you have forgotten another basic: power supply problems. Each of the lights in a portable light kit draws about 6 amperes of electric current. (That number is determined by dividing the watt power of a lamp by 100.) Most homes and other buildings with modern electrical installations have 20-amp circuits, but older buildings may have only 15-amp circuits, making the problem even more serious. So, a little quick mental arithmetic: Three 6-amp lights will draw 18 amps. If a 20-amp circuit is available you are hanging by a thread; if it is only 15 amps, don't even try. With the 20-amp circuit, *if anything else is on that circuit* you run a very good chance of blowing the fuses.

One reason for the blown fuses may be that you overloaded the circuit by trying to run all the lights from one floor plug. Furthermore, there is no sure way to figure out how the place where you are shooting is wired. If the electricians ran one circuit all the way around the room and attached several floor plugs to it, no

a   *b*

FIGURE 4-5. The effect of a "hot spot" in a picture. Everything is fine *(a)* until she moves her coffee cup into the picture *(b)*. When that happens the auto iris in the camera reads the brightness of that spot, closes down the iris, and the exposure on her face is destroyed. *(Courtesy of Will Counts.)*

matter where you plug the lights in that room you will have the same problem.

The answer is to try to take power from several circuits, perhaps by running an extension cord to another room or in from the hallway. That's also a quick way to solve the problem after you get the power back on.

There are two things you should do as a matter of routine. First, make sure you have plenty of extension cords with you and plug them into separate outlets. Second (and more important) think about it in advance.

Mixing Light   You learned in Chapter 2 about color temperature and the qualities of various kinds of lighting. Let's take this information in the field as we continue with the interview with the Nobel Prize winner.

The subject is in her office at the local university. It is a modern building with a dropped ceiling containing light diffusers and fluorescent tubes. When she turns the lights on, the room is flooded with diffused fluorescent light. Over her desk is a cantilever-arm lamp with a bright incandescent light. In addition, there are large windows along one wall admitting natural light. It is an overcast day.

You are confronted with a veritable cafeteria of light qualities. Depending on which light source you use, you will get different color temperatures, and therefore different quality pictures. The fluorescent lights will give you one quality, the natural light coming in through the windows another.

The problem with fluorescent lights is that they emit a wide range of color temperatures so that there really isn't one filter that can correct for fluorescent light. Fortunately, modern cameras with good white-balancing systems can help solve the problem. The trick is to be sure that the proper filter is in place and that the white balancing is done on the area of the picture where the subject's face will be. Careful placement of the target—right in the facial zone—will result in a white balance that will render the facial tones accurately and avoid blue or green facial tones, which are more distracting to the viewer than poor rendition of other colors in the background. Adding some quartz light to provide an overall boost in the light level will also help.

You will get some very interesting tonal quality in the picture if you decide to use natural light. But that choice depends quite a bit on where the natural light is coming from. If it is behind the subject you cannot use it because you will be shooting against it, and the auto iris will close down, putting the subject in silhouette. Moving furniture around is not a good idea, either. You may end up with the subject out of her normal environment and annoyed with you for rearranging her office. A network camera crew was ordered out of Canada after they moved Pierre Trudeau's office furniture around to get what they imagined was a ''more ministerial'' shot.

If you close the window drapes and light the office with your portable light kit, you will make it look like this famous woman only rates an inside office without windows.

So there are a lot of options, and the photojournalist must make a choice. Once that choice is made, however, lighting, filtering, and white balancing must be done to meet the lighting conditions the decision created.

Be sure to study your light setup and try to eliminate any distracting shadows that fall on the subject or the background: A shadow of the subject's head, shoulders, or arms on the background will move as the subject moves. Look also to be sure none of the light stands or cables is casting a shadow or is visible in the picture itself.

Barn Doors, Scrims, and Reflectors   Your light kit contains a number of accessories that you also want to put to use. **Barn doors** consist of a ring that fits around the light's lens and that contains small doors that can be opened outward from the sides and above and below the light. By adjusting these barn doors you

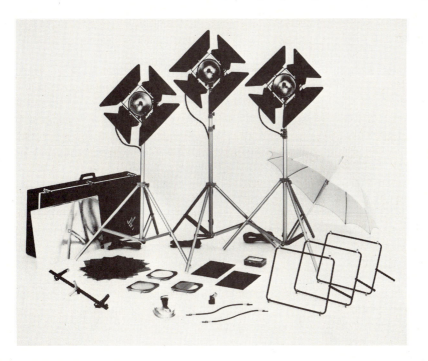

FIGURE 4-6. Field lighting kits contain barn doors, scrims, and reflectors to help control where and how the light will fall on the subjects or objects being shot. Barn doors can be opened or closed to prevent light from going where it isn't wanted. Scrims diffuse the intensity of the light and therefore soften shadows. Reflectors provide an overall flatter lighting condition and prevent glare on shiny surfaces. *(Courtesy of Lowel-Light Manufacturing.)*

can prevent the light from that instrument from going where you don't want it, or concentrate it where you do. **Scrims** are small round or square pieces of screening mounted in a frame that fit over the light lens and act to diffuse the light. Strong shadows caused by that light can be softened by using a scrim. Some light kits include folding reflectors that can be used to bounce natural or artificial light toward the subject to fill in or remove strong shadows.

It takes time to get these accessories out and set them up, but often the results are worth the time spent. They will help make the subject look as natural as possible and get rid of lighting conditions that will distract the viewer.

Natural Light Situations

In Washington, D.C., a great many interviews with government officials take place out of doors. Many times this occurs because the news crews can catch officials between appointments and they can make use of the natural light for a quick setup with an appropriate background—the steps of the Capitol, the White House, and so on. They also do this because sometimes there is no convenient place for a more formal setup. But it often appears that government officials do not have offices, and that reporters and photojournalists are not allowed inside the major government buildings—they just lurk around among the trees and gardens, and government officials come outside to visit with them when the officials decide it is convenient.

Sometimes you may have to meet your subject out of doors. When you have no choice because of time pressures, you must make the best of what you've got. But when you do have a choice about the location of the interview or story, your first question should be, Is the place I have chosen appropriate to the story? The second question is, What are the lighting problems there?

If the Nobel laureate is an ardent gardener, choosing to shoot the interview with her in her beautiful garden on a gorgeous summer day may be just the right thing to do. It will give the viewer some of the flavor of her private life and will put her at ease in an environment she enjoys.

Outdoor lighting setups look innocent, but that can be deceptive. Our subject has a garden full of roses surrounding a small pool with a fountain and with hedges and some trees nearby. You spot a bench near the pool and ask her to sit there for the interview. Roses need plenty of sun, so the chances are the bench and pool are in direct sunlight.

But it may be too sunny. Remember that sunlight comes from almost directly overhead during midday, and from sharp angles early or late in the day. There will be only one shadow, but it will be a strong one. The color temperature changes with the angle of the sun. People in sunlight tend to squint from its brightness or wear sunglasses. Being in direct sunlight is not very comfortable in hot weather.

A better locale would be on another bench beside the hedge and under some trees that provide light shade. There the chances are good that you will have a flat overall lighting situation and that you will be able to control it better. So you suggest that, and your subject is put at ease.

Whether it is bright or overcast outdoors, you will have several things to think about and control.

First, if you have to shoot in bright sunlight you actually might want to add some light—a battery-powered light held to the side of the camera by someone else to fill in the harsh shadows. Or you might want to use a reflector to do the same thing. The reflector is a better idea since it will be reflecting the same light (sun-light) as a source. Sometimes you can take advantage of a natural reflector, like the white-painted side of the laureate's home or a stone wall to one side. You will have to be very careful, however, because color reflects: If the house is painted green, you will get a green reflection from it.

Second, beware of the water in the pool; it will reflect sunlight like a mirror, and those reflections will move and change if a breeze is rippling the water.

Third, over in the shade the natural light will be flatter. Here, too, you might want to add some light (either battery powered or a reflector), since you want to get more light on the subject than on the background.

Fourth, you may have "natural hot spot" problems. Sunlight coming through the tree branches and falling on the subject or objects within the picture will be much brighter than the overall lighting. The auto iris will react to the brightness. Try to eliminate any hot spots by positioning the subject carefully. Beware of shoot-ing the subject with the sky in the background. It, too, will be a "hot spot," and you will risk having the subject appear in silhouette against the sky.

In both of the shooting situations discussed above two things are most important to remember. First, the natural light can be useful, but you must look carefully at the picture before you record it to be sure you have solved any distracting light problems. Second, the locale should be appropriate—if the subject never touched a clod of earth in her life, portraying her as an avid gardener is telling a visual lie.

SOUND—THE OTHER CHANNEL

The other major information channel of television news is sound. The sounds at a news event—even just the background sounds—are informative. They tell the viewer what it sounded like when the presidential candidate arrived, how the suspect talked, how the crash survivor felt about the experience. Relatively few people live in a soundless environment. Familiar sounds make the place more recognizable. New sounds provide a new experience for the viewer.

Researchers believe that the audience reacts to the way people sound when they talk. The voice reflects emotion. A foreign or regional accent is information. Pro-nunciation and enunciation give clues to such things as where the speaker comes from and how much education he or she has had.

Unfortunately it is often the pictures that get the most attention. The sound is made as almost an afterthought. But poor-quality sound can be just as distracting, just as aggravating, just as lacking in information as poor-quality pictures. There-fore, the time spent making sure the sound is of the best quality possible is as important as the time spent making pictures.

Chapter 2 established the basics of microphones and the sound system you will be working with. These basics will apply when you are working in the field.

The Camera Microphone

The first source of sound is from the microphone built into or attached to the cam-era. Unless something is done to prevent it, that microphone will deliver sound to the videotape recorder, where it will be placed on one of the audio channels—usually channel 2—on the video cassette. To prevent the camera mic from operating that way you must unplug it, or plug another microphone or blank mic plug, into channel 2. Most photojournalists let the camera mic operate whenever they are not using channel 2 for some other purpose so they can record the **ambient** (background) sound at the same time they are recording the video at the news event. News pictures without accompanying ambient sound do not have the sight-sound dimensions that will make the viewers feel as though they are at the news event.

Automatic Gain Control

Other sound is collected by microphones plugged into the audio amplifier of the VCR. The VCR amplifiers that handle the sound operate with an automatic gain control (AGC) function. That is, the AGC adjusts the loudest and softest sound levels to bring them down (or up) to an average level. Remember the word *average* because it has a lot to do with the sound quality you will achieve. AGC is convenient and requires no adjustments; you don't have to ride the gain to prevent loud sounds from blasting or raise low-level sounds so that they can be heard.

But this basic function has some problems. Because the AGC is always at work trying to average out the sound levels, the conditions found at some news events can create disturbing sound qualities in the recording.

If the reporter is standing close to a jet airplane as it taxies away for takeoff, the background sound will be very loud. As the reporter starts to talk the AGC will pull the background level down and his or her words will ride over it. If it is very quiet and the reporter is speaking in spurts rather than a smooth flow of words, the AGC will crank up the background each time the reporter pauses, and pull it down again when the reporter resumes speaking. In each case this "pumping" is heard as the AGC adjusts between the two sound sources and can be very distracting to the listener.

You can control "pumping" (1) by moving the reporter to a more balanced background sound situation; (2) by changing the type of microphone being used; or (3) by having the reporter move closer to the microphone.

That last paragraph contains the two cardinal rules for good sound operation:

✔ 1. Proper microphone position is six to eight inches away from the mouth for interviews and speech recording.
✔ 2. Use the proper microphone for the job.

You will recall from Chapter 2 that the normal ENG field kit usually contains four kinds of microphones: a hand-held omnidirectional, one or more unidirectional lavalier mics, and perhaps shotgun and transmitter mics. Now we will see how they can be used to avoid problems and provide good sound quality on the job.

Avoiding the "Ice Cream Cone Lick"

In a single-microphone interview, it is bad practice for the reporter to point the microphone at the subject while he or she talks, then point it back at him- or herself to ask more questions. If you have only one microphone it can't be helped, but it creates some problems.

1. The mic gets into the picture.
2. The reporter becomes a mic stand.
3. The reporter is tied down to the mic cord.
4. The subject is threatened by the mic.

When the microphone is conspicuous, it is distracting. Often the action looks like two people eating one ice cream cone; the reporter takes a lick, then the subject takes a lick, back and forth goes the microphone—usually right in the middle of the picture.

When the reporter holds the microphone at the end of that cord, the subject can simply walk away or move out of range. The very worst thing the reporter can do, of course, is to hand the microphone to the subject. Then the subject is in control of the interview and any chance of maintaining proper mic distance is lost.

It takes only a few seconds to provide the remedy. Use two microphones—hand held for the reporter, a lavalier clipped on the subject. Or use two lavaliers. Lavaliers are small and inconspicuous. They come with a small "jewelry box" of things that can be used to attach the mic to the speaker: a cord for putting it around the neck, a clip to fasten it onto a shirt or jacket, and a buttonhole clasp. The lavalier is quite unidirectional and can help eliminate disturbing background sounds if it is the proper distance away from the subject's mouth.

You should take care that the lavalier mic is as inconspicuous as it is designed to be. Drape the mic cord under a jacket or along the subject's side; don't run it across his or her chest so that it looks like a blood transfusion device. The mic should not be placed under clothing since the cloth can muffle the sound or rub against the mic as the subject moves.

With the subject's mic plugged into one audio channel and the reporter's mic into another, you have also provided for further control on each track level during the editing process.

Shotgun and Transmitter Microphones

Even the two-mic setup has problems. The mic cords are still leashing the reporter and subject to the equipment. You cannot attach a lavalier to a fleeing subject, and often it is very inconvenient to install long mic cord extensions so that the people in the interview can move around freely.

This is where the other two mics come into play. Shotgun microphones are one answer. They have a narrow angle of pickup and they can be aimed very carefully so that they pick up specific sounds from some distance away. Shotgun mics are excellent for picking up the questions at a news conference or the remarks of those at a public hearing. They can be put to good use to get the sounds of individuals in a group of people, or to single out one person from a panel of speakers, or to get the remarks of a news maker moving through a crowd or during a walking interview. They give mobility to both the reporter and the subject of the story. They have a drawback: Someone else must operate them at the scene if they are to be used effectively.

Transmitter microphones are another answer. Each contains a tiny radio transmitter that sends the sound the mic collects to an equally tiny receiver located on the camera or VCR. They have no cords to get in the way; the reporter can move freely. The mic can be attached to the subject like a lavalier so that he or she can move about without having to worry about a mic cord to trip over or drag along behind.

Transmitter mics do have disadvantages, however. The distance they can send their signal is limited. And because they use some of the same channels as other mobile radio equipment, they are subject to interference. A burst of transmission from the local construction company concerning exactly where a load of sand is to be delivered can blow your reporter right off your sound track. Even worse, you might get the voice of a reporter from a competing station doing his or her standup close. Solid objects that get between the mic and its receiver can block the signal completely.

Special Sound Problems and Situations

It would be convenient if all news events occurred in a sound recording studio where very sophisticated sound setups are standard. But usually ENG crews and reporters have to be able to cope with a wide variety of conditions in the field.

Other People's Microphones

At news conferences and public appearances by newsmakers, television news crews will often find that the people sponsoring the event have provided their own podium microphone for the speaker and a distribution system for the sound. These are usually called *mults* (for ''multiple sound systems''). They are set up with the idea that there will be one microphone for the news maker to speak into and enough places for the people who want to record that sound to plug into. This avoids the mushroom growth of microphones hiding a speaker and bad shooting angles for the photojournalists.

But mults have some problems. First, you have to know about them in advance so that you have the right kinds of connectors and microphones to hook into the central system. Second, you should be sure that whoever is providing the mults knows how to run them and has them in good shape. A 25-cent part in a distribution amplifier owned by ABC failed during the first Ford-Carter debate in 1976. All the sound was lost for twenty-seven minutes while the two presidential candidates stood there waiting to complete the debate.

There is no sure answer. One thing is certain, however. Recording the sound while pointing your microphone at a public address system speaker always results in poor sound. Avoid doing that at all costs. If this means carrying fifty feet of microphone cord with you, do it. And take a roll of tape with you so you can fasten the mic somewhere within that critical distance—six to eight inches from the speaker's mouth.

Other Sound Problems

In the field you can find as many sound problems as places to record sound. Some of these have to do with:

1. Acoustics
2. The manner in which the subject speaks
3. The environment where the sound is being made

Many books have been written about acoustics, but here are two of the most vexing situations that confront the TV news crew covering a story:

Hard surfaces will bounce sound back toward the microphone.
Soft surfaces will absorb sound.

If the interview is going to take place in a room with hard-surface walls you can be sure that the sound will bounce around like a gerbil in its cage. Unless you do something about that, your interview is going to sound like it was done inside the town water tank. So:

✔1. If you are getting a reverberation, work the mic closer to the subject.
✔2. Use a unidirectional microphone.
✔3. Move the site of the interview to a less resonant location.

Conversely, if the surfaces are very soft, they will absorb sound.

✔1. Again, work the microphone closer.
✔2. Or choose a mic with more omnidirectional characteristics.

When you are confronted with a subject who speaks very softly, you just have to get the mic closer.

One note here: People don't live, work, and play in acoustically perfect sound studios, so some of the natural sound ''feel'' of a location is needed to portray more accurately the location of the story.

It is dangerous—and unprofessional—to think that you will be able to handle sound problems during the editing process. Sure, you can raise the levels, but you must remember that adjusting the level for the speaker also raises the level of all the other sounds you recorded.

Background Sounds   Background sounds are something to check very carefully. They too can be sneaky. In a location interview where you have set up the subject and reporter facing each other so you can make the over-the-shoulder shot, you may have placed them in a position where their microphones will gather more background sound than you want. The subject may be standing in front of a very quiet area, but the reporter may be standing in front of an air compressor. Too much of that background sound may come in over the top of the reporter's microphone. Even if it doesn't, you will still find a significant difference in ambient sound levels while the reporter is asking the questions and while the subject is answering them.

If you set your microphone on a stand on the subject's desk, right next to a cherished antique clock, you will get the loud ticking of that clock throughout the recording and you won't be able to get rid of it.

Most of the answers to background sound problems come from the same thing that helps to solve visual background problems—the photojournalist's constant awareness of the environment in which the recording is taking place. You can move the reporter and subject away from the air compressor. You can realize the clock is there and put the microphone somewhere else.

Another background sound problem turns up when the reporter goes into a recording booth to record the narration written to go along with the illustrative scenes for the story. The material shot in the field will have a lot of good ambient, or wild, sound. The voice track the reporter has recorded will have *no* ambient sound. Unless something is done about that, the lack of ambient sound behind the voice-over will be very noticeable. Two remedies are possible.

1. As much as possible record the voice over and standups in the field with the same ambient sound in the background.
2. Mix the sound when the story is edited so that the ambient field sound fills in behind the narration.

Some background sounds will get you no matter what you do. The dog who has been sleeping soundly at his master's feet will begin to bark when you start the interview. Asking the dog to leave may adversely change your relationship with the subject. The telephone, which hasn't rung since last Tuesday, will ring during the interview; the loud air conditioner will come on; the baby will cry. All you can do is pray that it won't happen, but it will.

Special Setups An assignment that calls for the recording of music or any other special sounds requires special attention to the sound setup and careful planning.

If the story is about an important public hearing on a new wheel tax the city council is proposing, it may call for setting up a variety of microphones. You may have to provide a mic for each of the council members, a shotgun mic to pick up comments from the audience, and others besides. This will require the use of a mixer to control the various mics on the council table and elsewhere. Since the VTR has only two channels for sound, the mixer can be used to ride levels on the various mic locations and feed the mixed sound to one of the channels.

As cameras move into courtrooms, special attention must be paid to the entire setup. Where cameras are allowed, the courts usually have stringent rules about where and how cameras and microphones may be placed and when they can be used. Television wants access to courts, so the news crews covering those courts must be very circumspect and very cooperative. The worst thing that can happen is for someone to come bursting into the court chamber and start stringing cables and mic cords all over the place.

Music presents special problems for news crews. Although stereo sound for television is becoming commonplace, and better sound quality is being built into TV receivers, much TV news sound is not of hi-fi quality. Added to that is the fact that recorders—any recorders—operating on battery power do not run at a speed

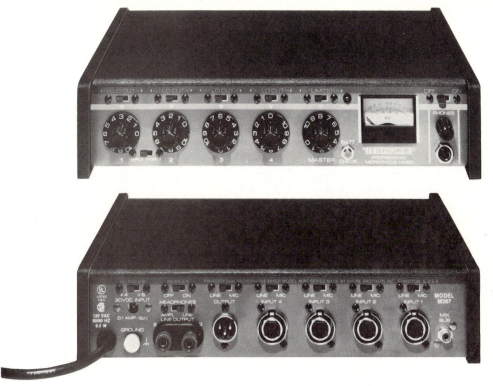

FIGURE 4-7. A small four-channel mixer such as this one is part of the ENG field equipment package. When a number of microphones are needed to pick up sound from a panel of speakers, they can be plugged in to this mixer and their sound controlled with the ''mixing pots'' (control knobs). The sound is then fed to one of the microphone inputs on the videotape recorder. Such mixers can operate on AC or battery power. *(Courtesy of Shure.)*

constant enough to record the wide range of sound frequencies created by a variety of musical instruments. If your assignment is to do a feature on the Fourth of July Pageant, don't just go to the dress rehearsal and point a mic or two at the performers. The chances are good that you will earn the undying hatred of those performers when they hear how they sound on your ad-lib recording.

You can do some things to improve the sound quality when recording music.

1. Use a converter to run the recorder on alternating current (AC). It will provide a much more consistent machine speed.
2. Record several of the musical numbers in their entirety with a good-quality audio tape recorder (also operating on AC).
3. Make a very careful microphone plot using good-quality microphones to get the best sound possible.

If you do this, when it comes time to edit the feature, you may have enough quality sound to mix with pictures to satisfy everyone, even the musicians.

The key to getting good-quality sound to go with the high-quality pictures you shoot is the same as for other operations: Use professional techniques and the right equipment. Think and plan ahead. Anticipate the problems and do something about them. It is not difficult to get good sound if you pay attention to it and believe in the need to get it. We use pictures *and* sound to tell the news.

MAKING IT ALL TELL A STORY

It's takeoff checklist time.

✔ 1. Camera ready?
✔ 2. VCR ready?
✔ 3. Lighting setup ready?
✔ 4. Mics, sound setup ready?

If everything checks out, from here on you can make pictures and sound. You are ready physically. But hold it. Are you ready mentally? What you accomplish from here on will be controlled more by that other level of consciousness—the commitment. The equipment is in place. Now it is time to concentrate on making the visual content work toward showing and telling the story in the clearest, most interesting, and most involving way possible.

This brings up a new list of questions. Some of them have already been hinted at. The answers to some of them will create frustration because they will mean you may have to change the physical setup. All of them, whether they deal with mechanics or aesthetics, relate to *what* you are getting on tape and *how* that will be used in putting the story together.

✔ 1. Is the camera location the right one?
✔ 2. How will the scenes relate to the subjects and the subject matter?
✔ 3. Have I got the proper cover material, and enough of it?
✔ 4. Have I got what is needed to ''tell'' the story?
✔ 5. Have I got what is needed for the editing process?

If you are on a spot news story you must run through this list at breakneck speed. If there is more time you have more time to think your way through it. But the list is there to be applied—always.

Point of View—Visual Awareness

We have already said that point of view is where you are shooting from: the camera location, the angle and size of the shot. Now, let's take point of view a step further—and in an aesthetic direction.

Interviews   Photojournalists find shooting interviews a daily chore and a boring one. People complain that there are too many ''talking heads'' on television news programs. But a talking head that is saying something interesting and significant is an important part of the daily news.

Someone said seeing Nikita Khrushchev pounding his shoe on the table at the UN and threatening nuclear war was riveting television news—even if the audience only heard Khrushchev speaking Russian. Seeing Lyndon Johnson, at the end of a speech, saying he would not run again for the presidency, seeing Richard Nixon in his tearful and disjointed farewell to his White House staff, seeing the TWA captain talking from the cockpit window as a hostage taker held a gun to his head, seeing the pope kneeling alone on the pavement as he prayed at a memorial to fallen workers in Gdansk—all were memorable television news events for viewers.

The key to it is, of course, that the subject is saying something pertinent or important. Part of the job of the photojournalist is to shoot interviews so that the viewer is allowed to see and hear the subject. Camera location and the placement of the subject in relation to the camera (and the audience) are all-important. (Look again at Figure 4-1.)

Note that the reporter is placed so that his or her back is to the camera, and the camera is shooting over his or her shoulder. The subject is facing the reporter and therefore is also facing the camera. By keeping the angle of the camera shot as close as possible to straight on, the photojournalist has the best chance to get a shot in which the subject is speaking directly to the viewer.

Note, too, that this setup gives the photojournalist several very useful shots. With a wide shot (LS) the subject and the reporter are shown together—the picture "says" this is an interview. With a medium shot (MS) the reporter's shoulder or head is included in the extreme edge of the frame—once again relating two subjects to each other. With the tight shot (CU) the reporter is eliminated and the subject speaks in closeup view.

A person being interviewed for television is being asked to do something unnatural. There's the camera, the lights, the other paraphernalia. He or she is tense or frightened. There's little pretense that it will be a nice, quiet conversation. So the subject will look at the reporter, who plays the role of security blanket, confidant, human receiver. The over-the-shoulder setup emphasizes this subject-reporter relationship and deemphasizes the threat of the camera.

Any variation on this setup that gets the subject and the reporter side by side makes for very awkward shots. In a straight-on two shot the reporter and subject are looking across the screen and their ears—not their mouths—are aimed at the viewer. There's also a hole right in the middle of the scene. If that hole contains a cage with two parakeets or a mobile which is turning slowly in a breeze, no one will listen to anything the subject has to say. In a one shot the subject is talking off the side of the screen.

The over-the-shoulder setup also helps establish the line of action. Whichever shoulder of the reporter you are shooting over, all of the action shots must remain on that side of the reporter and the subject. You can move the camera around anywhere on that side of the line of action to get cutaways or inserts, but if you cross to the other side you will violate the line of action. When the questions asked by the reporter are edited together with the answers from the subject, the subject will not be talking to the reporter. In fact he or she will seem to be talking to the reporter's back.

Reshooting the Questions with Reverse Angle
As noted in Chapter 3, in an interview done with one camera all of the shots have to be made over the shoulder of the reporter. It is a common practice after the interview is finished to shoot the questions over again with the camera pointed at the reporter. These reverse-angle questions give the editor a chance to cut from reporter question to subject answer in a series of scenes that duplicate what actually happened during the interview.

Here are important cautions about the practice of shooting reverse-angle questions after the interview is completed:

✔ 1. They *must* be the same questions asked in the first place.
✔ 2. You must shoot them in the presence of the subject. You don't want to be accused of mixing answer A in with question B.
✔ 3. You must shoot them all, since the interview will be edited. The one you didn't shoot may be the only one needed.

You must take great pains to make sure there is no change in the wording that might affect the meaning or thrust of the question. And your subject must be made aware of what you are doing.

Locale　If you are shooting a longer feature or a mini-documentary series, the chances are you will make visits to a number of locations in advance of the shooting. You will be looking for the best *locale* to shoot various segments of the feature or mini-doc so that the scenes shot give as true a representation of reality as possible.

For example: If you are shooting a feature about what carnival life is like for those who run the carnival, you will want to find locales that "show it like it is." You want to find places where the people eat, sleep, take a break, wash their laundry. You might want to show the endless drudgery of setting up and tearing down. To get those scenes you might follow the carnival to another town, or meet it before it comes to your city. You will want to shoot some scenes when the carnival is not crowded with customers to show what carnival life is like when the "tip" is not swarming over the rides, playing the games of chance, or filling their mouths with food.

During this kind of exercise, a good photojournalist's visual awareness is working at top speed. The well-trained eye is looking, always looking, composing shots, "seeing" shot angles, shot sizes, shot sequences. The mind is busy, too: This is the best place to get a cover shot; this is the best place to set up for an interview; over there I can get the carousel operator with the "three-rides-for-a-dollar" sign in the background; from here I can shoot the hamburger cook through the smoke; from this low angle I can shoot over the shoulder of that little girl to get the Alligator Man dozing on that folding chair.

Ernie Crisp, a famous TV news film photographer, had a phrase he shouted frequently at news film beginners: "Get down on your knees, you sinners." Crisp felt that while the tripod was a necessary device to get steady shots, too many TV photojournalists used it improperly. In relating story elements to each other the proper point of view is all-important.

"If," Crisp said, "you are shooting a story about kids in the first grade, the camera should be down at the kid level, not at the level of a standing adult. Kids sit in little chairs, they work at little tables, their world is down there and that's where the camera ought to be. . . . If you shoot only from tripod height you are not in the kids' world, you are in the teacher's world."

Sequencing　The mind's eye must work at all times to ensure sequence: Here's the long shot, here's the medium shot, and here's the closeup. Further, any element or person that is a focal point of the story should be "worked over" carefully.

Instead of just one shot of each basic sequence component, the photojournalist should make a variety of sequence shots. By changing the angle or location of the camera, by working around, over, or below the subject or object—always observing the line of action—you can get more interesting and informative shots and shot sequences.

For example: Let's say you are shooting the local university's track and field team while they practice for the NCAA indoor meet. You will, of course, interview the coach and some of the stars. But if that's all you get, you run the risk of a story filled with very dull "talking heads." The coach will inevitably say things like: "The team will have to give 110 percent"; "We're going there to run"; "It depends on the momentum we get from qualifying."

Instead, get the interviews first, and then "work over" the star pole vaulter as he practices. Shoot him full figure. Make closeups of his face, hands on the pole, arms cocked, feet and legs ready to make his approach. Shoot some scenes of him starting out, some more at ground level of his feet going by at full speed. Shoot some closeups of the end of the pole slamming into the vaulting box. Shoot several jumps from the end of the pit. Then shoot several inserts as he clears (or hits) the bar. Finally, shoot medium shots and closeups as he bounces into the landing pit.

Do the same for the best sprinter.

By working over the two athletes most likely to win you have illustrations for a story on team prospects that will be far more interesting than a couple of interviews.

The Box with the Window in It

Another element of visual awareness that must be considered is somewhat more abstract. The television audience is looking at what some have called a "window to the world." While that sounds dramatic, the concept is important.

The audience is looking at a pane of glass that is one side of a box. The frame around that glass represents the proscenium arch of a conventional stage. In a theater the audience sees the spatial relationship of two or more actors to each other, or one actor to an object on the stage.

The television audience sees the same relationships on the TV screen. And once they are established, the audience will remember the relationships of one subject or object to another, even if one of those subjects or objects is not in subsequent scenes.

If they first see a reporter and an interview subject in an establishing two shot where the reporter is on the left and the subject on the right, they know the reporter is still on the left when they see the subject in a one shot. If a painting and the artist who created it are shown in a shot, the audience knows the painting is still there in the same relationship to the artist when the artist is shown alone in a closeup.

The audience's ability to understand the relationship of two or more subjects or objects to each other in a picture extends to motion. Objects in motion—cars traveling around a race track, for example—go right to left if the point of view is from the inside of the track. They go left to right if the point of view is outside the track. The audience understands that after your scenes establish the point of view.

It is up to you to keep the point of view in mind so that the audience looking at the box will not become disoriented.

Closeups   Of all the shots a photojournalist makes when shooting a sequence, the closeup is the most important. People get more information if they can see the visual part of the news clearly. If they are provided with a closeup of the focal point of the story after the long shot and medium shot, they are told visually what that focal point is.

People retain more information from a person speaking on the screen if the speaker is shown in a closeup shot. Medium shots of speakers are just that—medium. Viewers get more involved in a closeup. They relate more closely to the subject. There are some indications they can actually hear better, perhaps because they listen more attentively.

When the focal point of the story is an object, the audience wants to see that object up close. Next time you are in a jewelry store look at how the customers behave. They lean over, or move closer, or put their glasses on to get a better look at the rings, digital watches, silver patterns. Television news can move the viewers closer to give them that better look.

Suppose the subject of the story is the batch of new boa constrictors born at the zoo. The audience will appreciate a closeup look at the babies on the screen, even though they probably would not move closer to the cage if they were actually there for the event.

Closeups, especially extreme closeups, involve some ethical and aesthetic elements that you need to think about while you are shooting them.

Many stations have policies dictating that blood and gore will not be shown, especially during the dinner-hour news. Many photojournalists, because of their ethical standards, simply refuse to shoot the closeup of the wound, the blood, the mangled arm, the head oddly twisted on the neck of the victim. They say that making these shots reinforces the widely held belief that journalists are ghouls who seek sensation. Others say that since there's a policy against use of such shots, there's no point in shooting them in the first place.

Yet there may be that one rare time when just such a shot is needed to make a vivid visual point. The videotape of the carnage when Anwar Sadat was assassinated in Cairo showed a number of scenes of an Egyptian officer who had only a bloody stump where one of his arms should have been. Those who used that scene in the coverage, like those who used the scenes of the bodies of Haitians washed up on a Florida beach, defended that use as showing just how awful the situation was. And the argument is still going on about whether some Pennsylvania TV stations were right or wrong when they carried pictures of a troubled state official who called a news conference and shot himself dead in front of the rolling cameras. Most stations edited the videotape at a point before the man pulled the trigger and did not show the rest.

Extreme closeups of people who are talking are very dramatic. Sometimes that extreme closeup tells the story better than any other scene—the exhausted face of the marathon winner, the dejected look of the election loser. But extreme closeups should be tasteful. The extreme closeup of a person who has a large wart on the end of his nose may actually distract the viewer. Because the viewer is looking with rapt attention at the wart and may even be commenting to someone else in the room about it, that viewer may not be paying much attention to the important things the person is saying.

Backgrounds   The photojournalist's visual awareness must extend to concern for what is going on in the background of a scene. When the action or objects in the background are more visually interesting than what is in the foreground of the picture the viewer may try to "look through" to see what is going on there.

A Chicago TV station decided to have its editorialist present the station's editorials on location. Each day, after the editorial was written, the editorialist and a crew would go to the scene of the subject and record it there. One editorial was about air pollution. The location for the shooting was in the city's air pollution control center.

In the foreground the editorialist spoke about pollution control and the need for stricter laws. In the background a man wearing a white coat and carrying a clipboard seemed to be reading pollution detectors and writing down the results on the clipboard. He checked, tapped a dial, wrote down the results, and moved to the next meter, where he repeated the action. Pretty soon the viewers were watching the man: "What dangers is he finding back there? Hadn't we better get in the car and drive to the country?" In the foreground the editorialist was offering a lot of good advice, but it is doubtful the audience heard it.

Even backgrounds that don't move can be so "busy" or visually curious that the audience is distracted. Interesting pictures on the wall, a plant that seems to bend toward the subject to bite her, a tree branch that moves in and out of the frame as the breeze blows, brightly colored objects, splashy wallpaper, all can overwhelm the focal point of the story. The photojournalist must see these distracting visual elements before shooting and work to control them.

Shooting B-Roll   It is time now to talk about the **B-Roll,** the illustrative scenes. Like visual continuity, the term comes to us from the days of film. Today some TV journalists call it "cover material." One of the most useful things about ENG is that the B-Roll can be edited together onto one video cassette along with sound-on-tape scenes.

Let's look at the photojournalist's in-the-field responsibilities concerning the B-Roll. Four main concepts are involved.

1. If you don't shoot the B-Roll scenes, you can't edit them into your story.
2. B-Roll material must follow visual continuity rules in the same way as any other visual sequence.
3. B-Roll material must specifically illustrate what the sound bite or narration is talking about.
4. Production effects are no substitute for good B-Roll material.

The primary purpose of B-Roll is to illustrate and illuminate, to explain things visually. A secondary purpose is to "cover" talking heads or **voice-over** (V/O) narration. So in shooting B-Roll, the photojournalist is collecting scenes that will go together to show the audience how something is done, what happened at a news event, or provide a closeup look at a process.

Here again visual awareness is the key factor. The photojournalist must look for the B-Roll scenes that best illustrate the story and gather them in ELS-LS-MS-CU-

ECU form so they can be edited into sequences. Good B-Roll material can be edited to match with the sync sound on tape (SOT), or to illustrate what the V/O is talking about. Good B-Roll material also should include the natural (ambient) sound (NAT-SOT) that goes with the illustrative pictures. This allows for interesting and creative sound mixes during the editing.

For example: The world's most famous diamond cutter has come to your city to cut a huge diamond into two pieces of the exact same size. He has agreed to allow you to videotape this process. It is both a news story and a feature.

He agrees to spend some time explaining what he is going to do before he does it. You ask him to tell and show what the process is and you videotape him doing that. You have his voice explaining and you shoot LS, MS, and many CUs of his hands, the tools he uses, reverse angles of his face, the diamond, and so on.

Then when the big moment comes you concentrate on it. You are rolling well ahead of time and recording the natural sound. It is very quiet now as he steadies himself, makes sure he has the angle of the cutting blade just right—but that silence is also part of the story. Now . . . he raises the mallet. Whack! There they are, two pieces. Keep rolling . . . he looks at them, holds them up, smiles, says: "There's really nothing to it if you study carefully, don't drink or smoke, and remain celibate for six months before trying it."

Now when the editor puts that raw material together he or she has all of the necessary sound and B-Roll scenes to make a very interesting and even exciting story.

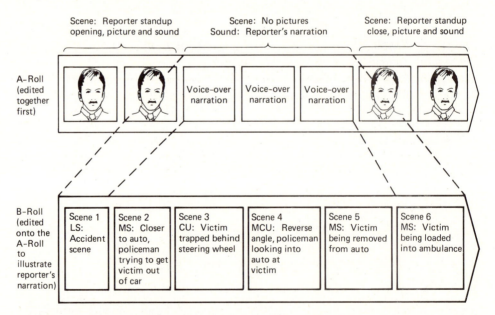

FIGURE 4-8. How B-Roll material is used to illustrate what a reporter or subject is talking about. Here the standup opening showing the reporter at the news event is the first scene edited onto the air tape. Then the reporter's voice-over narration is laid down, audio only. Next, the selected B-Roll scenes are edited onto the air tape in the space containing the voice-over narration, video only. Finally, the reporter's standup close is added to complete the story. B-Roll material illustrating what an interview subject is discussing is used in the same manner.

First the editor would use the establishing scenes to give the audience the locale. The V/O narration would tell what was going to happen.

Next, while the diamond cutter talks about and shows what he is going to do, the B-Roll scenes you shot during the demonstration are laid over his voice as he takes it step by step. You shot LS-MS-CU-ECU. You observed screen direction rules. You have both closeups and reverse angles of the cutter and the diamond, relating the two to each other.

What evolves is a little package that cuts between the cutter with sync sound and the B-Roll with the cutter's voice continuing on while the viewer sees what he is explaining.

Then, when the dramatic moment comes, the scenes of the actual cutting are edited together with the sound. The completed story is something like instant replay in sports. The difference is that you have shown the audience what is going to happen and then the real event. The B-Roll gives the viewer a better understanding of the whole story.

Not all stories have such dramatic B-Roll possibilities, nor would you always have so much time to shoot them. But most story locations have some B-Roll elements that can be shot and that, when edited into the sound, will help illustrate the story: there are bulletin boards with announcements, street and traffic signs, relevant objects, the places or things the sound is talking about. With all the fancy graphics we can now create we tend to fall back on them for illustration. Nothing will replace good B-Roll. That comes out of the photojournalist's eye and mind, not out of a digital brain.

Shooting for Edit   Two major concepts are involved in shooting for edit. One is mechanical, the other organizational.

The first concept has to do with tracking. Since the control track must be there for the edit units to lock together, you have to operate the tape recorder in a prescribed manner. We said in Chapter 2 that *only some* portable videotape recorders tell you whether the tracking is being put on the videotape successfully. If the one you are using does not include that feature, you will have to guess. But provided the recorder is working properly, there are several important things you can do to assure tracking. They should become automatic operations.

1. Record at least thirty seconds of throwaway material at the beginning of the cassette.

   This is to make sure there is enough tape with track on it to allow the editing controller to back up the tape—preroll—during the editing process without running onto the trackless leader material on the front end of the tape.

2. Record at least fifteen seconds of material (*after* the thirty seconds of throwaway material) after the recorder is started and before the beginning of any material you expect to use.

   This is to allow the recorder time to stabilize, and to assure you have good tracking *ahead* of the material you want to use so that the preroll can function during the edit.

3. Continue to record at least ten seconds after any action is completed before stopping or pausing the recorder.

TRACKING INSURANCE

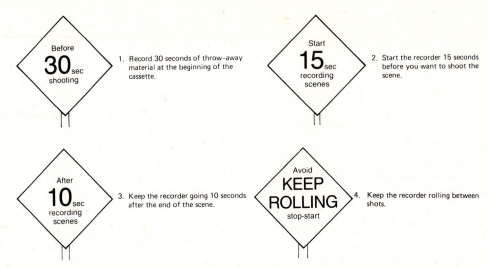

FIGURE 4-9. The steps to take to assure tracking.

This will ensure there is enough tracking *after* the material you want to use so that the rehearse-edit function of the editors will work. It will also ensure that the last few seconds of the tape segment will have tracking.

4. Keep the recorder running as much as possible.

Except when you are changing the setup or location, or taking a break, it is best not to stop the recorder. This is especially true between shots and on spot-news coverage.

It is better to have the camera movement, the shaky shots, the momentary views of the sky, or the toe of your left foot along with the usable material in one continuous flow on the tape than to have gaps in the tracking caused by stopping and starting the recorder. You can edit around poor visuals, but you cannot edit around a lack of good, stable tracking.

These four mechanical-operational functions should become standard procedures for the photojournalist. You want to have good tracking on all of the tape you record, both before and after the scenes you may use in the edited version of the story. If you try to run the recorder the way you would make snapshots with a still camera, that tracking won't be there where you need it.

For example: Your reporter team member is doing his stand-up closer. His last line is, "And that's the story from the XYZ bankruptcy hearing." Then you immediately stop the recorder.

No tracking will be under part of that sentence because the recorder erased the tracking that was on the tape parallel to the pictures of the reporter saying that line, and then put new tracking on a few seconds later. Since that sentence is about four seconds long, it will not have tracking "under" the last word or two because the tape hadn't reached the new tracking point. Without that tracking you will not be able to edit the reporter's closing line onto the "air" tape.

The same thing can happen to the front end of a tape segment. If the recorder is stopped when you see someone making a dramatic move or hear him or her start to say something, you have a problem. By the time you get the recorder rolling you will probably miss the action. Or if you do happen to catch it, the recorder will not have been rolling long enough to stabilize and get good tracking on the tape.

A second recording practice which will help in the editing has to do with editing in the camera. With film and its processing time photojournalists were cautious about shooting so much that editing deadlines could not be met. With videotape it is possible to shoot virtually everything that happens at a news event.

For example, a photojournalist got pictures of a prominent liberal politician being hit in the face by an egg thrown from the audience. He had stayed on and kept shooting most of the way through a long speech. The politician had some sparkling things to say about the egg-thrower and his or her sense of fairness and decency. Videotape allowed the photojournalist to capture that moment along with the other things the politician had to say.

But that's a mixed blessing. Overshooting is now rampant. It is so easy to keep running cassettes through the recorder while hoping something interesting will happen that the photojournalist loses all sense of discipline. It is annoying for an editor to have to scan through an hour of tape to find the forty-second essence of a story. News judgment needs to be applied firmly.

A more serious fault is random shooting. Sometimes a news event is so interesting visually that the beginning photojournalist acts like a novice glutton let loose at a groaning buffet table—a bite of this, a nibble of that . . . look over there . . . grab a snack of this, load up the plate with that. World champion eaters don't go about it that way. They launch a planned and sustained attack on the food and work their way through it with a method.

The photojournalist should do the same thing. Study the situation, size up the opportunities, and then carry out a methodical program to get all of the necessary and interesting visual material. It helps in the editing crunch if you can get the LS-MS-CU sequence shots, the cutaways, the inserts, and the reverse angles somewhere near each other on the tape. It also helps the photojournalist to remember to be sure the shots were made in the first place.

Pans, tilts, and zooms were discussed in Chapter 3. We told you their uses in visual composition and warned you they create problems during the editing process and for the viewer. It is how you shoot them, with the editing and audience in mind, that make them either usable or unusable.

When there is a motivated need to pan from one stationary object or subject to another, you must make the pan as smoothly and as slowly as possible. It is a good idea to practice the movement of the camera, or record the pan several times, to be sure you get the shot you want. You need to decide two things: where the pan will start, and where the pan will end. When you have decided:

1. Place your feet so they are pointing at *the spot where the pan will end*.
2. Rotate your body from the waist to point the camera at *the spot where the pan will begin*. Pan by pivoting from the waist. Do it with a slow and steady motion. End the pan by stopping and centering up on the object of interest. Hold the shot at the end of the pan for a few seconds longer than seems necessary. If the camera is mounted on a tripod you still have to pick out the start and end points before you make the shot, and make it slowly.

When you have to pan with a moving subject or object you have three more important things to remember.

✔ 3. Try to keep the subject or object comfortably in the frame.

✔ 4. If you can, try to keep the subject or object in the left or right two-thirds of the frame *away* from the direction it is moving.

✔ 5. At the end of a pan shot that is following a moving subject or object, *stop* the pan and let the subject or object continue on out of the frame.

All five of these actions will provide a usable shot for the edited story. The smooth pan from point to point will have a beginning and end. The following pan with the two-thirds composition will give the subject or object in the frame "room" to move in the direction of the movement. Stopping the pan to let the subject or object move out of frame will provide an ending to the shot and an opportunity for the editor to pick up the subject or object in any size shot in the next scene, thus avoiding a jump cut.

Tilts do not involve the same problems as pans. But there are three points you should remember: A tilt, too, must have a beginning and an end. Make it very slowly. Be careful that the tilt does not exaggerate the camera angle at the end of the shot so much that the view of the center of attention becomes wildly distorted, for example, as when a huge face looms over the scene like a vulture.

For zooms the same things apply. If you need to trim the size of a shot during the recording of a scene you can do it easily with the zoom. But do it very slowly, so slowly that it is almost imperceptible to the eye. Zoom to change the size of a shot of a subject, but do it *during the reporter's off-camera question*. This gives the editor a different-size shot to cut to when condensing the interview. During fast action on a spot news story, zoom to frame up the next shot while the tape is rolling. This gives the editor a well-framed shot to cut to *after the zoom is finished*.

Finally—to remind you again—the one zoom you should always make is the one that moves in to the tightest shot and focuses there. That will ensure that all shots wider than that will be in focus.

Just One More Shot, Please

ENG has had a great impact on the picture content of television news. It has made it possible to be almost anywhere and to get visual coverage of almost anything. And, some think, it is now too easy—so easy that it has dulled our sense of responsibility to the journalism involved.

You won't think it's easy when you are just starting out to do all of the things described in this section on making pictures. The complexities of running the equipment can be very daunting, but you must get past this point as rapidly as possible. Then you can join what is a rather distinguished group of men and women who work in visual journalism. You will share with them great satisfaction from knowing that what you did today gave the television audience a clear, honest, disciplined, and artful look at what happened in their world.

PROFILE

Larry Hatteberg has been chief photographer, executive news director, and anchor, editor, writer, you name it, at KAKE-TV, Wichita, Kansas, where he has worked for more than twenty years. In that time he has covered every possible kind of story in every corner of Kansas, the West, and in China, Hong Kong, Italy, New Zealand, and most points in between.

Competing with photojournalists from all U.S. television stations, as well as the three major networks and their foreign bureaus, Larry is one of only two photojournalists to win twice the coveted National Press Photographers Association News Cameraman of the Year Award. He has served as a faculty member of the NPPA Television News Workshop at the University of Oklahoma for many years and as a featured speaker for the NPPA "Flying Shortcourse" in New York, Chicago, Kansas City, Phoenix, and San Francisco. In 1979 he was a judge for the White House News Photographers Association. In 1980 he was elected president of NPPA.

Larry is nationally known as a photojournalist who cares about people. His "Hatteberg's People" program series is widely recognized for bringing out the personalities of individuals in very human terms.

TELLING THE STORY VISUALLY

LARRY HATTEBERG
KAKE-TV, WICHITA, KANSAS

Every day some technological advance gives us a new gadget that is supposed to help us do our jobs better. Some of them work; some of them don't. The cold world of the computer, microchips, and satellite technology has transformed us all from the chemical-mechanical world of film to that of videotape and "live shots" that just a few years ago were only dreams.

But even with all this fancy technology, it still all boils down to one thing. Photojournalists, and the reporters who work alongside them, are storytellers. The revolution brought by ENG has moved television a long way—technically. Journalistically, our profession has been turned upside down. We have technicians who are not photojournalists—and in some cases not even photographers—carrying around ENG cameras. Many of them don't care about our profession, and some don't even know what photojournalism is. They are there because of certain rules set by their employers or by virtue of membership in labor organizations.

We don't need more technicians. We don't need "shooters"; shooters kill things. We do need the very best photojournalists that we can find. We need people who understand how to tell a story visually and at the same time understand that it is journalism.

What kind of training and thinking will help us change? In broadcast journalism courses across the country there is emphasis on writing—students are told how to gather facts and how to put those facts into proper form. And there are courses in photojournalism where mechanics, composition, and pictures are given strong emphasis. What we need on top of that is to develop, for reporters and photojournalists alike, the ability to "think visually," and to "see visually."

ILLUSTRATIVE PHOTOGRAPHY VS. SEQUENTIAL PHOTOGRAPHY

The daily work of covering the news visually can be divided into two general categories: illustrative and sequential.

Illustrative photography is just that; it is usually used to illustrate the reporter's script. For example:

Visual	Narration
Helicopter shot of burned area	The fire burned more than one million acres of forest before fire fighters were able to bring it under control.
Wide shot of people inside school	A nearby school was used to house the four hundred persons made homeless by the flames.
Shot of investigators at campsite	This campsite is where arson investigators believe the fire may have begun, although no suspects in the case have been arrested.
Pix of unloading of truck	Meanwhile, food and clothing are being flown to Smithville from all over the state as residents respond to the disaster.
Mary Jones looking at remains of her charred home	But for people like Mary Jones, it will take more than food and clothes to erase the memory of the fire. (Sound bite)

Illustrative photography can be used effectively when time is important. It does not require matched action or great amounts of editing time to produce a story of this type. It communicates very simply what the viewer needs to know.

Sequential news photography is best used when the photojournalist has some degree of control over the subject. Wide shots, medium shots, and closeup shots in sequence with matching action shots are usually the trademark of sequential photography.

Sequential photography requires a high degree of skill in both the photojournalist and the editor. It is the closest to "Hollywood" shooting that most photojournalists will ever come. Almost anyone can shoot illustrative video, but mastering the art of sequential photography requires an artistic mind, an ability to sense the story and find the pictures that will portray that sense, a feeling for the human equation, and great discipline.

WORKING WITH PEOPLE

If it were possible for television photojournalists or photojournalism students to be invisible, our work would be much easier. Since we are not, each of us must develop our own techniques in working with people. It is easy to get so involved with the technology that you forget you're working with a human equation—you and the subject. How you and he or she communicate will mean the difference between a successful story and one with little meaning.

It begins with attitude. Always treat people the way *you* would like to be treated. Because you work for a television station or a network doesn't give you any special dispensation where manners are concerned. Most of the time you will be in someone's home or on their property.

Respect the property of others. Doing things like putting gaffer tape on expensive wallpaper and then pulling the tape and the wallpaper off at the same time will not endear you to those you are trying to cover. Don't put heavy metallic objects on top of expensive furniture, thus running the risk of scratching it. Don't move furniture around unless you ask permission; you wouldn't do that if you were visiting in someone's living room, and you are a visitor no matter how much "glamour" goes with your job. You can be sure that if the personal property of your story subject is damaged by your carelessness, the rift between you and your subject will become as large as the Grand Canyon.

If damage does occur, offer to compensate the person for the damage. To ignore it will continue to foster the notion that those of us in television are high handed, arrogant, and disrespectful.

Attitude is involved in any kind of story, whether it is a fire, natural disaster, news conference, or some other spot or general news story that makes up the bread and butter of the newscast.

In these cases you will most likely be on a secondary relationship level with most of your subjects. What that means is you, as a photojournalist, will only be dealing with that person for a moment or two before moving on to another shot.

For example: At a fire you are taping three firemen holding a hose and pouring water into a burning building. Your three- to six-shot sequence will include a wide shot, a medium shot, and a closeup shot. While taping that sequence you may or may not have had conversations with the firemen. It may have been just a short sentence: "Hey, guys, tell me if I'm in your way." By saying, "Tell me if I'm in your way," you have acknowledged their importance and are saying that you, as a photojournalist, are willing to work with them. By saying nothing a subconscious rift develops between you and the firemen. They may tell you to move before you get the shots you need. By working with them, you may even get shots you hadn't planned on.

Perhaps the most difficult and most criticized situation for a photojournalist is taping someone who has just lost their home or a loved one, or who has been an eyewitness to a tragedy. The question is: How do you do it and still retain your integrity as a human being?

The first rule is to avoid putting the camera and microphone into someone's face without asking their permission. I don't think this rule applies to most other situations, but it surely does on those stories where emotions are running high and the individual to be photographed is not a public figure. Instead it is someone who, through no action of his or her own, has been caught up in the event.

The first thing the photojournalist should do is to put the camera down and walk up to the subject to be photographed. Tell that person who you are and spend some time with them so that condolences can be expressed about the loss or the fearful experience they've had. The secret here is that the photojournalist must be genuinely concerned or supportive. You can't fool people—you must *feel* the way you speak. Then, after words of condolence or support, tell the individual that you know this is a difficult time for them, but it might help someone else if he or she could tell the viewers what happened.

If you approach the story that way, several things will happen. Because you have stopped to talk with the person for a moment to express your feelings to them, you don't come off as some insensitive and bloodthirsty newsperson who's only in it for the gore. You do show that you are a sensitive person who is just doing his or her job. Then, by telling the subject that his or her version of the incident may help someone else who might have to face similar problems, you are saying that there may be a positive side to this tragedy after all—and you are only trying to help.

ETHICAL ATTITUDE

Each of you must decide for yourself what your limits are in covering a story— the scope of your photojournalistic ethics. In a recent motion picture about the news business, a newspaper editor says: "I know how to write the facts and I know how *not* to hurt people. But I don't know how to do both at the same time." It is a dilemma that we, the photojournalists who are among the first on the scene, face every day.

Is it tasteful to show a woman screaming with anguish as they pull the body of her son out of the water? Do you tape someone who's been burned in an explosion and show them in closeup detail? Do you show an uncovered body on the air? Only judgment by reasonable and experienced journalists based on a specific situation should prevail.

At emotional crime scenes and violent events no good is served if you lose your head along with everyone else. It will work against you to talk back to law officers while they're doing their jobs, even if you think they are acting improperly.

If you believe you've been wronged, then discuss it rationally later, either with the officers or with their superior. Don't create a scene unless you believe your life to be in danger because of some officer's action. You are there to record on tape the factual events of life. When someone interferes with your job, it is only natural to want to blow up and recall all of your First Amendment rights.

But those rights don't automatically admit you to crime scenes or allow you to disobey any law enforcement officer. In truth, you have the same rights as any other member of the general public. No more, no less.

FEATURE STORIES

My favorite area of working with people is the feature story. There is sort of a universal feeling among photojournalists that they have "arrived" when the assignment desk gives them time to go out and do a nice feature piece. The problem is too many reporters and photographers botch the job even before the tape has been recorded. There are several possible causes for this.

Many reporters and photographers worry more about their equipment than about the person they are about to tape. Photojournalists must know their equipment as well and as intimately as they know a wife, husband, or other loved one.

The mechanics of taping must become second nature to the photojournalist. In fact, you shouldn't even have to think about the equipment as you are taping. Your entire thinking process should be directed toward the subject. How is what you are shooting relating to what the subject is saying? How can you make this person relax? Are you getting the shots you need to tell the story? Those are the kinds of thoughts you ought to be having, not whether the exposure is correct, the right buttons have been pushed, or the tape is rolling.

When you meet your feature subject for the first time leave the equipment in the car or van. In most cases your subjects aren't interested in your equipment—in fact, they are terrified by it. Without your gear you will be free to talk with the subjects and get to know them.

At first talk with them about what *they* are interested in. Talk about their garden, their kids, their stamp collection, their nice furniture—anything but why you are there. They already know that, and so do you, so what's the point of discussing it? In the time you spend talking with your subjects you are, in effect, becoming friends with them.

Again, you have to be genuinely interested in people; you can't fake that and shouldn't want to. Probably one of the reasons you decided to become a photojournalist is that you are interested in people. Most people you will work with can spot a phony smile a mile away.

Whether you take five minutes or an hour to get to know your subject it will be the most valuable time you spend on that assignment. Why? Because the more you give of yourself to your subject the more your subject will give back to you on the tape. People find it much easier to talk to friends than to strangers. You will remain a stranger unless you take the minutes we've been discussing to get to know your subject as a human being.

Don't make a big deal about your equipment. It's scary stuff to outsiders. When you have finished getting to know your subject and it's time to bring in the gear, do so carefully. Keep the conversation going and continue to reassure the person that there is really nothing to what's going to happen next, and that they'll do well.

HUMANE LIGHTING

Light the scene as simply as possible. Be professional about it but don't go into complicated lighting setups. As quietly as you can, try to figure out how to plug in the lights so that you don't end up blacking out the entire area with a blown fuse. Don't get into a big discussion of this with the subject either; he or she will be nervous enough already. There will be enough cords and lights and other paraphernalia to worry about anyway, so keep it as simple as you can.

HUMANE SOUND

One of the most valuable tools you can use with your subject is a wireless microphone. It's important for several reasons. Once a wireless mic has been placed on your subject, he or she will be more likely to forget about it than if you have the mic cord running from them to the tape recorder like a heart monitor cable. Further, with a wireless microphone there is nothing tying you to the subject; you can move around much more freely without disturbing him or her. And because people tend to forget they're wearing the mic, they usually say things in a more natural way. When the subject feels more at ease you get a truer representation of what the person is really like.

Absolutely the worst thing you or the reporter can do in a personality story is to hold a microphone in front of the person while doing the interview. Nobody likes to talk into a microphone stuck in his or her face. It looks horrible in the picture, it makes the subject uneasy, and it makes editing difficult.

Lavalier mics are better. The wires are still there but lavalier mics are somewhat less conspicuous to subjects so they forget their voices are being recorded.

THE REPORTER EQUATION

About the reporter's role in all this: In personality stories you and the reporter must remember that the *subject* is the most important person in the story, not the reporter. In these stories the reporter should be heard and not seen. I know that this goes against many station policies, but so be it. Television journalists must understand that people want to see real people, not reporters. Reporters are not real people. The person who is being interviewed is the real person.

Also, the whole story should be more than an interview. You don't *interview* people in personality stories; you have *conversations* with them.

What do I mean by conversations? Let's say you are doing a story about someone who carves lifelike figures of birds out of wood. What many reporters do is to have the cameraperson tape a brief sequence of the person carving the birds. It is the standard long shot—medium shot—closeup sequence that is basic to television news.

That's fine, but then what do they do? They have the person stop carving so they can do an interview. This takes the subject out of context and puts him or her in front of the TV camera to answer questions. What has happened is that the subject has been moved from a natural environment to a foreign one and is now expected to perform for the camera.

That is all wrong. The result may be a sound bite, but seldom will it be memorable. The subject usually makes one of those "I carve birds because it makes me feel good" answers—not exciting stuff, not natural, not personal.

Instead, why not let the subject continue to carve the birds, but don't ask questions, just have a conversation.

You or the reporter might say, "I'm impressed that you have the patience to do this painstaking work."

They might reply, "It's not patience that lets me do this, it's an inner peace I get when I make with my hands one of God's beautiful creatures. If they bring a smile to someone then it doesn't matter how long it takes; a simple smile makes all the work worth it."

Now there's a nice sound bite and you haven't even asked a question. The reporter must introduce topics to discuss and then lead the subject towards his or her natural way of saying things that will make the sound bite memorable. The reporter should let the subject do most of the talking. The editing will organize the story and make it clear to the viewer.

Another benefit of taping someone as they are actually doing their work is that it is photographically easier to edit. If the sequence leading up to the sound bite has been of the subject carving the bird, then the sound bite scene shows the carving continuing; it makes the whole piece flow more smoothly and keeps the tempo and pace moving.

It is important to try to keep the people whose personalities you are trying to capture as comfortable as possible in their own environment. Have them do a variety of normal things if there is no real central visual focus to the story. Talk to them while they are getting into the car, or walking, or going through the refrigerator, or feeding the cat. People talk when they are doing those things in real life. There is no reason for them to be still and posed in front of the camera to be able to speak. It is important to remember what you are trying to do—show that person the way he or she lives, works, thinks, talks.

Personality and feature stories are the most difficult to do well. However, if you, as a photojournalist, will remember to befriend the subject before you start the taping; keep the equipment out of the way and as unobtrusive as possible when it is there; take advantage of the natural surroundings to put the person at ease; and let the subject be the star of the piece, you will find these stories rewarding to you, to the subject, and to the audience.

The job of a photojournalist has never been more important than it is to-day. Over the past thirty-five years we have all learned to deal with an infant that has grown into a giant, global telecommunications industry. Television and the computer have carried us all into a communications revolution. They have given us ways to communicate that we never thought were possible.

But with all the technology comes pressure. We, as photojournalists, must continue to understand that our job is storytelling. More than ever before, our industry is crying out for communicators—people who can tell stories about others visually. We don't need more shooters or more photographers who only understand focus and f-stop.

The greatest compliment we can receive as photojournalists is that we are good storytellers. Give me a person who can *visually tell a story* and I'll show you a photojournalist who can communicate with the world.

Editing

5

I n all forms of journalism there is underlying tension between those who gather the raw material and fashion it into stories and those who take all of the material aimed at an edition of a newspaper, or magazine, or television news program and produce a finished product.

The news gatherers like to boast that the program would be nothing without their persistent digging, organized minds, and glittering writing talents. They see themselves as the front line, the shock troops, the wide receivers, the soloists who make things happen.

Those who shape the news material into the finished product, called editors and producers in television, see themselves as sages who make sense out of nonsense, the bastions of accuracy and judgment, the guides and mentors of the somewhat overbred, high-strung, frivolous reporters.

Every profession has its own mythology. It gives its practitioners a sense of mystery and dedication. It is mostly bunk, but it has a nice ring to it.

Editing is essential. It is perhaps more essential to *clear communication* of thoughts, ideas, and information than the news-gathering function. All journalists must have excellent news judgment; editors simply need the most. All journalists must be able to focus, clarify, condense, synthesize, and analyze huge amounts of raw material. Those skills are central to the editor's job.

In addition, editors are packagers. They bring the story, segment, and program together to make an understandable and coherent whole. To do this well editors must be the guardians of the concepts of structure and linear news. Close attention to these two basic concepts is the key factor in:

1. Eliminating randomness
2. Giving focus to the significant and interesting elements of the news
3. Providing pace, mood, and tone

4. Assuring a logical progression through stories, segments, and entire programs

Finally, editors provide guidance—a second or third mind to give meaning, clarity, direction, and form. No matter what job in television news you aspire to, you must understand the editing process because (1) it affects all those other jobs, and (2) it is essential to clear communication.

THE EDITING PROCESS

The first idea to keep in mind is that the editing process begins at the moment stories are chosen for coverage.

Just the choice itself means that one story has been selected over another because the journalists think it is more interesting, significant, or important. And having chosen, the journalists begin to think of the possible content, shape, and focus of that story, how it can best be told, what illustrative elements will be needed, how it will weigh in importance with the other stories chosen for the newscast.

Second, the editing process never stops, because everyone has to think about it all the time. Reporters, photojournalists, crew members, and technicians working in the field must have news judgment. They are, after all, making the first editorial decisions on what is important and significant about the story they are covering. They gather the raw material, avoid the extraneous, and try to get all of the facts (and pictures and sound) that may be needed to tell the story visually.

Third, the editing process, like the reporting process, begins with an absolutely essential question:

What is this story really about?

A famous documentary producer once said one of the most important things he does at the beginning of the editing process is to give the program a title. That, he said, forces him to think about most of the other priorities such as structure, focus, and direction. The title may be honed and polished, but it is a primary editorial decision. It is very much like asking, What is this story really about?

EDITING VIDEOTAPE

The first step in the process of editing videotape is much more concrete, but it is no less important.

Logging

With the raw material at hand, the first step is to make a careful log of its content. That is, each video cassette is played back and a list of all the scenes is made. It must include every scene—those that may be out of focus, poorly exposed, poorly framed, shaky, or otherwise obviously useless—along with each scene's exact location on the tape (counter number, time code number).

Time spent in careful logging is time saved later, so logs should be as accurate and complete as possible. And while logging, the editor can begin to make some judgments about which scenes will work best and the linear order of the story. If someone else is going to operate the editing machines, the log becomes his or her record of where the material to be used is located on the cassettes. The cut sheet or scene list—the list and order of the scenes to be used—grows out of the log.

In electronic news gathering some logging and preliminary editing decisions don't even have to wait until the raw material is in the newsroom. Reporters and/or field producers can view the material just shot, log it, and dictate editing suggestions on their two-way radios. Or they can view the material as they are riding or flying back to the television station and make notes and decisions as to which scenes will be used and in what order. It is also standard procedure to log all video and sound as it is being received from the microwave back at the station during a live shot. More editing is being done right in the field. ENG and SNG vans equipped with edit packs, and even compact production switchers can handle packaging of stories with all but the most elaborate effects.

Standard Editing Procedures

Editor-controller equipment packages operate somewhat differently depending on the way the manufacturers lay out the various functions. You will have to learn the specifics of the ones you are working with. Furthermore, most stations have their own peculiar ways of doing things. Most have standard procedures designed to cut down on errors and poor-quality results. Most of those have to do with the potential pitfalls of tracking, discussed in Chapters 2 and 4.

Let's suppose that you are sitting at a typical editing console, log and cut sheet in hand, about to use a widely accepted standard procedure. In front of you are two record-playback videotape machines with TV monitors that show you the pictures and sound from each machine. You will have an editing controller, an audiotape record-playback, a mixer, and perhaps a time base corrector and character-special-effects generator. Figure 5-1 shows a typical editing console setup.

All of the editor-controller packages are conformed left to right, or from top to bottom. The source machine is on the left or on top; the record machine is on the right or on the bottom. The editing controller will be either between or to the side of the VTRs. All of the other units you will use should be within arm's reach.

Virtually all edits today are made in insert mode. Therefore:

STEP 1. **Put a fresh cassette in the record machine and lay down a control track on it.**

FIGURE 5-1. A typical ENG editing bay. On the table is the editing controller, which operates the two videotape recorders. Its controls allow the editor to move the tape cassettes in either machine, to locate the edit points, and to select the kind of edit wanted. Above are the video monitors the editor uses to view the tapes for selecting edit points and to check the edits during preview or while they are actually being made. To the right of the controller is an audio mixer used to dub and mix audio onto the air videotape. *(Courtesy of the Winsted Corporation.)*

Do this in the following manner: Feed color bars or black to the machine; some sort of routing switcher or internal system will do this at the touch of a button. Record the color bars or black on the videotape cassette in the record machine. Many stations routinely "track" all cassettes daily. The first time you find someone slipped up and hasn't done that will be the last time you will trust that it *has* been done. A cassette with no track on it will not edit.

Make sure that you have tracked a space on the cassette that is *much longer* than your edited story is going to be since you don't want to run out of track before it ends. One final pre-edit preparation: Rewind the record tape to the beginning, roll it forward fifteen seconds, and edit a countdown leader onto it.

A countdown leader is just what it sounds like. Ten seconds are displayed on the tape, counting down from ten to two. No number one is displayed, so that one second of black will be on the tape just ahead of the first pictures. By dubbing this onto the beginning of your story tape, you provide a simple way to cue the tape for playback and a visual countdown for the director as the tape is rolled into the newscast.

STEP 2. **Put together your A-Roll.**

The **A-Roll,** or basic edited story, may contain several things. If you are editing an interview, the log and shot list will show what portions of the interview you have chosen as well as the in cues and out cues.

In editing an interview or speech excerpts, simply lay down those sound bites, both video and audio, in the order you have chosen after laying down whatever opening scenes you have selected. You can edit the sound bites together without worrying too much about things like jump cuts and other distracting visual material because you are going to cover those with cutaways and inserts from your B-Roll material later (see Figures 5-2 and 5-3).

If you have voice-over narration to be illustrated with B-Roll pictures, lay down the narration sound first (see Figure 5-4). The narration should be recorded in advance by the reporter and will have been delivered to you on an audio cassette or CART along with the video cassettes.

Remember that these machines will edit both video and audio, or video only, or audio only. The appropriate switches on the record machine control these functions.

To lay down narration set the record machine switches so that you are recording *audio only, on channel 1*. (You may want to use the camera mic sound on channel 2 for ambient sound.) You have timed the narration and know exactly how long it is, and exactly how long you want each scene of the B-Roll video that will illustrate the narration.

STEP 3. **Insert the appropriate video.**

In the first A-Roll situation (Case One) below you have your voice-over narration and interview excerpts edited on the sound. You must now go back and insert, *video only*, the B-Roll scenes for the narration and the cutaways and inserts that will cover the jump cuts. What cutaways and inserts? The ones you, or your photojournalist, were so careful to shoot in the field.

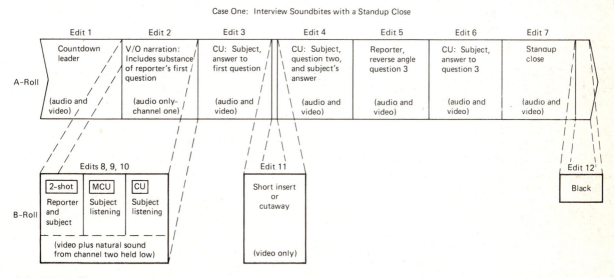

FIGURE 5-2. The steps involved in editing a story containing sound bites from an interview and a standup close. After the first seven edits create the A-Roll, the B-Roll material is laid over the V/O narration, the cutaway is inserted between sound bites one and two to cover a jump cut.

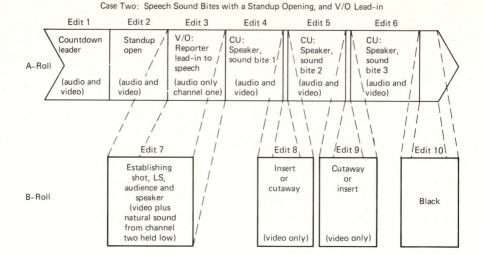

Case Two: Speech Sound Bites with a Standup Opening, and V/O Lead-in

FIGURE 5-3. The editing of a story in which a news maker is delivering a speech. The first six edits create the A-Roll with sound bites. The last four edits insert an LS establishing shot of the speaker and audience over the V/O lead-in. Inserts and cutaways are placed between the sound bites to avoid jump cuts.

Case Two presents a similar situation; you have to lay down the standup open and then three sound bites. Again, inserts or cutaways must be inserted between the sound bites to avoid jump cuts.

In Case Three, containing voice-over narration, you now go back and insert, *video only*, those B-Roll scenes you have chosen to illustrate what the narration is talking about.

If you have a standup open and close, you will, of course, lay down the open right after the countdown leader and the close as the last scene of the story.

You have just edited a video story with video and sound. But you still have one more thing left to do.

STEP 4. **Record black immediately after the end of the story.**

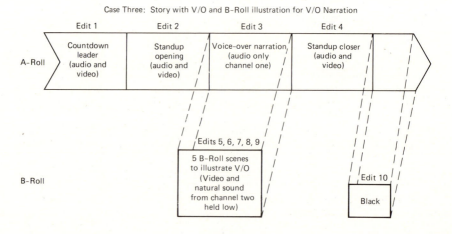

Case Three: Story with V/O and B-Roll illustration for V/O Narration

FIGURE 5-4. The editing of a story with a standup open and close and narrated V/O scenes from the news event. The first four edits lay down the countdown leader, standup open, V/O narration, and standup close. Then five more edits insert the B-Roll scenes over the V/O narration.

To do this, feed black to the record machine. Rewind the tape to about fifteen seconds from the end of the story, play the tape, and punch the record *and* edit buttons at the exact moment the story or standup close ends. This will prevent any extraneous video from getting on the air if the control room director is slow on the next take. A little black on the screen is preferable to random scenes from last week's news that were on the cassette before you edited this story.

The three editing procedures outlined above are very basic. They do include, however, all the moves you must learn to make with the editing equipment.

Some Audio Procedures

Most editing bays contain equipment designed to allow you to edit in sound other than that which is on the raw material (source) cassettes. This may include an audio mixer fed directly to the video machines or a separate audio console with audio cassette and CART (cartridge), reel to reel, and disc turntables. Many stations seem to prefer a setup that connects audio cassette and/or audio cart playback units through a relatively simple four-channel audio mixer.

If more elaborate audio mixes are needed they can be prepared elsewhere and dubbed onto audio cassettes or carts for insertion onto the videotape during the editing process.

Even a simple four-channel mixer with a reel-to-reel or audio-CART record-playback unit is quite flexible. And it can be used to balance between channels when you want to incorporate wild, or ambient, sound under voice-over narration.

Recording Separate Audio   To feed audio from another source—such as the voice-over narration in Case Three—to the video editing ensemble, you must first set the sound levels. Most audio mixers will include a button or switch that will provide a 1,000-cycle tone—a reference tone that can be used to establish levels.

Note that most videotape recorder-playback units have audio limiters on them. Turn them off when you are setting levels, and be sure to turn them back on when you have finished doing so. If you don't do this, it is possible to misadjust the levels in such a way that the videotape machines will raise the background noise to a very high level during periods of low or no audio. This can be very distracting to the listener and can destroy the effect you wanted to create.

Now, with the limiters off:

1. Turn on the tone on the mixer and set the level on the mixer volume unit (VU) meter at zero VU (100 percent modulation). Put the needle right at the beginning of the red. It will stay there, since the tone is constant.
2. Place the record videotape machine in record mode.
3. Adjust the audio level controls on the record videotape machine to show zero VU (100 percent modulation) on the channel one or channel two VU meters, or both.
4. Turn the limiters back on.

What you have done will assure that the same level that comes out of the mixer is being recorded on the videotape. This also lets you do all of your mixing and balancing with the mixer rather than with the VTR controls. This is preferable because you are dealing with only one "mixing pot" (control knob or slider)—you have already established the level by feeding the 1,000-cycle tone from the audio recorder and matching it on the record machine. Adjustments can now be made easily with the mixer pot.

Once you have set the levels on the record videotape machine correctly, you are ready to begin more sophisticated audio work. Most of the situations you will encounter will fall into one of these two categories: using the mixer to balance between two channels of the videotape; or using the mixer to add narration, music, or wild sound to the tape.

Balancing Between Two Channels

In some circumstances it may be necessary to reduce the level of one channel on the videotape relative to the other during editing. For instance, you may have sync sound (SOT) recorded at the scene of the news event with wild sound recorded at the same time on the other channel of the videotape. In this case the wild sound would probably be on channel two (from the camera mic) and the narration on channel one. If the wild sound from the camera mic has to be reduced, you can use the audio mixer to do it.

First, use the mixer tone to set the level on the record videotape machine as outlined above.

The mixer usually can be set up so that it carries sound from the source to the record machines, so you will want to connect one of the pots on the mixer to channel one on the source machine, and another to channel two on the *same* machine. You will play back the sound from source to record during the edit, and control the levels through the mixer.

At this point you must use your good judgment:

✔ 1. Play the tape on the source machine and set the levels to achieve the balance you want.
✔ 2. *Listen* to those levels; get the balance the way you want it to sound. (The meters don't tell you everything.)

Finally, simply recue the source and record tapes and make a normal edit with the controller. The sound will be balanced the way you want it.

Laying Down Narration on Part of a Video Story

Frequently you will find you want to put voice-over narration on a part of a video story. This occurs when you want to use some prerecorded voice-over narration and some sync-sound interview material. Or you may have a standup open and close, prerecorded voice-over narration, and sync-sound interview.

The two most common situations you will encounter are:

1. Putting down narration before the video has been laid down.
2. Putting down narration along with the video.

Again, the first move is to establish the proper levels. In both situations, it is wiser and easier to use the editing controller to make the edits since it is much more precise.

In the first instance, cue the source machine to any arbitrary point on the tape it contains and let the automatic functions of the editing controller make the actual edit while you roll the prerecorded narration at the edit point.

In the second situation, cue the source machine to the exact edit point you want and insert both video and narration at the same time. Here's how to do this. When you have both videotape machines cued, and the prerecorded narration connected to the proper audio channel on the record machine, start the edit. When the machines complete the preroll and rundown and begin the edit, the record machine insert or record light will come on. When that light comes on, start the audio cassette or CART with the narration on it; the narration will be recorded on the videotape. The editor will do the precision work while you roll the cassette or CART when the insert or record light comes on.

Mixing Narration with Wild Sound *Mixing* means blending sound from two different audio sources. There are many times when doing this will help make the "main sound" clearer while you still retain the other sound on the other audio channel of the videotape.

Assume now that the narration is prerecorded on an audio cassette or CART, and that wild sound is on channel two of the tape in the source machine. For instance, the videotape of last night's important basketball game has been edited to present the highlights of the game. On the tape is the sound of the crowd cheering as the home team won the game with a flying fast break. Your sports reporter has

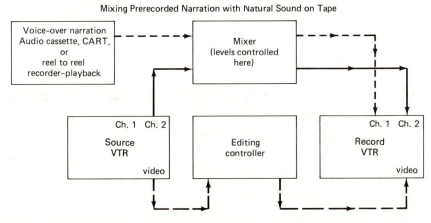

FIGURE 5-5. Mixing two sources of sound during a video edit. In this case prerecorded voice-over narration has been cued up on an audio playback machine and run through the mixer to channel one on the record VTR. The natural sound on tape (NAT-SOT) picked up by the camera mic is on channel two of the video cassette in the source VTR. It is fed through another mixer pot to channel two on the record VTR. Thus the levels of the two channels of sound can be adjusted to hold the NAT-SOT at a low level while the V/O narration is allowed to come through at full level. The video scenes are transferred from the source to record videotape through the editing controller.

written narration describing the action and has recorded it on an audio cassette or CART. You are going to mix the narration with the cheering.

Connect the audio cassette player through the mixer to channel one on the record machine. Connect channel two from the source machine through the mixer to channel two on the record machine. Roll them and set the levels where you want them. Recue the audio cassette or CART machine and both videotape recorders. Make the edit as you normally would. When the red insert or record light comes on, start the audio cassette machine to add the narration to edited pictures of the game along with the cheering.

Backtiming Narrative Inserts

If you have prerecorded narration, wild sound, and sync sound, you can, of course, edit the narration and wild sound as we have just described. Then you would make another edit to add on the sync-sound interview or other story material that is to follow the narration. But that can cause a video or audio jump, or both.

Instead, let's **backtime** the narrative inserts, and insert them in the proper length of time ahead of the place where the interview or other sync sound begins. Since you won't have edit where the two join, you won't have a jump, either.

To do this, use the time counting features found on most modern editing controllers. You will have noticed that as you move the videotapes in the source and record machines the counters, or readouts, have been timing the tapes in minutes, seconds, and frames. If the editing controller contains a memory unit, you can use these readouts to tell the controller where to start and stop the edits. If not, these readouts can also be used as stopwatches to tell you the length of each scene, the length of each sound bite, and the length of the finished story.

Suppose you are trying to hold the interview subject's audio or other sync sound

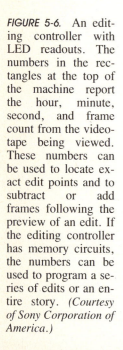

FIGURE 5-6. An editing controller with LED readouts. The numbers in the rectangles at the top of the machine report the hour, minute, second, and frame count from the videotape being viewed. These numbers can be used to locate exact edit points and to subtract or add frames following the preview of an edit. If the editing controller has memory circuits, the numbers can be used to program a series of edits or an entire story. (*Courtesy of Sony Corporation of America.*)

as a low **sound bed** under the prerecorded narration, and then bring it up to full level at the proper time.

✔ 1. Time the narrative insert *exactly*.

✔ 2. Set up for editing through the audio mixer, just as if you were going to mix narration with wild sound.

✔ 3. Roll the audiotaped narration and set the proper level. Recue the taped narration.

✔ 4. Roll the videotape and set the proper level for the videotape sound. *Make a mental note of the position of the audio mixer pot controlling the videotape sound and turn it down so only a very low level of that sound will get through.*

✔ 5. Recue the source videotape, and note the exact tape time.

✔ 6. Back up the source machine one-half to one second more than the length of your narrative insert. For example, if the narrative insert is exactly eighteen seconds long, back up the source videotape until the timer shows you are eighteen and one-half to nineteen seconds *before* the point you want the sync sound to begin.

✔ 7. Enter this point as your source videotape edit point. (The extra one-half to one second is to allow for your reaction time in starting the audiotape machine, and raising the interview audio or sync sound at the end of the narration.)

✔ 8. Cue the record machine to the proper point and perform the edit with the controller as you normally would.

✔ 9. When the red insert or record light comes on, play the narration on the audiotape machine.

✔ 10. At the end of the narration, make two quick level changes. First, raise the level of the source videotape sound to the proper level using the pot on the audio mixer. Then pot down the audiotape level.

If all has gone well, you should have brought up the sound level of the interview or sync sound at exactly the proper time, and you will have a very smooth transition with no jump in either the video or audio continuity.

The "Lip Flap" Problem

The "Lip Flap" Problem   When you use any video that shows a person talking, the audience expects to be able to hear those words. When you use those pictures without the sound, you automatically create a **lip flap** problem. The mouth is moving, but the words are not coming through. This problem usually develops when you try to use a medium or closeup shot of an interview subject, without the sound, as an establishing shot. The subject is talking with the reporter, but the audience can't hear what he or she is saying.

A simple sequence will solve this problem:

✔ 1. MLS two shot, subject and reporter chatting.

✔ 2. CU, subject, listening to reporter.

✔ 3. MS, over the shoulder of the reporter, subject listening.

With these three scenes you establish the reporter-subject interview relationship, establish the subject's face, and set up for the answer to the first question.

Of course, there are different combinations and different shot angles that can provide variety to these kinds of establishing sequences. But if you consistently do it this way and insist that the photojournalists give you these shots, "lip flap" will disappear from television news.

Live Narration   Of course, it is possible to have someone in a recording booth or studio do live narration, but we would like to discourage you from doing this. First, it is difficult to cue a live narration with the precision that is needed to prevent jumping in either too soon or too late. Second, by putting the narration on tape you don't tie up that person or the studio for long periods of time while you try to get a "keeper."

On the other hand, there are occasions where the live narration involves description of a complicated series of scenes on the videotape and needs to be carefully paced to those events. In this case putting the narration on the videotape as the narrator watches the scenes may be the most practical solution.

Editing B-Roll

We have already introduced you to the concept of B-Roll from the point of view of the photojournalist working in the field. We said the whole procedure starts with getting good B-Roll material at the scene. That procedure continues and comes to its logical conclusion in the editing of the raw material. Doing it well at both ends of the production process is one of the most creative elements of television news.

Remember the rules:

🗸 1. B-Roll must be illustrative.
🗸 2. B-Roll must have sequence.
🗸 3. Special effects are no substitute for good, illustrative B-Roll.

In the logging process the editor is looking for B-Roll scenes that will illustrate, explain, and illuminate what the speakers are talking about.

If the story is a feature showing someone doing something unique—such as the diamond cutter—it is the B-Roll material that will tell the story. All of the "talking heads" in the world, no matter how fascinating they are, cannot substitute for good B-Roll that *shows* the audience what is happening.

If it is a simple interview, or even a spot news story, there are still scenes that are needed in editing to illustrate the tenor and circumstances of the interview or the details of what happened at the spot news story.

That brings us to the second rule. A B-Roll segment must have sequence just as an entire story must have sequence. It must have a beginning, middle, and end. It must match words and pictures just as carefully. The scenes in a B-Roll sequence are really a small visual story within the larger visual story. Too many times we see B-Rolls that seem to have been put together in a haphazard, random manner—

in the days of film such B-Rolls were tagged ''sweepings from the cutting room floor.'' Now, they are ''cold, leftover cassette.''

Since you are trying to illustrate what the narration or the subject is talking about, all of the rules of visual continuity come into play. You want to carry the audience into that illustration using long shots, medium shots, and many closeups. You want the B-Roll to flow and move forward.

If you are working on the story of the diamond cutter, you have an interview with the diamond cutter telling how he cuts a diamond into two equal pieces. And you have B-Roll material showing him doing it. Edit the first part of the interview as sync sound (SOT), and go back and put in cutaways and inserts to cover the jump cuts.

Then edit the part where he describes what he is going to do, again just cutting it on the sound. Here you don't have to worry about the jump cuts because you are going to cover all of that with the B-Roll pictures.

Look carefully at the raw material from which you will construct the B-Roll, and select those scenes which are most illustrative of what he is saying. Then arrange those scenes in a sequence.

Sound	Scene
''The first thing to do is to be sure the diamond is tightly fastened to the dop with lead and plaster.''	MS: Diamond cutter's hands holding diamond in the dop. CU: Diamond in dop. ECU: same as above.
''Then, we mark the grain line so that we are sure the cut will follow the crystalline structure of this particular diamond . . . and so divide it into two equal parts. . . .'' (SOT)	Insert ECU: diamond cutter's eyes looking down. Insert CU: hands marking line.
''This takes a lot of study. Every diamond is different, so there is a lot of time spent and a lot of skill involved in figuring out just where the grain lines are, and how they can be used to make the cut. I'm sure I have it right . . . we will see.''	MCU: diamond cutter.
(Reporter narration, V/O: ''Now Darrell Drake, making the actual cut. . . .'') (SOT)	MS: Diamond cutter, intense concentration.

(No sound from him; just the ambient sound since he's not talking.)

MS: Another angle, he picks up mallet, places cutting knife on diamond, replaces it.

CU: Knife on diamond

ECU: Same as above.

(SOT)
''Now. . . .''

CU: Mallet taps knife three times, then comes down hard, making the cut.

(SOT)
''There, another success. . . .''

ECU: Diamond in two pieces.

MS: Diamond cutter, holds up the two pieces. Smiles.

CU: Cutter's hand holding the two pieces.

SOT continues as the diamond cutter says he wasn't worried, etc.

MCU: Cutter

Notice that several B-Roll segments are intercut with the sync sound. The B-Roll has been edited to fit the diamond cutter's narration and has shown the audience the process with closeups, just as if they were there leaning over the cutter's shoulder. When the sync sound is being used the diamond cutter is seen speaking, and when the B-Roll scenes are shown they are matched to what he is saying.

The B-Roll scenes also give visual continuity. You move from a medium shot to very tight shots of his hands at work, the diamond, and the results. Several times you have cut back to scenes with the diamond cutter in them to help reestablish the relationship between the medium shots and the closeups. If you stayed on closeups only, that relationship might become blurred in the viewers' minds.

Notice that this story has two time sequences: the first during the demonstration, the second during the actual cutting. A short reporter narration V/O was inserted to tell the audience that from there on they are going to watch the real event.

When you get to that moment you and the audience are grateful that it is shot close up—that's what we came for. Let the ambient sound carry the load. This is not the time for words.

End the story by using the sync sound of the diamond cutter expressing his relief and satisfaction. If you were to end the story with the shot of the two parts in the diamond cutter's hand it might be adequate, but the audience really wants to hear how he feels and probably needs help in coming down from the tension of the high moment before moving on to the next news event.

Problems   In the edited story above, it is obvious that you have all of the shots needed to take maximum advantage of the B-Roll possibilities. The photojournalist has been careful to shoot all of the scenes from the same side of the line of action, so you don't have screen-direction problems. And there are many good closeups to use to bring the audience close to the focal point of the story.

The sound, particularly the ambient sound, is very useful. The diamond cutter has "talked you through" the process and demonstrated what he is going to do. You can then cut the demonstration scenes to fit his "play-by-play" narration and to prepare the audience for what they are about to see.

If you had not had that sound—if, for example, he is reticent in telling about his exotic profession—the reporter would have had to write and record voice-over narration. But it should be very loose. If the narration filled all of the scenes with words, much of the tension of the climactic moment would be lost.

As was noted in Chapter 2, you will find very few set rules about scene length. The two major ones to keep in mind are:

✔ 1. A scene should be long enough to let the viewers get a good look and absorb what they are looking at.
✔ 2. If you have a scene where you want the audience to absorb a great deal of visual and aural material it must run longer than a scene with minimum complexity.

Yet scene length has dramatic possibilities. As you get closer to the big moment, you may want to shorten the scenes, particularly those inserts that cut between the hands at work and the face of the diamond cutter expressing concentration. Then, when you get to the actual cutting of the diamond, you may want to start that as early as possible so that you have a scene that says to the audience, "Now—hold your breath." And you surely would not want many fast-paced cuts in the video to destroy the tension.

The best guideline to follow in editing a story like this is to ask that key question: "What is this story *really* about?" The answer is not "about a man cutting the world's largest diamond." The real answer is "about a man *actually* cutting the world's largest diamond." Adding that one word gives focus to the story. You are going to show the audience something it has never seen before. The early part of the story explains what is going to happen, and, even though the diamond cutter uses some technical terms, the audience can see generally what he is talking about. Then the audio and video carry the audience up to and through the critical act— *actually*—and through to the end where everyone can breathe a sigh of relief.

Other B-Roll Applications   You won't have such good B-Roll material all the time. The only thing that would have made the story more dramatic is if the diamond cutter had goofed and broken the gem into a million pieces.

Other more common situations usually do not include such good B-Roll possibilities. Yet almost any story is improved with the insertion of B-Roll that is illustrative of what is being said.

Take a more prosaic story, one about people working their way up through a line to get their unemployment checks. This can be shot and edited in a very routine manner. It will look routine when it is aired. Or it can be shot with some attention to the B-Roll possibilities, which can be used in the editing to show and tell the story more effectively.

If all you have to work with is a series of medium shots of people standing in line and of the people behind the counter handing out the checks, the visual material will not show the audience what it's like to have to go to the unemployment office to get the weekly allowance.

A run of medium shots is like looking at someone's snapshots after they get them back from the drugstore. You know that if you have made snapshots of an event that itself had a beginning, middle, and end, you often arrange those snapshots in that order. While you show them to someone else you sometimes provide a "narration" that may sound like: "This is before he was going to jump into the lake; there he is, ready to jump; there's the splash—I didn't shoot fast enough—and there he is all wet after he got out." You constructed a sequence even though all of the snaps were medium shots. Of course, there isn't a lot of detail in the shots, and there are no closeups, so the "story" you've shown and told isn't very interesting.

But the story of the unemployment check line can be made more interesting, and more meaningful if B-Roll scenes can be edited into the story to help focus it.

The photojournalist should do the following:

✔ 1. Concentrate on one or two individuals in the line after shooting some scenes of the mass of people.

✔ 2. Give you closeups of the individuals and the actions they had to take to get their checks.

Among these scene possibilities are:

MS and CUs of the individuals
CUs of their faces
CUs of their hands as they receive the checks
CUs of the face of the clerk handing out the checks
CUs of the clerk's hands
CUs of the hands of the applicant signing for the check
MS and CUs from both sides of the counter but on the same line of action, from the applicant's point of view as he or she gets closer, and from the clerk's point of view as he or she does business with the applicants

With those scenes to work with you can edit the story for voice-over narration so that it shows:

Scene 1. LS: "A large number of people showed up today to get their checks."
Scene 2. MS: "The lines were long but things went efficiently and the applicants were patient," or "It was a mess and the applicants got impatient."

Then, with the B-Roll material showing one person going through the process, it might look like this:

Scene 3. MS: Person third from front of the line
Scene 4. CU: Face of same person, now second from front of the line
Scene 5. CU: Clerk looking at same person
Scene 6. MS: From behind the counter, looking over the shoulder of the clerk
Scene 7. MCU: Person receiving check from clerk
Scene 8. CU: Person's hands signing for check
Scene 9. MS: Person thanks clerk, turns and walks away out of the frame

This sequence could be edited in as the narration is telling the audience the average amount each person received, how many are getting close to the end of their allotment, and so forth. It is much better than a series of medium shots showing people's backs because it personalizes the activity and allows the audience to identify with the individual who is going through it. It also shows that the process is easy; or that the process is long and boring; or that you'd better get there early, or whatever.

In interview situations, the opportunities for B-Roll material are often even fewer. But perhaps the subject has something he or she wants to show the reporter, or wants to conduct a simple demonstration connected with what is being discussed. Even if the story is about something as simple as the new tourist brochure the chamber of commerce is going to publish, you have chances for shots of hands holding that brochure, opening it up, closeups of the cover, the inside pages, the pictures it contains.

It may be difficult to shoot those scenes while the interview is going on, but they can be shot after the interview is completed. The effort should be to show the brochure as well as talk about it. Remember, the audience will quite naturally want to see it.

DEALING WITH SPECIAL SCENE PROBLEMS

Cutaways and Inserts

The editor should always keep in mind the differences between cutaways and inserts and their appropriate use.

Cutaways should be suited to the action. Like those standard shots of the reporter listening to the subject, they are used to cover jump cuts and to establish and reestablish the relationship between the subject and the reporter. A cutaway, like a shot of the collection of miniature elephants on the subject's desk, may or may not be appropriate. If the subject is the state Republican chairman those elephants become a part of the story. If the subject is the head of the local Planned Parenthood chapter and the story is about a new series of lectures about contraception, the elephants are a visual non sequitur.

Inserts should take the viewer closer to the action. They are used to emphasize and illustrate what the subject is talking about. Even when they are used to cover jump cuts they often work better than cutaways because they provide emphasis and focus on the objects or actions the subject is discussing with the reporter.

Zooms, Pans, and Tilts As Editing Problems

Some years ago the faculty of the National Press Photographers Television News Workshop came up with four very unofficial but graphic names for various kinds of zooms.

1. Zoom: a shot moving closer to the subject or object.
2. **Mooz:** the reverse of a zoom, pulling back from the subject or object to include more in the scene.
3. Zoof: a zoom that ends up out of focus.
4. Moof: a mooz that ends up out of focus.

Of course, zoofs and moofs are unusable and tell you something important about the skill of the photojournalist who shot them.

Scenes that include a zoom or a mooz are useful in editing only if they are *motivated*. That is, they must purposefully take the audience closer to an object or subject to provide a closeup look or pull back from a closeup to show the relationship of the object or subject to something else relevant to the story.

For example, a zoom starts from a two shot showing the back of the reporter's head in the foreground, then moves to a MCU of the subject. It might be very useful if the reporter's V/O narration tells about the question asked of the subject. It shows the audience the relationship between the two people and allows the viewer to "lean closer" to hear the answer—it is motivated.

A mooz that starts with a tight closeup of an object and then pulls back to reveal that the object is part of an exhibit in a store window is also motivated. It catches the interest of the audience and then shows the object's relationship to other objects and its location.

Each of these shots and all of their counterparts can be put to good use by an editor. But they take up precious time. Once the zoom or mooz is started, it must be allowed to continue until it is completed; you should not cut on a zoom or mooz. These shots might be appropriate for the beginning and ending scenes of a story. Nevertheless, it is almost always better to cut between the scenes within a story rather than waste the time letting the zoom or mooz carry the viewer from one size shot to another.

Further, except in very special circumstances—such as using the motion of zooms and moozes to create an effect—you should studiously avoid cutting from zoom to zoom, or mooz to mooz, or any other combination: The audience will become disoriented. And you should avoid frequent use of zooms and moozes; they rapidly become visual clichés.

Finally, zooms and moozes are almost never a substitute for the LS-MS-CU sequence of scenes cut to appropriate length. It may seem that the zoom encompasses the long establishing shot, the medium shot that comes next, and ends up in the closeup that should follow. Lazy editors use them because it means they don't have to make three edits to get to the closeup. But the zoom used that way takes a relatively longer time to move the visual story forward. Editing the LS-MS-CU into a sequence may not be quicker in the editing room, but the sequence that results is usually more forceful in getting the story started or beginning a new segment within the story.

Moozes that focus tightly on an interesting object and then pull back to reveal its setting and relationship to other objects or subjects in the scene have dramatic possibilities. Sometimes it is a good idea to use such a shot at the beginning of a sequence as an attention getter. You show the viewers a closeup of something interesting, maybe something they cannot figure out. Then you let the shot pull back to show how that object relates to the story they are looking at.

For example: A tight closeup of a Super Bowl Championship ring on the finger of a hand, then a mooz back and tilt up to a medium shot showing that the person wearing the ring is the new quarterback that the local NFL team has hired today is an interesting way to start the story of the announcement news conference.

Or a shot might begin on the hands of an artisan performing some delicate work on a strange-looking object, then pulls back to show the artisan and the object. It turns out the person makes flower holders out of old auto engine valves. The visual story shows how she does that. The audience doesn't recognize that the object is a valve in the first shot but finds out what it is as the story develops. The main thing to remember is to use these shots in editing where they are appropriate. Use them sparingly. They often are not a good substitute for a series of cuts which will focus on the center of action more quickly.

USING SPECIAL EFFECTS

Many ENG editing complexes, TV station control rooms, and post-production suites contain stunning arrays of machines that can create special video effects. These range from simple machines that generate and insert words on the screen to electronic palettes on which an artist can add features to already existing pictures or create entirely new pictures with an almost infinite range of colors, lines, and brush-stroke widths.

Some image manipulators can shrink an image down to a pinpoint then send it spiraling across the screen, leaving a trail of afterimages as it goes. Others can turn an image around like a revolving bank thermometer sign and reveal a different image on the other ''side.'' Images can tumble, roll, cartwheel, and zoom off to infinity. No doubt there are computer graphics generators on the drawing board whose stunts are limited only by the imaginations of their creators.

You can get quite a bit of heat out of a confrontation between those who say the image manipulators are a danger to television journalism and those who say audiences are becoming more visually sophisticated all the time—and therefore desire graphics and understand them.

One side says it is possible to re-create with graphics scenes of events that could not possibly have been covered with videotape or live equipment. They can be made to look remarkably real, as a visit to any video games parlor will prove. If, the proponents say, the information used to create the graphics is absolutely accurate, then the renderings will be absolutely accurate.

Such talk chills opponents to the marrow. They point out that no graphic representation can be the real thing, and they worry that the false portrayal—no matter how lifelike—can be too easily mistaken for that real event. ''You are showing people something that never happened,'' they say. Further they worry that if the graphic creating is done by people less responsible than journalists, the door is opened to hoaxes of catastrophic consequence.

It is easy for an editor to get caught up with these technological wonders—and the argument that surrounds their use. Clearly when that use creates appropriate and useful visual information they can be important tools. When they are used to cover up the obvious fact that good video, especially good B-Roll and appropriate illustrative material, is missing, they are just crutches. Let's look at some of these special effects and some practical applications.

Character Generators

These machines, referred to as *Chyrons*™ or *fonts*, create a few words, a few lines, or even a screenful of words that can then be inserted in, or edited onto, other video. The word Chyron™ is the commercial name for one brand of character generator, just as font is short for Videofont™, another brand. Others refer to them as *CGs*. We will use *font* since in that form it means ''typeface.''

The most common font is a **lower-third** super, that is, a line or two of words placed in the bottom third of the picture frame to identify the person speaking. Some stations' procedures call for the lower thirds to be put on the videotape at the time it is edited. Most insert them live during the broadcast.

Fonts perform the important function of identifying the speaker by name and title visually. Even though that speaker may be identified in the voice-over narration or by the anchorperson reading the script in the studio, lower thirds should always be used and inserted as quickly as possible after the picture of the subject appears.

FIGURE 5-7. One frame from a videotape showing a lower third super used to identify the subject who is speaking. These words are created by a character generator and are inserted onto the tape or are superimposed during a broadcast through the control room switcher. *(Courtesy of Will Counts.)*

FIGURE 5-8. Character generators, graphics generators, and frame storers can be used to add a wide variety of information to the video frame. Here characters have been developed as special effects to add to a bumper about the regatta. The action within the video frame could be frozen, or the racing boat could speed on out to the frame as the videotape rolls on through. *(Courtesy of Laird Telemedia, Inc.)*

You probably don't have to use a lower third to identify the president, Yasir Arafat, or a handful of other readily recognizable people in the world, but you should use them on all unknowns, and always if there is the slightest possibility the audience won't recognize the subject.

If the audio portion of the story contains the voice of someone who has not been identified visually, a font that reads "Voice of _____" should be inserted while that voice is being heard to help further with identification.

It is common practice to use a lower third only the first time a subject appears in the story. However, if that person appears again much later in a long story, and if reidentification is important to the clarity of the story, do it again.

A major problem with lower-third fonts, especially ones that are two or three lines long, is that they cover the mouth of the speaker in a closeup. CBS News solved the problem several years ago by moving the lower-third font to the lower left-hand edge of the screen. The alternative is to look for a shot of the subject that is loose enough for the lower-third font to appear below the subject's chin and then cut to a tighter shot as soon as possible.

Depending on how sophisticated (and expensive) they are, character generators can do many other things to add visual interest and clarity. Most provide either upper- and lower-case or all upper-case letters. Some provide different typefaces, some have drop-shadow letters that have three-dimensional characteristics. Some provide for a border around the edge of the letters to make them stand out more clearly. Many allow for the letters to be colored, or the color can be added through a switcher, or the letters or words can be made to blink on and off. All of these functions can be called up with the touch of a button or two.

Besides providing the lower-third supers, character generators can be used to position words and symbols almost anywhere on the screen, to make lists and scroll them up or down, or to make words move horizontally across the screen. Character generators that have memory capacity can store and retrieve regularly used lower thirds or symbols like the station's logo. They are also widely used to present and update sports scores, election results, and other tabular information.

An editor has to think carefully about the possibilities for using the character generator to provide additional information on the screen, about the design and layout of the material, and about the appropriateness of it. This is because the words and other symbols added to the television picture call attention to themselves. They can, and sometimes should, distract the viewers' attention.

You have probably seen the weather warning march across the bottom of the TV screen just at the high moment of drama in the movie you were watching. Certainly the weather warning is important and in this situation the distraction is part of a valuable service. But watch out if you are going to include a lower third, the station's logo, and "Skycam 2" over some very interesting video shot from the helicopter. You are likely to have so many layers of video on the air that the audience is forced to look through this visual picket fence and is so distracted it loses everything.

The editor must also try to keep the words to a minimum. The TV screen is small. People read at different speeds. A whole screenful of words must remain there long enough for the audience to read it all the way through *twice*. If the message is an important one—perhaps the numbers to look for on cans of food being withdrawn from sale for health reasons—you would probably want to have the narrator read the words as they appear on the screen. That way you would be more certain that the message got through.

If the words are a list of three or four important points from a new government report, the narration and the words on the screen should be keyed together. Merely putting words on the screen, hoping the audience will read them, usually is not very effective communication.

Frame Storers and Frame Manipulators

The new technology of digital-computer–generated video is very much with us and is growing all the time. Computers can be used to generate words and pictures, store them, and bring them up onto a TV screen in almost any form. They are limited only by the amount of memory capacity that they have and by the imaginations of the people who program them.

Frame storers can take one frame of video, hold it in a memory, and return it to the screen on command. These frames can contain almost any visual material—one frame of picture from a videotape, a chart, a table, a piece of graphic art, or anything else.

Before 1974, networks and stations reporting election returns had to construct massive scoreboards in their studios. Today most of the precise and speedy vote totals and the graphic frames they appear in come from computers.

Graphic frames are created by artists and then stored in a computer. The vote totals also are fed to the computer. With the touch of a few buttons the totals are electronically inserted into the frame and brought up on the video screen. With other computer programs sampling the vote and providing projections, the hopeful candidates get the good or bad news just as they are lowering themselves into their favorite chairs for the election night ritual.

Frame storers and frame manipulators have many uses in television news editing. The frame storer is like a huge filing cabinet for visuals and graphics of all kinds. Hundreds of video frames can be kept in the memory for instant retrieval. Thousands more can be stored on videotape for retrieval within a few minutes. New frames can be created using camera shots of still pictures or drawings, fonts, computer-generated effects, a frame from a videotape, and other switcher-generated effects.

An editor confronted with a story—for instance, about the local or state economic conditions—often needs to combine the video, interviews, and voice-over narration provided by the reporter with graphic material created during the editing process. The videotape shot in the field can provide topical scenes. Then words, phrases, lists, numbers, percentages, or dollar amounts can be added using the font and special effects.

The special effects usually come from a switcher, where a variety of sources of still or moving video can be mixed by keying, splitting the screen into segments, wiping, scrolling, dissolving, or superimposing one video image over another. With the touch of a button, the screen can be cut up into halves, quadrants, or almost any type of segmentation, and different video can be inserted into those segments.

Suppose you want to show the cover of the latest city government report on one side of the screen and a list of the four major points made in the report on the other. The report is set up in front of a studio or graphics camera, and the camera is positioned so that the report fills the left side of the screen. Then the list of four major points is entered into the font and positioned on the right side of the screen. The font is also programmed to scroll those four points upward on command. Color can be added behind the scrolled material. Voice-over narration that will "read along" with the font list has already been laid down on the videotape that will contain this segment of the story. Then the switcher effects are set to split the screen into two halves, so that the camera shot of the report fills the left half and the font material the right half. All video signals are fed to the videotape recorder, and the TV screen will show the report and its major points while the narration gives emphasis to them by repeating them. The font can just as easily be programmed to add the points on the screen one at a time as the narration proceeds.

Switchers can also be set up to provide circles and rectangles that are brighter than other portions of the screen. And the more sophisticated ones will make the edges of those circles, ovals, or rectangles hard or soft. Thus, you can "vignette" the edges as a photographic portrait studio would, or highlight a line, sentence, or sentence fragment from a page in a document. Again, the narration might repeat those words as the audience views them.

Then you have the ultimate special effects, things called Squeeze Zoom™, CBG-2, Chyron 4, ADO, ADDA, and Quantel™. These and other electronic effects systems provide the ability to zoom into any part of a video frame and to insert that portion of that frame into any portion of any other video frame.

Sports event producers have made startling use of the Squeeze Zoom™. The pictures of an event's action can be moved to a small portion of the screen with results, averages, and other tabular material added while the action continues. Or interviews with a star player can be inserted while the player continues to perform. Almost any combination of split-screen and frame-insert effects and continuing live action pictures can be created.

But such uses don't have to be limited to live sports coverage. An editor can use this equipment to create all sorts of graphic and video combinations to be edited into videotaped stories.

Artwork

Every station has an art department. The graphics specialists who work there spend most of their time creating material for commercials. More and more news departments are using the art department or creating their own graphics sections to provide the charts, graphs, maps, and other illustrative material needed to help explain a story more clearly. A good graphic artist can be a great aid to an editor looking for ways to illustrate complex stories. Simple line or bar graphs can be created and then shot with a studio or ENG camera or graphics cameras and frame storers for insertion into the story. Where stations have computer graphic capabilities, those graphs can be animated and put onto videotape for editing with voice-over narration or other B-Roll applications.

One of the most exciting innovations in computer graphics has been the explosive development of machines to display the weather. Even an amateur can create animated computer graphics sequences from symbols and maps already stored in the memory. These can then be mixed with weather satellite pictures and other materials to show how the weather has been, is now, and will be. So far, these machines have been used mostly by meteorologists, but there is no reason other applications cannot be made to help illustrate other stories in a newscast.

The Editor's Choice

We started this section with you sitting in front of an editing console ready to do some simple editing. It has ended up with you in a big control room filled with machines that can do all sorts of wonderful things.

Everyone in television news these days is, or should be, visually conscious. After all, we work in a visual medium. The important thing to remember is to use the capabilities of the equipment to provide more information and to do so with clarity. Editors must avoid sensory overload for the viewer. Too many things that blink, wipe, dissolve, scroll, and read all at the same time can lead to confusion. The viewer may be dazzled but may also mumble: "What was *that* all about?" You should keep it simple and make sure that what you are creating adds focus and clarity to what you are trying to communicate.

Reporting

6

Reporters are the shock troops, the nerve ganglia, the heart of the news-gathering system in any journalistic enterprise. Reporters go out and gather the facts and process them into news stories. They usually do the initial writing and editing of those stories. Without reporters, there would be no news.

In television reporters also go on the air. They are seen doing their work in the field and in the studio. The audience knows and respects them. Most reporters are proud of their profession and wouldn't want to be doing anything else.

''Reporter'' is a romantic title, and we create specific connotations when we put an adjective in front of it, such as investigative reporter (all reporters investigate), economics reporter, field reporter, general assignments reporter, and so on. A reporter might covet only one title more: correspondent. That title is even more romantic, especially at the national network level, where the aura of the term gives it a connotation that is very heady for the person who has the title.

In this chapter we are going to look at how television news reporters use ENG technology to report news stories. We'll look at some examples of basic story types such as spot news, feature news reports, and live coverage from the field. We'll consider techniques of ENG field reporting, various problems that crop up to challenge the field-reporting team, and what field reporters come up with to solve those problems.

But first let's check the basics of news reporting that beginning journalists (and unseasoned students just starting out) must know about.

RESEARCH: LOCATING INFORMATION AND SOURCES

Reporters have several ways of gathering facts and information, the raw materials of their news accounts. They search and research through such records and documents as police blotters, courtroom transcripts, courthouse files, and so forth. And they look at other written or recorded information, everything from meeting minutes to PR handouts from the annual report to the printed program.

Most newsrooms maintain library files of news tape and scripts of all local coverage. Reporters who have beat assignments routinely keep their own files concerning major elements of that beat and the personalities on it. These files may include newspaper and magazine article clips by subject and other background information about a topic. Surely they will contain the reporter's notebooks and lists of public, private, and unlisted phone numbers—including the numbers of those public phones and booths at "watering holes" and other locations their best contacts frequent. When the name Lee Harvey Oswald surfaced after President Kennedy was assassinated, a reporter scored a worldwide scoop by digging into her files to get out her notes from an interview she had had with Oswald in Moscow many years before. A Chicago radio reporter got early details on the death of a mayor by quickly locating the number of a pay phone in a bar where he knew a key contact made a regular stop for a pick-me-up no matter what was happening.

Reference works and computer data banks are another standard source of facts

FIGURE 6-1. Whether they use typewriters or video display terminals to do it, reporters gather the facts and try to make the facts, and the pictures that go with them, work together to tell a complete story. (*Courtesy WBNS-TV, Columbus, Ohio.*)

and background information. But you must know how to use these sources in order to take good advantage of them and avoid wasting precious time hunting through them, trying to figure out what kinds of information they contain, and how it is organized and indexed. Time is usually critical, and you need to find what you are looking for quickly.

FIRST-HAND REPORTING

Journalists also witness things. They watch critically, and listen carefully at events as observers and eyewitnesses. They learn to keep their eyes and ears open. They teach themselves to be attentive, and they become very skillful at these techniques of fact gathering. Most reporters master the art of taking notes, and they devise their own system of abbreviations and other ''shorthand'' notations and symbols to keep track of what they witness.

Covering Beats

Television news organizations have different staff structures regarding the reporting jobs the staff will handle. Some have a beat system, others call some of their reporters ''specialists'' and designate general areas such as education, statehouse, politics, science, and so on.

The beat system is a traditional journalistic structure that was set up to assure that someone on the staff was covering important news-producing spots such as City Hall or the sheriff's office. The idea of specialists implies the reporter has special knowledge or training about a field, such as economics, the professions (like medicine) or institutions (like the legislature).

If you are going to cover a beat or if you are going to cover a specialty area, a number of common and unique things can help.

1. Know the territory. If most of your coverage is going to be done within the confines of a building or headquarters, you must become as knowledgeable of the layout and functions in that building as the oldest denizen of the place.

It is too easy to fall into bad habits about this. The regular trip from the parking lot through the same door to the same space every day leaves you unprepared to find your way when something unusual happens. Take time to explore and learn the history of the place. Especially learn where there are telephones, electric outlets, useful stairways, windows where your crew might run a cable or a microwave dish, and where the best place to park a truck is. When you have to go live, you won't have time to find the building superintendent.

2. Know the people. Get to know the little people as well as the big ones. One truism says that an army is really run by its sergeants. The same idea is true about most other institutions.

It may be useful and ego boosting to hobnob with the mayor or have the governor or senator call you by your first name, but if you always have to explain who you are to those in outside offices, reception desks, gates, and security checks, you're going to be slowed down when it counts. Besides, if you make friends with them, these people can be extremely valuable sources of inside information—not the quotable kind but the fill-in-the-blanks kind—and they don't give out those kinds of goodies to strangers.

✔ 3. Know the rules of the game. All public institutions, professions, businesses, and private social and cultural institutions operate under a set of regulations. These may be statutory laws, common laws, ordinances, legal contracts, articles of incorporation, mandatory or informal codes of ethics and practice, or even teachings and customs that have, over time, become rules of conduct for those who subscribe.

A reporter following a specialty needs to know what the rules are. You can't cover the courts well without understanding what the law says about how the criminal justice system should work or how lawyers can operate and what the rights of the accused are. You can't cover the school board or the city council well without knowing about what the laws let those institutions do. You can't cover science and scientists without understanding how and why they are dedicated to the scientific method. Once you know them, you have to be able to explain all these "regulations" to your viewers in language they can understand.

✔ 4. Know the subject matter. You never stop being a student or having to do your homework.

You must continue to study—with special attention now to the world of the people and institutions you are covering. You need to know the nomenclature, the culture, the issues, the major debates, and the history and background of that world. That means reading everything you can get your hands on, discussing this world with the people who live in it, and being forever curious about it. And again you have to figure out just how to explain it in ways the viewers can comprehend.

INTERVIEWING

Of all the things a reporter does to gather information about a story, the most basic is interviewing. The interview is the one main way a reporter gets facts on which to build a story. Interviewing is the backbone of the reporting process, and interview results are the backbone of a news story.

Reporters talk with people who are concerned with or know something about a news event. In other words, they interview people. Some reporters build their professional reputation on and become very well known for their skill at the craft and art of interviewing. And interviewing is just that, both craft and art, part "science and technique," and part "interpretation and feel." Perhaps you have your own favorite reporter, a person whose interviewing skill and intuition you both admire and envy, someone who can do an interview that makes you say, "They make it look so easy. How do they do that?"

Interview Planning

Here is the main idea for doing a good interview, the main advice all the experts give: preparation. A good interview does not just happen; it requires careful and detailed planning and preparation. Good interviewers do both. "Gee, wouldn't it be great to be as good as Mike Wallace," you muse. It is well known among reporters that Mike Wallace prepares his interviews, and that he prepares them meticulously.

So you will want to get into the habit of the professional approach and plan and prepare your interviews. But before you start writing out your interview plans, do a little analysis. For purposes of analysis, interviews can be classified according to their objective. What kind of information, basically, are you after in this interview? Is the main purpose of it to produce facts, such as the cost of the project, the amount of the contract, the results of the vote, or the terms of the agreement? Or is the basic purpose to get opinions, for example, the reason for the loss, the seriousness of the situation, the meaning of the decision, or what the political candidate sees as the main issue of the campaign? Still another possible purpose is to reveal to the audience aspects and dimensions of the personality and life style of the interviewee, whether he or she is a beauty contestant, sports hero, Oscar nominee, or lottery winner. Asked another way, is the fundamental purpose of the interview to inform, to persuade, or to impress?

Of course, no interview satisfies just one objective exclusively. Facts and opinions get intermixed, and the manner in which someone answers a question can override the words themselves: Sometimes *how* a person answers tells more than *what* he or she answers. But frequently one objective is the main goal of the interview. And it will help you to obtain that objective, focus your preparation more sharply, and think more clearly about planning the interview if you first think through your basic purpose.

Interview Research

There's that word again, *research*. Having spent time thinking about what you want this interview to accomplish, you should then start your research by learning as much as you can about the person to be interviewed and about the topic of the interview. We've already talked about the many sources of facts and information you can turn to—scripts and tapes of your own past newscasts, newspaper and magazine article clips, news releases and PR handouts, printed programs, transcripts of speeches, and other sources for background and older information. Reference works such as *Who's Who*, bibliographies, and biographies can help a lot. The city directory (as distinct from the telephone book) lists a wealth of information about residents of a community. On the campus the faculty-administration-student-staff directory is usually packed with all sorts of background and current information about the university community. (A word of caution: The publishers of compiled facts and other information do not guarantee the complete accuracy of the material, so keep alert and make a habit of cross-checking your information.)

Given this purposeful research of background information, you are then ready to work up questions. Think up questions. Lots of questions. As many questions as you possibly can. Sometimes other staffers may join in the thinking process. That's called "brainstorming." In brainstorming you all think of as many questions as you can, and someone writes them all down. You make big lists of questions. Try to keep the viewer in mind because the viewer is the ultimate target for the answers.

Don't worry about the exact wording of the questions. That comes later. Avoid making judgments about them. That comes later, too. In one such session, a particular reporter had a habit of criticizing the questions being suggested by other reporters with comments such as, "Nobody cares about that" or "That's a dumb question." Finally another staffer in exasperation blurted out, "Look, friend, either think up or shut up!"

Interview Organizing

With a full set of questions you are ready for the next step in the process, organizing. One part of organizing is to group the questions into categories so that they're not jumping around all over the place and going back and forth in random fashion. You should try to avoid having to say in an interview, "While we were on the subject of *X* I should have asked you. . . ." or words to that effect. Occasionally you will have a good reason for going back to something touched on earlier in an interview, but generally it is preferable that the interview move forward, not backward.

Another part of organizing is to rank the questions according to their importance. Frequently you'll be able to sequence a progression of questions that leads step by step to the more important ones. You'll have your main questions, of course, and you'll want to have some secondary questions as well. And then, just to be safe, have some back-up questions.

During this time of sifting, sorting, and organizing your questions, you should weed out those which have little or nothing to do with your topic, those which are mundane, those whose answers are already well known or could be easily learned just by doing a little research. Having done your research, you'll recognize questions that fit the "don't use" category. Also, don't be too intent on fitting every last question into some category. Some questions will not fit no matter what scheme of categorizing you use—they just seem unrelated to any others in the pile.

As you organize the questions also start working on their wording. Try to hear how the questions sound, and try to hear them as your guest is likely to hear them. Don't be so ready to accept the first phrasing that comes to mind. Rather, be super critical of the rough-draft wording. Is this question clear? Can it be interpreted in more than one way? Does it have words with fuzzy meanings in it? Nothing will slow down an interview more quickly than the guest saying, "I don't understand what you mean," or "What do you mean by. . . ?"

Does your wording make the question open-ended or close-ended? An open-ended question is just what the label implies. It lets the respondent take the answer in any direction he or she wishes. "How do you feel about. . . ." and "What do you think of. . . ." are examples of open-ended wording. Some experts believe an open-ended question is a good way to get an interview started because it helps to create a more relaxed atmosphere, allows the guest to hear the sound of his or her own voice, allows a release of built-up nervous tension and anxiety, and generally makes for a smooth and easy start to the conversation.

A close-ended question focuses the answer by reducing the guest's options for an answer. ''Will you vote for or against the motion?'' is a close-ended question because it narrows the range of possible answers. Of course, the person answering might reply, ''I haven't decided yet,'' or ''I plan to abstain,'' so just how ''closed'' a close-ended question is depends on exactly how it is worded.

During this evaluation of the wording of questions, you will want to look carefully too at whether your question might be a ''yes-no'' question. Q.—Do you play the piano? A.—Yes, I do. Q.—Do you enjoy that? A.—Yes, of course. Q.—Do you play any other instrument? A.—No.

If you take the time to say aloud each of your proposed questions, try to hear it as your interviewee is likely to hear it, and try to anticipate what the answer might be, you'll avoid some of the most common pitfalls of interviewing. Mostly it's a matter of deciding what you want to know and then making the wording clear, precise, and specific. Keep asking yourself, ''What, exactly, do I want to know?'' and ''Will this question ask for that information?''

Should you write out the final versions of your questions? Some beginners find that this helps overcome their anxiety; it gives them a sense of confidence to know that if their mind goes blank, they can fall back on a written list. However most seasoned reporters seem to agree you should not read questions to your guest. It is better to practice asking the questions aloud during your preparations, and then let the exact wording of the questions occur normally and spontaneously during the interview, not memorized, not written out, but not spur-of-the-moment, either. In other words, the questions are planned and rehearsed but then delivered impromptu.

In the time just before the interview, should you tell your guest the exact questions you are going to ask? Journalists are pretty uniformly agreed you should not. The risk is that the answers may sound canned, rehearsed, and lacking in animation and spontaneity, or hesitant and tentative. When the guest is told exact questions before the interview what often happens is that he or she gives an answer in practice and then, when the light goes on, gropes to re-create that exact answer. On the other hand, it is standard procedure to tell the guest what areas you will cover so that the questions don't come pouring down out of the blue, catching the guest by surprise, breaking concentration, and making him or her less able to deal with the question effectively.

Below is a summary and review of traditional dos and don'ts of conventional interviewing. Following that you will find excerpts from the transcripts of two broadcast interviews. Here's what to do: Read over the list of dos and don'ts, and then examine the excerpts to see how many dos and don'ts you recognize.

✔ 1. Don't put answers in the subject's mouth.

Q: How do you feel about the drug problem?
A: Well, I feel that it's, uh, uh. . .
Q: A serious problem?
A: Yes, a serious problem.

Q: And what do you think should be done about it?
A: Well, I feel the police, and the parents, should uh, um. . . .
Q: Be held responsible?
A: Yes, the police and parents should. . . .

✔ 2. Aim the questions at specific points, not broad areas.

Q: Do you like animals?
A: Yes, I guess so.
Q: What kind?
A: Oh, bigger ones, I guess.
Q: I see. *All* big animals?
A: Well, no, not all, mostly big jungle animals.
Q: Do I have this right, you like all big jungle animals?
A: I didn't mean that, I meant those that are nice, you know, that don't kill other animals.
Q: Then you like big jungle animals that don't kill others for food, is that it?
A: Yes.
Q: Well, why didn't you say that in the first place?

✔ 3. Remain impartial. Keep your opinions to yourself.

Q: How do you feel about this total lack of respect among our teens for anyone over thirty? Do you think this animosity came about because of the arrogance of the older generation?
A: Well, I really doubt all teenagers harbor the animosity that you mentioned. Many of them are fine youngsters, the same kind of children we were when we were their age. And I hardly think arrogance describes the older generation.
Q: Yes, but don't you think teens should be held responsible for all this damage to dorms, and the drinking after football games and general lack of respect for. . . .

✔ 4. Don't mimic each answer.

Q: Which of the four seasons do you like best?
A: I like them all, but I prefer the winter months.
Q: I see, you like them all but prefer winter. Do you like winter sports, is that it?
A: Skiing, yes, but not the others.
Q: Okay, just skiing, no others. Good. And do you have any hobbies?
A: Oh, yes, I play the piano, and I collect pine cones.
Q: I see, play piano and collect pine cones. Good. What do you, uh, do with the pine cones, by the way?
A: I eat them in winter.
Q: Yes, of course, you eat them in winter. . . .

✔ 5. Don't assume and presume. Just ask straightforward questions.

Q: I suppose the torn ligament means you're through with football.
A: Through? Through with football? Heavens, no. The doctor says I'll be back good as new in four, five weeks.
Q: I assume you feel the same way I do about the drug problem, and so the question is, really, what we should be doing about it.
A: First of all, I don't even know how you feel about the drug problem, as you call it. I don't even know for sure what the problem is to begin with; maybe you can explain to me what you mean and then we can discuss it. . .

✔ 6. Don't interject meaningless comments into answers, comments such as ''I see,'' ''Uh-huh,'' and the like.

Q: What do you think about this school situation?
A: Well, clearly, it's quite serious,
Q: Uh-huh.
A: And quality instruction has been allowed to slip because of. . . .
Q: Um.
A: Because of too many frills and distractions, and. . .
Q: I see.
A: And not enough of the basics like reading, and writing and. . .
Q: Right!
A: And arithmetic, especially arithmetic.

✔ 7. Don't waste time with questions that have obvious answers.

Q: Your official title is dean of journalism, is that right?
A: Right.
Q: And you've been dean since 1979, right?
A: Correct.
Q: Meaning, this being 1989, you have been dean for about ten years.
A: Yes, that would be ten years, correct.

✔ 8. Get your facts straight.

Q: You've been playing the trumpet for how long?
A: I have never played the trumpet. My instrument is the French horn.

✔ 9. Don't ask multiple-part questions. Take it one step at a time.

Q: When will you move to Bloomington, when will you actually begin your new job, will your family be with you, and by the way, what does your family think of your taking this new job?
A: My wife is all for it, and the kids think it's great. What was your other question?

✔ **10.** Don't monopolize the interview. If the question takes longer than the answer, something is wrong.

> **Q:** In 1962 your were a member of the Federation of Actors and ran for the presidency of that group. You were defeated by Ronald Credge, who went on to become the nation's first astronaut. Since that time you have been at odds with the space administration and have even threatened to expose them for what you charge as their waste and corruption, isn't that true?
>
> **A:** Yes, basically that's all true.

✔ **11.** Do not answer questions.

> **Q:** Why is the bail set so high?
>
> **A:** Because this man is accused of murder. If you were in my shoes, wouldn't you set it high too?
>
> **Q:** I see your point. If he asks for a hearing, will you grant it?
>
> **A:** It would be a mistake to grant such a hearing, don't you agree?
>
> **Q:** You pose an interesting question. Why would it be a mistake?

✔ **12.** Look at the subject and listen to the answers.

In order for the other person to speak naturally, that person needs to have someone to talk to, needs to have someone listening. We will have more to say about listening later in this chapter. The point here is to avoid the bad habit of first asking a question and then tuning the person out while you review your notes as you mentally prepare your next question, glance around into space or watch something in the background. Watch the other person and listen to the answer. Often the answer will include a key comment that ought to be followed up or cleared up. Also the answer may contain an "opening" that he or she puts there on purpose so that you will have an easier transition into the next question. Or perhaps the interviewee isn't being candid in the first answer. He or she may feel uncertain as to how you, the questioner, are going to react to the answer, whether you can be trusted not to embarrass him or her with an unkind or thoughtless reaction to the views he or she is expressing. The first instinct is to answer cautiously while gauging the atmosphere of the situation. Or the guest may seem tense, answers terse and mechanical; the whole interview may seem to be going nowhere. You must be able to read these clues, verbal and nonverbal, and to react to them to get the interview back on track. If you sense a hesitation in an answer, you might respond, "In addition to that, are there other. . . ." Your leading of the interviewee with the expression "In addition to that" may help resolve the situation. Another question that has proved effective in many interviews is the simple "Give me an example of that" response. Viewers and listeners (and readers) love examples. If you do not understand the answer, don't just ignore it and allow the conversation to proceed. Stop to clear things up. A straightforward approach is probably best, something like, "Let me get this straight, did you say. . . ." or "I didn't understand that last point, would you mind going over it again?" Be careful about starting a response to a guest's answer with the expression "In other words, what you are saying is. . . ." Had they wanted their answer in other words, they would have put it in other words.

A DISASTER. . . AND A SUCCESS

With these dos and don'ts in mind, let's now look at excerpts from the transcripts of two actual broadcast interviews, looking for examples of dos and don'ts from the real world of interviewing.

Announcer. "Program Previews," usually heard at this time, will not be heard this evening because of the following special interview.

Interviewer: Well, thank you very much, and we have the distinct pleasure and the honor of chatting with Mr. Victor Borge. Would you, uh, just say a few words sir so, uh, they'll believe that you're actually here? We've been waiting for you for some thirty-five, forty minutes.

◄ *An awkward beginning at best. The statement fails to frame and direct the interview; worse, it gives the guest nothing on which to base a reply. Worst of all, the statement appears self-centered (the audience isn't interested in what the interviewer has been doing).*

Borge: Really!

◄ *What else could he say? (One would hope he'd let this pass and forget it.)*

I: And you've been on the way from N———.

◄ *The interview still is headed in no direction, and the guest still has not been given a question to respond to.*

B: That's why you have been waiting.

I: (laughing) That's why I've been waiting. And, uh, this type of conversation is the type of conversation I suspect that, uh, you'll be, uh, presenting in your performance tomorrow night.

◄ *Why "suspect" anything? Why not just ask the first question in a straightforward manner?*

B: Not necessarily. I have no one to talk to.

◄ *Shot down from the very beginning!*

I: Oh! That's right. You do do a, uh, uh, one-man show.

◄ *How obvious can you get?*

B: I do do, yes.

I: And I understand that this is, uh, at the present time. . . .

B: (interjects) Do do.

I: Ha ha, this is the, I, I, this is not going to be easy for me, sir, I suspect I'm up against. . .

◄ *By now it has become clear that the interviewer had nothing prepared to open this interview. Of course, that is one good reason why the interview may be "difficult." The fact that Borge is a "real professional" (what other kind is there?) has nothing to do with the present difficulty. Perhaps Borge, being the professional that he is, has now decided to ask the reporter a question in an attempt to settle him down.*

B: You're doing very well so far.

I: I'm up against a real professional.

B: Nooo, I wouldn't say that. Um, I would like to know the program that's been cancelled out, what was that?

I: Uh, just records and, uh, the programs coming up.

B: Oh.

I: We would much rather, uh, chat with you than listen to records and hear what's coming up. And incidentally, in some sense, sir, this is a, uh, preview, because we're previewing, uh, your performance tomorrow night. And we might get the plug in now, I suspect. Tickets are available at the student union, and your performance is at the field house.

◀ *Borge still hasn't been asked what he's doing in town.*

B: Oh, is that so? I thought it was inside.

I: It's, uh, it's inside, the field house is inside, sir.

B: Inside what?

I: Uh, you've got me on that one. I suspect it's, um, uh, er, inside the city, how's that? Okay? I, I want to know more about your performance though, uh. . . .

◀ *Since Borge is still waiting for a specific question, how can he tell more about his show?*

B: Well, I've told you everything I know.

I: You haven't prepared it? No, I'm sure you have.

◀ *At last! A straight question, and Borge gives the interviewer an opening to follow up on.*

B: Yes, to an extent, I would say.

I: Uh, you do some of the routines you, uh, uh, have done, um, in, uh,

◀ *He blew it, and turned the interview to a new and unrelated direction.*

one-man show you did in New York City.

B: Yes, uh-huh.

I: I, uh, was fortunate enough to, uh, catch that program in New York City, and, uh. . .

B: You enjoy it?

I: I enjoyed it very much.

B: Good.

I: And I also enjoyed the, uh, bow you had the, uh, paid, uh, employees, uh, take. Why don't you tell us about that?

B: Well, there's nothing much to say about it. They come in and take a bow. I do a one-man show, and I get a little tired of bowing all evening, so I. . . .

I: Well, the point, uh, is that, um, there are a number of, uh, musicians and a number of, uh, stagehands that have, uh, to be at your performance, is that correct?

B: That was in New York. We had eleven stagehands and five musicians.

I: And, uh, you asked them to come out and take a bow to, uh, make a point, I suspect. You don't have these problems, uh, in the Midwest, do you, the union problems with the, uh, uh, stagehands and the, uh, musicians?

B: I don't have a problem with them, uh, but I don't think we have any problem whatsoever with stagehands or any unions for that matter. They just tell you what. . . .

I: What you can do, and, ha ha, you do it and you have no problems.

B: And that's no problem, that's right.

I: You have been, uh, a comedian for how long?

◄ *Meaning okay, what's your question?*

◄ *Once again, the audience isn't interested in the interviewer.*

◄ *The question is too general, which is why he gets the answer he does.*

◄ *The point, the point! When are we going to get to it?*

◄ *The interviewer's point appears to have something to do with union "problems" Borge has experienced, but the statement is poorly phrased, and the guest rejects the inference that in the past he has not been able to "get along" with stagehands and other unionized theater workers.*

◄ *Surely the interviewer could have researched this, but given that he didn't, he should have listened to the answer and then followed it up. Also, the in-*

terviewer does not make clear why he believes that Borge's answer amounts to a suggestion that his music is "humorous."

B: Oooh, let me see now, that's very difficult to determine actually. Ever since I was four years old, I guess.

I: You have been a, uh, performer on the piano for how long?

B: Same amount.

I: Uh, you're suggesting now that your music is humorous? I do know that you, uh, that you, uh, play humorous music, but you play it very well, and you also play, uh, serious music.

B: Yes.

◀ *The interviewer has not taken charge and deserves this answer.*

I: Do you have some albums, uh, that you have recorded, uh, of serious music?

B: No.

◀ *And this.*

I: You do have some albums that are, uh, uh, comedy.

B. Yesss.

◀ *And this.*

I: (chuckles)

B: I, I don't speak very much, do I?

I: No, you don't speak very much, and uh, I'd rather this was, uh, an interview with you rather than, uh, uh, my talking so much, and I'm trying to, uh. . .

◀ *This is a key point in the interview. The host wishes the guest would respond even though he has not prepared the interview, does not have a progression of questions to ask, and apparently does not know how to proceed. The guest is losing hope.*

B: Well, would you ask me, ah, let me see now, what question can you ask me? (pause) You go ahead.

I: Yes, well, uh, I'd like to, uh, to, uh, find out if, uh, if you, uh, find college audiences, uh, different than, uh, general audiences. Is it, uh, more fun performing with a college crowd?

◀ *A glimmer here; although the question is hesitant and presented somewhat tentatively, it is the first interesting question to be asked.*

B: Definitely. . . .

I: (interrupts) Now I. . . .

◀ *And Borge is willing to get into a discussion of it even in spite of the interruption.*

B: (continues) Because they are more hep, they are faster, they are um, they understand everything almost the moment it is done or said.

I: The, uh, uh, young people then react with a lot more spirit, a lot more vigor?

B: Not necessarily young people, but um, educated people. . . .

I: The, uh, performance then. . . .

B: (continues) They probably hear better than older people.

I: Yes, I'm sure they do.

B: And faster.

I: And faster.

B: Yeah.

I: The, uh, performance that you will give for the, uh, university people then, is it very much the same as the performance you give for, uh, a general audience, or do you change your material somewhat?

B: It's a better performance because, uh, they understand it better. But it's the same performance.

I: You've been, uh, travelling for, uh. . . .

B: I have to, we've come from Omaha.

I: Yes, I mean in general with your, with your show, you've been on tour for some time.

B: Yes, for years.

I: And, uh, this current tour has, uh, been for how long?

B: This is a very short one, about eight days.

I: You are, uh, you arrived in N———, as I understand, just a short time ago, and came directly to N———, and, uh, I'm interested in knowing where you came from.

This answer gives the interviewer several interesting avenues of questioning to pursue. All he has to is listen carefully and then respond with a follow-up question.

But that is not exactly what Borge said. The interviewer failed to listen carefully.

Clearly Borge is listening to the interviewer very carefully, and just as clearly, the interviewer

(interrupting again!) is not listening at all to Borge.

The interview has settled down here and shows promise of getting at some information that is both interesting to the audience and at the same time relevant to the upcoming Borge performance.

This is an abrupt shift to an earlier topic, already covered.

The point was made earlier.

Ask a general question. . . .

and get a general answer.

Strike two! Borge answered that twice already.

B: Omaha.

I: And, uh, you performed there?

◄ *Strike three!*

◄ *One wonders what the interviewer had in mind—Borge is surely not making chopped liver.*

B: Yes

I: How many nights did you stay in Omaha?

B: One.

I: One-night show, huh?

◄ *There's either an echo or a parrot in here.*

B: Yes.

I: Packed house?

B: Oh, yes.

I: I'm looking over at your agent and he's nodding yes, too. And from here where do you go?

B: Now that's a good question. Now to go over to my agent again and ask him.

◄ *This question is okay and this line of questioning might lead to some good information, but look more closely at it. The questions are actually more appropriate for the agent than the performer. Borge does the normal thing by directing these questions to his agent. Also the questioning leads nowhere, distracts from details of the local performance, and stops the interview in its tracks.*

I: All right, uh, George, where does, uh, Mr. Borge go from here?

Agent: (off mic) Madison, Wisconsin, and then Milwaukee.

I: Madison, Wisconsin, and then Milwaukee. And then?

B: Home.

Agent: (off mic) No.

B: Oh, I beg your pardon.

Agent: Louisville, Kentucky.

B: Oh, Louisville, Kentucky.

Agent: And Owensboro, Kentucky.

B: Oh, come on now, that's the end, and then home.

I: And then home. So there's, uh, approximately, uh, four to six more per-

◄ *What was the point of this line of questioning?*

formances and, uh, then back to New York.

B: Right.

I: Uh, will you be, uh, taking it easy when you return, uh, or will you be going on another tour very much like this one?

◄ *Okay, the question is legitimate, and the audience may now begin to learn something about the guest (even though we still have not learned anything about his upcoming local performance).*

B: I never take it easy. There is no time to take it easy.

◄ *This answer gives the interviewer a perfect opening for follow-up questions.*

I: Can you tell me how you, uh, go about getting your material? I personally find it very humorous. I'm interested and, uh, how much of it is, is, uh, prepared and how much . . . .

◄ *And again he blows it. He misses the opening and the questioning turns abruptly away from that promising area to something very different. This very likely is unsettling and confusing to the guest.*

B: (interrupts) Well, my whole speech today was prepared.

◄ *There is a tone of exasperation in this exchange, but if the interviewer grasped this overtone, nothing came of it in the follow-up question.*

I: The speech that we've done . . . .

B: Yes, and no, and no, and yes.

I: But I'm referring to the, uh, actual performance. How do you, how do you acquire your material?

◄ *This is a legitimate question.*

B: Well, it all depends on the audience, more or less, usually more.

◄ *And another perfect opening for some follow-up questions to learn what the answer means.*

I: You, uh, go, uh, along and, and make these items up as the performance, uh, uh, you react with the, uh, the group?

◄ *Groping, hesitant, but at least it keeps the interview moving forward in what appears to be an area of interest.*

B: Now and then, yes. I have, of course, a basic routine, and that's why I have to go from town to town, because I can't use it more than once.

◄ *The guest is responding now, and here is the opening, a basic routine, an area to be explored with further questions.*

I: Well, many of these, uh, items that you'll be doing tomorrow night, uh, are on, uh, record already, aren't they? Some of the things that you've done are almost classics.

◄ *Once again, a missed opportunity to explore the upcoming local performance by asking more questions about "the basic routine" (it's as though the interviewer didn't hear that) and a shift to something that was touched on very early in the interview. Also once*

B: No, it's quite a different program now.

again, an assumption, rather than a question.

◄ *And again the assumption proves to be wrong. This answer, that the program is "quite different," would make an excellent transition into a line of questions about the local performance.*

I: It is?

B: Yes.

I: Will you be doing the, uh, routine, uh, that I suspect you call the punctuation routine?

B: Yes.

◄ *But this following set of questions, while interesting, is not moving the interview into any productive or promising area.*

I: Uh, would you be willing to just give us a moment or two of that so we can hear what it sounds like? It's one of my favorites.

B: Um, why, I don't think so, because it requires explanation and a lot of, a lot of, um, preparation.

I: But in any case, uh, we won't be too disappointed because we can, uh, hear that tomorrow night when you appear in the field house.

◄ *This material shows promise of moving the questioning toward information about the local performance, which is (or ought to be) a main focus of the interview.*

B: Definitely.

I: How much, um, uh, serious music will you be presenting? We have, uh, a rather fine music department here, and . . . .

◄ *Fine, now we finally may be getting to the main point, the local performance.*

B: I know that.

I: And I'm sure some of the people would be interested in, uh, hearing you play seriously.

B: Oh, I play now and then, now and then a couple of selections.

◄ *Here is the opening for some follow-up questioning.*

I: Uh . . .

B: Chopin, Liszt.

I: And I know that, uh, you have been known to, uh, play Chopin and call it Liszt, and play Liszt and call it Chopin, uh, I don't think you'll have too much success fooling people here with this, but, uh, but . . . .

◄ *The thrust of this comment is okay, but wordy. Remember, the idea is get the guest to do the talking, and clearly the reference to "fooling people" is awkward at best.*

B: Well, I, I never try to fool them, but I can't remember the name sometimes.

I: Ha ha, as I recall, you also have a routine where you, uh, try to remember, uh, is it your family's names?

B: The children's names, yes. We have five children, that's a lot of children. But they don't come when I call them anyway, so . . . .

I: You have, uh, five, uh, children. Where do you live permanently? Are you from New York?

◄ *The question (really two) is not clear, hence the answer given.*

B: No, I'm from Denmark.

I: No, I mean now. Where are you living?

◄ *The interviewer fails to ask a more direct question, causing further misunderstanding, which is enough confusion to open the door to another burst of ad-lib banter. In other words, the guest has no serious and focused questions to answer and so goes off on a tangent.*

B: In, uh, Connecticut, oh, right now I'm living right here. In the N——— hotel.

I: The N——— hotel.

B: I almost missed the four o'clock elevator, going down, the one that goes down, you know.

I: There's one that goes up, too.

B: Yeah, well the four o'clock goes down. I almost missed it.

I: I'm glad you made it because, uh, you were able to arrive here at our station to chat with us this way.

B: But you said I was late.

◄ *Take special note of this—the guest heard the unfortunate reference to being late and has not forgotten it.*

I: Well, you were late, but it wasn't your fault, and we'll have to excuse you on that basis. Uh, I know that, uh, that you, uh, will be, uh, getting to the field house on time, I hope, tomorrow night.

B: Definitely.

The interview at this point meanders through several harmless references to the time and place of the performance, punctuated with more quick-witted replies by Borge as the interviewer gives the details of the location and time.

I: (continuing) Well, once again, we'd like to remind our listeners that, uh, Victor Borge will be appearing here on the campus tomorrow night, uh . . . .

B: I don't think I have given any of the listeners a clear picture of what I am going to do, actually.

◄ *Another key point—the interview has now come nearly to the end, and a main point of the guest appearance, the forthcoming performance, simply hasn't been explored.*

I: You know, uh, I have to say this, that, uh, when you came here, uh, and you walked in the door, we didn't have much of a chance to chat. And, uh, I'm very glad that we've been chatting this way. But, uh, you know, for an interviewer . . . .

◄ *The fact that the host and his guest did not have a chance to chat informally may explain in part why the interview was so haphazard, but the lack of chance to meet and talk before the interview was not the main problem. The lack of interviewer preparation and the host's implied assumption that this interview would therefore "take care of itself" combined to create this disaster.*

B: It really gives you good exercise.

I: You bet. Because for an interviewer, the most difficult, uh, job is to, is to, uh, uh, respond to a, a one-word answer, and I, uh, know you were pulling my leg, uh, because . . . .

◄ *One can sympathize with the interviewer, but again he is wrong. One-word answers are frequently the result of poorly worded questions. And the most difficult job for an interviewer is to try get a good interview without solid preparation.*

B: I never touched you.

I: Uh, it's been, uh, it's been a great pleasure and uh, uh, I want to thank you very much for coming over, and I want to complete what I was saying, and that is that, uh, tomorrow night at eight o'clock you'll be appearing in the field house. And the time again, eight P.M. Tickets are available still; you can, uh, pick them up tomorrow beginning at eight o'clock. The ticket office is closed right now.

And here, for comparison, is an excerpt from a television interview by Harry Reasoner:

Reasoner: Dr. N——— is recognized as one of the world's authorities on languages. He's a professor at N——— University and the author of a lot of books. Just looking at languages as an expert, which, uh, which is the best, would you say?

◄ The question is short, concise, direct, and clear.

Guest: English is very practical, very flexible, extremely usable, concise. It is by no means the most, uh, euphonious language in the world. It has some pretty tough sounds to the ears. I remember when I first came to this country, some of the people on the boat said that English sounded like cats meowing.

R: Which would you pick for beauty?

◄ And so is this one.

G: Well, I'm prejudiced, but I suppose my native tongue would be my preference.

R: Italian?

◄ Reasoner was listening to the answer, didn't fully understand it, and instead of just going on to the next question, clarified it.

G: Yes. Well, it's the most musical language. Certainly it is the best language for singing.

R: Speaking again from the standpoint of practicality and flexibility, what's the worst major language you can think of?

◄ Notice the logical arrangement and progression of the questions.

G: Well, the one that I have some slight familiarity with that impressed me as being the most difficult, the one that I've had the toughest time really learning, is Vietnamese.

R: Vietnamese?

G: Uh-huh.

R: Because of the tonal quality?

◄ Follow-up.

G: Yes, the tones, and the glottal stops.

R What are the shortcomings of English? Are there things that you worry about in it?

G: The, uh, worst shortcoming of English is the tremendous spread between the pronunciation and the spelling. Or to put it another way, the fact that the spelling is awfully, awfully archaic.

R: What are the particular strengths of English? Now you mentioned flexibility, are there others?

G: Ah, the flexibility, conciseness, the fact that you can say what you are out to say in probably the smallest number of words and with the greatest directness. A business letter in English, for example, will occupy a certain space. Now, you try translating that same business letter, with all the nuances, into French, or Spanish, or Italian, and you'll get almost twice as long a letter.

R: How many words altogether are there in the English language?

G: I would say that a fair guess right now would be about a million words, of which no man knows more than about a hundred thousand.

R: Is that so?

G: You know one word out of ten in your language.

R: What about the influence of television and radio on usage and on phonetics?

G: The influence of, uh, television and radio on language and phonetics is tremendous, overwhelming. It is the biggest force that has ever operated in the world. Ah, it reaches everybody, and every person is a potential willing and unwitting imitator of what he hears. In other words, your television, especially the television but also the spoken movies and the radio, are in the process of obliterating local dialects in all language.

◄ Reasoner has been listening to the guest's answers. . .

◄ and here's the proof.

◄ Notice how short and concise the questions are and how they focus attention on the guest and his answers.

LET'S HEAR FROM THE INTERVIEWEE

Interviews with various kinds of experts who are visitors to the community are fairly common story assignments for television reporters. The guest usually is prominent at least in his or her own field, and sometimes, of course, will be famous and well known to the general public. The point is that such assignments happen so often that unless the reporter does something about it, they all start sounding and looking pretty much alike—dull and shallow. At best they have predictable questions and standardized answers, and at worst they can be total disasters, as the Victor Borge interview shows.

Two Chicago professors and free-lance writers, Connie Fletcher and Jon Ziomek, did a study of just this issue.*

Connie teaches at the Loyola University department of communication, and Jon at the Medill School of Journalism at Northwestern University. They interviewed prominent people who had been guests on various TV interviews to see what they had to say about their experiences with reporters. The celebrities' strongest complaints included:

1. Reporters who show up unprepared and say so
2. Reporters who show up with one or two preconceived notions and ignore everything else
3. Reporters who talk more about themselves than about the celebrity
4. Reporters who act bored or distracted by other things so they don't listen carefully

Fletcher and Ziomek say that research is the key to getting good results from an interview and that what the researching reporter should look for is the question that is brand new or seldom asked. They advise: "Research your subject like a prosecutor who wants to win every time. Look for clues as to what the celebrity wants to say but hasn't, or what the celebrity stopped saying ten years ago, or what the celebrity shies away from, or what has been buried under piles of standard questions and angles for years."

They also offer a number of tips on how to get the most out of the interview once the cue light goes on:

1. Reinforce everything they say. "That really helps me, this is really interesting."
2. Let them talk about what they're doing in town. That's their reward for doing this for the twenty-fourth time.
3. Give them a compelling reason to keep talking—the provocative, unusual, and sensitive questions may bring them to actually enjoy the interview. Most celebrities have larger-than-average egos.
4. Get them out of the "usual quotes" rut by responding more positively to the unusual or to the sidelights and unexplored territory.
5. Use *reflective listening techniques*, that is, play back a summary of what they have said: "That made you angry?" "Why did he say it wasn't your best?" "What was it about that situation that made it work so well?"
6. Let them ramble, but don't be afraid to redirect the interview to where you want it to go: "This is really interesting, and I want to get back to it, but right now I'd like to ask you about. . . ."

*"How to Catch a Star," *The Quill,* December 1986, pp. 32–36.

7. Never denigrate or put down the subject by giving or showing your personal reaction to what they have said.

8. Try to get what you wanted and need from the interview, but don't be so stiff you refused to follow into new and interesting areas if the celebrity heads in that direction.

Interviewing is the main way broadcast journalists do a couple of important things—gather information from people and obtain the recorded material needed for sound bites. We have given you some prescriptions for how to prepare yourself, some techniques to try, and some standard approaches.

Alternate Approaches

Even though these lists of dos and don'ts (and there are many other such lists) cover the basics of interviewing, you can do interviews in other ways as well.

In his essay Larry Hatteberg describes the way he goes about interviews when he is profiling people. Tom Pettit has said that reporters should not be afraid to ask "the dumb question." By that he means that sometimes it is wiser for the reporter to just take on the role of the average viewer and ask the questions the viewer might ask, even if the questions go against the image of the well-prepared, well-back-grounded, experienced reporter we all would like to portray. Bob Dotson uses what he calls the "Columbo technique" (see page 213).

In the introduction to *The John McPhee Reader,** the editor of the book, William L. Howarth, tells us how the famous author goes about the interviewing he does for his extremely successful nonfiction books and articles. Howarth says that when McPhee does an interview, he tries to keep his mind as blank as possible: "He has found that imagining he knows a subject is a disadvantage [because] that will limit his freedom to ask, to learn, to be surprised by unfolding evidence." He says McPhee believes an interviewer doesn't need to pretend ignorance because most stories are full of surprises, and the reporter should resist the temptation to "bluff with a show of knowledge."

Howarth admits that this sometimes makes McPhee seem dull witted. He repeats answers and even garbles up what the subject has said so that the subject has to provide a new answer. That gets the subject to elaborate and perhaps amplify and simplify until McPhee has virtually everything the subject knows about the topic. For McPhee, the ideal interview is one in which he listens without interrupting.

The things he learns in one interview lead to other interviews and also tell him what things he needs to research. (He does not use a recorder because he thinks they inhibit people.) When McPhee hears the same stories the third time, he stops interviewing and begins the writing job.

That job includes first transcribing his notes. He says that process is like the way a magnet attracts iron filings—as they take shape, he gets ideas about how the story will be structured. Then McPhee reads the notes over and over, producing more notes and more impressions of how the story will develop.

*William L. Howarth, ed., *The John McPhee Reader* (New York: Vintage Books, 1978), pp. 7–33.

A lot of things in this description of how McPhee works are not possible for a broadcast reporter. Clearly we have to have sound and **actualities.** We usually don't have as much time as he has. And none of us is a world-famous author. But think of the parallels to what Bob Dotson and Larry Hatteberg say in this book.

Follow It Up   Carl Hartman, a veteran AP correspondent who covers international economics from Washington, says that reporters need to guard against being just transmission belts for the obtuse and sometimes misleading language used by bureaucrats and public relations people. He says, for example, that ''no comment'' and denials should be handled with more precision, either with follow-up questions or copy that focuses sharply on just exactly what was said.

When you get a ''no comment,'' Hartman says, it may be that your question was improper and what your source is really saying with the no comment is, ''You're asking me a question that you know it would be wrong of me to answer.'' He suggests that your reply to ''no comment'' in such a situation could be a polite: ''I didn't ask for comment; I asked for facts.'' And Hartman says, reporters should be precise about just what was asked that produced the no comment answer.

Evasions also need follow-ups.

Statement:	''The subject wasn't discussed at the meeting.''
Follow-up:	''What was discussed?''
Statement:	''To my knowledge, that didn't come up.''
Follow-up:	''How complete is your knowledge?''
Statement:	''I won't discuss anything so silly.''
Follow-up:	''What is silly about it?''
Statement:	''We never discuss personnel matters.''
Follow-up:	Hartman says that it is perfectly legitimate for the reporter to point out other times when personnel matters were discussed.

Denials are somewhat more complicated because they have the reputation of the person or the institution behind them. Hartman says that reporters should look carefully at exactly what is being denied. He points out that former national security advisor Robert McFarlane ''categorically denied'' in November of 1986 that he had been in Iran ''last month.'' McFarlane had visited Iran, but in May, not October.

It is important that the reporter be professional about such jousting. Hartman says reporters should:

1. Report statements by officials as precisely as possible (a good reason to play the tape and save the sound bite for later use).

2. Avoid implying your own conclusions. (The facts may prove you wrong next week.)

3. Not be afraid to point out what a statement does or does not include or where other facts point elsewhere. (Part of your job is to give the audience the facts so it can make its own decision about who is telling the truth.)

THE SPECIAL ROLE OF LISTENING

Researchers estimate that we humans spend about 80 percent of our waking hours communicating—reading, writing, speaking, and listening. That's eight minutes out of every ten we're awake, forty-eight minutes out of every hour.

Another fact, according to the experts, is that just a little more than half this communicating time, 55 percent, is spent in a combination of reading, writing, and speaking. In other words, we spend 45 percent of our communicating time in listening. A big problem is that, without realizing it, we often listen quite badly.

For example, most of us know from our own experience that when we're listening to a joke, story, or the details of some adventure, we're not really listening at all; no, we're impatiently waiting to respond with a similar story of our own in a sort of "Can you top this?" contest. The act of listening does not come naturally, and it does not come easily. We can, however, analyze this activity and our own listening habits and then teach ourselves to become much better at it. The very first step in that process is to become aware of the importance of listening, to become conscious of how well or how badly we do it, and what difference that makes.

A student intern who was doing television interviews with county extension folks on homemaking topics reported in one of her progress reports that she felt the best interviews from her point of view were those that went smoothly. She meant those in which the guests were very articulate and talkative, people who would respond readily, people who would answer a question almost before the question was asked, indeed, people who would talk even without questions being asked. The student's point was that all she had to do to conduct the interview was to get the person started and then sit back and relax and take it easy.

That's a widely shared view about what makes a good interview, and it's a wrong view, a misconception about the nature of face-to-face communication. Good communicating requires effort from both the speaker and the listener. Good listening is crucial to the process. Good listening is not passive; you just don't sit back and let the speaker speak on. Good listening is a much more active process than that. The listener shares half the responsibility for a good exchange of ideas.

The listener must listen to the words being spoken, of course, but it is much more involved than that. Another thing the experts tell us, for example, is that in the typical face-to-face communication situation, the words being spoken (the verbal part of the message) carry a startlingly small part of the meaning of the message, considerably less than half of it.

What we listeners get as the meaning of another's message comes from such other things as the speaker's rate and pattern of pauses and silences, intonations (the up-and-down pattern of voice inflection), facial expression, posture, hand and finger movements, gestures, and other nonverbal cues. Even how the speaker is dressed influences the meaning we get out of a message. Not only that, we're told that a message is subtly affected by room lighting, wall coloring, furnishings, ambient sound, and a variety of other environmental factors.

To be a good listener, you must first of all focus your complete attention on the speaker and keep it there. Second, you must studiously avoid sending the speaker nonverbal signs of impatience, boredom, and inattention. Signs of inattention include checking your notes, staring off into space, looking around at what is going on in the background, tapping the fingers or the foot, glancing at your watch, sitting on the very edge of your chair, straightening your trousers or tie, brushing back your hair, adjusting your skirt, and so forth. These nervous mannerisms are guaranteed to make your guest ill at ease and convert a creative tension of heightened awareness that should exist between yourself and your guest into a destructive tension of distraction and dismay. Your inattention will ruin the atmosphere of the interview.

To be an active listener you should watch the speaker and pay attention to the words being spoken and to the guest's nonverbal cues. Your job is first to integrate and then to interpret all this information so as to be able to understand what the speaker means rather than just what the speaker says. Often when the process doesn't seem to be working well, you can help straighten out the situation and clarify the meaning with a statement or question such as, "It sounds like you're saying that. . . ." or "As I understand it, your point is that. . . ." or "Am I correct in hearing you say. . . ?"

Lastly, as with any other skill, you can practice good listening, and you can get better at it with practice. Here is a game you can play with a friend to get yourself started. First, you have to agree on the rules of the game, and the only rule of the game is this: Let your friend start a conversation by making a statement to which you must respond. However, before you are permitted to respond to the statement, you must tell the other person what he or she said. When your friend agrees that you got the message right, and only then may you respond. Then, before your friend is allowed to reply to your response, he or she must tell you what you said, and you must agree he or she got it right. A little exercise of this kind will go a long way toward raising your awareness of the hazards of communication and the importance of careful, active, critical listening to the process.

To review:

✔ 1. Two-way communication is an active process for both the speaker and the listener.

✔ 2. The nonverbal part of a speaker's message is as important as the words being spoken.

✔ 3. Look at and listen to the speaker. Your actions are as much a part of the message as the speaker's words and actions.

✔ 4. Practice your listening skills regularly.

FIELD REPORTING: GENERAL STORY ELEMENTS

Having reviewed the basic tools of reporting—(1) research, (2) first-hand information gathering, and (3) interviewing of various kinds—we now turn to the matter of putting those skills to work on ENG assignments in the field.

There is a good deal of argument about which part of a television news field report is the most important. Some experts discuss whether it is the opening or the closing. Others say the crucial part of a story is the middle, its development and progression, its "story line." But these are differences of degree, not of kind. Everyone agrees that the open and the close are both vital to the ultimate success of the package. So it simply makes good sense to give special attention to all elements in the story.

The Opening Segment

The lead will be either "soft" or "hard." A soft lead is somewhat nonspecific and rather generalized. It flows naturally from the story **lead-in,** read live by the anchor in the studio, to introduce the report. In contrast, a hard lead is much more direct and specific, a sentence or so zeroing in on the most newsworthy element of the story, and thus, a lead that stands by itself. Let's look at the hard-lead technique first.

```
              HARD NEWS FEATURE WITH HARD LEAD

         Video                         Audio

ANCHOR ON CAM      Next in the news, a dream come true for
                   Yourtown Mayor George Arfield. Our man
                   Stanley was there, and filed this report.
VTR STANLEY        SOT (hard lead)
                   Mayor George Arfield officiated at ground-
                   breaking ceremonies this morning for the
                   city's proposed new domed stadium. Under
                   sunny skies. . . .
```

With a hard lead, the basic newsworthy facts are laid out in a direct, declarative sentence. The lead sentence captures the essential point of the story. The lead-in to the story read by the anchor acts as an introduction to the report, but these two elements are different in tone and thrust. The lead-in doesn't get to the essential news point of the story, but the story lead does just that.

When the story is written with a soft lead, the connection between the anchor lead-in and the story lead becomes much more direct. The story lead-in introduces the report, and the story lead picks right up on the tone and theme of the lead-in without even interrupting the story flow. The soft approach makes for a smoother transition from the studio anchor to the VTR field segment. The field reporter picks up right where the anchor left off.

```
              HARD NEWS FEATURE WITH SOFT LEAD

         Video                         Audio

ANCHOR ON CAM      Next in the news, a dream come true for
                   Yourtown Mayor George Arfield. Our man
                   Stanley was there, and filed this report:
VTR STANLEY        SOT (soft lead)
```

```
It had been the mayor's pet project for
years. . . going back even to his days on
the city council. This morning under sunny
skies he was beaming as he. . . .
```

Notice how with a soft story lead the reporter doesn't get right to the news point, but rather starts the story with a look back at how (or when or where or even why) this occasion began. Many television newspeople prefer the soft-lead approach because of its smooth transition from anchor desk to field report. Of course, you will want to vary the approach because a newscast with a large number of either kind of lead becomes predictable and begins to sound too repetitive. Story content should be a main factor in your decision as to which kind of lead to use. On a breaking story with some stunning development (the mayor unexpectedly and dramatically announces his resignation, effective immediately), you certainly would not want to keep the audience in suspense with something indirect like, ''The mayor summoned reporters to his office this morning with what we all thought was going to be some sort of routine announcement, so you can imagine our surprise when he. . . .'' In this situation the story fairly cries out for your lead to get to the point immediately.

With either technique, though, you must keep in mind the fact that the audience needs to be stimulated to watch. It is as though the audience is asking, ''Why should I even be interested in this?'' Your opening should provide an answer to that question even before the audience gets a chance to think about it. The opening should be a grabber.

It is true that you cannot communicate effectively with an audience until you have its attention. But remember that it is not just a matter of getting attention. You should get the audience focused on your report in a way that is relevant to and consistent with your material. The opening must be related to the content of the story; the purpose of the opening is not just to get attention, but to help the viewers understand the meaning of the story. You want an opening with a point. When a speaker begins a speech by telling a joke, and it turns out that the joke was just for laughs and had nothing at all to do with the speaker's message, the audience will feel cheated. A good joke with a point that illustrates a speaker's message is much better for two reasons. One, it avoids the audience's having that let-down feeling, and two, it helps the speaker get the message across by focusing audience attention on that message, by reinforcing the message.

Actuality: Interviewing in the Field

If you are planning to include actuality in your report—a sound bite of a news maker giving a reaction or the statement of an eyewitness, for example—think through what you want to learn from the news maker and frame the wording of the questions carefully. The goal here is to get short, concise answers that are clear, informative, and to the point. But you also have to keep in mind what it is that you do not want if it can be avoided, and that is either a yes-no answer or a nonstop answer. It is easy to blame the subject when you get either a yes-no response or a long-winded talker. But the truth is that much of the reason for the clipped or windy response may go back to the question that was asked or to nonverbal cues you send out during the reply.

For example, some reporters "jump" on answers, that is, they fire their next question even as the last syllables of the previous reply are being spoken. This not only makes the editing of the tape more difficult, but it also may be sending a message of impatience to the person answering the question, a nonverbal "Hurry up, now!"

Controlling for Time

If you get a long-winded answer, you might narrow the question or sharpen the focus and ask it again. But remember the earlier advice about avoiding the expression "In other words, what you are saying is. . . ." This is almost always a mindless expression, a crutch, and the problem with it is that you are putting words in the subject's mouth. The subject may quickly agree with what you said just to get the interview over with, but it may not be what he or she really wanted to say.

You can also control for time by keeping your questions short. The goal of the interview is to let the other person do the talking and in his or her own words. Throughout your childhood, people probably told you, "Don't interrupt." But you may have to if the speaker is rambling on and on. You can interrupt strongly or gently. If you crash in and override the subject, not only are you being impolite, but you also risk frightening your subject and destroying his or her train of thought. However, you can interrupt more gently. Listen closely, then say something like, "Pardon me, that's very interesting, let's go back over it," or "Just a second—can you explain this point for me?" However you phrase the break, try to put the blame for it on yourself without sounding foolish. Members of the audience want to get the subject's ideas, and they will appreciate your efforts to steer the guest and help him or her understand. People who are used to being interviewed for TV know they should keep their answers short, and experienced interviewers have expressions to take advantage of this fact. Charlayne Hunter-Gault of the "MacNeil/Lehrer NewsHour" has mastered the live interview technique of getting the guest to wrap it up as time is running out with expressions such as, "To sum that up now in the thirty seconds we have left. . . ." or "Can you answer in just a few words, we have just fifteen seconds. . . ." and so on. When the interview is live (as on the NewsHour), you find ways to control for time, or else.

For recorded interviews remember that most of your actuality is going to be edited before it gets on the air. You should leave a pause between the end of an answer and the beginning of the next question or at the points of interruptions so there is room for the edits to be made cleanly. The point made previously in this section is that it is not a good idea to jump right on top of a subject's answer with a new question. It is much easier to remove "dead air" during an edit than it is to try to find a tiny space in that split second between the last word of an answer and the first word of your next question. Editing your actuality tape will go a lot more smoothly if you have reverse-angle questions, a technique discussed in detail in Chapter 4. To review the main points from that section:

✔ 1. The re-recorded questions must be the same questions you asked the first time.

✔ 2. You must re-record the questions in the presence of the subject. This is an external check on the accuracy of your phrasing of the question: You don't want to be accused of recording the subject's answer to a question and then putting a different question in front of that answer in the editing process.

✔ 3. You must re-record all the questions you asked in the interview, since the interview will be edited. The one you didn't re-record may turn out to be just the one needed.

Get to the Point

While you and your crew are gathering the raw materials of a story in the field, at some point in the process you have to come to a decision, you have to answer a key question. It doesn't matter whether you are a beginning student intern at the campus station or a twenty-year veteran journalist. The question is asked in different ways, but no matter how it is phrased, it must be asked and answered. And the question is:

> What do these facts add up to?
> What is this story all about?
> What is the point of this story?
> Now that I've got the facts, what have I got?
> What does it all mean?

However you phrase the question, try to answer it as precisely, as specifically, and as briefly as you can. A single, short declarative sentence would be ideal. But wait! Not so fast. Be suspicious of the first, and thus perhaps the easiest, answer that comes to mind. Someone said, "When faced with the obvious, look elsewhere." The answer to this question is so important to your story that you must work on it, think it through, look at it again, mull it over, and think it through again from the top, from underneath, from up close, and then from a distance.

This mental work is not easy. But it makes the rest of the work to finish the story a whole lot more pleasant. For it is at this "What does this story mean?" point that you are approaching the most creative part of the work of packaging a field reporting assignment: organizing the material into a news story. And remember, you are packaging just exactly that, a story, something with a beginning, a middle, and an end.

Standups

Another standard feature of many field report packages is the standup, or standupper. The standup is a short monologue delivered into the camera by the reporter.

The reporter needn't be standing by the way. Some standups are delivered while the reporter is seated, some are done while he or she is walking. In presenting your standup, look right at the viewers. Imagine they are the lens of the camera and talk with them through it. Look relaxed but disciplined. A standup is no place for groping and hesitations, fumbling, stammering and searching for what you want to say, or punctuating every other phrase with the meaningless "ya know."

Reporters have at least three basic techniques for getting standup material ready for a straightforward delivery with good eye contact: memorizing, extemporizing, and ad-libbing, also called "winging it."

A term borrowed from the legitimate theater, **quick study** refers to a performer who memorizes lines quickly and effortlessly. Of course, memorizing words and delivering them well are two different things. Many fine actors and actresses agonize endlessly to commit lines to memory just as some pedestrian performers have a script firmly in mind after only a couple of readings.

For the TV reporter, the main problem with the technique of memorizing is that the delivery is very likely to look and sound stilted and mechanical. It may lack spontaneity even when it's done without a mistake. Furthermore, total disaster (or an endless succession of retakes) lurks in the background waiting for the reporter who loses the train of thought while pouring out the memorized lines.

In his writings the late President Harry Truman used *ad lib.* in place of *et cetera.* He would write a list of things and then "ad lib., ad lib., ad lib." Obviously he used the term to mean "and so forth." The expression *ad lib.* really means "to improvise" from the Latin "at one's pleasure." Improvising a standup is something you will probably have to do sometime in an emergency. But ad-libbing usually doesn't lead to the kind of precision you want, and as an alternative to some concentrated rehearsal and preparation, it is just plain foolish.

In the extemporaneous method, you have a better chance of avoiding the stiffness of delivery from memory and the looseness of meaning that ad-libbing can cause. You've already read and thought about the extemporaneous method; we covered it (although we didn't call it that) in the section on interviewing where we discussed the best way to work up your questions. First, you get the main points of the standup and the order in which they come firmly fixed in your mind. Next, you run through the delivery a couple of times to set the pattern in your mind. You may—in fact you undoubtedly will—use different words and expressions each time you run through the standup. Only the main points and their sequence remain unchanged. Then when you do the **take** you let the exact wording come out spontaneously.

Body Language   Try to avoid nervous mannerisms that tend to be distracting to an audience. If you're using a hand-held microphone, hold it firmly, but try not to "white knuckle" it. Don't open and close your fist around the mic in a nervous rhythm with your delivery. If you wear a ring, don't hold the mic with the ring hand; you will get a clicking sound on the audio track. Keep the mic clear of all objects and clothing so that taps, rubbing sounds, and clankings don't drown out what you are saying.

"Stand up straight," your mother said. Distribute your weight evenly on your feet, get into a comfortable position, and stay there. If you rock from side to side or back and forth during the shot, the camera will try to follow you and you will look as nervous as you probably are. Keep your head steady and avoid nodding repeatedly to punctuate your phrases.

About the way you dress: It sometimes seems that the first thing anyone does on getting a job as a reporter is to buy a trench coat. Nothing is really wrong with that except that it has become a fashion cliché. You should dress so that you look presentable, professional, and businesslike. Avoiding calling undue attention to yourself by your attire. Save the trendy, mod, high-fashion stuff for your leisure time. If all your subjects are wearing rodeo outfits, it's probably because that's what the story is about. It may be appropriate to wear casual clothes on some assignments, but you will look as silly in a big hat and a flowered shirt on the rodeo assignment as you would wearing a plumed helmet to interview the Queen's Household Cavalry captain. Of course, sloppy attire is never justified. How you dress in private is your business. How you dress on the air is another matter.

Watch Your Language

Be professional in the way you talk off as well as on the air. Badmouthing, flippant remarks, and profanities may entertain your photojournalist and crew, but such behavior is also ill-mannered and adolescent. Around cameras and microphones, horseplay and loose talk are not only bad habits, they're dangerous habits to get into. If it gets on tape or especially on the air, it can get you fired or hunting for a good lawyer. A good rule is: When there's a microphone or camera around, assume it is on and talk and act accordingly.

When you record, use good diction in your delivery. Avoid slurring words, running the last syllable of one word onto the first syllable of the next, or skipping entirely over syllables. Slow down. Most flubs and fluffs are caused by carelessness and speaking too fast.

Be sure your pronunciation is correct. This includes not only the words you speak in your narration or standup, but especially the names of persons and places. Don't put on airs. Water is not pronounced "worter" by most people. In Chicago it's "Go-the" Street. If you pronounce it "Gurr-tah," the bus driver won't let you off. Only the Kennedys and the upper-class British pronounce junta "junter." In the spring of 1982, nobody ever figured out whether it was "Argenteen" or "Argentyne"—even on the same newscast, though they could have looked it up.

Always ask your subject how his or her name is pronounced and then pronounce it that way yourself no matter what the spelling actually "looks" like. Sometimes you are going to have to approximate the pronunciation of foreign words and proper nouns. Get as close as you can and, most important, practice it so both you and your subject are comfortable with it. That way you stand a better chance of being able to rap it out with confidence and avoid pronouncing it different ways in the same story.

Speaking for Edit

We've already talked about the editing problem that results when you leave less than a split second of space between the last word of one answer and the first word of your next question. The same principle applies to your standup. When you get your cue that the recorder is rolling, remain silent and still for a few seconds (a good way is to count silently to five) and then begin. When you get to the end, stand motionless and remain silent for a few seconds (again, a silent five count). This procedure will put a little editing space on both ends of your standup, which will give the videotape editor some room during the editing process. If you begin right at the cue, there may not be room to make the edit at that point. At the end of the take, if you immediately break and ask "How was that?" there'll be no space in which to cue the end of the edit. The edit may either lose the last syllable of the last word of the take or include the first syllable of the first word following the end of the take. Either way is very sloppy editing, but hardly the editor's fault.

When you are recording voice-over narration try to keep your energy level and your concentration up so that you are projecting and relating to the audience just as much as when you are doing your on-camera standup.

Many stations ask their reporters to "label" their standup or V/O takes, for example:

> Sports Ace, standup open, take one
> Enterprising Reporter, transition, take two

And so on, until they get a take they can live with.

Some station procedures call for the reporters to count down audibly at the beginning of each take, for example: "Sports Ace, standup open, take one . . . in five, four, three, two. . . ." (Pause silently for one beat, then go.)

If something like this is standard procedure in your case, be sure to make the silent count in the same rhythm as the spoken ones. Nothing is quite as frustrating to an editor as a countdown that leaves no space after the final audible count, or leaves four or five beats before the narration begins.

If you have trouble getting a satisfactory version in three takes, one of two things may be happening. One, maybe you are just not mentally ready and well enough prepared to begin with. What the takes amount to, then, is rehearsal, something you should have done before recording. Or, two, maybe you are striving to be perfect. You want to do the best you can, of course, especially in this kind of work, where being merely good is not nearly good enough. But remember also that absolute perfection is rare—maybe impossible—and if you botch it today, you can learn from that and excel the next time out.

Ending It

The closing of your story is at least as important as the opening, maybe even more important. You've aimed your opening squarely on the mark, and you've gathered actuality to develop the news point. Now you should tie it all together with flair. Whether you close with a standup or with V/O narration, the important thing is to make the content of the close relevant to the point of the story. If you are going to sum up or recapitulate the two or three important points of the story, make sure that what you say in the closing grows out of what has gone before.

Content-analysis studies in which researchers try to determine if the reporting was fair and balanced sometimes show that bias can occur more frequently in lead-ins, openings, and closings, than in other parts of the story. As reporters try to focus the story on the news point, they sometimes do not take enough care to avoid words that connote an opinion. For example, the anchor lead-in to a story might be something like this:

```
        Video                         Audio
ANCHOR, ON CAM        It was a bad day for state Democrats;
                      statehouse reporter Doug Huber has the
                      story. . . .(VTR HUBER)
```

Huber's story must provide the evidence to support that lead-in assertion. Or if Huber makes the assertion in his standup opening, the support for it must be in the packaged story content.

Huber could use the same idea in his closing instead:

```
     Video                          Audio
VTR HUBER        So it was a bad day for the state Democrats,
                 as they lost another round in the
                 courts. . . .
```

The story should already have provided evidence that Democratic Party interests were damaged by the court action.

Nothing is intrinsically wrong with such a lead-in, opening, or close if the evidence is clear. But reporters are reporters, not editorial writers. It is just as wrong for reporters to insert their own opinions, characterizations, or judgments into stories as it is to insert conclusions that are not clearly supported by the facts simply for the sake of a nice, tight ending or a clever turn of phrase. Prepare the closing carefully. Rehearse it enough to be sure that you get the result you want and that it is a proper, sensible, clear conclusion to the story.

You Are a Member of a Team

The relationship of the reporter, beginner or professional, and the crew is a very important element in field reporting. The relationship must be a positive one if the team is to be effective. Perhaps it is not absolutely necessary that crew members like each other personally, but it is essential that they get along well professionally. Without this professional compatibility, it will be very difficult to get the raw materials needed to make the story jell. On the other hand, when all crew members are working together, they complement one another's efforts, and a more complete story is likely to be the result.

When differences arise—and they're bound to—the problem must be faced and

FIGURE 6-2. In the field the reporter and the photojournalist work together to gather the facts, visual information, interviews, and eyewitness accounts. This raw material will be combined and edited to make the finished story. *(Michael D. Sullivan.)*

worked out. Out in the field is no place for "the silent treatment." This point is so important and so basic that the late Frank Kearns would sometimes devote an entire lecture to it. Kearns, a veteran CBS-TV News foreign correspondent who capped his professional career with twelve years as a professor of journalism, emphasized to his students that reporter, photographer, and soundperson simply had to be on the same wavelength. As Kearns put it, "You've got to talk these things out and keep talking them over until you do come to an understanding."

As the team reporter you must also respect the equipment and the problems the other members of the crew may have in operating it. That is why we've put so much emphasis on learning the parameters of the technology. You cannot detach yourself from the need to protect the gear so that it will continue to work properly. As the reporter you will often be cast in the role of team leader, so your attitude toward the operational and environmental problems you find at the scene of a spot news story may be reflected in how other team members go about their work. If you don't take care to protect equipment when you're working in the rain, it sends a wrong message to the crew.

Keep the words *please* and *thank you* at the top of your vocabulary. Television news brings together you and the other members of your team, and then you are all in contact with members of the general public. So the need to say "please" or "thank you" will come up. You can express these sentiments in many ways, and a little courtesy goes a long way toward assuring cooperation both from the team and from the public. Of course, it must be sincere. If you do not feel it, better that you say nothing. But a well-placed and well-timed expression of thanks costs you nothing, and you may be amazed at the dividends it can return.

COVERING SPOT NEWS

Spot-news stories are breaking events, usually fast-moving, spontaneous, and chaotic. They include such things as fires, explosions, vehicle accidents, hijackings, shootings, floods, and other events of violence and disaster—natural or human caused—that come under the umbrella of what some people call "down-side news."

Television news departments (the more progressive ones, at least) have "disaster plan" policies and procedures, which we discuss elsewhere in this book. Similarly street reporters (at least the more skillful ones) have professional habits that help them prepare for their coverage of spot news as thoroughly as possible in the shortest amount of time. It is partly a competitive and winning attitude. These reporters play "What if" games—"What if, right now, I had to fly out of here and cover a furnace explosion at P.S. 105?" "What if the phone rang right now and the word was that the mayor had just collapsed and died of a heart attack?" The goal is always the same, staying on top of the news in a highly competitive field, not only being first but, more important, being right.

So being mentally prepared and mentally flexible for the unpredictability of spot news is a good start toward being ready when spot news breaks. And when it does, you will either be between assignments or already out in the field working on something else. If it is the first case, you gather yourself up, get as much briefing as can be crammed into a few minutes, and get to the scene with your crew as fast as you can. If it's the second case, you and your crew stop or rapidly conclude the coverage you are on, pack up the equipment, and move quickly to the new location.

Experienced reporters will tell you that this shifting of mental gears is one of the more difficult things about television news field reporting. You have all your attention and mental energies focused on the original assignment, and then in midstride you must break off that story and turn to an entirely new and unrelated event. Often it is an event filled with confusion, chaos, and perhaps even danger to yourself and your crew.

Hazard Training

Let's pause for a minute to think about safety. Here we want to distinguish between the professional and the student.

Occasionally television news field reporting may involve risks to the crew. News directors and the crews themselves worry about these dangers and the odds. It is stupid to drive to the scene so fast that you have an auto accident before you get there. Helicopter pilots and reporting crews can recognize a dangerous situation; they follow preflight checks and flight rules scrupulously. And even with all the precautions and safeguards, accidents do happen; newspeople are injured, and some are killed, while on assignment.

At the scene, professional crews are alert to dangerous situations and try to stay out of them. Being aware of risks means that when newspeople take risks, they do it in a calculated way and not thoughtlessly.

It is never too soon for you, the student, to practice common sense, to sharpen your instincts, and to protect yourself and your crew from danger. Remember this: Your professor does not want you endangering yourself or your crew, no matter what the class assignment is. On the contrary, your professor's first concern is that you stay well away from such harm. At a construction site with heavy equipment in operation, stay well out from under moving cranes; keep well back from bulldozers, earth movers, and other machines. Stay away from exposed electrical power lines. Avoid leaning out of a tenth-floor dormitory window to get that great high-angle shot that's "going to earn you an A." Don't set up in the middle of the superhighway for that great into-frame–out-of-frame sequence. Don't set up the tripod on loose, shifting ground. If you are carrying the camera and recorder, watch where you are stepping and be aware of what's to the side of and behind you. Look in the viewfinder to see what's in front of you, and when you see something coming toward you, don't just assume that whatever it is will miss you. At some point (sooner rather than later) take your eye away from the viewfinder to see if your position is safe. Don't run a drop cord from the house to poolside to run the equipment from AC power, then get into the pool, mic and all, to do that "innovative standup." As in all other phases of this work, your good judgment is always needed.

Problems of Spot-News Reporting

Throughout this book we deal with the various elements of covering a spot news story for television. At the end of this chapter is an essay by Lynn Cullen of WTAE-TV, Pittsburgh. The essay is filled with detailed tips from the reporter's point of view. For now we will look at some of the general problems.

1. Time pressures and fact gathering
2. Sources
3. Shaping the story
4. Clarity of expression

1. Time Pressures and Fact Gathering

Start out by assuming that you won't have enough time to get yourself fully ready to go on the air. You are the vanguard person at the story. You must learn to capture the basic framework of the story as rapidly as possible: the who, what, when, where, and the how and why. It may seem that those are so basic they don't need to be mentioned again, that "it goes without saying." But it is worth repeating the basics. The first four—who, what, when, and where—are usually easier to get than the last two, how and why. In fact the how and the why may not be determined for hours or days after the event, if then. You don't want to leave them out of any story, but you must be on guard against speculating in the early phases of coverage.

You will be under other kinds of time pressures. The goal is to get as much information as you can and get on the air as fast as you can. You may already have been given time limits: The next newscast is going on the air in thirty minutes; you are going into it live for two minutes, thirty seconds. Or a newscast is already on the air, and the station needs facts for a bulletin. Or it's forty-five minutes to air time, and you are expected to deliver a story before the newscast is over. Whatever the situation, the clock is ticking like a time bomb, and it is up to you to meet the deadline. When they explain the procedures for using the oxygen masks on air-planes, they always say, "Breathe normally." Whether that's possible is a good question, but of course you should try. Plunging into a spot news story requires as much level-headed thinking and acting, as much "normal breathing," as you can muster.

So you race around to find out what you can. If you stick to the key story elements already mentioned, you have a better chance of getting what you need than if you go about it in random fashion without plan and without purpose. But those basics will not come in any set order. You may get the what before you get the who. The when may not be exactly clear. You know where you are, but in reporting the where you need to be precise, exactly where. There might be some facts that point to the how and why. You need these, but you also need to be cautious in assessing what you know or think you know about this event. You may not be able to get all these basics in your first sweep of fact gathering, but you must try to be as complete as you can be.

You also need to begin to think about interviews and eyewitnesses as soon as you can.

2. Sources A cardinal rule for any reporter is: "Be sure of your source." At a spot news event you frequently can't be certain. But here are some things to think about:

1. Who's in charge here?
2. Where is the official source?
3. Where and from whom is the information coming?
4. Who is here whom I know?
5. Does this story have "sides"?
6. If yes, who are the spokesmen or women?
7. Is what I'm hearing different from what I'm seeing?
8. Have I seen something others have not seen?
9. What can (should) I do about that?
10. Do some people here, including official spokespersons, have a vested interest in what has happened?
11. What can (should) I do about that?

Clearly many of the answers to those and other questions like them depend on your ability to evaluate the information you are getting in the confusion of the moment. Some of the sources will give you basic facts. Others will give you opinions based on the little knowledge they may have at the moment. Some will try to get their version on the air for self-serving reasons. Part of your evaluation will come from comparing what you are seeing with what you are hearing and from comparing what you are hearing from one source with what you are hearing from another. Part of making sense of all this will come from your own common sense and gut instincts. Does what you are hearing make sense? Is it logical? Is it a reasonable explanation for what is happening? Does the demeanor of the source— whether the person looks directly at you, his or her facial expression, posture, and so on—convey an impression of sincerity? Does the information you're getting come from more than one source? If not, you can verify it, or have you checked it with other sources? Is this source in a position to know—firsthand, secondhand, or even less directly? If the source quotes someone else or starts saying, ''I was told,'' or ''I heard,'' or ''Someone said,'' you know right away you'd better talk with that someone for confirmation. Is this information official, unofficial, or rumor? You never report a rumor. You do check out a rumor.

What you must try to do in the time available is come as close to the truth as you can. Many things may be unknown. There's a good chance that some of the facts you gather from your sources will turn out later to be wrong or incomplete. In the heat of the moment, people can and do simply misstate something or misunder- stand what you want. It is unfortunate that errors get into spot news stories. They should not. But when you feel sure you've done your best under the circumstances, errors should be few and far between. And you should work as diligently as you can to see that any errors are corrected just as quickly as possible.

3. Shaping the Story

At a spot news event, time to think is the most precious time of all because there is so little of it. But you must take enough time to put shape to your story. Seasoned live reporters say that the trick is to stick to the basics and keep it simple both in language and in structure. If you are on the air live, tell what you know. Don't speculate. Be willing to admit what you don't know. Re- member two essential ingredients of news judgment: what is important and what is significant.

You are trying to reconstruct for the audience the main elements of the event. Often keeping a chronological outline in your head or in your notes will serve as a good guide to how you ought to tell the story. Keep it straightforward and simple. You might begin by saying, ''To take it from the top. . . .'' or ''Here is what happened, and what we know so far. . . .'' and then outline the important and interesting facts. Develop and finish one element of the story before you go on to the next. Avoid jumping back and forth between elements whether you are dictating a bulletin or doing a tape report or a live insert. If you have a little time to write something out, keep the direction of the story going forward. Organize it. A simple, tight report of the known facts in some sort of logical sequence is preferable to something that meanders around. And, of course, almost anything is better than a random delivery of unevaluated facts, rumors, speculations, and ''somebody said''s.

As in the hard news feature reporting situation, the way you end the story is crucial to the impression the audience takes away from your report. Here is where you and your audience will come together on the point of this story, on its meaning. An excellent technique for ending is to summarize the main news points that you have just made in your report, but briefly. This is usually much better than trying to do a ''mood'' ending or offering your opinions about how grim, stark, humbling, terrifying, or whatever it all has been.

In fact, be wary about waxing eloquent in any segment of your report. As Harry Reasoner once observed. ''There's a very fine line between eloquence and hot air.'' A classic piece of newspaper lore illustrates the point. A reporter covering the great Johnstown Flood of 1889 got carried away and wired his lead: ''High atop a mountain peak, God viewed nature's awful destruction below. . . .'' The reporter's more down-to-earth editor at the other end wired back, ''Forget flood! Get interview with God!''

4. Clarity of Expression   Chapter 7 is devoted entirely to news writing. But let us emphasize here that all the rules of simple, tight, easy-to-understand writing that apply to the presentation of a script also apply to the material you prepare, extemporize, or ad-lib in a spot news situation. In fact, the guidelines should be applied with even more discipline in the field. It is very difficult to maintain proper syntax and grammar if you allow yourself to get involved with a lot of compound or compound-complex professor-type sentences. You wouldn't do that in your scriptwriting; you shouldn't do it in the field, either. You should always try to:

1. Use declarative sentences.
2. Keep all verbs in the same tense throughout the story.
3. Make pronoun references clear; if you have any doubt, substitute the proper noun for the pronoun. To write (or say), ''An unidentified assailant shot the police officer through the shoulder with his own gun last night'' leaves the meaning of ''his'' dangling.

If you use big, colorful words, you run the risk of conveying a wrong meaning or impression or overdramatizing. If you use a simile or metaphor in an extemporaneous or ad-lib situation, take care to make sure the reference is apt. Sometimes just the right phrase will come to you. You get a thrill out of that, and your audience gets a wonderful insight. But be wary—a slip and you'll find yourself standing there with egg on your face.

Summary

Field reporting with or without electronic news gathering equipment calls upon the reporter to use all of his or her ability to gather facts and background, to organize and edit, and to tell the story in a logical and clear manner. Interviewing is both art and science, and preparation is a key to good interviewing. Good listening skill is essential.

In the hard news feature the aim is to make the story as complete as possible. In the spot news story the reporter strives for reportorial completeness, but time often cuts this process short. The aim, therefore, is for the best available version of the facts at the moment of coverage.

Because time restrictions do not permit you to tell everything you've learned about a story during the gathering stage, your ability to make news judgments is crucial. Deciding what is the main point of the story is the single most important choice you have to make.

PROFILE

*L*ynn Cullen is a native of Green Bay, Wisconsin. She studied at Northwestern University and earned a journalism degree from the University of Wisconsin at Madison. After graduation she spent seven years as a reporter, anchor, and talk-show host at WISC-TV, Madison.

In 1981 Lynn moved to WTAE-TV in Pittsburgh, where she is the "Offbeat" reporter. She also produces specials and does half-time reports for Pittsburgh Steeler telecasts. She has won four Pittsburgh Press Club Awards for her reporting, numerous Associated Press Broadcasters awards, and a national Women in Communications award for a series about sexual harrassment.

Lynn, who herself was included in two of Dick Clark's TV bloopers programs that aired in both the United States and Great Britain, says she prefers stories about all the things that don't usually get on television—the outtakes—and doing reports that are humorous or heartwarming.

GOING LIVE, BEING LIVE

LYNN CULLEN
WTAE-TV, PITTSBURGH

Rumor has it that when opportunities for dodging bullets are in short supply in television news, war correspondents like to keep in professional shape by doing live inserts for the six o'clock news. Perhaps that's a myth, but it is not a surprising substitution. Both jobs offer the adventuresome reporter the same kind of thrills, if not the same ultimate risks.

Done correctly, a live report can be television news at its best, providing the viewer with eyewitness immediacy, information, and drama. Done incorrectly, it can be uproariously and unintentionally funny to the viewer, while the reporter who ends up DOA—Dead On the Air—seldom considers it amusing. That is why live-shot reporters, like war correspondents, must possess the best in reportorial skills and a more than casual knowledge of basic survival training.

Of course, few live reports are as risky as facing enemy fire in a war zone, although a few do come close to that. But first, let's take a look at the gentlest of the genre: the planned live event that happens during a newscast.

It could be a testimonial dinner for a local civic leader or a rank-and-file union vote on a tentative contract agreement that, if accepted, would end a bitter, month-long strike. Perhaps the governor is coming to town for a closed-door briefing with county officials regarding the proposed location of a hazardous-waste dump in the far corner of their bailiwick.

Because the meeting itself is planned, the producer and the reporter will have the luxury of planning their coverage. They will know, for instance, that a group of angry and frightened citizens who live near the proposed site is planning a noisy greeting for the governor. And they will know his arrival is scheduled for five o'clock, one hour before air time. It's a perfect opportunity for what is sometimes referred to as a wraparound, or more inventively, as a "Sony Sandwich"—a taped and edited package, coupled with a live introduction and tag from the reporter at the scene.

Since the meeting between the governor and the county officials will be occurring behind closed doors during the newscast, it is their comments beforehand that you will want to tape and package. And because the demonstrators will be waving their signs and hollering before, during, and after the meeting (fully aware, of course, that the news will be on the air and they will be on the news), their protest will provide both a dramatic backdrop for the live report and a spokesperson for a live interview.

How do you, the reporter, approach this assignment? Chances are you will be given no more than two and a half to three minutes to tell the story. That includes the live introduction, package, interview, and tag. Organization then becomes the key factor, and that should begin in the truck on your way to the scene. Simply shelve the small talk and instead talk shop with the crew. After all, you are all in this together.

Their concerns will be with logistics such as finding a place to park the remote unit and figuring out how to get the signal (and consequently your report) from the scene to the station. If, as is possible, they must operate from a location a few blocks away from the action because an uncooperative building or hill is blocking their transmission, that fact will have an impact on how you can perform your job.

But let's assume the best—that the truck can park and operate well at the scene, and that you've arrived a comfortable thirty minutes before the scheduled five o'clock appearance of the governor and county commissioners. Even though they may not yet be in attendance, it's a safe bet your competition is, so you need to get to work.

Go straight to the demonstrators and like that mythical Martian ask one of them to take you to their leader. Then, while you are talking to the group's spokesperson, you should be doing two things: getting the spokesperson's concerns and what he/she plans to do about them down on paper; and gauging how good an interview that person is likely to give on camera. If you find someone who is distractingly nervous or inarticulate before the fact, imagine how tongue-tied he or she may become with the camera on and thousands watching. So, say thanks for the valuable information, ask him or her to point out some other protesters you should question, and then go quickly to find someone who *can* talk.

What you are looking for, ideally, is a person who can respond intelligently to the politicians' statements and can do it in terse twenty- to thirty-second "bites." That niggling time allotment may seem preposterous at first glance. But if you remember that the producer has given you just two and a half to three minutes to do the entire report, it begins to appear almost generous.

At any rate, line the person up. Make certain he or she will be at your truck ten or fifteen minutes before air time. And don't forget the correct pronunciation and spelling of his or her name, and any title he or she may claim. You will need to radio that information back to the producer so that it can be "supered" on the screen during the live shot.

It's probably getting close to five o'clock, so your photojournalist should already be videotaping some B-roll video for the package: shots of the protesters, their signs, any visible security precautions taken by the police, establishing shots of the scene. If you have a minute—and try to work so that you do—you now need to organize your thoughts on how best to tell this story and to figure out what questions are likely to elicit the most newsworthy responses from the governor and the county representatives. You're going to have to work very fast and hard in the next sixty minutes, so efficiency is one of those things "devoutly to be wished" to paraphrase a certain melancholy Dane. You might wish you'd done a little spring training with the local football team, because if the governor's not in a particularly talkative mood, you might find yourself in one of those car-to-door press stampedes where you'll need your microphone, a good bit of moxie, and the muscle of a middle linebacker.

Let's assume you survive the governor's arrival, even manage to grab a good, tight sound bite from him, and that you also have a less strenuous opportunity to interview one of the more articulate commissioners. It's 5:10 and you have the lead story, but a major portion of it is not yet written, fed back to the station, or edited.

Unless you have an unusually well-honed memory or were wise enough to carry a small audio tape recorder during your interviews, you'll need to review the scenes that have been shot on the truck's monitor while the engineer transmits the raw video back to the station and into the hands of an increasingly impatient editor. Your concern now is to pick out the parts of the governor's and commissioner's interviews you want to incorporate in the package, and to write down their verbal in cues and out cues so that you can radio them back to the producer.

Once that is done you've got to get the script for your package written. It is, of course, wise to bear in mind that the editor will need a minimum of fifteen minutes to put it all together in time for the six o'clock program open. It is, however, paralyzing to dwell on this disquieting fact. Just bear it in mind, and keep your package simple and straightforward.

Quickly outline the major points you'll make during the live opening stand-up. Only rough it out, though, and get on to the edited report, because that has top priority. It should run no longer than a minute and a half, and its end should be scripted to allow for a smooth transition into the live interview with the protester. For example, if the package concludes with the governor's promise that all interested parties and points of view will be heard before any decision is made, you'll be in gravy when the camera returns to you and the protesters are chanting in the background, hoping the governor will hear them through the closed doors of the meeting room. You could, of course, make reference to that very point and then move effortlessly to the live interview.

But meanwhile, you're still in the remote truck, and ready now to record your voice-over narration track and transmit it back to the station. When that's done you can get on the two-way radio and give the producer specific instructions about the package, the in cues and out cues, and any names or locations that should be inserted over the video. Maybe you'll want to down a few Rolaids about now, but don't waste time because you've still got to construct carefully the live portions of your report. It is not wise, however, to script these segments verbatim. You're not going to have a TelePrompTer™ from which to read the words; nor should you lose all eye contact with the audience by having your nose firmly planted in your scribbled copy. Memorizing the script also presents problems for most reporters. There's always the danger of forgetting the lines, or perhaps worse, reciting them in an unnatural, stilted manner. Have some faith in your ability to tell the story simply, as if you were talking to a friend. Help yourself by jotting down key words, phrases, or statistics that will help if you should lose your train of thought. It's a good idea to write down the name of the person you'll be interviewing live. It's one of those things you *can* forget, and that's embarrassing.

After having said all that, let me suggest that it would be wise, nonetheless, to have a very good idea of what your opening and concluding statements will be. No good reporter wants to stumble into a report or mumble out of it. You are the only person who knows where this live presentation should start and where it should end.

I'm guessing it's now about ten minutes to air time, which means you'd better comb your hair, join your photojournalist, and turn your attention to the subject, who is more than likely suffering from cold feet, clammy hands, and a dry mouth. If you're smart you'll try to calm him or her down. It's in your own interest to make the subject feel as relaxed and comfortable as possible under the rather unrelaxed circumstances. By all means tell him or her exactly what's going to happen. Tell him or her to look at you, not at the camera, during the interview, and to try to keep their responses short and to the point. Be as reassuring and calm as you can, given the fact you may well be a nervous wreck yourself. It's not improbable that the feeling most reporters get before their first live shot is very much like that of the novice parachutist before the first jump. The only difference seems to be prepositional in nature—one will be *on* the air and the other *in* it. Both are living somewhat dangerously.

Before we take the plunge, though, let's get a better idea of where we are. I suggested earlier that the protest would make an ideal backdrop for the live report. But will it? The last thing a reporter needs in the background is a crowd of mugging yahoos—people who wave wildly and inexplicably scream, "Hi, Mom!" That can be distracting and should be avoided whenever possible. But if the demonstration or crowd is relatively civilized, peopled with folks who will continue to do whatever it was they were doing before your camera arrived, then the more the merrier. Their presence will give life and immediacy to the report much more readily than the letters L-I-V-E superimposed on the screen ever can. And if you're especially lucky, your mobile truck will be outfitted with a rooftop platform where a camera can be placed to photograph over the heads of any rowdy troublemakers, yet still give the viewers a clear picture of the scene.

It's time now to lend me your ears because one of them must be fitted with a contraption called an IFB, which stand for *interrupted feedback*. It is an earpiece connected to a small receiver that clips on a belt or can be hidden in a pocket, and it's your personal lifeline to the support crew back at the station. Through it you will be able to hear program audio and the director's instructions. If he or she is good at the job and reassuring by nature, you'll get a countdown to the report just like Mission Control: "About five minutes till we come to you . . . How about another mic check? . . . Two minutes, Lynn . . . ten, nine, eight . . . and you're on the air."

It was Ringo Starr who said, "All you gotta do is act naturally." It's a deceptively simple suggestion, but it's a good one. The live shot reporter is certainly not in anything approaching a "natural" situation, although the good reporters will appear not to have noticed that. So when air time comes and the photojournalist's finger points in your direction, here are some tips on assuming the natural look:

Try to speak in a normal tone of voice and in a normal cadence.

Eyeball the camera lens as if it were an old friend and tell your story with as much feeling and enthusiasm as you can muster.

Whenever possible, make reference to the scene and include the viewers: "These demonstrators, as you can hear, seem to have their doubts about that. . . . This so-called briefing is going on right now behind those locked doors. . . ."

Don't worry if you have to refer to your outline. It looks perfectly normal, and in some instances can underline for the audience just how quickly your cameras have brought them to the scene—so quickly you're speaking from scribbled notes!

Back to our hypothetical live shot and some potential wrinkles that can develop. For instance, it's possible that you'll be leading effortlessly into the taped package when the director's voice breaks into your thoughts with the order to "stretch." What that means is that there is some sort of a problem on the other end with getting the package on line and you'll have to stall. The direction to "stretch" is as unwelcome to a reporter as the suggestion to "tread water" is to a drowning man. A seasoned, unflappable reporter, however, would use the occasion without batting an eyelash to tell the viewers all those little details she'd had to jettison because the two and a half to three minutes wasn't enough time to tell it all. In this situation a good gift of gab comes in very handy.

Eventually, the director will give you either the good news that the tape is ready or the unwelcome information that it's not going to play at all. If it is a no go, you'll have to ad lib a summary of the report as best you can, do the interview with the protester, throw it back to the studio, and then count to ten between clenched teeth. Technical difficulties, you see, are one of the pitfalls of live reporting and continually remind us how relatively new all this electronic gadgetry is.

If the package is there as scripted—and it usually will be—you should use the ninety seconds in which it is playing to reassure the subject and to remind him or her in a pleasant way that nice, short answers are best. If, despite this, the subject begins to ramble when the moment of truth arrives, don't be afraid to jump in at the first punctuation mark and redirect the conversation. This is not an easy thing to do, but it should now be apparent that good live reporting as a whole is not an easy thing to do.

At a spot news event the reporter often must go live with very little information and within minutes of arriving on the scene. Here television has a tremendous advantage over newspapers, and if you're lucky, you'll beat out your competition, too. But some of the examples that spring to mind here also raise serious questions about journalistic responsibility in volatile situations.

To illustrate here is another hypothetical situation: An armed man has taken hostages in a downtown office building. Some shots apparently have been fired. You and your cameras have just arrived on the scene. One thing that you must remember at all times is: Don't get in the way of the police. It's your job to report the story and bring the viewers as close to the action as possible, but it is certainly not your place to get involved or to alter the situation in any way. Unfortunately, some reporters and producers have made questionable and potentially catastrophic decisions in situations like this one.

For instance, showing the location of police sharpshooters on the roofs of adjacent buildings during your live report could be helpful to the hostage takers, if they have a television set available—and they easily could have access to one. Showing police crawling toward the getaway car they've agreed in the negotiations to provide, but then continuing to show them letting the air out of the tires might be wonderful video for your purposes, but also could cause a nervous TV-watching gunman to explode. At night, simply turning on your bright television lights could spook a cornered gunman, or transform an unruly crowd into a rock-throwing mob.

There's another type of remote report. It is one to which the adjective "gratuitous" easily applies. I know you've seen them, many of them, as a matter of fact.

The poor reporter stands, microphone in hand, at the now-deserted scene of some story that happened hours before and ended long ago. Why is the reporter still there? Probably because station management thinks its viewers are still struck by the sheer wonder of this new technology and because station management is still struck by the cost of it.

For the reporter, though, the gratuitous remote presents a bit of a problem. What to do? My advice is to try your best not to look foolish or furious, keep the introduction short, get right to the package since there's nothing going on where you are, do a quick live tag, and then head right for the nearest watering hole.

Going live merely for the sake of going live is still a problem in many markets, and unfortunately, such indiscriminate use of television's live capabilities only serves to minimize the impact of on-the-spot coverage in those situations where it is truly warranted.

Here are some more helpful hints.

1. The live interview puts the reporter in an exceedingly vulnerable position.

First of all, it's quite possible that despite your most earnest efforts, the subject will be a dud. He or she will either talk too much and say too little or, worse, answer your questions in monosyllabic yeses and nos. In such cases the smart reporter will have an alternate line of questions in reserve, just as well-applied assertiveness training may help when you are confronted with the nonstop talker. Also, you will get only one shot at each live report, so you must be concerned with the quality and coherence of your questions. In a taped interview the reporter can even be lazily conversational if that approach will get the desired responses. If the question sounds foolish, it can be reworded and asked again or simply edited out of the piece. But no such escape routes are available to the live shot reporter. A stupid question asked is a stupid question aired. Most live shot reporters would have a comfortable nest egg set aside if they could collect a dollar for every word, phrase, or question they wish they'd never uttered.

2. In certain live situations, some say ideal ones, a picture is truly worth a thousand words.

When confronted with such a situation the reporter (who is never, incidentally, paid by the word) might want to remember that fact and keep quiet, letting the natural sound and video do the job for a while. A spectacular fire or a parade are two disparate examples of possible opportunities for this kind of reportorial restraint. Although many reporters would never think of it, there are times when they should get out of the way and let the camera take center stage without superfluous commentary.

3. Contacts are your master weapon.

If it's a big story (let's say the decision in a spectacular criminal trial), all the stations in town will be going live at the same time and all will want the same people live—the district attorney, the defense attorney, perhaps the defendant. If a reporter is to stand any chance of getting a commitment from any of the principal players to talk to him or her first, the calls, the contacts, the professional relationships that have been established before the fact will be the decisive factor.

4. The IFB as friend and foe.

Those earpieces (IFBs) I mentioned earlier that feed you the director's instructions and program audio are wonderful when you are feeling alone and vulnerable. But if you are trying to ad lib a cogent paragraph or two about the story you're covering, it can be very distracting to have to listen to, "Wrap it up, please," or, "Twenty seconds, Lynn," or, "Throw it back to Don." To take all that in, keep your delivery smooth, get out on time, and never let the viewers know you're suffering sensory overload, amounts to nothing less than a mental juggling act. Don't worry if you should drop the ball occasionally. It happens to the best.

5. Wind is always unwelcome at a live shot.

This is especially true for female reporters who sport longer hairdos than most of their male colleagues. Trying to do a serious report while looking like an English sheepdog is not a comfortable situation. Combs and hairspray are unisex; barrettes or headbands can be indispensable for female reporters and should always be taken along just in case, the same as foam wind protectors for the microphones.

6. How you look on the air is important to your credibility.

This may not be a popular idea to raise. But the reality of the business is that television reporters are supposed to look neat and attractive on the air. Some pancake makeup, a hairbrush, and just plain good grooming between times will prevent the way you look from distracting the audience. Of course, your first priority is to get the story, but you are also expected to look presentable when delivering it.

7. Always dress for the weather (advice your mother would give you if she only knew).

If it's wintertime and your station is not located in a tropical zone, always dress warmly. If it's snowing, blowing, and cold, lined boots, gloves—you can't take notes wearing mittens—and a hat are essential. I once found my-self stuck outside during an interminable hostage situation. The temperature was well below freezing and I had a flimsy coat that was not up to the job, open-toed, high-heeled shoes, and no hat. My mouth actually froze that night, so when I went on the air I could not shape my lips to pronounce certain consonants. Needless to say, I was as embarrassed as I was cold.

8. A prop can be apropos.

A prop or visual aid can be very useful, especially if video is difficult to come by.

Let's say a pipe in a huge natural gas tank has sprung a leak and five thousand people have been forced from their homes because of the danger of an explosion. It's a big story, and you are in big trouble, because the police are keeping you far away from the dangerous tank and far away from the pictures you need. Even though you have video of the evacuees leaving and video of the emergency crews arriving, you still have *no* video of the very thing that is causing all this chaos. What do you do?

The reporter who actually found herself in this difficult position employed three tools at her disposal: her reporting skills, her inventiveness, and her can of hairspray. Using her reporting skills she learned the leaking pipe was no more than six inches in circumference, about the same size as the can of hairspray in her purse. So on her live tag she simply traced her finger around the base of the hairspray can, illustrating in a very visual way the irony of such a small object creating such a big problem. It was very effective.

9. Show some leg; or, Take a walk.

Since these are called *live* shots, it is not a bad idea to look alive during them. Nowhere is it written that a reporter must stand stock still, cemented to one spot.

Try starting a report offscreen and then walking into the establishing shot. Or if you're reporting on a drop in automobile sales, for instance, start the report by getting out of a car and then move through the dealer's showroom until you encounter the salesperson who is to be your interview subject. To enhance and lend immediacy to a spot news report, you could retrace the steps an armed robber took leaving the scene of the crime.

The idea here is to be creative. But please be careful! I once started a live shot in an elevator, pushing the "open" button so as to reveal myself as I began my intro. It was very dramatic. The only problem was, the doors shut on me while I was still talking.

10. Be prepared.

If the director has told you you'll be on in a minute or so, get yourself in position *immediately* and stay put. That "minute or so" could become seconds if something unforeseen happens. Nothing looks more unprofessional than getting caught off guard when the anchor introduces you.

And on the other end, when you've finished your report and thrown it back to the studio, always stay put and maintain eye contact with the camera until the director gives you the all clear. You don't want the camera to catch you dropping your mic and leaving as if you had more important things to do.

So that's the advice from the trenches. Live reporting is probably one of the most difficult jobs television can offer to a journalist. Not all reporters can do on-the-spot reporting well, and few excel at it. But this much should be apparent from what you've read here: Only the thick of skin, the fleet of foot, and the quick of tongue need apply.

Writing: The Leavening Agent

7

PRINCIPLES

Experienced broadcast news writers refer to various principles that are guides to good radio-TV news writing. The number of standards and how they are worded vary from expert to expert. But their principles usually include the following ideas:

1. Broadcast news involves a group in a team effort. Therefore a standardized and uniform set of rules for the preparation of copy is a must.
2. Broadcast news lacks permanence. The listener or viewer has no chance to go back over parts of a story not clearly understood. Thus simplicity and ease of understanding are primary news copy requirements.
3. Nearly all the written portions of broadcast news programs are presented orally, that is, the sender speaks the text and the receiver hears it. Thus the writing style approaches ordinary conversation.

This last item, a conversational writing style, is often recommended as the number-one standard of broadcast news writing: "You should write the way people talk."

With news writing principles such as these as a foundation, many rules and guidelines to good broadcast news writing have been accumulating going all the way back to the beginning of radio and radio news in the 1920s and thirties. The guidelines are constantly being changed and improved because, for one thing, electronic news technology continues to change and improve.

WRITING WITH WORDS, PICTURES, AND SOUND

In this chapter we are interested in the question of how to adapt these basic broadcast news writing skills to ENG. A main focus of this chapter is on how to combine good voice-over writing and motion pictures. The idea is to combine words and moving pictures into a coordinated and unified news account, a story in which the words and pictures are purposely created and edited to synchronize with and complement each other.

This kind of writing is challenging and made even more so by other factors. Often other things besides text and motion pictures are folded into the ENG story mix to make the story even more interesting and informative, to give it more impact and more realism. These ingredients may include natural sounds, standups, sound bites, and even in special circumstances, graphics, other visual embellishments, and perhaps even sound effects. So although the focus of this chapter is on the craft of **keying,** that is, making text and visuals mesh, good skill at the fundamentals of broadcast news writing is crucial. And that is where we now turn.

BROADCAST NEWS WRITING: A REVIEW OF THE BASICS

Simplicity—In a Conversational Style

Broadcast news copy should be written with an eye and an ear for simplicity and in a writing style that is conversational. A lot of basic advice is available about these two fundamentals.

1. Write Short, Direct, Simple Sentences
The short sentence is a bread-and-butter writing tool for broadcasting. But experienced writers know that news stories consisting entirely of short sentences tend to sound choppy and singsong when read aloud. Conversely, long sentences are not bad just because they are long. Long ones made so with dangling phrases, clauses, and dangling attributions make the story difficult to read aloud and difficult to grasp. Here are some examples:

> **Weaker:** For the first time since the spaceship *Challenger* exploded January 28, 1986, killing all seven crew members, electricity surged into the shuttle *Discovery* on Monday as NASA began readying the ship for the first post-*Challenger* flight, an official said.
>
> **Stronger:** Space officials at NASA turned on the electricity in the shuttle *Discovery* for the first time today.
>
> **Weaker:** The civilian unemployment rate was down to a decade low of 16 percent in July, the government said Friday in a report released by the Bureau of Labor Statistics.
>
> **Stronger:** A government report released today shows the unemployment rate last month at 16 percent, the lowest rate in ten years.

Weaker: In his first public comment since the recently completed congressional Iran-Contra hearings, President Reagan will give his general views about that testimony in a televised address to the nation next Wednesday at 8 P.M.

Stronger: President Reagan will go on television Wednesday evening. He will give his views of the testimony given to Congress during the Iran-Contra hearings. The president's talk will begin at eight o'clock.

2. Use the Active Voice   Because of those personal elements of the television news delivery system we talked about in Chapter 6 and perhaps especially because of the immediacy of broadcasting, news writers show a preference for the active voice over the passive. As you will recall from your English composition class, in the active voice the subject of the sentence *takes* the action, for example: The president signed the bill into law.

In the passive voice, the subject of the sentence *receives* the action, for example: The bill was signed into law by the president.

3. Read It Aloud   But remember, we're talking here about *preference*. No newscast is or should be constructed entirely in the active voice, it is only the more basic of the two forms. And in the final analysis, the true test of the conversational quality of a piece of news copy comes when the text is read aloud. The proof is in the listening. If it *sounds* fine to you, chances are it will sound that way to the listener. Therefore it is very important that you get into the habit of reading your copy *out loud*. Read it aloud as you type it; chatter at the typewriter or keyboard. Try it out. If it sounds stiff when you read it, it will sound worse when the listener tries to understand it.

4. Avoid Abbreviations and Symbols   Abbreviations are rarely used in broadcast news copy; symbols in place of words, almost never. For example:

Weaker: The accident, which occurred at the intersection of S. Jones Ave. and W. Adams Blvd., caused a 90-minute traffic jam-up in the So. Hills area.

Stronger: The accident happened at the intersection of South Jones Avenue and West Adams Boulevard. Traffic was jammed up in the South Hills area for about ninety minutes.

Weaker: B & D Coal Co. Pres. James Black says 3rd qtr. profits are going to be 7.5% higher this year as compared to last year's figure.

Stronger: B and D Coal Company third-quarter profits are up. Company President James Black says the increase over last year's third-quarter figure is seven-point-five percent.

Exceptions to the abbreviation rule are *Mr.* and *Mrs.* when used together, *Dr.* for doctor, and abbreviations that are supposed to be read aloud—F-B-I, T-N-T, C-I-A, U-S-A. Note that these are typed in caps (capital letters) and hyphenated. They are expressions so familiar that they are easily recognized by all the audience.

5. Use Contractions   Well-placed contractions will help make your story sound more conversational when read aloud by giving it a sense of ease, cadence, and flow. We use contractions freely in our conversation, but not all of them. Some contractions sound awkward, and we rarely speak them because they don't sound right. An example is the contraction "it'll" for "it will." But for the most part, contractions brighten everyday conversation. They are to broadcast news copy what seasonings are to food: Small amounts in tasteful combinations are great, but use carefully—don't mix anise and sage. Here are some examples:

More formal: Bauer said he is certain he will be a candidate for student body president.

Less formal: Bauer said he's certain he'll be a candidate for student body president.

More formal: The Environmental Protection Agency says it will announce new standards for clean water later today.

Not improved by contraction: The Environmental Protection Agency says it'll announce new standards for clean water later today.

More formal: Council members said the money is not available.

Not improved by contraction: Council members said the money's not available.

More acceptable: Council members said the money isn't available.

A variation: Next in the news, a vacation idea that definitely is *not* for the timid.

Comment: If you want to emphasize the negative, don't (do *not*) use the contraction.

6. Be Extra Careful with Names

The general rule for names is to notify the audience that the name is coming by putting some alerting words or sentences ahead of it.

People listen to and watch news amid distractions—the kids want in, the dog wants out, and so on—and they are likely to miss the first few words of a story. Or until they hear the first few words of a story, they don't even know whether they're going to be interested in it. Thus writers avoid beginning a report with any crucial information such as a person's name or indeed with any proper noun. Most authorities recommend the person's middle initial be dropped unless very particular identification is needed. Omit the names of obscure persons and places if they are not meaningful to the story. When you use a name for the first time in a story, use the full name; in subsequent references the last name is enough. A title normally precedes the name, although this is varied for ease of listening; if the title is long and unwieldy, it should be shortened or perhaps written as a separate sentence.

Weaker: Bill Jones, the 16-year-old son of Dr. Thomas L. Jones, chemistry department chairman of research and graduate studies, was presented the Governor's Heroism Medal this morning for saving a life while on duty as a guard at the city swimming pool.

Stronger: The teen-age son of Chemistry Department Chairman Dr. Thomas Jones—16-year-old Bill Jones—has received the Governor's Heroism Medal for preventing a tragedy at the city swimming pool.

7. Use Phonetics   Words that are difficult to speak aloud—the spelling doesn't indicate how the word is supposed to be spoken—must be given special handling. First, of course, you must learn the correct pronunciation. Then type a phonetic into the script. This should be done each time that word occurs in the text. For example:

> **Weaker:** A teenager seeking to learn the fate of Lebanon's lost Shiite Moslem leader hijacked a Lebanese airliner today.

> **Stronger:** A teenager seeking to learn the fate of Lebanon's lost Shiite (SHEE'-EYET) Moslem leader hijacked a Lebanese airliner today.

If two words in a row need the phonetic, keep these words together in the original and in the phonetic version:

> **Wrong:** The program featured the famous pantomimist Marcel (MAR-SELL') Marceau (MAR-SOH').

> **Right:** The program featured the famous pantomimist Marcel Marceau (MAR-SELL' MAR-SOH').

8. Be Wary of Numbers   Numbers are especially difficult for the viewer or listener to grasp. The general rule is to round off a number unless the exact number is significant. Some helpful rounding terms are:

> about
>
> just over (or under)
>
> nearly
>
> slightly more (or less) than

Another technique is to write the number into the text twice, first as an approximation (rounded), then as the exact figure. You would do this where the *exact* figure is important.

> **Exact figure not vital:** Police said the burglars took just over 21-thousand dollars.

> **Weaker:** Burglars escaped with 21-thousand-247 dollars, police said.

> **Exact figure stronger:** Police said the burglars took just over 21-thousand dollars—the exact amount was 21-thousand-247.

For very large numbers (any number over a thousand), the standard technique is to use a hyphenated combination of figures and spelled-out words, for example, "50-thousand," "six-billion."

> **Weaker:** The legislature has approved an emergency money bill of $3,497,800 for relief work in tornado-stricken. . . .

> **Stronger:** The legislature has approved an emergency money bill of just under three-point-five million dollars for tornado-ravaged. . . .

Weaker: Foreigners last year were granted 31,476 patents, or 46% of all U.S. patents, and Americans got 38,124, or 54% of the total of 70,600 patents issued, U.S. Patent Office officials announced today.

Stronger: United States Patent Office officials report that last year foreigners received more than 31-thousand U.S. patents. That's not quite half of the 70-thousand-plus granted during the year. The rest, a little more than 38-thousand—or 54-percent of the total—went to Americans.

Fractions are written as words and hyphenated.

Weaker: The mayor said 3/4 of the money had been spent.
Stronger: The mayor said three-fourths of the money had been spent.

9. Use Standard Punctuation

Follow traditional punctuation rules for the most part. Here are a few additional things to consider about various punctuation marks.

1. The question mark is rarely used in broadcast news. A news story should answer questions, not pose them.
2. The dash and the ellipsis (a row of three periods) seem okay (either one, but be consistent) where a pause in the delivery for emphasis or dramatic purpose is wanted.
3. The comma is a very useful punctuation mark; it helps make the meaning clear and helps the phrasing of the delivery. But the comma can be overused, and it can be misused. If you rely on short, declarative sentences as your basic style, you won't need a great amount of punctuation. If you set off a phrase with commas, be sure you include one comma at the end of the phrase as well as at the beginning. That helps the newscaster find the end of it.

10. Spell Correctly

If you're not certain, look it up. Bad spelling invites problems at the microphone. Besides possibly causing poor delivery, misspellings are psychologically harmful: If the spelling is in error, could the facts be also? Simplified spellings—''nite,'' ''frate,'' ''tuff'' ''kwik''—do not work well in broadcasting. Avoid them.

11. Direct Quotes Need Special Handling

The scripting of a direct quotation is another sticky area for the writer. Experts generally agree that the direct quotation should be short—a few words, a line at most—and to the news point. However if you're going to quote at length, the idea is to break it up into several shorter ''takes'' that can be interspersed in the text. The audience needs to know the exact material being quoted, of course, and many (though by no means all) writers find the words *quote* and *unquote* (or *end quote*) to be awkward and not suited to a conversational writing style. What some writers do is insert word equivalents to take the place of the printed quotation mark. Some of these equivalent expressions are

And these are her exact words. . . .

This is the way he put it. . . .

She added, and again I am quoting. . . .

Weaker: Hospital officials say the patient's condition has been upgraded quote ''from serious to stable'' unquote, and that he is now quote ''out of immediate danger'' unquote.

Stronger: Hospital officials say the patient's condition has been upgraded, in their words, ''from serious to stable'' and they add he is now, again using the hospital's words, ''out of immediate danger.''

TV NEWS WRITING—A COMBINATION OF SKILLS

Use All the Tools

As we said at the start of this chapter, television news writing is not just words, but words and sounds, voices, faces, scenes, lighting, background, color, motion, editing, combining, mixing, sequencing, and producing. Bob Dotson from NBC News says:

> If you show me a good television writer, I'll show you a guy or a girl who is also a good television director, who is also a good television producer, who is also a passable lighting person, who also knows something about audio. We have to tell these stories with all the tools we have.

A number of years before Dotson made those comments, CBS-TV's Fred Friendly made just about the same points:

> We are all writers: the editor who selects the film, the guy who writes the copy, who plans the broadcast, they are all writers. Writing is really only the final act of what people do. . . . If you do your work well, most of the writing is done by the people in the program—and by the sequence of scenes.

With the concept that ''writing'' for television news is a complex combination of jobs—gathering the facts, choosing the story focus, selecting visual material and words, and putting it all together into a package that is going to go into a program with other stories in a planned arrangement—let's look to the researchers to see what they can tell us about the best way to proceed.

WHAT RESEARCHERS SAY

John Robinson and Mark Levy of the University of Maryland recently published a book that focuses on the research that has been done about television news in the

United States and other countries.* Their book summarizes the theories and findings of mass-communications scholars from a variety of fields and reports on their own research into how much people understand of what they see on television news. They challenge a lot of propositions, suppositions, myths, and warmly held beliefs. Among these myths are:

1. Television news programs are the main source of news for a majority of people.
2. Because that is true and a lot of research shows people remember only one-quarter to one-third of what they watch on television news, the world is in terrible shape.
3. Journalists know best when it comes to selecting what is news and preparing it for broadcast.

Robinson and Levy say that a lot of the data alleging that myth one is true comes from asking the wrong questions in the wrong way. Myth two is in question, they say, because it calls for human perceptions—which are often misleading and distorted. Myth three fails, they say, when those journalists fail to take enough account of how people receive and process information from television.

These researchers say that if television news is not the main source of people's information and is not as influential as some say, it could be if journalists make the news as understandable as they can. Because television news is transitory, quick, and a mass of complex aural and visual messages, they say, the final test is not how much information is acquired, but how much of it is understood.

One Day's News—One Week's News

Robinson and Levy did their major recent TV news studies outside the laboratory. They asked real viewers about real newscasts they had watched in normal (in-home) viewing situations in the United States and Great Britain. They asked people what they could remember from newscasts they had just watched (recalled) and then asked them what the main point or gist of the stories was (understood).

One study covered a week of network newscasts. The results agreed with other studies that have shown low recall. But since they probed more deeply, their data show higher numbers. About 62 percent of the viewers remembered something about the stories, but less than half of the week's most important news was understood by those viewers.

In another study of one day's network newscasts, about one-third of the viewers in the United States and Great Britain understood the stories in that day's news.

Those results clearly show that there is a serious problem in getting the news to the viewers. There are a number of factors that Robinson and Levy think help recall and understanding.

*John P. Robinson and Mark R. Levy, with Dennis K. Davis, *The Main Source: Learning from Television News* (Beverly Hills, Calif.: Sage Publications, 1986).

1. Prior knowledge. People who had previous information about the stories, either about the stories themselves or about the area or issue the story focused on, did better on recall and understanding.
2. Education level. Better-educated people also did better. Better-educated people also read more (and more serious) newspapers, listened to more informational radio, and felt they were better able to understand TV newscasts in general.
3. Attention. Those who paid close attention got more out of the newscasts. (But only one-third of the American viewers said they were able to watch without being interrupted.)

We might have been able to predict that those factors would be important without this research, and there is not much we can do about them. But it is important that Robinson and Levy have the proof and that they also conclude that while television news has a "Teflon quality," the book includes some ideas about things that we can do that will help the viewers understand better.

Content and Structure

W. Gill Woodall, an associate professor of speech communications at the University of New Mexico, has summarized experimental and observational research and related it to the journalistic guidelines we often use to structure news content.* Woodall points to recent studies from Sweden that show that the five W's and H so dear to us may not work as well for television as we think they do. First, he says they are not equally important, and not all stories include all these "criteria." Second, he says that the why angle is the one most often left out, and that that is the one that increases comprehension the most.

Woodall and many others say that repetition and redundancy help people remember and understand. Thus if the pictures and sound material in a story repeats and backs up person (who) and place (where) elements, viewers will remember those elements better.

But these researchers also say that it is the cause-and-effect element (why) that helps the most in understanding. Woodall agrees that this creates a problem for journalists, since the why angle of stories is often the most difficult to determine, and speculation on why could hurt journalistic credibility and objectivity, especially if the speculation turns out to be wrong. Yet cause-and-effect elements are so important that we need to make every effort to get them into our stories.

Words

How about vocabulary? Over and over again the researchers have found that we need to be more sensitive to the fact that we, as journalists, know a lot more about the news than the viewers do. And we are verbal chameleons: We pick up and use

*Robinson and Levy, pp. 133–158.

the technical terms and the vocabulary of experts. Such expressions as ''bilateral agreement,'' ''leading economic indicators,'' and ''economic embargos'' get into scripts and roll off the tongue with great ease. Sound bites from experts are filled with similar terms. Few viewers understand them, and the researchers urge us to explain them or use alternative language that helps the viewer comprehend.

Pictures

How about the visual material? Experiments reveal three factors that most help people understand the visual material. Woodall says they are:

1. Vividness: compels attention and starts powerful mental images to work on understanding.
2. Concreteness: provides details and specifics about people and what happened.
3. Linking: the connection between the visual information and news content.

Robinson and Dennis Davis, a professor of speech communication at Southern Illinois University, say that further analysis of the British and American TV newscast surveys shows that vivid and concrete pictures which were loosely linked to story content hurt comprehension, but that vivid, concrete pictures that were tightly linked to story content helped people retain and understand the news.* This was especially true when those links dealt with cause-and-effect elements. A warning about ''vivid'': Some evidence indicates that pictures that are too vivid actually hurt comprehension, apparently because they create such strong mental images at the time they are seen—and drive everything else from the viewer's mind. But they may be remembered for a long time.

Story Types and Newscast Structure

What does the research tell us about what kinds of stories people understand best and the effects of where they are placed in the newscast?

Robinson and Davis say that the first stories and the last stories are usually well understood. But lead stories that contain a lot of extraneous and unrelated angles, words, pictures, and graphics can be poorly comprehended. Closing stories were always understood better, perhaps because they are usually quite visual and high in human-interest elements. Good comprehension of stories in the middle of the newscasts seemed to be connected to how much personal relevance the stories had—oil and gasoline prices, a truck drivers' strike that blocked major roads, and changes in national health insurance policies, for example. Or the audience understood and remembered stories better if they contained famous individuals doing something unique—the pope in Poland—or were about unique situations such as a plane crash.

*Robinson and Levy, pp. 196–197.

Here are a couple of lists of helpful and less-helpful story characteristics that may hold some surprises for journalists and their news judgment traditions.

HELPED UNDERSTANDING:

1. Length: longer stories are always understood better—includes stories with longer anchor on-camera time.
2. Human interest.
3. Personalization.
4. Excitement.
5. Unusual story structure.
6. Surprise: a large number of unusual elements.

NOT SO HELPFUL TO UNDERSTANDING:

1. Conflict.
2. Proximity.
3. Relevance of the story to society.
4. Relationship to viewer's own group or culture.
5. Prominence.

Notice some of those words, such as *conflict, proximity,* and *prominence.* A lot of research remains to be done—and the researchers emphasize that all the time—but it may be that some of our most strongly held beliefs are not as potent as we think.

And a note about grouping stories together: Producers often group stories about similar topics, or the same topic but in different locales, within the same program segments. In fact, it is described in Chapter 8 as one common way to go about structuring a newscast.

Woodall reminds us of the recent findings of Barrie Gunter and his colleagues at the British Independent Broadcasting Authority, from a series of experimental studies that concern what the researchers call ''pro-active interference.''* That is: When viewers see and hear a series of stories that contain many of the same elements, they may have trouble remembering most of the stories after the first one. So grouping a series of stories under some generic theme such as ''Local Crime Today'' may result in a blur of stories and a real chance the audience will transpose the details from one story to another.

Gunter says a way to prevent this is to use production techniques: changing the format from tape with V/O for one story to anchor on-camera narration for another similar story or including other aural and visual elements that make it clear to the viewer where the story is going.

Gunter's research suggests that it is hard to follow stories that are grouped together, and that such visual crutches as generic B-Roll film, file tape, and generic graphics may confuse more than they illuminate (see Chapter 11).

*Robinson and Levy, pp. 211–228.

How Can We Help?

Levy, Davis, and Robinson go beyond the usual research summaries that say much more work needs to be done. They try to relate the research on TV news comprehension to what they call "newswork." They say that "news that informed as it 'told'" might in the long run attract larger audiences.

For some general steps, they recommend that journalists work harder at anticipating future events and prepare to explain them better. It might be a good idea, they say, to try to find out how much prior knowledge people have about future subject *x* and begin to build a common body of knowledge about it.

They are firm when they recommend that we stop assuming the audience knows as much as we do about the news. They complain that journalists are too much concerned with the latest details and not concerned enough with the background. Updating is fine, but if the audience has little prior knowledge, you can't update a vacuum.

Specifically they recommend:

1. More repetition and redundancy. But they don't mean just repeating things. They mean that every story should be organized around a main point, that the story should build up to the main point, and that all elements should contribute to the main point and its various implications.
2. Emphasize why the story is important.
3. "Slow down" the news with tighter, better-structured reporting and more demanding and reflective writing. Highlight the historical context as well as the latest angles.
4. Be explicit; don't expect the audience to get hidden, implicit messages.
5. Separate similar stories from one another. Avoid having the stories melt together.
6. Make extensive use of graphics to handle statistics and other quantitative information.
7. Tell the story in human terms whenever possible.
8. Explain technical or specialized terms. Avoid jargon.

Robinson and Levy's recommendations may sound familiar to you because they do emphasize things that we have talked about in this book. The recommendations also attack some things that we have perhaps taken for granted. But it is helpful to look at how scholars think we could improve the way we communicate. Often they've "got the data to prove it." And we need all the help we can get.

TV NEWS COPY: THE MECHANICS

A page of television news copy is typed in what is called the "split-page" format. The copy is typed on standard-size (8½- by 11-inch) sheets of unruled paper (see

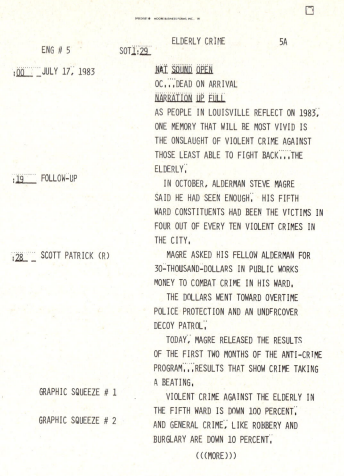

FIGURE 7-1. A typical television script page. Information needed by the control room director—time cues, cues for the insertion of graphics, roll cues for videotape—go in the left-hand column. The script narration itself, and any other sound information, goes in the right-hand column. *(Courtesy of WAVE-TV, Louisville, Kentucky.)*

Figure 7-1). The two kinds of information on a typical page of text are (1) video and audio cues and (2) words to be read aloud.

The video-audio descriptions (cues) are located in the space to the left of the page and the material to be read aloud (text) is typically located on the right side of the page, which splits the page vertically. There is no one standard way to divide the page into right side and left side. At some stations the dividing line is exactly in the middle; in others the text is typed across nearly the whole page, and cues are squeezed down the left margin, or the text is squeezed down the right third of the page. In some newsrooms all cues are typed in caps and all text in "down style" (upper and lower case). In other newsrooms this is reversed. And in still others all information (cues and text) is typed in caps using a typewriter with an oversized typeface (and no lower case). You should, of course, follow the format everyone else is using. The important thing is to be consistent.

Because the production of a television newscast requires so many people and such a high degree of coordination among them, multiple copies of the script are necessary—perhaps just a few in smaller operations, but up to a half-dozen or more in the larger news organizations. Technology is changing these details too, of course. Multiple-copy forms, such things as script packs and carbon books of copy paper, are giving way to terminals, screens, and other tools of computer technology. Where typewriters and terminals coexist, the technology has even produced a tele-copier that takes a page of typewritten material and electronically converts it to a computer file. Changes along these lines are sure to continue, and there are those who foresee the day when paper may vanish from the newsroom. When a Tele-PrompTer™ is used, special script forms are needed so that the cues and text will fit on the screen; but electronic teleprompting is now a reality, and that technology, too, is rapidly becoming paperless.

TV News Copy: Adapting It to ENG

Because the words and the pictures must work together to tell the story, writing text for a voice-over requires that the writer have not only a solid grasp of the fundamentals of television news writing but also a solid understanding of how a motion picture story is put together, the role and function of narration, and the interdependence of the picture, word, and sound portions of a story. The work of the writer and the videotape editor must be coordinated so that the visual and aural ingredients are unified and fitted into a third entity, the complete story.

Which Comes First?

This brings us to another question, one that has been discussed for so long now that we should probably term it a "classical argument." The question is: Should the pictures be edited first and then the narration written to fit? Or should the text be written first and then the pictures edited to fit?

One stock answer is that television is a visual medium, and therefore the word is subordinate to the picture. By that theory at least, the visual part—the motion pictures—should be edited first to tell the story visually. Then the text can be written to coordinate with and complement the picture part, to round out and finish off the story. As you might have guessed, the answer is not that simple, and even when that may be the right answer, it may be the right answer but for the wrong reason. The question is important enough to merit a closer look.

Recall the discussion of the idea of structure in Chapter 3. The story requires structure. Of course, it is true that television is a visual medium, but that does not really help us to understand the relationship between words and pictures in a TV news story.

Television is more than a visual medium; it is a narrative medium. And in any narrative the words provide structure for the story. Nonetheless the debate on the question continues. Here's Bob Dotson on the subject:

> This is not the classic argument between Is it the reporter who's more important? or Should the pictures tell the story? The point is that everything is of equal importance going into an assignment.
>
> If you have tremendous pictures . . . well of course you don't put any copy in there. But on some other stories the copy may become more important.

So it's more than just that classic argument, Which is more important? The point is that the reporters and the camera people in the field ought to be aware of all the tools and not just rely on this wonderful technology we have back in the studio to flip-flop scenes when we get the wrong screen direction—if you worry about screen direction at all—and all the things that technology has been able to backstop us with.

Voice-Over

As you get down to the business of starting a text for a V/O story, you will need two sets of facts: (1) facts about the news event, the five Ws and H of conventional on-camera news reports; and (2) facts about the edited version of the motion picture part of the story. Armed with this information, you are ready to begin the task.

Story Facts

Television news writers sometimes refer to the facts related to the news event—all the facts that they have—as the **dope sheet** or "poop sheet." The dope sheet consists of information about the event and can include such things as the reporter's notes from direct observation, notes on interviews with eyewitnesses or participants or others at the scene, newspaper clips, magazine articles, background research culled from reference works or computer data bases, a printed program, a public relations handout or package of information—just about anything that will shed light on the story.

Visual Facts

As for the facts describing the video material, the profession has no accepted uniform or standard set of terms to describe the various elements of the video. Nevertheless you will need a shorthand description of each scene of the picture story and its running time in seconds. In order for us to consider this further, however, some agreement on terms is essential.

The smallest visual unit of videotape is called a frame. A series of frames with the same content makes up a **scene,** or variously a **shot,** or **take.** Let's stick with **"shot."**

When a videotape recorded at a news event is ready for editing into a story, the first thing that happens is that someone, perhaps the writer, reporter, or video editor, logs each shot, as discussed in Chapter 5. Now sometimes in the real world no log is made; shots are screened and so forth, but nobody actually makes a log. Why? For one thing, logging can be tedious. And a bother. (Nobody ever said television news was easy or lacking in tedium.) But skipping the step of logging is a mistake, perhaps a big mistake. Bob Dotson again:

> I really don't ever write the final draft until I have personally logged every shot. And I do a double log. And you can do this sometimes on a general news story. It doesn't

take that much longer. Try doing this sometime: You log your shots. You also log your natural sound. So that when you get to the writing side of it, and you say, ''Well, I've got to say this, because this is an important part of the story.'' Then, you suddenly realize that, ''Hey, Joe Blow already said that.''

For not just the sound bites but the natural sound, you know there was back here a cat crying, and at the point where the cat is important, why don't I just let the cat cry instead of me saying, ''A cat cried tonight''?

So if you do a dual log—I'm talking general news, obviously on spot news you don't have time for this—if you do this dual-logging system, it's a lot easier to write, because you do know what you've got hidden there. Sometimes things will pass through that you weren't aware of because you were busy getting information, or writing, or whatever when you were on location.

Okay, so you do your log. Using the log, the videotape editor, the writer, or the reporter may now decide how much of which shots will go into the edited version of the visual side of the story and in what order. In making the edited version, the editor might rearrange the sequence of the shots, shorten their running time, break a shot into shorter segments and intersperse these among other shots, and use other editing techniques discussed elsewhere in this book to turn the raw videotape into an edited motion picture story. One with continuity, we hope.

Now we need another term, this one to describe an edited segment. Remember, we're calling unedited segments *shots*. We'll call an edited segment a **scene.** If a log is compiled by listing in sequence the content and running time of each shot on the unedited tape, then a scene list is a listing, in sequence, of the content and running time of each scene in the edited version. Some newsrooms refer to these scene lists as ''cut sheets.'' Armed with the cut sheet and the dope sheet, you are now ready to write the V/O text.

Writing voice-over narration—text to go with motion pictures—has a certain element of precision about it. The running time of the picture story clearly limits the number of words that can be fitted into that time, and what the pictures show (content) and the order in which they show it (sequence) clearly force a parallel development of the accompanying text. Bob Dotson again:

I walk into a story, and I do it the same way every time. I do the ''fly-on-the-wall,'' you know, do the ''Columbo,'' I just kinda sit around and eavesdrop on the situation. . . .

And then I start thinking of it in terms of building blocks. Where is the camera? Where is the sound? What have I got to say?

I write constantly. I don't take notes; I write constantly. I try to write what I call ''the corners of the picture,'' things that I know the camera can't show, things that people tell me that aren't in the sound. I'm constantly writing it down.

Word-Picture Match

A very basic need in this kind of writing is to make the words and the pictures work together to tell the story. For example, suppose the story is about local reaction to a new drug-paraphernalia law passed by the state legislature. The scene shows a store countertop with items on display—packages of cigarette wrapping papers, snuff boxes, and so forth. It might start like this:

```
       Video                        Audio

Merchandise          Customers find in these shops all sorts of
10 secs.             merchandise related to the use of drugs--
                     from papers to snuff boxes.
```

The writing here is backward; it is not well linked with the visual. The words and the pictures are not working together. The audience is looking at "merchandise," but the text is talking about customers. Clearly the pictures cannot be changed (unless shots of customers are available), but the matter can be resolved rather easily by recasting the sentence so that merchandise is the subject of the sentence. You could change the sentence to read:

```
       Video                        Audio

Merchandise          All sorts of merchandise related to the use
10 secs.             of drugs--from cigarette-wrapper paper to
                     snuff boxes--is for sale in these shops.
```

Getting the words and the pictures in sync takes some time and thought, and a lot of practice, until you get a feel for the techniques involved. Earlier we talked about chattering at the typewriter, reading your script aloud as you write it. Now we have a new problem—writing, reading the script aloud, *and* keeping one eye on the pictures that will go with the words. Of course, where the pictures are compelling, keep the writing out of their way; where the pictures do not give their own meaning, then the writing must play an entirely different role.

Keying: Keys to Word-Picture Fit

Writing to the Picture   If you write a text that is directly related to what is being looked at while the text is being listened to, you are using a technique called "writing to the picture," or **direct narrative.** This is what you do when you write text so that the name of a person in the story comes up in the narration just slightly ahead of or at about the same time that face of that person appears on the screen. This technique is also called "keying." An accomplished writer can deftly weave details into the narration in such a way that at key points all along the story what is being looked at and what is being listened to match and mesh with each other perfectly.

```
                         CUT SHEET
BANK ROBBERY
              Scene                    Scene Time/Cumulative
                                              Time
MS, Exterior of bank                   04/04 (seconds)
MS, Money on bank lobby floor          06/10
MCU, Money on floor                    04/14
CU, Hand holding $50 bill              04/18
MS, Police talking to Mrs. Louis       04/22
MCU, FBI taking fingerprints           05/27
MS, Police talking to newsmen          04/31
MCU, FBI questioning Hayes             06/37
MS, Police examining holdup car        07/44
```

Take, for example, standard videotape coverage of a story of a branch bank robbery. The robbery is routine except for one thing. The robber was so nervous he dropped part of the loot on the floor of the bank lobby as he was leaving, and a customer in the bank ran after him to tell him about his loss. The pictures show a crowd of people standing around looking at the money on the floor and closeups of the money. Later there is an interview with the ''good Samaritan'' who tried to be helpful.

In editing the tape, those pictures of the money and the interview with the ''good Samaritan'' are included. The pictures of the money, in fact, are scenes 2, 3, and 4 in the cut version. Therefore, the writer has to figure out how to explain why the money is on the floor and the significance of those scenes as they are viewed. Obviously, those scenes and the explanation should come before the interview. This structuring of the visual part of the story is logical and dictates the way the story is written even before the first word goes on paper.

Writing Away from the Picture   If, on the other hand, your text covers aspects of the story that cannot be shown, your text at those points is said to be written ''away from the picture.'' Another term for this approach is **indirect narrative.**

While the pictures are unfolding the visual part of the story, the text may be covering *why* the event happened, or *how,* or it may give perspective by telling how what is being looked at relates to what can't be shown. For example, a story showing the president visiting a poor family hard hit by inflation may relate more to the unpopularity in Congress of the president's program to combat inflation than it does to the visit itself. So while the pictures are showing one aspect of this political fact, the text is adding context. In another example, pictures show rescuers in icy lake water pulling a child out. Narration adds facts that the pictures cannot show, for example, the temperature of the freezing water, how long the boy was under water, and so on.

The skillful writer may use this in-and-out (direct and indirect) weaving pattern, synchronizing the narration to the pictures at some points and adding background and additional nonvisualized facts at others. In other words, the text is written to complement the pictures, to flesh them out, fill in blank spots, to give added meaning, context, understanding, clarity—as Dotson says, writing the corners of the pictures.

Avoid Visual Reference

It is important to link the text and the pictures firmly at those points where words are needed to explain to the viewer what's going on. But there are weaker and stronger ways to firm up the linkage. Keep in mind that while you want the words and pictures to go together, you also want the text to be independent of the picture, or another way it is sometimes put, you do not want to *stop* the pictures with the words. The text should not duplicate the picture by telling viewers what they can plainly see. Also the text should avoid direct visual reference. Expressions such as "The president, *seen here* getting out of his car" or "*seen here* falling down the plane's steps" are usually unnecessary and are considered unprofessional and amateurish. The same holds true for the expressions "As you can see," "Shown here on the left," and other similar visual references.

However, do you remember the phrase "Apply the rules thoughtfully and carefully"? A picture shows two men handcuffed together, walking toward the camera on the sidewalk outside the Federal Building, both dressed similarly. Nothing stands out there, and the story is that the chief of detectives is returning a convicted murderer to his jail cell. Direct reference to which person—"the one on the right (or left)" is the detective, and which is the criminal, is not only permissible, it is *mandatory*.

Timing

Beginners in the art of voice-over text writing have no clear notion of how much text will "fit" a given scene in the scene count. This formula has proved helpful and allows the beginner to gain some "feel" for the quantities involved:

Guideline **Three Words Maximum Per Running Second of Video**

Counting words is tedious, however, so there are script formats that provide other guidelines. With a split-page format and a standard pica typeface, a thirty-five-character line of copy will take about two seconds to read, a forty-five-character line about three seconds to read. Thus in a five-second scene, a writer will have about two and one-half lines of script space, or about fifteen words to "fit" the narration to the scene. Ten seconds of picture will use up five lines, or thirty words, and so on. Line count is a rougher way of estimating text length, but is quicker.

These formulas are merely starting points and must be adjusted for a variety of individual variables, for example how rapidly or slowly an individual anchor reads; whether the story pace is quick or slow; and, when line counting, line length and the size and pitch of the type. The type size on a TelePrompTer™ may be larger, so word count—the basic three-words-per-second—remains a useful guide to how much narration can fit into a given amount of scene running time.

Keeping in mind these formulas, study this example of a cut sheet and a script developed from it, keyed and edited to fit.

CUT SHEET

```
FLU SHOTS STORY
              Scene                Scene Time/Cumulative Time
MS, BUILDING (ESTABLISHER)        05/05 (seconds)
CU, SIGN                          02/07
MS, LADY ENTERS                   04/11
MS, WILES                         04/15
CU, WILES                         03/18
MS, WAITING ROOM, SLOW PAN        10/28
4 CU SHOTS, RECIPIENTS            20/48
MS, KAPP GETS HIS                 09/57
```

The writer knows from the cut sheet that because the tape begins with the "where" of the story, the text will have to begin with the "where" also. The writer will have to work the text for about 30 to 35 words, 11 seconds times 3, down to the end of the third scene, "lady enters." The text should now state the name of the county health supervisor, Doctor Wiles, whose picture will come up on the screen at this point, 11 seconds (and 30 to 35 words) into the story. Getting the name "Doctor Wiles" to occur about 30 to 35 words into the text thus "keys" the name and the picture. From there on the picture-word story is further advanced to a point about nine seconds from the end of the videotape, where the reporter himself (Kapp) is shown getting his injection. Finally the writer knows that the entire text must not exceed a maximum of 171 words (57 seconds times 3) or 28 lines of two seconds each. Once the text reaches or exceeds that total, it must be edited down to a word count a bit shorter than that maximum so that the text will have "breathing room." Here is a draft of the V/O text followed by an edited (final) script version:

SWINE FLU STORY, FIRST DRAFT

```
ANCHOR, ON CAM                       Monongalia County's swine
                                     flu vaccination program got a shot
                                     in the arm today.
                                     We get the details now from
                                     reporter Gene Kapp.

VTR, KAPP              (SOT)
MS, BUILDING ESTABLISHER   05/05     Area residents received their
```

CU, SIGN	02/07	flu shots at the Monongalia County Public Health Center on Collins Ferry Road as this season's first
MS, LADY ENTERS	04/11	supplies of the new vaccines were made available to the public.
MS, WILES	04/15	Health officials were happy with today's turnout, about two thousand people total.
CU, WILES	03/18	County Health Director Doctor
MS, WAITING ROOM, SLOW PAN	10/28	I-A Wiles gave a brief summary of the program and asked each person getting a shot to fill out a registration form.
		Wiles explained that there are two types of vaccine. One is
CU, 4 SHOTS RECIPIENTS	20/48	called bivalent (bye-VAY-lent)--it is for anyone who is 65 years of age or older.
		The other type--called monovalent (MAH-noh-vay-lent)--is for persons between the ages of 18 and 65.
		Wiles said that supplies of both types are plentiful locally.
		He stressed that these vaccines will protect you only from the so-called swine flu, and not from
MS, KAPP GETS HIS	09/57	any of the various other strains of flu sickness.
		He noted that there haven't been any reported side effects from those using these two new vaccines.
		So I got my shot . . . and believe me, it didn't hurt a bit.

—0—

First of all, the draft of the text is too long—178 words or 31 lines for a time frame that will accommodate only 171 words or 28 lines maximum. Also the two shots of the medical doctor come up on the screen well before the name occurs in the text, suggesting that most editing should occur in the front part of the text. Lastly, in order to give the text breathing space, we need to edit out about 15 to 20 words or 3 to 4 lines to bring the total down to about 160 words, or 26 lines.

SWINE FLU STORY, FINAL VERSION

ANCHOR, ON CAM   Monongalia County's swine

flu vaccination program got a shot
in the arm today.
We get the details now from
reporter Gene Kapp.

VTR, KAPP	(SOT)
MS, BUILDING ESTABLISHER	05/05

Area residents received their
flu shots at the Monongalia County
Public Health Center on Collins
Ferry Road.

CU, SIGN	02/07

MS, LADY ENTERS	04/11

Health officials were happy
with today's turnout, about two
thousand people total.

MS, WILES	04/15

County Health Director Doctor
I-A Wiles gave a brief summary of

CU, WILES	03/18
MS, WAITING ROOM, SLOW PAN	10/28

the program and asked each person
getting a shot to fill out a
registration form.
Wiles explained that there
are two types of vaccine. One is
called bivalent (bye-VAY-lent)--it

CU, 4 SHOTS RECIPIENTS	20/48

is for anyone who is 65 years of age
or older.
The other type--called
monovalent (MAH-noh-vay-lent)--is
for persons between the ages of 18
and 65.
Wiles said supplies of both
types are plentiful locally.
He stressed that these vaccines
will protect you only from the
so-called swine flu, and not from
any of the other strains of flu
sickness.

MS, KAPP GETS HIS	09/57

He noted there haven't been
any reported side effects from
those using these two new vaccines.
So I got my shot . . . and
believe me, it didn't hurt a bit.

--O--

So the edited version of the script is now down to around 165 words, a much
better overall fit with the running time of the tape. Pencil editing to remove excess
words has fine-tuned the timing. Notice also that because the editing was done
mainly in the first twenty seconds or so of the script, the edited text keys much

more closely to that part of the report where the scenes of the doctor are on the screen.

Overwriting

Thus the text editing has resulted in a correction of what is quite likely the single most frequently occurring weakness in beginner-written voice-over scripts: overwriting. The problem is not only that the text spills over the running time of the tape, but also that the viewer drowns in the words and isn't given a chance to correlate the pictures and words into one unified entity. Keep in mind that the pictures are giving visual information, and the text is filling in the gaps, providing facts needed to understand what the pictures are showing. In this case, watching is primary, listening secondary. Similarly if the report contained "natural sound" (the background or ambient sound at the news event) that was compelling, natural sound could be primary and text secondary at key points in the story. At those points any words would get in the way, and you would need to "write silence" into the script.

Careful Pencil Editing

Voice-over writing technique calls for economy of words and compression of style. A handy trick students have found useful in helping them achieve leaner, spare prose is to write the first draft of their text to just about the exact count of the videotape running time. Thus if the tape runs 60 seconds, the text will run to 180 words; for 90 seconds of tape it would be 270 words, and so forth. After drafting the text, the trick then is to pencil-edit (remove) about 10 percent of the words. For example, in a 180-word text, you should cut 15 to 20 words; in a 270-word text, 25 to 30 words, and so forth. Students are amazed to learn that this can be done with no damage to the content, clarity, or meaning of the text. In many cases it improves clarity by getting some of the wordiness out without taking away any significant information.

Another adjustment to the formula may be needed because of the mood of the news event itself. Some stories are exciting, happy, fast moving. Others are languid, soft, slow. Still others are sad, emotional, shocking. Each requires a different approach in writing narrative for it.

Voice-Over with Sound Bites

A special writing problem is created when the voice-over story contains an actuality or sound bite, a sound-on-tape statement from a news maker. The scenes will have been edited to build up to that point in the story, and your text also. The word or line-count formula should help you avoid the text quantity problems of *underleading* (or undercutting) and *overleading* (or upcutting) the sound.

On the air you can recognize underleading when the narrator reads the text right up to the end of the lead-in line, right to the sound bite, and then you hear an awkward silence while the narrator (and the audience) waits for the last part of the scene to run up to where the sound bite begins. Overleading, just the opposite problem, results when the final words of lead-in text spoken by the narrator override the first words of the sound bite.

Each of these problems is easily avoided, but you do have to take care to count accurately. For example, if the visual material for voice-over narration is 20 seconds long, at which point the sound bite begins, the voice-over text should be a maximum of 60 words (the 3-words-per-second formula) and then pencil-edited to adjust, probably by removing five words or so (10 percent of the copy) to allow breathing room. An out-loud rehearsal allows the anchor to get the feel of the copy, and final adjustments can be edited then.

A variation on this kind of voice-over report is the story with a V/O introduction, then a sound bite, and then a V/O tag. Here is an example:

```
                      WBOY-TV
                     SHOT LIST

FAIRMONT GENERAL HOSPITAL STRIKE
Video, strikers on picket line video is similar      12/12
throughout
SOT bite                                             20/32
Video to end                                         07/39


---------------------------------------------------------------


Slug: FGH Preview              TOMORROW MORNING, NEGOTIATIONS
Date: 10-21                    WILL GET UNDERWAY ONCE AGAIN IN THE
Writer: Jeff Hertrick/late     FAIRMONT GENERAL HOSPITAL STRIKE.
                               SINCE THE STRIKE BEGAN AUGUST 31st,
                               THE HOSPITAL HAS HIRED 82 REPLACEMENTS
                               FOR STRIKING NURSES.
                               THOSE REPLACEMENTS HAVE BEEN PROMISED
                               PERMANENT EMPLOYMENT.
vo/sot/vo tag. . . . . . . . . . . . . . .BUT LOCAL 11-99 SAYS THE REPLACEMENT
:00 Upper/Fairmont             ISSUE IS THE KEY STUMBLING BLOCK TO
                               RESOLVING THE STRIKE.
                               THE UNION SAYS THE HOSPITAL MUST
                               AGREE TO KEEP ALL STRIKERS BEFORE AN
                               AGREEMENT CAN BE REACHED.


        sot . . . . . . . . . . . . . .


                                     -----------------------------
:16     super/ Vickie Tennant
        cue/ ''problem with that'' :32
                                     -----------------------------
v/o tag. . . . . . . . . . . . . . . . . . . .HOSPITAL ADMINISTRATOR ROBERT
```

PTOMEY SAYS HE HOPES ALL ISSUES AND
CONCERNS OF THE UNION WILL BE
RAISED DURING TALKS TOMORROW.

total rt/:39

The problem here is to create a text that adequately introduces the story, including 12 seconds of voice-over material (in this case 34 words) that leads directly to the sound bite, and then a 7- to 8-second tag, also voice-over (in this case 20 words) to conclude the story.

Lastly, the writer is striving to create not only the right amount of text but also an informative and understandable lead-in to the story's sound bite.

Lead-Ins

A more important problem, not mechanical but editorial, concerns the *content* of the text and especially the lead-in to the sound bite, the sentence that introduces the news maker's statement. First of all, the news maker's statement is an important part of the story because it gives the audience not only the content of what the speaker said, using his or her own words, but also the richness and dramatic effect of the speaker's speech, tone of voice, facial expression, perhaps gesture, and all the other things that combine to convey the meaning of the words spoken. An actuality incorporated skillfully into an ENG field report is an example of using the unique tools of television news to their fullest.

Your challenge in working up this report is to capitalize on this unique opportunity with introductory material that focuses audience attention on the speaker and on what he or she had to say. You want your text and sound bite lead-in to be better than merely "good." A key to "great" is to know exactly what the speaker said in the sound bite. Armed with this knowledge, you are ready to create a text and a lead-in to the actuality that highlight this element of the story, to guide audience attention toward the speaker and the speaker's message, thereby making the meaning of the story clearer to the audience.

The lead-in to the sound bite should establish clearly who is speaking, and it should set up the content of the sound bite. Your text might go to the question of the significance of the news maker's statement or the effect it is likely to have, or your lead-in might summarize that content, paraphrase it, or clarify it. Often the text before the lead-in to a sound bite will explain where and under what circumstances the statement was made. The important thing is to make clear (1) who this person is, (2) the context in which his or her statement was made, and (3) what the news maker said.

The Echo Effect

Watch out for the "echo effect," also called "parroting," in which the text lead-in uses the respondent's exact words. For example, the story may be about a judge's ruling in a child custody case.

Weaker:

```
(Text Lead-In)          The judge said this case was unusual
                        and that therefore he would take
                        exceptional cautions for the children's
                        safety.

SOT Sound In--Cue:      ''This court will take exceptional
                        cautions for the children's
                        safety. . . .''
```

The combination of the narrated lead-in followed by and using the exact wording of the judge's comments on the tape illustrates the echo effect. Do not use the speaker's exact words in the text lead-in:

Stronger:

```
(Text Lead-In)          The judge said the main thing he wanted
                        to do in this case was to protect the
                        children.

SOT Sound In--Cue:      ''This court will take exceptional
                        cautions for the children's
                        safety. . . .''
```

Reinforce the Sound Bite Content

Whatever your script for the text lead-in, check that the text refers to the issue the news maker is discussing. Make sure you understand the sound bite and then paraphrase, summarize, outline, digest, and condense, as long as your lead-in avoids the exact words of the sounds bite.

Be Specific   A specific lead-in is better than a vague one:

Weaker:

```
(Text Lead-In)          When asked what he thought about the
                        president's reinstatement of
                        registration for the draft, Herrick had
                        this to say:

SOT Sound In--Cue:      ''It's probably the worst
                        decision. . . .''
```

Stronger:

```
(Text Lead-In)          Herrick was especially critical of the
                        president's decision to once again
```

require 18—year—olds to register for
the draft:

SOT Sound In——Cue: ''It's probably the worst
decision. . . .''

The first lead-in is weak because it doesn't give a hint as to what Herrick said in the sound bite. It stops the story's information flow, stops the forward movement of the story in its tracks. The second example not only avoids the awkward and wordy text (''When asked'' and ''had this to say,'' both of which state the obvious), but also reinforces Herrick's statement by alerting the viewer to the thrust of what he said.

Here are other examples:

Weaker:

(Text Lead—In)   Defensive end Delbert Fowler has played
under both coaches. And Fowler talked
about some of the changes the new coach
has begun to make.

SOT Sound In——Cue: ''Now, you'd better be on time or
you're in trouble. . . .''

Stronger:

(Text Lead—In)   Defensive end Delbert Fowler has played
under both coaches. And Fowler says a
big difference is the discipline.

SOT Sound In——Cue: ''Now, you'd better be on time
or. . . .''

Weaker:

(Text Lead—In)   Wilson told W—X—X—News about the main
idea behind the Jaycees.

SOT Sound In——Cue: ''The whole purpose of this thing is,
we want the members to. . . .''

Stronger:

(Text Lead—In)   Wilson said the main idea of the
Jaycees is to promote the self-
development of its members.

SOT Sound In——Cue: ''The whole purpose of this
thing. . . .''

In today's television news, the function of the in-studio on-camera news anchor is often one of introducing the reporter who covered the story. From that point on, the entire story, including the lead and story introduction, the voice-over narration, and other informational materials (on-the-scene interviews, standuppers, transitions, closer) is recorded in one complete package onto the ''air'' videotape.

For example, the reporter and crew may go to the scene of a news event and begin the coverage in what might be called the ''normal'' way, with the photographer gathering the visual material with natural sound and the reporter gathering factual information and doing interviews with eyewitnesses or others directly involved in the story. Then, choosing a key location at the scene of the event (often one showing the ''where'' of the story), the reporter may do an on-camera standup introduction to the story, a standup transition or closer, any combination of these, or even all of them.

Editing the Package

Back at the station, the reporter may sit down with the videotape editor and pick out the sound bites—the wanted portions of the interviews—plus the desired take of the standup open, transition, and close, all of which are going to be used in the packaged report.

Next, the reporter may write the voice-over text that fits between these various sound-on-tape elements, then narrate this text into the story to bridge the sync sound elements. The reporter may take this script to a sound recording booth to record it on an audio cassette, CART, or reel, or the narration may be recorded directly onto videotape, depending on the newsroom's technical setup.

Then the videotape editor is ready to cut the story and piece it together. Onto the master video cassette goes audio and video from the standups and interview sound bites and the recorded narration that bridges those sections. The editor then returns to the raw videotapes to select B-Roll scenes where appropriate and perhaps the natural sounds that go with them. These are then edited onto the master tape *over* the voice-over narration that bridges the picture-plus-sound bites laid down earlier.

One advantage of this editing sequence is that it is very economical and saves reporter and writer time; it is a most efficient way to package a field report.

The Snapshot Effect

But the technique is not without its problems, at least one of which is pretty severe. In the process of looking for B-Roll scenes or shots that appropriately ''cover'' the voice-over narration, the editor risks losing the sense of visual story line, the continuity, the visual ''flow''—the ingredient that converts a series of scenes into a story. The danger is that the shots may end up looking like a bunch of unrelated snapshots in a photo album, scenes chosen just to "cover" the narration rather than to establish and advance a visual story line. The fundamental weakness of this technique–and you're likely to see it any night of the week on your local television newscast–is that the visual has been made secondary to the writing, which would seem to stand on its head the conventional wisdom about the value of the visual and the role of the text. The result is what RTNDA President Ernie Schultz refers to as the "illustrated story." And he's not the only one making that observation.

File Footage Sins

This book refers several times to what Reuven Frank, former NBC News Division president, has said about television news. He has spoken about these issues a number of times during his long and distinguished career. In a keynote address to the Radio-Television News Directors Association in December, 1980, Frank said:

> Satellites and portable cameras and miniaturized tape have put us within instant range of everything happening everywhere. That is what we used to long for. But the result has been a kind of bulletin service that provides information no different in essential nature from what comes by other media, radio or print. Because we can bring all the news, we therefore must. It is rare, however, that the information is other than the words, or that the value is other than the speed of dissemination.
>
> What television does uniquely, the transmission of experience—what was it like?—is a rare and accidental accomplishment. Pictures, when they are available, are matched to words. The words come first—not pictures. I daresay there are people in this room who have never seen pictures put together to tell a story and then words fitted into them, as needed, to fill in, to underscore, to bridge gaps. Almost nobody writes silence any more.

Eyewash   Frank was especially critical of two visual techniques that are fairly widespread in television news. One is the use of file footage and library tape to visually "cover" the text of a story (called **eyewash**); the other is the use of electronically generated graphics and other production elements to "dress up" the visuals over the narration. Of these two practices Frank said:

> We keep files of pictures to show when there is nothing else to show, truck shots down the aisles of supermarkets, wheat pouring into a boxcar, a slow zoom into the Capitol dome. I understand you have a word for this—eyewash—pictures that can go with any words . . . And then there are the graphics. Television is a visual medium, so there must be graphics, devices that give forth numbers and letters, and split screens, and zooms and starbursts, and insets and flipovers.
>
> I will give you a rule: A device can only enhance, and if there is nothing there in the first place, you can't enhance it.

Frank's remarks make interesting reading, especially when compared with Barrie Gunter's research, reported earlier in this chapter.

Summary

✔ 1. Type the story on standard-size sheets (8½ by 11 inch) of clean paper inserted vertically into the typewriter. Double-space all text using the split-page format and all caps or lower-case form as dictated by newsroom policy.

✔ 2. Each scene in the videotape and its running time must be typed into the video column on the same line of the text where it occurs (comes on the screen) and matches the narration.

✔ 3. Do not overwrite the text. The formula ''three words per second'' is a maximum and should be adjusted downward as the individual circumstances of your story and the situation dictate.

✔ 4. Sentences should be short, but vary the length for better listenability and copy ''flow.'' Avoid long, involved sentences with many words separating subject and verb, dangling modifiers, puzzling pronouns-antecedents, dependent clauses, compound constructions, and the like. Short words are better than long words.

✔ 5. Where ''keying'' is necessary, match the words to the pictures very carefully by counting words or timing them to the running time of the scenes, so that identification and descriptions of action match the visual material. You want the on-air person to be talking about what the audience is watching.

✔ 6. Do not state the obvious. The audience can see what the pictures are showing. Tell the audience what the visual material means, not what it shows.

✔ 7. Do not stop the picture flow with words (''shown here on the left''). Avoid making visual references unless it is absolutely essential to avoid misunderstanding or misidentification.

✔ 8. The text should complement the visual, but it also should be capable of standing by itself.

✔ 9. When the pictures (or sounds) are especially compelling, especially exciting, or especially dramatic, write so that the text anticipates this highlight by explaining its impact or significance, or by following it with a similar explanation—with silence (no text) artfully used to let the picture (or sound) speak for itself.

✔ 10. When the visual or sound material is especially strong, do not try to jam too many words on top of it. The audience will be concentrating on the interesting visual material, and you will not be able to punch a lot of facts through that concentration.

✔ 11. Read your text aloud as you type it. The style of the writing should approach the conversational. Write the way people talk. Avoid jargon and stuffy wording; use action verbs and descriptive adjectives and adverbs. Try to match the mood, pace, and tone of the visual material; avoid words that are stonger than the visual.

✔ 12. Keep the text lean and loose. Give the audience time to see *and* listen.

Producing and Delivering the News with ENG

8

It is axiomatic that technological change dictates organizational and operational change. At the BBC in England, the editors used to call the news-gathering function "the intake department." Over the years they dictated that this function should not be confused with the production function. "Intakers" should be concerned with getting the news from where it happened to the people who will shape it into understandable messages. They should not be concerned with what happens to the raw material in the processing of it.

Today it seems dangerous to apply this as an analogy to what reporters and camera crews do in the field as compared to what editors, writers, producers, and ENG coordinators do in the newsroom. ENG provides speed; that speed has knocked down the walls of many compartments.

Reporters and remote crews have two kinds of time: quick time, when the live tape or live report must air as fast as possible, and extra time, the chance to get more depth into the stories and to stay at the story location to report the latest developments up to and during a newscast. For those inside the news operations, ENG technology has meant dealing with expanded news horizons and content in what turns out to be about the same amount of preparation time. Newscasts are longer; more air time means more room for more material. There is more visual volume, more raw material to digest. There is more of everything except minutes on the clock in which to get the raw material ready to go on the air.

Therefore, editorial control becomes more important. No matter how large or small the staff may be, the jobs of those who gather the news and those who bring it together and put it on the air are intimately linked. Television news is no place for loners. Of all forms of journalism, putting together a newscast is the most team oriented. Whether it is a one-minute update, a local insert in the morning network news programs, a thirty-minute or sixty-minute dinner-hour local news, or a three-

FIGURE 8-1. Ann Compton, ABC News Correspondent. *(Courtesy Donna Svennevik/ABC News.)*

hour extravaganza in a major market, the way the teamwork goes determines how successful the newscast will be.

At a conference on press responsibility conducted by the Gannett organization, then ABC News White House correspondent and veteran Washington reporter Ann Compton gave an insight into the world of television news on two different levels—local and national.

She said:

> When I started out in Roanoke, Virginia—back in the Third World of television news . . . I often thought up the story, drove myself there [and] on rare occasions picked up the silent camera and shot the cover footage myself.
> I screened the film, often did the splicing myself, wrote the lead-in for the anchorman and then went back and rewrote the whole process for the 11 P.M. news later that night. . . . I never felt more creativity than I did back in those days; it is far less creative at the network level. . . . Where I had real impact and felt the greatest sense of responsibility was reporting for a local station covering half the state of Virginia.*

Correspondent Compton said it is much different at the network level.

> . . . When I do a minute-and-fifteen-second spot on "ABC World News Tonight," consider the cast of characters that goes into putting that spot together. There are three network correspondents for ABC, NBC, and CBS working at the White House each day; there are two full camera crews and a lighting technician. There is a research staff

*Quoted in "Editing in the 80's," Part V, *The Gannetteer*, March 1982.

back in our [bureau] with computer access to a myriad of clippings and resources that we need in putting together, for instance, a spot on the unrest in Poland.*

And other members of the team are at work.

There is at least one producer back in the shop who does nothing all day but screen all the video that might go into my spot, be it from our library files in New York, be it stuff that we've shot today and have sent back to the office, or be it things sent in from our affiliates or our bureaus across the country.

There is one senior producer in Washington who not only screens my script but coordinates to make sure that I do not step on the toes of any other correspondent.

There is one desk editor who does nothing but read the wires and concentrate on the other news sources that are commenting on Poland so I can have access to all the information I should on the story.

There is one videotape editor who puts my pictures together so they don't look like a patchwork quilt but instead flow from one scene to another.

There are two senior editors who review my script and fit it in with the total lineup of "World News Tonight."

And there is an anchorman who more often than not writes his own lead-in to my script. . . . The strength of that lead-in often enhances the value or quality of the spot.†

Ann Compton's account of her team vividly shows the difference in staff size and responsibility between small market stations and a network. It is obvious that there is an economy of scale at work. In the small station where Ann began the levels of responsibility were few in number; the reporter served as reporter, photojournalist, editor, and writer. Editorial and content control was firmly placed on her shoulders. At ABC News she has a large number of people helping her and supervising her coverage.

Even in the Roanoke station it is a good bet that today more people are involved in producing the news than when she was there. The emergence of ENG is part of the reason.

NEWSROOM STRUCTURE AND OPERATIONS

Whether the work is done inside or outside, it begins, expands, and results in a final product in a newsroom. There news directors, assignment editors, producers, video editors, writers, reporters, photojournalists, and technicians come together to "manufacture" the product. A hierarchy is aimed at maintaining a chain of command.

At the top is the news director, sometimes a vice president for news. He or she establishes and runs the budget, hires and fires, and has the ultimate responsibility for everything that goes into and comes out of that news operation. He or she is hired or fired by the station's general manager. The successful news director today

*Ibid.
†Ibid.

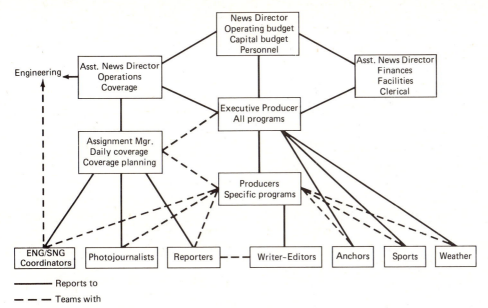

Engineering

| Reports to
- - - | Teams with

FIGURE 8-2. The newsroom team. This organization structure is typical for a medium-size newsroom. While the news director and his or her assistants are in overall command, this structure puts heavy responsibilities on the assignment desk and the producers who plan and manage the coverage and news program production.

is one who can handle the budget, supervise the operation so that it turns out quality (and popular) news programs, and motivate the staff. News directors today say you should study economics, business practices, technology, journalism, and especially, they say, how to get that motivation—what the coaches endlessly call "momentum." As one news director said, "Some days I think I should have majored in abnormal psychology."

Next in authority are assistant news directors, producers, and assignment managers or editors. They are in charge of the operational functions. They are expected to direct the hour-by-hour, minute-by-minute news gathering, preparation, and production. If there is more than one assistant news director, they may have specific assignments like budget control or supervision of technical liaison with the engineering department along with operational supervision.

The Assignment Desk

At the heart of any news operation is the assignment desk. Here sits the linchpin figure: the assignment editor or manager. He or she is supported by people with titles such as news manager and managing editor, and by ENG and SNG coordinators. A station's news-gathering success is keyed to the successful functioning of the assignment desk. The desk is the main source of coverage planning and execution. Its personnel maintain sometimes elaborate files on news stories that are coming up, sources, and where they can be quickly located. It also keeps a lookout for new angles on breaking stories and follow-ups on continuing stories. Its personnel, in sum, must know what has happened, what is happening, and what is going to happen.

The speed with which stations can and must react to news and deliver the cov-

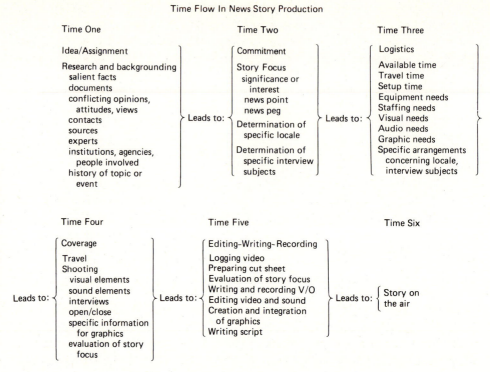

Time Flow In News Story Production

Time One		Time Two		Time Three
Idea/Assignment		Commitment		Logistics
Research and backgrounding		Story Focus		Available time
salient facts		significance or		Travel time
documents		interest		Setup time
conflicting opinions,		news point		Equipment needs
attitudes, views	Leads to:	news peg	Leads to:	Staffing needs
contacts		Determination of		Visual needs
sources		specific locale		Audio needs
experts				Graphic needs
institutions, agencies,		Determination of		Specific arrangements
people involved		specific interview		concerning locale,
history of topic or		subjects		interview subjects
event				

Time Four		Time Five		Time Six
Coverage		Editing-Writing-Recording		
Travel		Logging video		
Shooting		Preparing cut sheet		
visual elements		Evaluation of story focus		Story on
sound elements	Leads to:	Writing and recording V/O	Leads to:	the air
interviews		Editing video and sound		
open/close		Creation and integration		
specific information		of graphics		
for graphics		Writing script		
evaluation of story				
focus				

FIGURE 8-3. A television news story requires a great deal of planning that sometimes has as much to do with the logistics and mechanics of the medium as it does with the subject matter of the story itself. However, all of these elements must be taken into consideration for the story to make it onto the air.

erage puts a great deal of pressure on the assignment desk. Yet there is more to it—the human factor. Assignment managers must be psychologists, too. Since they are the people who are most frequently in touch with the news-gathering personnel, they have to be motivators. To get the most effort out of the staff they must know the strengths and weaknesses, the likes and dislikes, fears and foibles, even the personal relationships between staff members.

If your first professional assignment is as an assistant on the assignment desk, it is a good place to be because you will be in the center of the action. It's a good place to start before you move on to being a reporter or photojournalist or video editor, since you will get a better knowledge of the whole news operation. If you aspire to be a producer, it is *the* place to start.

The Producers

Producers are very important people. At the top is an executive producer in charge of the content, order, news judgment, and production of all news programs. Then come line producers—the 6 P.M. producer, for example. In larger operations there may be segment producers who have responsibility for perhaps a portion of a lengthy newscast, or the live inserts in a newscast, or a particular special report or department within a newscast. Then come assistant producers and production assistants who work for producers in a wide variety of tasks.

The producer's role in TV news is closer to that of the managing editor of a newspaper than to that of the producer of a motion picture or a Broadway musical. Producers in the entertainment business—that's where the title comes from—buy scripts, hire actors, rent the theater or sound stage, and gamble that the show they are putting together will make a lot of money for the investors and themselves.

News producers are commanders, directors, managers, organizers, and, above all, journalists. They make most of the news and production judgments. They have a lot to say about what stories are covered, how they are covered, and who covers them. They decide the order of the program and the amount of time allotted to each element in it. They often do a lot of the writing, particularly copy for anchors involved in a news special with a lot of live inserts, or live coverage of a breaking story. They take or get the blame when things go wrong or wrong decisions are made. It is a truism that if the program goes well the anchors and reporters get the credit. If it goes badly, no matter what the reason, the producer gets the blame.

What every news program producer is trying to do is provide a mix—hard news, features, consumer information, life-style elements, editorial opinion, special segments, weather, and sports—that will give the audience a satisfying package of information, even a little entertainment. They want to leave the viewers with the feeling that they have seen and heard about most of the events that have happened in their community that day.

The producer is another linchpin figure in the TV newsroom. A Washington news vice president said: ''I give my producers a great deal of power and responsibility. If something goes wrong I don't call the anchor, I call the producer. I expect them to have all kinds of news judgment and to be in command of everything.''

A Columbus news director: ''I have a lot of arguments with my producers about news judgment. Some of them are so production oriented that they sometimes obscure the content with the production flash. That bothers me. . . . There is some truth to the claim that we have to be as clean and fast paced as the entertainment programs we compete against. But, the successful producer in the long run is the one who . . . [can] control the production elements [to] enhance the story telling, not overwhelm it. That takes judgment and it has got to be in the direction of the journalism.'' A news consultant based in New York thinks the new technology has given the producers a lot more power along with a heightened need to stay on top of the processing of the raw material. ''They are at the end of the pipeline . . . they control what goes out . . . so they've got to be able to watch the material as it comes in, and then control what is done with it. . . . They must be there all the time shaping the content, checking it for accuracy, completeness, aptness, and deciding how it fits into the rest of the newscast.''

It's both hurry up and wait. ''You have to be able to wait for later developments,'' says the news director of a New York network-owned station, ''then push for the deeper coverage ENG and SNG can provide. The producer has to be capable of directing a change to add new material 10 minutes before airtime or right in the middle of the story.''

Flexible and firm in Chicago: ''They've got to organize things quickly, and be flexible and firm at the same time. It's the rule now to hold off until the latest fact is in, then commit. And for the 10 P.M. program, they've got to be able to think 'new.' What new things can we do to this story to make it better, fuller, and more satisfying for those who also saw it at 6 P.M?''

A juggler of facts and splash in San Francisco: ''They have to juggle more balls in the air at the same time. The first thing is to take care of the information content. Yet, you can have the best information in the world and if the program has a lot of production errors people will tune away. It's a tough balancing act between content and production values.''

Producers are also at the center of any live reports. While the most exciting live reports are those that interrupt other programming to bring the audience running coverage of a breaking story, most live reports come in regularly scheduled newscasts. These then can be called ''planned live.''

For example, at the regular morning editorial conference a decision is made to do a live insert from City Hall, where an important council committee will be debating a major decision. The best estimate is that the committee will vote in favor of it, and that that vote will come shortly before the 6 P.M. news begins. But at the editorial conference it is also decided that the live report will include pretaped material covering other angles. These include:

The impact of the decision on the area of the city most affected

How the city's action may affect a bill now going through the state legislature

The impact of the action on the political futures of city officials

Other reporters are assigned to work up material on these angles. At 6 P.M., the reporter is live at City Hall announcing the committee decision. He or she includes the pretaped packages on the other angles within the report. This is called a ''live wrap.''

Putting these live wraps into the regularly scheduled program is tangled with problems for the producer. He or she may have constructed a tightly timed program that now becomes a ticking bomb. The reporter must be able to tell the story quickly and concisely within a given time limit. Interviews may run too long. Getting the pretaped material into the live wrap calls for precision in the control room. If the report is to include questions and answers between the studio anchors and the field reporter, they must go back and forth crisply. No matter who goofs, the responsibility rests right on the producer's shoulders.

What counts the most is the producer's ability to keep firm control at a time when being flexible leads to either success or disaster. A Boston news director tells us just how important that ability is: ''Live means less control. The producers are in charge, but someone else has that segment of the program in their hands.''

In Detroit: ''There is a much bigger chance to make a wrong decision when you are live. Those who make too many wrong decisions aren't producers for very long. Like quarterbacks, their pass completion average is the thing they live or die by.''

In Minneapolis: ''Live makes the programs really difficult to plan. No longer can they say, 'This story will be one minute thirty-three seconds with a seventeen-second lead-in!' It must be engraved in stone somewhere that no live report ever ran short. . . . Producers must be ready to rebuild the program one minute before air time or put it back together in some coherent form [if something goes wrong] during the program.''

An executive producer in Los Angeles says that live inserts have made the news programs free form. "The producer knows that he or she will have some of this and some of that, but only a tentative idea about how long each of those is going to be. They've got to plan on what they can drop or add but still get everything in. . . . People who can do it and have it make some sense . . . and still come out on time . . . are gems."

Executive producers have the real power. They oversee the operations of the producers and the programs or program segments they produce. They also supervise the news-gathering activities, the staff, the content—everything.

Some are more executive than others. In Minneapolis an executive producer claimed he was at home in time for dinner almost every night. In Los Angeles an executive producer is awakened by his clock radio, which is tuned to an all-news radio station. He makes some phone calls to his assignment desk even before he gets out of bed to determine how his station's coverage plans are progressing. As he eats breakfast he watches his station's morning news reports and makes some more phone calls. As he drives to work he listens to the morning network news programs and his station's local inserts on a specially equipped car radio that can tune to the audio portions of the local TV channels.

Throughout the day he barks, cajoles, grumbles, molds the activities of the staff and the content of the news by close supervision of every phase of the day's work. Then, when the dinner hour news is over, he holds a meeting to talk about what will happen on the late evening news and the next day.

Told about those calm, at-home dinners his Minneapolis counterpart enjoys, he said, "I don't believe it for a minute; they must not have ENG yet."

Technicians and Technical Coordinators

Also in and around the newsroom are the technicians. Usually they report to the head of the engineering department, not the news director, so excellent liaison between the two departments is crucial to smooth operation of the technology they oversee. The engineers are vitally interested in the quality of the pictures and sound going out to the audience. The journalists are vitally interested in the clarity and understandability of the content of those pictures and sound.

It does no good to have fuzzy pictures and sound that people can't see or hear, just as it does no good to have stories that are so badly written and edited that the audience can't understand what the news program is trying to communicate. Both the engineers and the journalists must have as their primary goals the highest technical and content quality that can be achieved.

The number of people who work on the two sides trying to achieve these goals varies with station size. And station size and union jurisdictions vary the things that journalists can do in terms of operating the technology. In smaller stations the journalists may be able to operate cameras, video editors, and even play back of tapes into newscasts. In larger markets the union contracts may dictate that technicians will run the machines while the journalists tell them what content is desired.

Some of the division of labor depends on where that labor is being performed. You can usually count on technicians running the machines in the station's control

a

FIGURE 8-4. Many TV newsrooms don't look much different from a newspaper newsroom or a large central office. The staff of WTHR, Channel 13 in Indianapolis, gets ready for another dinner-hour news program *(a)*. But the place where the assignment desk and producers work tells you where you are *(b)*. This nerve center monitors coverage, editing, incoming video signals, police and fire calls, and the progress toward air time that the staff is making. *(Courtesy of WTHR-TV, Indianapolis.)*

b

rooms and technical areas. That is their domain, their turf, and you risk at the least sharp words and perhaps outright banishment if you start to fool around with their switches, buttons, dials, scopes, switchers, special effects, and the like without first asking permission. It can take hours to get a control room back to normal function after some curious (and ignorant) person has wandered around turning things on, off, up, down, open, closed, twiddling, and tweaking. Most engineers like to operate like aircraft commanders—with preflight checks and all switches in the proper position. They do not take kindly to fiddlers, and no one would want to have it any other way.

In the field, the divisions become somewhat more logical. Here technicians will certainly be running the most sophisticated parts of the gear. While the photojournalists make the pictures and sound and the reporters get the facts and report them, the technicians get the mobile equipment up and running and keep their eyes on the dials. Yet automation and computerization are coming along rapidly and in the future you may find equipment that almost anyone can run.

What the engineers also do—and with ENG it is essential—is maintain the equipment. Here their skills are vastly different from those of the journalists. The machines we use are highly complex. They do break down, and except for some basic field trouble-shooting procedures anyone can learn, fixing them is an engineering job. That requires special training, thousands of dollars worth of test equipment, and a good supply of replacement parts.

One of the most frustrating things about ENG gear is that it usually starts its decline with a partial failure—some function unexpectedly stops, but only for a split second. By the time you have said, ''Hmm?'' the thing is working again. That split-second failure probably will not repeat itself when you report the problem to the maintenance folks, and the equipment will operate perfectly as soon as an engineer gets it on the test bench. Then, of course, the same problem will develop the next time you are in the field.

Although it is hard to imagine, what you and the engineers really would like is for the machine to fail totally. As one technically minded friend said, ''What I really like is to see smoke—not a lot of smoke, but a little. When something smokes you can usually find the burned place so it is much easier to spot the problem and fix it.''

Nobody really wants smoke. Most well-run stations have a preventive maintenance program designed to keep the equipment operating at peak efficiency. That will go a long way toward catching problems before they become problems. The broadcast journalist can help a lot if he or she will do three things religiously:

1. Follow the procedures set by the engineering department for operating the equipment.
2. Respect the equipment and treat it gently.
3. Report problems immediately.

ENG/SNG Coordinators

This brings us back to teamwork. Between technologists and journalists is a growing group of people who are called ENG coordinators. They provide the operational liaison between the engineering and news departments. They see to it that the needed facilities are ordered from the engineering department, plan facilities' use, innovate ways to use ENG and satellite technology for news gathering and production, and supervise and monitor its use when ''on line.''

When news is breaking the ENG coordinators are right in the middle communicating in two directions: to the engineers and to the editors and producers. During less dramatic times the ENG coordinators work on crew and technician scheduling, assignment of editing rooms and equipment, monitoring production flow, and technical planning for future remote coverage.

Portrait of an ENG Coordinator   In San Francisco, Al Topping is an ENG coordinator who lives a frenzied and what seems to be a very romantic life. He wears cowboy boots and a fringed leather jacket. He has a jeep for getting around on the ground, and he frequently goes up in the helicopter to see how things are going from the air. He has an unquenchable thirst for getting the news on live, and first.

He likes two parts of his job better than the others: riding the microwave system during a newscast, and planning live remotes that beat the competition.

"My job," he says, "is to embarrass the competition by doing it first, fast, and better. I like to get outside and follow the crews. They work better when they know I may show up in my jeep anywhere, anytime.

"We may have as many as eight or nine live shots during any day. The key elements as to whether we use live ENG are time and the size of the story. That decision is based on the distance we'd have to travel to get it and get it back, and whether using the ENG as a delivery system will get it back in time for a news program."

Topping is a true child of the technology. "I really like to ride that microwave system during a broadcast. We might have those eight or nine live shots planned but we've only got six microwave towers on the tops of the mountains. So sometimes we have to use the same tower antenna for two different stories, and they may be back to back.

"I'm right there in the hot seat, talking to both ends. It gives me a great sense of power to sit in the control room and call the shots, especially when one story is on the air, and the next one is coming in from the same relay tower. [When that happens] we can't see in advance whether the picture for the second story is ready. It's a thrill when they both work."

It may be a thrill to Topping, but such a ragged-edge approach is not often appreciated by others in the control room.

"You know," he muses, "there are not a lot of directors who can take this. What you need is a bright kid with the reaction time of a pro quarterback, and who is dumb enough to take a remote picture live if I tell him it's going to be there. Older directors who've been burned wouldn't do it, but our guys do, and we don't miss too many of them."

The next best thing Topping likes to do is the planning that results in good coverage. Good planning as to locations for cameras and crews and their mobile units can do a couple of things, he says. "It can let you get the story without 'getting into' the story. And it can protect your people.

"We had excellent coverage of the demonstrations which followed the sentencing of White [the man who was convicted of killing San Francisco mayor Moscone]. We did it without getting into the story or getting anyone hurt. Another station in town had a crew beaten up because they were too close and too vulnerable."

Topping's plan called for a series of short microwave relays over the top of a tall building and down into a parking lot on the other side so that the news van was well away from the demonstrators.

But Topping is proudest of his plan for the coverage of the release of Patty Hearst from prison. It involved landing a helicopter on top of a mountain in a snowstorm.

FIGURE 8-5. A control room that puts the programs on the air. In KARE-TV's control room all of the technology comes together to meld the pictures and words of the anchors in the studio with all of the videotape, microwave, satellite feeds, special effects, digital graphics, and the appropriate sounds that go with them into an on-time, high-quality, error-free production. KARE-TV, Minneapolis, Minnesota. *(Courtesy of Television/Broadcast Communications Magazine.)*

His eyes glittering brightly, Topping said, "That helicopter was used as a microwave tower to get the signal back to the station. We were the only ones who got the story live. It was like a war operation."

Those coordinators who handle SNG work with their satellite crews, trucks, and satellite control points. It is likely that today Topping would have used a satellite mobile unit on top of that mountain instead of the helicopter, and the link would have been made more easily.

Studio and Control Room Personnel

We have one more place to look into on our tour. That's the studio and control room from which the news is aired. Sometimes the "studio" is actually part of the newsroom itself. The anchor desk and the visual area behind the anchors' seats, the weather production area, and all the lighting instruments that go with it may be over in one part of that newsroom. When programs go on the air, cameras and their TelePrompTer™ rigs and related equipment are wheeled in or brought out of storage and the newscast comes from the newsroom. Some stations that use newsroom sets or that do live remotes from the newsroom arrange things so that the activities of the news staff become the background. If that's the case the people shown in the background should be on their best behavior. Reading a newspaper or eating a bologna sandwich doesn't portray the kind of intensity the audience expects.

More traditionally the studio is in a separate location. It contains a huge news set—they get more elaborate design and graphic attention all the time. Studio cameras, TelePrompTers™, the weather area with radar screens, keying screens, perhaps an interview area, are all permanently lit to provide the best pictures possible.

You may see more technicians. Camera operators stand behind their charges and move them, zoom, focus, pan and tilt on command over the intercom from the director in the control room. You may see a TelePrompTer™ operator who keeps the script moving at the proper location and speed so the anchors can read it smoothly while seeming to look right at the audience. You may see lighting technicians who adjust the instruments and their brightness, but that is usually done beforehand.

Larger stations certainly will have a floor director, who provides cues and human support for the anchors. The floor director is a very important person. He or she takes commands from the control room director and relays them to the on-air talent. The relay will be made by hand signals when the studio is "live," or by terse voice commands during the playing of a tape or commercial: "A minute thirty to the end . . . commercial coming up, speed up . . . slow down . . . wipe the sweat during the next tape segment . . . calm down . . . wake up. . . ."

A floor director with whom one of the authors worked killed a rat once by stomping on it with all the aplomb of a maître d' while the program went on without pause. Be nice to the floor director if you are going on the air; one who is not your friend can do all sorts of subtle things to ruin your concentration.

Through a door, or perhaps farther down the hall, is the control room. In here are the people who get that news program on the air. Some technicians run the audio board, turn microphones off and on, ride levels, play back audiotapes, and so on. Others will run the video switcher and perhaps the character generator. Still others will supervise the electronics, control the quality of the pictures from the studio cameras, play back videotape packages, switch to the microwave, the satellite, or whatever.

The star of the control room is the newscast director. He or she and the technicians who run it preside over a massive switcher through which goes all video, studio or remote. The switcher also provides all special effects, simple or elaborate. The director takes the program script and directs the technicians, studio crews, and on-air talent through the program. The director gives orders for any function to be carried out:

> Roll opening tape . . . dissolve to camera 1 . . . cue George . . . camera on Jane . . . take 2 . . . roll VTR 18 . . . take VTR . . . stand by, remote one, we're coming to you in 5, 4, 3, 2, . . . take remote one . . . stand by, camera one . . . stand by, George, for crosstalk to remote . . . stand by squeeze zoom . . . stand by, Quantel . . . stand by, black . . . go to black. . . .

On the director's shoulders rests all of the responsibility for a smooth, clean production—one without awkward pauses while a VTR rolls through the countdown; one without the wrong camera on the air; one with everything coming up at the exact second it's needed. Directors need strong nerves and quick reaction time.

They need to be able to read a script, watch all the pictures, listen to the audio, watch the clock, give the studio crew and anchors instructions, get new instructions from the producer and pass them on, anticipate the next action, and join the network program following the news without missing a beat.

PLANNING THE NEWSCAST

Now that you've had your tour it is time to look at how newscasts get put together and on the air.

The planning of a newscast begins long before air time. Parts of it may be set up days before. Other segments may come from special assignment reporters or special units of the news operation that have been assigned investigative stories, series, consumer affairs, and features. Regular weather and sports segments have been blocked in for approximate lengths. Of course, it will contain coverage of the scheduled events and the breaking news of that particular day. And commercials—never forget those.

Syndicated Services

Some of the news content may come from outside sources. Each of the three national networks has jumped into SNG to create a service for its affiliates. ABC calls it NewsOne and its system Absat; CBS has NewsNet; and NBC operates Skycom. The idea is for the network newsrooms and bureaus to act as collecting points for video and sound coverage from the network intake and from the network affiliates' efforts. Then this material is fed to the affiliates on the network satellite links. In the ABC and CBS systems there are a number of feeds of national and regional video stories each day at scheduled times. When there is a major story breaking the network systems can pick up affiliate coverage and send it out on a spot news basis. The satellite links can be used for unilateral coverage by or between affiliates.

Also, many stations subscribe to other syndicated services that, for a fee, provide a huge variety of news and features. These include special material about health, handling money, hobbies, commentary—almost anything people are interested in. Stations that are members of broadcast groups often exchange stories among stations in the group. Others make arrangements with cable news services to take material from them and share their own coverage in return. Or stations may have their own regional or national bureaus. Now that satellite transmissions are a regular activity for stations all over the country, getting a news story of interest to the local audience from some distant point is much easier and more economical. For more on this, see Chapter 11.

The News Hole

At the beginning of a news day a newscast is very much like the dummy of a newspaper or a magazine. The ads have been sold and are laid out. What is left, the *news hole,* is blank, waiting to be filled in by editors and producers. The size

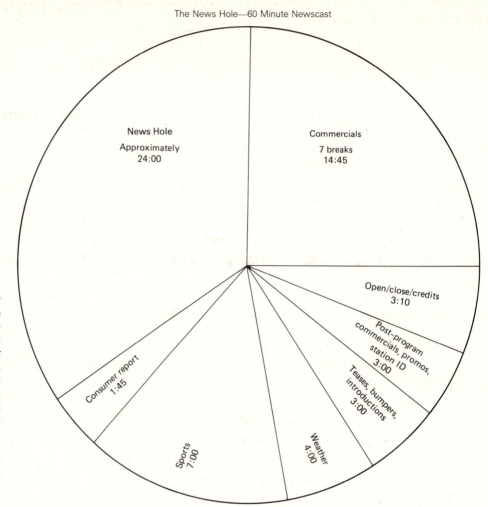

The News Hole—60 Minute Newscast

News Hole
Approximately
24:00

Commercials
7 breaks
14:45

Open/close/credits
3:10

Post-program
commercials, promos,
station ID
3:00

Teases, bumpers,
introductions
3:00

Weather
4:00

Sports
7:00

Consumer report
1:45

FIGURE 8-6. Every second counts in the news hole for a typical 60-minute television newscast. After all of the production elements, such as the opening and closing, bumpers, teases, and introductions, and the commercials are subtracted from the total time, slightly more than 32 minutes is available for news, weather, and sports.

of the TV news hole varies with the number of commercials and the length of the program. However, it is quite rigid. At the networks some 22 to 23 minutes of time is available. For a local station with a thirty-minute newscast the news hole can be much smaller after the time for the weather and sports is blocked out. In an hour news program there may be about 32 to 35 minutes of news space or quite a bit less; again it depends on the amount of commercial time sold and regular content and production features.

The Editorial Meeting

Whatever the amount of time, the specific planning usually starts early in the news day. There is an editorial conference attended by the news director, executive producer or designate who runs the meeting, producers, the assignment desk, reporters, ENG/SNG coordinators, and sometimes the photojournalists. Here the previously

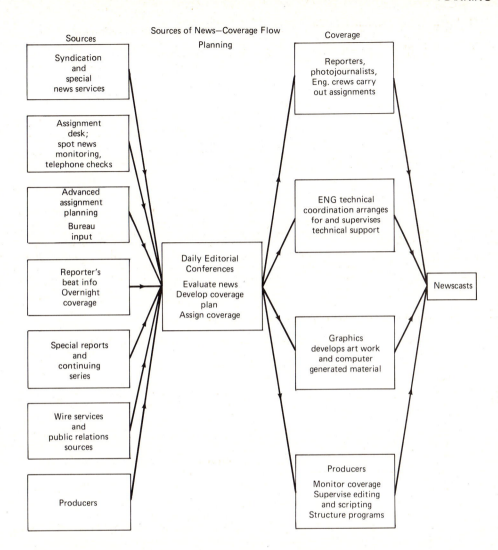

FIGURE 8-7. Coverage flow. Ideas for news stories and other elements in a newscast come from a wide variety of sources as the day begins. In most stations these ideas flow into and out of the daily editorial conferences. Then the staff gets to work to gather, edit, and produce newscasts that will contain a mixture of the most important, significant, and interesting information available.

scheduled material, the news opportunities, the continuing series, and a more exact time for weather and sports are blocked out. Whoever runs the meeting expects the others both to bring hard material—stories, segments, series that are or will be ready to run—and to contribute to general discussion of how scheduled stories and breaking news will be covered.

There usually is a good bit of give and take in which the roles of the producers, news managers, and assignment editors are crucial. The assignment desk has been setting up the day's activities. Its editors will have a list of story possibilities, follow-ups, new angles, and other coverage plans, in a relatively detailed form. This list is often called the "outlook" report. It grows out of the extensive advance files the desk keeps—wire service reports, newspaper clippings, publicity releases, notes from beat reporters and the planning staff, and suggestions from the staff at all levels. The desk editors also watch the competition's news programs, get telephone tips, viewer reactions, and brainstorms from almost anyone. They also know what coverage has already taken place overnight and during the early morning hours and who is available for assignment.

The producers will have a similar list and may also have ideas about importance, news judgments, story length, and approach. The reporters who will be getting assignments will pitch in with other ideas and suggestions. Reporters with regular beat assignments will add comments about possibilities from their beats.

When this meeting breaks up the result should be a plan for the day's coverage and clear knowledge of who is to be where and how the coverage is to be carried out. The assignment desk then prepares a more detailed outlook report and probably a "troop movements" report, copies of which go to all concerned. The producers begin to sketch in a tentative rundown for their newscasts. Reporters, photojournalists, and crews take off to get their jobs done.

Because there will be a number of newscasts during the broadcast day, a similar, though shorter, meeting for those involved in the late evening news may take place later on. Here staffers just coming to work go over what has been planned and look for further opportunities for coverage later in the day.

Coverage Management

Meanwhile, the assignment desk personnel are at work carrying out the coverage plans. This involves a number of activities that go on at the same time. They include liaison with the producers, reporters, editors, and the ENG/SNG coordinators or engineering department. If remote units are needed for a scheduled story the orders for those probably will have been given as soon as the need was known. There are only so many mobile units and camera-tape crews available, so careful planning is a must.

Assignment desk editors undoubtedly have their own fantasies about what a perfect day would be like. That might be a day in which the entire staff is available, all facilities are working and available, there are enough people and facilities to meet all opportunities, and the planning has been so good that there are no surprises.

Chances are about ten million to one that such a day ever will happen. If it ever does someone will write it up. They will gain international fame lasting about as long as it takes for the diaries of dead despots to be unmasked as forgeries. The nature of news is that it happens when nothing and no one is available to cover it, at the wrong time, and in a place that is very difficult to get to. There is never enough equipment or staff to satisfy the needs on a busy day.

Shaping the Coverage   As the day goes on the time for the newscast gets closer with every tick of the clock. Now the producer's role becomes even more important. Some stories will turn out to be duds. New stories or better angles to planned stories will pop up. Since ENG and satellite delivery provide more flexibility for broadening and deepening coverage of planned stories, the producers will be thinking in this vein as the routine of getting the raw material in and processed goes on. They will be asking things like:

1. Does this story have another angle?
2. Have we got the right approach?

3. How does this story relate to the others in the newscast?
4. Has this story changed since we started?
5. What is interesting and significant about this story, and how can we take advantage of that?

They will also be on the lookout for new stories that are developing and revising their program plans as they come in. In fact, producers are constantly working with a rundown sheet, revising it, reordering it, and changing the program lineup as the news develops. (Fig. 8-8 shows a typical rundown sheet.) Some producers have developed rather exotic tools to help them in their newscast planning. Many use some sort of "menu board." It may be as simple as an inexhaustible supply of mimeographed forms with blank spaces where plans can be scribbled. Or it may be a more elaborate ring or hinged notebook with plastic-coated Magic Marker cards to write on and shuffle. Or it may be some Rube Goldberg contraption with slots into which typed story slugs can be inserted and rearranged. With computers and video display terminals this sort of "thinking man's rundown" process is at the producers' fingertips.

No matter what method is used, the producers are constantly evaluating the components that will go into the newscast. They monitor coverage carefully by talking with the reporters and photojournalists and by watching it as it comes in and is edited. They direct the script writing, voice-over narration, and use of special effects to enhance the meaning and production values, constantly shaping, revising. There are a lot of key questions:

1. Have we got it?
2. Have we got it right?
3. Are these the important angles?
4. Is it clear? pictures? words? graphics?
5. Is anything missing?
6. What can we do about that?
7. If live coverage is involved will what we planned work?
8. If it doesn't what can we do?
9. Is what we plan to do with production elements appropriate?
10. What else can we do to make sure this is interesting, significant, *and* understandable?

Many producers seem to spend most of their day going around the newsroom looking as though they were balancing the world on one shoulder and the universe on the other while suffering from a terribly stiff neck. But don't get the idea that they are alone in the process. A great deal of discussion takes place in the newsroom. In fact, how well the producer communicates the ideas he or she wants is one of the important factors in personal success and getting the program on the air in its best form.

In any command situation communicating with those who carry out the orders is usually as important as, if not more important than, issuing the orders themselves. The end result is the program itself. Nothing has been accomplished by the coverage plans, or their results if the program doesn't work. What has been gathered together should become a mix of interesting, significant, informative, illuminating, well-ordered video stories, readers, special segments, that use crisp, clear writing, graphics, and meaningful and appropriate production values to make it work.

ORGANIZING THE NEWSCAST

By now air time for the newscast is rushing closer and it is time to bring specific organization to the material which has been prepared. You won't see neat piles of script, video cassettes, and rundowns yet. In the crunch of getting the program on the air, editing and writing may continue right up to air time, and even while the program is actually on the air. But the producer is the person who must bring order out of the hurly-burly. Scores of things have to be checked and cross-checked and more orders given and carried out. There are story angles to sharpen, story focuses to clarify, the link between words and pictures to tighten, production elements to add or discard. Through all this *timing* is never out of the producer's mind.

The Rundown

The producer has been wrestling with the rundown virtually all day. That grand plan he or she had after the editorial meeting is probably a shambles. Stories that seemed to be lead material have turned out to be less important and significant. Other stories that seemed to have less strength now have become stronger. Breaking news may have become dominant.

What the producer has in front of him or her—version 1 or version 15—is a series of news segments that are established between commercial breaks. One or more of these segments will be reserved for sports. Another segment will contain the weather. Still another one may contain a special department of the newscast—Gripe Vine, an editorial, consumer affairs, commentary—that is a regular feature of the news program.

The Lead

Producers generally believe that selection of the lead story is a crucial decision. Journalistic tradition has had a lot to do with shaping this belief. Newspaper editors spend a lot of time deciding which story will get the main headline on page one and which other stories are important or significant or interesting enough to join it there. Much has been made of a comment attributed to Walter Cronkite that television news is a headline service. Cronkite also said that all of the words in a TV newscast would not fill the front page of a newspaper.

Too much has been made of this. On the one hand, TV news has made so much of the lead story decision that we have trained the audience to believe that the lead story is the most important story in the newscast.

On the other hand, a TV newscast is much different from the front page of a newspaper. While page-one editors try to get the important news on it, they also give a great deal of thought to the mix of stories that will go on it. Many want one or two major national or international stories, a major state story, a major local

```
NEWSCENTER 13 AT 6:00 FRIDAY 11/25/83                          6:00:00

SNEAK (TREE LIGHTING )(LAFAYETTE FATALS)(XMAS SHOPPING )(CARRIAGES ):30
NEWS OPEN  SKY REMOTE                                              :30


   1  Christmas Tree              vo-vtr/vtr CK window      H   mc   :20
   2  Tree Lighting Preview    GND-SKY-REMOTE/vtr CK window  J   rvw  1:30


   3  Lafayette Traffic Fatals    vo-vtr           (WIPE)   H   mc   :20
   4  Traffic Toll                vo-vtr                    H   mc   :20
   5  700 N. Goodlet Shooting Folo vo-vtr/start CK window   J   dw   :25
                                                 (WIPE)
   6  Harris Trial Advancer       vo-vtr                    J   dw   :20


   7  Christmas Shopping          REMOTE/pkg/vtr CK window  H   nr   1:45
   8  Tippecanoe Mall Shopping    pkg/vtr CK window         J   rvw  1:30
   9  United Christmas Service    vo-sot                    H   gp   :45
  10  Tree Lighting (FLOATING)  GND-SKY-REMOTE/start CK window  H  rvw  2:30
  11  Weather Preview Intro       3-Shot                    J        :10
  12  Weather Preview             vo-vtr                    B        1:00
  13  Sports Preview Intro        2-Shot/CK window          H        :10
  14  Sports Preview              vo-sot                    D        1:00
  15  Tease/Bump 1                vtr/font(HIGH FRONTIER )  J/H      :20
      1st Break
      1:00Marathon/:30Hooks/:05/:30Datsun/:05Awards                 2:10


  16  Soviet Missiles Reaction    vo-vtr/start CK window    J   mc   :20
  17  Pulse 1                     V9/font                   J   mc   :20
  18  High Frontier               pkg/V9 CK window          Hmc/jl   2:30
  19  Newsroom Update Intro       2-Shot/CK window          J/H      :10
  20  Newsroom Update WHITE HOUSE STATUS  vo-vtr            BRUCE    :30
  21  Deason/Shortened Sentence   vo-vtr                    H   mc   :20
```

FIGURE 8-8. The first half of a typical producer's program rundown. Each element of the program is listed in the order it will occur. The central column shows the production elements involved with that story: The story slugged Christmas Tree will include voice-over-videotape (v/o-vtr), and videotape played on the Chromakey™ window behind the anchors (vtr CK window). The right column indicates which anchor will handle each story, the reporter involved, and its running time. *(Courtesy of WTHR, Indianapolis, Indiana.)*

story, and a very interesting feature. They will also include pictures to illustrate some of the front-page stories, stories carried inside the paper, or sometimes just a very interesting picture that can stand alone. The newspaper editor thus selects and puts together a package of stories and pictures designed to catch and hold the attention of the reader regardless of what other parts of the paper the reader may move to, and to lead the reader to the inside pages.

The TV news producer is also a packager, but because of the way the audience receives the news from television—that key concept of structure and linearity—the packaging is done much differently. The TV viewer is not like the newspaper reader who can start anywhere and select anything throughout the paper. The viewer cannot stop the forward movement of the newscast or jump ahead or go back to something that has already been presented.

Therefore, the producer must construct the entire newscast with forward movement clearly in mind. The audience must follow along as the newscast progresses. While selection of the lead story is important, the effect of its selection is different. That decision does at least three things:

1. It gets the audience's attention.
2. It affects the content of the entire first segment.
3. It affects the content of subsequent segments.

Suppose, for example, that you are the producer and that you have two or even three major stories on a given day. One is a major development in the Middle East, another a major local economic story, the third the tragic death of a top rock star. There are those producers who would say you cannot make a mistake; any one will work. There are others who will go for the rock star story every time with the rationale that such a story can happen to the star only once. Still others will say that the local economy is more important than either of the other two. There will be those who opt for the Middle East story because of its peace-or-war, oil-or-no-oil, or U.S.–Soviet implications. And a few will say the death of a rock star is *never* as important as other more substantive local, national, or international stories. (Yet when Elvis Presley died, two of the three national networks led with it, and the murder of John Lennon got top play on all three. Both stories were also on page one of most newspapers.)

If you decided that the rock star story is your lead you certainly will get the audience's attention. And you certainly will have affected the way the first and subsequent segments go. Yet there are always people in the audience who don't care about rock stars no matter what happens to them, and who will think you are pandering to the lowest common denominator if you select that one over the other two. There are also thousands in the audience who do care and will be very interested in the story. The same thing can be said for the Middle East and the local economy; though the pandering charges may be dropped, new charges of being dull or repetitious may be added.

It is very dangerous to prescribe formulas, much less formats, for such decision making. This is because the moment they become doctrine or policy they also can lead to poor judgment. If the policy is that all newscasts will lead with a local story, what do you do on the day the president is shot or it looks like World War III has begun? At least the policy should be modified to read: All newscasts will lead with a local story—except when something else is more important.

Journalism texts spend a great deal of time with the characteristics of news judgment and toss around words like ''immediacy'' and ''propinquity.'' It is good to study these words even if it is just to learn what they mean. But at the risk of being simplistic, try these three words as guidelines for lead story decisions:

1. Significant

✔ **2.** Interesting

✔ **3.** Important

Some will quibble. They'll say significant and important are the same thing, but we contend that something can be important without being significant—though we will not argue that the opposite is true.

There are as many personally held theories about what constitutes a good lead story or the proper content of a newscast as there are producers. In his book *Newswatch: How TV Decides the News,* Av Westin, a vice president of ABC News, says there are three parts to his formula.*

✔ **1.** Is my world safe?

✔ **2.** Are my city and home safe?

✔ **3.** If my wife, children, and loved ones are safe, then what has happened in the past 24 hours to shock them, amuse them, or make them better off than they were?

Westin says that those are the questions the audience has in mind when it sits down to watch the news on television. He also says that stories in category three seldom take the lead position, though they do, he feels, belong in the newscast.

The Segments   No matter what lead story decision the producer makes, it affects the content of the rest of the first segment and the following segments. That is because the segments themselves must be structured just as the entire newscast must be structured. Each may be thought of as a small newscast within the larger one. Each carries the audience forward. Each makes up a part of the bigger structure of the entire program.

Although there are many variations that can be created, let's consider several commonly used segment categories:

1. National
2. International
3. Local
4. Topical
5. Geographical

The first three look very much like three segments of a newscast. You could say: "Aha! I will lead with the major local story, and the first segment will be all local news." Then you could move on to the national news, then international, then sports, weather, and the closing feature.

Nothing is particularly wrong with that newscast structure. You wouldn't want to do it in the same order every day, but it certainly is much better than a random selection of stories thrown at the audience without any attention to two other important concepts: logical order and logical progression.

*Av Westin, *Newswatch—How TV Decides the News* (New York: Simon and Schuster, 1982), pp. 62–63.

Your newscast should be orderly and linear. Some stories relate to each other. It is a good idea to look for and think about using these relationships even within categories as broad as national, international, and local. We know that the audience doesn't like to be bounced around through the news. Viewers become confused if the first story is about Congress, the next about the Japanese computer industry, the next about a storm in Kansas, the next about a new video game which is sweeping the country. Some of these stories may be related. Let's see what we can find. If the story about Congress has to do with raising trade barriers to the importation of Japanese computers, and the video game is made by the Japanese, then it might be good judgment to link these stories together. The story would have a *logical order,* and a good transition would provide a *logical progression*. Unless there is some wild angle to the Kansas storm story—if it destroyed the factory that manufactures the video games in the United States—it doesn't relate. And even if that unlikely angle was a part of the storm story, remember the operative word *logical*. Not all stories relate to each other no matter how hard you bend, mutilate, or twist them.

Watch out for categories that are too broad. It is often counterproductive to think of categories like national or international as boxes into which you can throw all the stories that occurred in the United States or all the stories that happened outside the country. Some of them won't fit into the box, no matter how big you make it.

So, let's look at topical and geographical for a different perspective. Here we immediately think of "cue words" like economy, labor, weather, crime, Latin America, the Far East, Canada. Here we often find some more useful relationships. When the anchor says, "In the local economy today," there is a geographical word and a cue word, "local" and "economy." We are setting up to use both *logical order* and *logical progression*. All the stories in this package should relate to the economy, and they should be local. Not all of them will be—nor should they be— pounded and squeezed so that they do. The links must be obvious and real. And remember what we said in Chapter 7 about a string of stories that are very similar— lack of audience attention can blur the details.

Stories that fit into a geographic zone often work well together. Sometimes they do not. If there is a series of stories out of Latin America that have to do with failing monetary systems there may be not only logical but also real relationships. A story or segment that brings these together and shows how the monetary policy of one country affects that of another and how United States monetary policy affects them all can bring much more understanding to the audience than a series of stories that does not explain and illustrate the relationships.

Sometimes the day's news brings a series of seemingly diverse stories from one geographic zone: a volcano here, a flood there, bad crops elsewhere. Here geography works with less effect. The topic—broadly—"nature" may be more useful. But, beware of too much cosmic topicality. The Four Horsemen of the Apocalypse syndrome—Death, War, Famine, and Pestilence—must be applied very carefully.

Some stories simply stand alone and no amount of examination will result in that blinding insight you hope for. What to do with them? Try these things:

✔**1.** If it is a very important story, especially if it's local, put it first, then go on to something else.

✔ **2.** If it has feature possibilities it might go last.

✔ **3.** Or if you get a tiny insight, put the story at the end of a segment.

✔ **4.** Put it together with some other "stand-alone" stories.

Level of Interest

Since the TV audience cannot be selective about what we give it, its only recourse when something uninteresting or insignificant comes along is to "tune out." The most drastic action viewers can take is to tune out literally—change channels or turn the set off. Usually they just turn off their minds.

The problem is made more complex by all of the distractions that can interfere with close attention to the news. The kids are underfoot. Dinner is being prepared. The neighbor is using that electric drill again. The phone rings. The folks in the next apartment are fighting. The TV news producer must try to arrange the order and progression of the program so that the highest level of interest is maintained throughout the program. The ideal would be that everyone paid attention all the time. That's impossible because the news program carries things some people aren't interested in, like sports, the markets, Flag Day at the elementary school, and parking problems for people who own three fancy cars.

We cannot force them to listen to and watch everything. But producers can do things with the order and progression of the program that will at least result in renewed interest.

✔ **1.** They can try to be sure that each segment begins and ends with a story that is interesting, if not significant.

✔ **2.** If they have "lead" stories that did not make *the* lead, they can use those stories to lead other segments.

✔ **3.** They can make wise use of features, particularly at the end of internal segments.

✔ **4.** They can look at the news value of sports, weather, and other departments and place those segments accordingly.

✔ **5.** They can divide up a major story, putting the primary elements at the beginning, coming back for details, sidebars, and other angles later.

✔ **6.** They can update major stories later in the newscast.

In looking at the order of the stories and the order of the segments of a newscast, one thing the producer should try to avoid like poison ivy is structuring the newscast in descending order of importance. Obviously no one would want to hold back the major news from the front of the program; that's what the audience tuned in for in the first place. But if the program is ordered from the most interesting or significant story to the least interesting or significant story, the interest level goes down from the beginning to the end. Halfway through the newscast the audience may have turned to other things.

Timing

One of the most important single factors in broadcast news is timing. Scheduled news programs start at a precise minute and second and end the same way. A seventy-second news update wedged into the prime-time evening schedule is just that—forty seconds of news headlines, and a thirty-second commercial. Nothing will wait for the end of that small news segment; it must begin and end precisely on time. If the program is thirty minutes or an hour in length that is all the time available.

Even then you really didn't have thirty minutes or one hour. Before anything else is done the time for commercials, the opening and the close, and "bumpers"—production transitions between news segments and commercials—must be subtracted. Other commercials, those sold adjacent to the newscast, come out of the total. For example, most news programs will be followed by at the least a thirty-second or one-minute commercial and a ten-second station break; that can cut the total amount of time available to 29:20 or even 28:50 right off the top.

The typical arithmetic for finding the actual amount of time available for news, weather, and sports in a thirty-minute time block looks like this:

30:00	
− 00:30	(adjacent commercial)
− 00:10	(station break)
− 06:00	(6 minutes of commercials)
− 01:00	(6 ten-second bumpers)
− 00:30	(length of program opening)
− 00:20	(length of program close)
20:00	

Without doing anything more than that, the producer has learned that there are only twenty minutes for news, not thirty. Then, take out the time for weather and sports—let's say 3:30 for each. That totals seven minutes, so now there are only thirteen minutes left for whatever amount of news a given day may bring.

The producer does the above arithmetic early in the day after checking the station program log to determine the number of commercials and subtracting the known length of the production elements, such as the bumpers and open and close. If it is a heavy news day, he or she has already told the sports and weather anchors they can have only three minutes, or 2:30, and listened to their screams with tolerance and firmness. Time gained is one to two minutes.

Now the trick is to fit the news into the fourteen to fifteen minutes available. Doing that is a major, continuous, and very precise task.

First, each story is given a tentative length when it is assigned. Reporters, writers, and tape editors are given a time frame within which to work. They are told, "Your story will be a major one; you can have two minutes, or two minutes fifteen," or "Forty seconds max!" or even "Twenty seconds, firm." These times are very tentative at this point since they are based on what the producer *thinks* the story is going to be worth even before it is covered. A lot of things can change.

Second, these tentative times are written in with the story slug on the first rundown of the day. They are transferred to new rundowns as those are developed.

Third, all times in the first rundown are added up to see whether the total comes anywhere close to reality. If it doesn't, some preliminary but drastic reassessment has to be made. Producers develop a rather precise feeling for approximately how many stories can fit in a thirty-minute or one-hour newscast and quickly get the knack of sketching out a reasonable estimate of what is possible within the time available. New rundowns are made, adjusting story order and length, as news gathering and processing continues.

Fourth, the newsroom peace-keeping negotiations begin. As new tentative times are assigned the noise level from protests gets higher. The producer must remain firm, but must also listen to legitimate arguments from reporters, writers, and editors who are putting forth reasons why their stories can't possibly fit in the smaller time frame given them. And the producer must keep on top of the stories as they are being processed to make sure the agreed-upon times are met.

Usually everyone wants more time, but if someone figures out a way to shorten a story it is good news to the producer, who must juggle both time and information. The important and significant facts and visual material must be in the story. Unnecessary details must come out. The news hole will not get bigger.

Fifth, the final program rundown is completed. Very precise timing is required at this stage. All the completed stories and those being finished up now have actual running times. These actual running times go on the final rundown and are totaled up. If it happens to be that one day in a year when everything goes just right, the total will match the total time available. If it isn't that day, further adjustments and fast decisions are called for. Stories may have to be dropped or added or changed from a story with video and sound bite to a voice-over read by the anchor. New scripts must be prepared to reflect all changes. Perhaps there is time for a quick video edit to take out a second sound bite. Perhaps the story can be moved to a later segment to give time for such an edit. Any of these changes alter the timing within the newscast and its total running time.

The producer can do three things to help keep accurate account of the time:

1. Add up the tentative time allocations as soon as a first rundown is made.
2. As the story times change from estimates to actual, adjust the total program time by adding or subtracting the difference between the two from the total program time.
3. As early as possible, learn to add or subtract minutes and seconds in your head.

It is very difficult to add a whole column of minutes and seconds without making a mistake. Mistakes made that way tend to become embedded in the rundown. The sensible thing to do is to add or subtract two numbers and then write down the difference after each computation.

For example:

Story	Estimated Time	Actual Time	Difference
Mayor	1:20	1:30	+10
County Fair	2:00	2:10	+10
Brush fire	:50	:45	−05

Obviously, the difference between the estimated time and the actual time has added fifteen seconds to the time available for stories so far. If all the changes have been subtractions rather than additions, twenty-five seconds have been gained. That is nice because it doesn't take long for a few seconds saved here, and another few saved there to add up to twenty to thirty seconds, time enough for an additional story or to add more details to a scheduled story. That is why so much attention is paid to compressing and tightening stories and segments.

The worst way to go about determining actual time as opposed to estimated time is to try to add all the estimated and actual times in two long columns of minutes and seconds—especially if you try to do that in a rush as air time gets closer. There are just too many chances for mistakes. Working with the subtotal of two figures and the gross difference between estimated time and actual time is much easier and more accurate. Of course, determining the timing should go on constantly; waiting until the last minute can lead to real disaster.

One other timing point the producer will want to know is the running time of the program as it plays on the air. Some stations have standard final rundown sheets that include all timing elements. One column shows the running time of each story, and another shows the running time of the program to that point. Stopwatch in hand, the producer can check off each timing point as it is met. If material has to be dropped or added, the decision can be made immediately.

One of those might look like this:

Event	Time	Running Time
Start	00:00	00:00
Open	00:20	00:20
Mayor	01:30	01:50
Fair	02:10	04:00
Fire	00:45	04:45
Bumper #1	00:10	04:55
Comml #1	00:60	05:55
Congress	01:20	07:15
U.N.	00:40	07:55
Space	02:00	09:55

And so on, through to the end of the program.

Backtiming

As a last check on the timing many producers switch to backtiming after the final program rundown is completed. This provides a security blanket that will help the producer assure that the program gets off the air on time.

Although there are many variations, the simplest backtiming method starts with determining from the station's program log the exact time the program is supposed to end—let's say 28:30 for a thirty minute program, or 58:10 for an hour-long newscast.

With that figure established and with the final rundown sheet in hand the producer begins by *subtracting* the time for each element of the newscast from the end time, moving *upward* from the bottom of the program rundown. Some producers backtime all the way to the beginning of the news program. Others pick an arbitrary point, say, the beginning of the last or next-to-last commercial break.

Backtiming thus gives producers a ''point of no return.'' If they find the program is running long or short at that point, they can either add or delete material, or tell the anchors to speed up or slow down so that the program comes out exactly at the time prescribed on the log.

A final note to this kind of arithmetic. It is a good idea for anyone who thinks he or she may become a producer to start practicing addition and subtraction of minutes and seconds in his or her head. At least one manufacturer makes a hand calculator that will do this, and computer terminals can be programmed to keep instant track of time. But if you rely on those crutches you may find that your hand calculator battery has run down, or you're away from your terminal when you most need to do your sums.

Bumpers, Teases, and Other Production Effects

Another part of the producer's mind has to focus on production elements of the program. Many stations use what are called ''bumpers'' between the news segments and the commercial breaks. These do several things. They act to tell the audience that there is a break and they can provide information.

Bumpers are usually designed to promote upcoming stories. They can be as simple as having the anchors say, ''We'll be back with more news after these messages,'' or the more curt, ''And now this. . . .'' Or they can be short segments that use some or all of the special effects from that elaborate switcher in the control room.

In most stations, the bumpers are standardized: a brief headline superimposed on the screen while the anchor reads the same words. Theme music may be added. More elaborate bumpers employ rolling video or still frames and animated graphics that whirl or flop words or pictures about upcoming stories. Some stations use bumper time to include more information such as markets, farm prices, the pollen count, commuter train schedule reports—tiny visual-only stories that will not be mentioned elsewhere.

There is not much difference between a bumper and a "tease" except that the tease is just that—written and produced to stimulate curiosity so that the audience will stay tuned in to see what the tease was about.

Producers are usually responsible for the writing and production of bumpers and teases. Bumpers should include information and should be written so that it is clear to the audience what is coming up after the commercial. If video from an upcoming story is to be included in the bumper, the scenes shown should be carefully selected so that they show a key element or a highlight of the story. Random video scenes from the story will not whet the appetite to see more or add information. If the bumper includes words on the screen—a headline—great care should be taken to assure that their meaning is clear. For example:

"Next, the End of the World?"

That is startling, all right, but the viewer may not see the question mark in the short time the phrase is on the screen.

How about:

"Next: Prices Going Up"

That's pretty routine, but if the story is about *farm* prices going up, the headline should say so.

Cleverness, style, and taste are a part of bumper production.

"Next: Futbol and Football"
"Coming Up: Skirts"

The first is clever, making the play on words. In Europe soccer is called, and often spelled, "futbol." So when there are both a soccer game and a football game in town and the next stories are about them, this bumper may cause a chuckle and be remembered. The second, presumably about the new fall fashions, is sexist and tacky.

Bumpers with video and production effects are often quite tricky to produce. They usually are put together as separate tape cuts and played back separately from the other video stories. Many stations purchase bumpers designed specifically for them by outside production houses. With the format designed to link with the design of the station's news set, program intros and endings, promos, and media ads, current information for specific newscasts can be added on a daily basis.

Keys, Windows, and Pictorial Graphics

Almost all newscasts make use of some kind of on-set graphic presentations. This is another producer responsibility, and the new technology has made this area bloom.

FIGURE 8-9. The key window. At WSAZ-TV, Huntington, West Virginia, the anchors report in front of a Chromakey™ window that is isolated at the back of the set. Any video source can be inserted into this space electronically so that it is combined with the picture of the news anchor, as the air monitor on the left shows. Other set designs incorporate the window into the set wall. *(Courtesy of WSAZ-TV, Huntington, West Virginia.)*

The simplest form of this is the traditional "window" behind and to either side of the anchors. Sometimes the set contains one window centered so that the anchors can sit on either side of it and it can be seen by the audience to the left or right of whichever anchor is speaking. In the old days, slides were projected from behind the set onto a translucent screen mounted in this window.

Today it is more likely that the window area is quite different. What happens, in its simplest form, is called chromakeying. The window is not a window at all. It is a part of the set wall with a frame around it, but in that frame is an opaque area painted or lighted green, or blue, or almost any color. With the control-room switcher set up to use the selected color for the **Chromakey**™, any other video signal can be electronically inserted into the broadcast picture in that space.

The additional video signal can come from a number of sources. It can be from another camera that is taking a picture of a graphic mounted on an easel in the studio, or from a slide projector in the control room. It can be moving video from a tape, or live video from a remote source. Or it can be one frame of video from a frame storer.

On the air the two video sources—the studio shot of the anchors in their set and the stills, frames, or video keyed into the window area—come together as one picture. To the audience it looks like the keyed material is actually in the window. In the studio all that is seen is the painted or lighted wall.

Some stations that do many live inserts arrange for the picture from the live remote to be projected into the window space so the anchors can see it. Others provide the combined picture on television monitors placed off the set so the anchors and weather anchors can see it there and seem to be talking about the picture in the window although they are really talking to a colored rectangle on the set back wall.

More elaborate electronics can get rid of the window entirely. Control room switchers containing these special effects can insert any video signal into the studio picture without the Chromakey™ target.

Although the mechanics of all of this is very much a part of the technical operation, the use of such effects is a journalistic decision. The graphics represent an opportunity to provide additional information for the viewer. Thus, the producer makes the decisions whether to use such effects or not.

Many stations subscribe to special services that provide generic graphics. By generic graphics we mean vertical or horizontal artwork, perhaps including words, that can be used in the window to accompany stories. They are things like slides, stored video frames, drawings, or other artwork that shows flames along with the word "Fire," or a picture of a "Saturday night special" pistol, with the words "Gun Control" or the word "Crime." The all-time favorite must be the drawing of a Capitol dome, which is used everywhere to depict "The Government" or "The Legislature." There are map services that sell graphics depicting various news-related areas of the world, like the Middle East, the city of Beirut, San Salvador, China, and so on. Network affiliate feeds send graphics packages for stations to insert with their own graphics equipment.

Many stations call on their own art departments to prepare their own generic graphics or specific ones as the need develops. Thus, the producer has at his or her command a file of these graphics which can be called up from slide files, frame storers, or graphics generators. Or new graphics can be ordered as the need arises.

Whatever the source, the producer must think about the proper use of such keys. The important thing to remember is that they are, intrinsically, more information on the screen. If they serve as cues or prompters for the audience as to what the story is about, or provide some details about the exact location of the story or the face of the news maker in the story, they relate to the story in a positive way. If they are inappropriate because they are difficult to figure out, or don't really fit the subject matter of the story, they can have a negative impact because they are distracting. The test is whether the graphics add information or help focus the story, or make it more complete and easier to understand.

Using the Talent

Another part of the producer's job is to decide how best to use the on-air talent. The anchors (usually there are several), reporters, and weather and sports anchors represent a resource. Besides the fact that they are hired to perform on the air, the way they are used during the program is an important production factor.

If the producer decides that the anchors will simply alternate stories, he or she does not take advantage of a number of things:

1. The way stories are linked together by topical, regional, or geographic categories affects which anchor should read or introduce the story.
2. A switch from one anchor to another can be used to change direction or topic within a newscast segment.
3. Switching anchors can be used to change the pace of the newscast.
4. Some anchors handle some kinds of stories better than others.
5. Some formats call for a certain anchor to handle certain stories.

Suppose, for instance, that the lead to the newscast is a roundup of major events that happened that day in the state legislature. All of that material, including the video stories by reporters on the scene, should be anchored by one person. If the next major story or group of stories within the segment moves to a major local drug crackdown, another anchor should handle it. Not only will that decision give the audience a nonverbal cue that the story subject and locale are changing, the switch will keep the pace of the program moving.

Switching anchors can also be a useful way to change the subject matter completely. If the newscast contains a series of stand-alone stories, alternating the anchors will provide some nonverbal punctuation, and may even refocus the audience's attention.

Of course, the anchors should not be switched within a story or between the opening and closing of a story that includes a video report.

Sometimes the format dictates the anchor. If, for example, there is a formal or informal custom that one of the anchors always reads a closing feature, the audience rapidly becomes accustomed to that and looks forward to it. Sometimes one of the anchors has special expertise, or does a frequent "reporter's notebook," book reviews, or reviews of local entertainment—or even an editorial commentary.

Switching anchors for sexist reasons fortunately has gone the way of the dinosaur. We are long beyond the day when women read "women's stories" and men handled the gory stuff. Yet sometimes one or the other of the anchors should be the one to present the story because he or she has a particular interest in the story or a knack of handling the material that relates to the audience in a special way. In this situation the fact that the anchor is male or female is a resource to be considered, not something that dictates the choice.

The use of reporters on the news set is another variable for the producer. Reporters are seen all the time covering stories from the field. But it is sometimes a good idea to bring that reporter into the studio to present portions of a story. This technique is used frequently in the presentation of investigative reports. There it strengthens the credibility of the reporter and the report. It can also be used when the reporter has been an eyewitness to a particularly interesting breaking story, or has had an interesting experience in developing the story.

GETTING IT ON THE AIR

Now, the big moment! It is air time. All of the work of the entire news team will come together during a sustained, high-anxiety effort that requires precise execution and professional attention.

The staff has been working all day to bring together the physical components of this complicated human-technical effort. They are:

1. A complete script containing all of the words to be spoken, and all of the timing and technical cues the newscast director will need
2. A stack of video cassettes, all properly labeled
3. A rundown sheet for the tapes
4. A rundown sheet for the graphics

5. A rundown sheet for the font operator, giving all the words for lower-third supers, scores, weather words, and so on
6. Anchors in the studio, director, producer, and technical staff in the control room
7. All fingers crossed

Various stations do things various ways. One is to put all of the above information in the script and let the director make sure that all the various elements like videotapes, graphics, and fonts are ready. But that puts a lot of responsibility on one person's shoulders. Because several people have to perform a variety of functions in the control room and studio during the airing of the program, another system may call for the producer to provide individual rundown sheets for each function.

No matter what system is used, the script must contain all necessary information. At this point it becomes the essential production tool and guide.

As you know, the script contains two columns of information—the production information the director will need to function as commander of the technology and the words the air talent will speak.

Below is a transcription of a WAVE-TV, Louisville, Ky, script. The director's information is in the left column, the anchor's material on the right. Words in parentheses explain the cues:

```
              SCRIPT WITH ANCHOR V/O AND SOUND BITES
              Video                              Audio
/OC David [on camera,              Contracts with four city
Anchor #1]                         employees' unions apparently
                                   will expire tonight without
                                   settlements.
                                     About 16-hundred workers
                                   are involved.


ENG #_____ [tape
#_____]
 VO NATSOT [voice-
over, natural sound on
tape]
 VO: 12 [Voice-over                  Among those without a
lasts 12 sec]                      contract are the firefighters,
                                   who this afternoon resumed
                                   negotiations with the city.
                                     Early settlement is
                                   the exception in labor talks.
                                   Both sides today were
                                   optimistic, but cautious
                                   about specifics:
SOT FULL: :27 [sound               (((SOT)))
on tape up full, lasts
27 sec.]                           IN CUE: ''IT IS HARD TO . . . .''
```

```
Insert: Ron Gnagie
Firefighters' Union
[lower-third super]
--- Charles Roberts
City Negotiator
 [lower-third super]          OUT CUE: ''AM VERY CONFIDENT.''

VO NATSOT: :15                Also unsettled are police,
[Voice-over, natural         firemen and oilers, and
sound on tape, lasts         teamsters. All are expected
15 seconds]                  to continue working while
                             negotiations go on.
```

Now, let's look at this script page carefully to see what it provides as a production tool. The director would take all the pages of the completed script and mark them up with his or her own written-in reminders. The first thing in the video column is a simple indication that one of the anchors, David, is on camera. In this instance, since David will be on camera 3, that notation would be written in next to the /OC command.

The command VO NATSOT means, as indicated, that David will read this part of the script as a voice-over with videotape that contains natural sound from the scenes on the tape. The director needs to know this so that he or she can tell the audio operator to open David's mic and hold the tape sound underneath the narration. The director also sees that this portion of the narration that David will read is twelve seconds long.

SOT FULL means that the sound on the tape, the sound bites, must be brought up to full volume—again a command the director gives to the audio operator. The script also shows those sound bites will run twenty-seven seconds.

The inserts below SOT FULL indicate that two lower-third supers will be inserted when the two speakers are seen and heard. The font rundown will instruct the font operator to put those names and titles into the character generator. The director will tell the person running the switcher when to bring them up on the screen.

After the sound bites, the closing to the story is again read as a voice-over by David, and the script notes this will take fifteen seconds.

Note that the in cue and out cue are placed in the audio column of the script. This is because they are part of the *sound* that will be included in the story. This brings up another rule: All video-directing commands go in the video column; all audio-directing commands go in the audio column.

The internal time cues, such as those indicating the length of the voice-over narration and the sound bites, are put into the video column so that the director will know the length of those individual elements as well as the length of the entire story. Many directors use stop watches that can display both elapsed time and split times. Thus, like an athletics coach, the director can keep track of both the running time of the entire program and the timing of each element of each story.

Let's look at another script page, one which includes a completely packaged tape story by a reporter.

Video	Audio
/OC LAURETTA	School officials are glad to get the 350-thousand dollars allocated by Fiscal Court yesterday. But even with the good news, an old problem may be made worse. Reporter Jeff McConnell says there'll be no more subsidy to anyone.
ENG #8 [tape #8]	(((SOT)))
McConnell [reporter's name]	NARRATION UP FULL
Insert: Jeff McConnell WAVE-TV reporter [video is McConnell standupper]	IN CUE: . . . ''IF SCHOOL OFFICIALS . . . .'' OUT CUE: . . . ''TRANSPORTATION SUBSIDY. . . .''
Insert: Yesterday [video is scenes of yesterday's confrontation between Dumeyer and McConnell]	NARRATION UP FULL Catholic school officials like D.K. Dumeyer had no comment yesterday. And even a day later he still wasn't ready to talk about where to find the 675-thousand dollars to transport first through eighth graders to parochial schools. In fact, Dumeyer told me by phone it could be two weeks before they are prepared to talk.
[video is :10 McConnell doing this bite on camera in the field]	IN CUE: . . . ''BUT TODAY. . . .'' OUT CUE: . . . ''THE FISCAL COURT. . . .''
[Video is B-Roll from scenes shot at Public School Headquarters]	NARRATION UP FULL Catholic school and public school relations were already less than good after the county school board came out against tuition tax credits for private schools. So what will Dumeyer's decision do to that relationship?

```
   Insert: 4:12      IN CUE: ''THE PARENTS. . . .''
Ingwersen [the
video is of an       OUT CUE: ''CHANGE THE FACTS. . . .''
interview with
Mr. Ingwersen]


   LIVE OC TAG         Meanwhile, county school officials
[Live on-            still haven't decided which of two or
camera tag by        three plans it will decide on to get
Lauretta]            the rest of the money needed for
                     optional busing.
```

This script serves a dual purpose. It is a "map" for both the videotape editor and the newscast director. It was written by the reporter to provide the voice-over narration that he put on audio tape before that audio was edited together with the pictures on the videotape. It also contains the in cues and out cues for the sound bites he chose for the package. And it tells the video editor where the voice-over narration should be brought up to full level. Finally, it provides video directing information—the lower-third inserts—so that the newscast director can order them put on the screen at the appropriate time.

Even though all of McConnell's story was packaged on a video cassette, the script is included in the program script so that the director and anchors can follow the packaged story as it plays. Also, there are elements of it that must be performed while the program is on the air.

A script for a news program must include all program elements. If a bumper and a commercial segment are to follow the story about the school system, there would be pages or at least notations after the school story indicating that the bumper and commercials are the next program elements. Those notations would indicate which bumper and which commercials are to run in that time. If McConnell had reported his story live, the program script would contain a page indicating where the live remote was to come from, the anchor's lead-in, time limits, and what videotaped segments are to be rolled in along with their in and out cues.

The Videotapes

There are variations in station procedures regarding how the videotape segments are played back into the program. Some stations dub the three-quarter-inch cassettes prepared by the news department onto one-inch video CARTS or even two-inch reel-to-reel tape. Although some quality is lost in the dubbing, some technical corrections and improvements in the tape quality can be made during the dub so that the air picture is more stable. With current improvements in video editors and the tape itself, many stations now skip this step and play the cassettes directly into the program. Whatever system is used, great care must be taken to assure that the right tape is played at the right time. Therefore, an accurate rundown sheet is a necessity.

Producers must be sure that changes in the tape order made during the preprogram planning are copied onto that rundown sheet.

Words and Effects

The same thing is true of whatever video effects are to be inserted into the program. Care must be taken to make sure the lower-third supers are spelled correctly, and that the right one goes in the right place. No one wants to have the wrong name appear as identification of the speaker in a sound bite. Besides being sloppy, it could lead to a libel suit.

Any other video effects to be used must also be indicated on the script at the exact point they are supposed to appear. It is up to the producer to make sure the script tells the director what is desired. Otherwise mistakes are made and the post-program review results in a lot of shouting matches. The director's job is tough enough without having to guess the intentions of the producer.

Summary

"It's 11 o'clock, do you know where your children are?"

That phrase precedes the late news on many stations across the country. It's a reminder to parents. It also signals to TV news personnel that the most important time of their day has arrived. No matter what else has happened that day the time has come for everyone involved to get sharp. The entire effort can either come off smoothly and professionally or it can go down the tube in a flurry of missed cues, wrong tapes played, anchors looking around wildly trying to figure out what to do next, and much evil language bouncing around the control room.

Precision of execution is what is needed. In the control room, the producer and the director share the burden, but not in equal parts. The producer has brought the program to the director to execute. In the preceding six or seven hours the producer has made myriad decisions—story selection, content, and length; program order and timing; production elements to be included. Now the director takes the helm. He or she must see to it that what the producer has created gets on and off the air without a blip.

Yet the producer may still have to make many decisions in the event of a technical or human failure—a VTR refuses to play back a tape, an anchor gets lost in the script or makes a mistake, a live report fails to come up on time. The producer must decide what to do next.

If the tape machine fails, the producer and director must keep the program going—back to the anchor quickly for an apology to the viewers. If the anchor has made a misstatement, it must be corrected as soon as possible. If the live report fails, the questions are: Will the technicians be able to get it on immediately, soon, later, or not at all? If the remote is lost completely, there's a big hole in the program that must be filled with something else. If the remote works but runs badly overtime because the news maker rambles on and on, something will have to be dropped to get the program off on time. These are producer decisions and they must be made quickly and firmly.

Directors are like the helmsman and duty officer on a battleship. Their job is to keep the ship going at full efficiency in the proper direction and speed prescribed. The producer is like the commanding officer who makes decisions like slow down, speed up, turn to port, fire the guns, advance, retreat. Retreat is seldom an option. Producers, like naval officers, are supposed to "put themselves in harm's way." No matter what happens, the reality is that there will be a newscast at a certain time of day and that it will run a certain number of minutes and seconds. The larger reality is that the precision with which the producer makes news and production judgments, checks the details, anticipates problems, and has alternative plans to solve them leads to the crisp execution of a program that is clear, informative, and satisfying for the audience.

When it all comes off smoothly there is a huge sense of accomplishment. When it doesn't the producer must inspect everything he or she or others did that caused the failure. Post mortems about program failures are no fun. If it has been "that kind of day" you will make only one more discovery. When you get to the parking lot you will find you left the windows rolled down and the lights on, and the battery is dead.

Producing Live News

9

The flowering of the new technology in television news comes when news departments are called on to use it for their coverage at the scene of a news event. That activity is, of course, the most dramatic, most difficult, and most rewarding development in ENG. Using the technology to bring the viewers the news as it happens requires the utmost in careful planning and management teamwork, and a little bit of luck.

PLANNING

The luck factor is always there but it can be reduced in importance by a good operational plan—one that can be applied across time and the vagaries of each individual news story.

First, you have to know what your technical resources are. Then you have to figure out a way to use those resources efficiently, economically, strategically, and logically. Major elements of the plan must deal with facilities and technical support, staffing, programming, policy and decision making, and editorial control.

The components of such a plan will look something like this:

1. Facilities and technical support: What have we got to work with, where is it, who's available to run it?

2. Staffing: Who will produce, who will edit, who will report, who will supervise?

3. Programming: Will this be used in regular news programming? Will we do bulletins, special reports, one or more wrap-ups? Will there be continuing coverage, will the story last a long time? When will it be time to stop the coverage?

✔ 4. Policy and decision making: Who will call the shots? Who has the responsibility? Are the responsibility lines clear?

✔ 5. Editorial control: Who will maintain an overview of the coverage? Who will monitor the coverage? Who will provide liaison with the field? Who will check facts and keep additional information flowing to the field? Who will monitor the writing, editing, and production elements?

No single producer, writer, editor, reporter, photojournalist, assignment desk editor, or technician is going to be called upon to make all these decisions. The ultimate authority lies with the news director and the general manager of the station. The generalized checklist above is full of decisions only they can make. But other decisions within that checklist clearly are to be made by those farther down in the table of organization. If the news director has to make logistic and operational decisions at the same time he or she is called on to supervise, administer, and make go or no-go decisions, it is too big a load for one person.

Thus, every station has, or should have, a game plan which has been worked out in advance and is well known and understood by its staff. Without such a game plan and a clear description of responsibilities, people working in the flurry of live coverage may not know when they are supposed to concentrate on their part of the team operation, when they are supposed to ask for guidance, or what to do next.

There's an analogy with the term itself—"game plan." In the huddle between downs, the quarterback speaks some mysterious language: "Red right 7, 85 out, fly left on three." Everyone in the huddle knows that the play will be the halfback (red) off right tackle (right 7), and that the right end (85) will fake a short pass and then block the defensive corner back while the left end will run straight down the sidelines (fly left), and that the ball will be snapped on a count of three.

When the teams line up, if the quarterback sees a defensive change which reduces the chances of the play's success, he can call an audible signal which changes the play. If someone doesn't hear the signal or forgets what to do, the play doesn't work.

A quickly called game plan for a television news operation may sound quite a bit like the one the quarterback called in the huddle: "You produce, you coordinate, you edit, you write, you report. Everyone keep me informed. Now go!"

Production of a story when using the mobile equipment can be very simple or very complex. Let's take a simple case.

The Story

The assignment is to take the news van to the airport and cover the arrival of a senator returning home after a visit to Russia. The van will microwave the material back to the station for editing and use in the noon news program. A longer version and a sidebar interview with the senator's wife will be prepared later for use in the dinner-hour news.

This is relatively easy because the assignment desk has known the senator's return date and time for several days. It has ordered facilities—the van and crew and the intake of the microwaved material. The decision to microwave the report was made because the senator is arriving at 11:30 A.M. Time is too short to deliver a videotape any other way.

The reporter has known of the assignment for twenty-four hours and so has researched it and prepared a list of questions. The producer of the noon news will monitor the feed and, with an editor-writer—and some radioed editing suggestions from the reporter—will see that the story is edited and the script written for the noon anchor.

It all goes well; the senator makes some very provocative comments on U.S.–Soviet relations. The senator's wife gives interesting details about the trip. During the afternoon the reporter will recut the story for the 6 P.M. news and edit and write script for the sidebar interview with the senator's wife.

The Story Changes

The wire services also covered the senator's arrival. By 4 P.M., there is an uproar from the State Department in Washington. Spokespersons there deny what the senator has said and accuse him of upsetting some very delicate negotiations.

The assignment desk reacts. Where is the senator now? Can we get him to respond? The reporter drops whatever she is doing, checks her notes, and gets on the phone. Quickly she finds out the senator is in a meeting at a local hotel with party leaders, doesn't want to come out of the meeting just now . . . meeting will end at about 5:30 . . . is due at cocktail reception in the same hotel at 6 P.M. The 6 P.M. producer, the desk editor, and the reporter decide that a mobile unit will be dispatched to the hotel. The reporter will go to the hotel to set up to do either a live-delayed or live shot for the 6 P.M. news.

Remember "keep me informed"? Chances are good that the news director or executive producer has been keeping an eye on what the operational staff is doing. If someone had anticipated there would be a reaction, plans could have been made earlier. Nevertheless, something has to be done quickly, and the new plan is acceptable. Except the boss says, "Hell, everyone will be wanting reaction . . . the place will be swarming with the competition . . . anyone got any ideas?"

The desk editor says, "The radio traffic indicates channel 10 is setting up outside the party room and plans to go live from there."

Enterprising Reporter raises her hand. "I've got something. I know the senator well, his wife, too. They're staying in a suite. I'll bet he's going to change clothes for the party. Can we get into that suite so that I can grab him before he goes downstairs? Could we do a live shot from there?"

ENG Coordinator: "Sure, we can use the mini [short-range microwave] for a double hop—out the window to the truck, from the truck back here. But someone's got to get us in and we'd better also set up where Channel 10 is. . . ."

Enterprising Reporter: "I'll get us in the suite; you set it up."

News Director: "Okay, but we better have the backup location too, otherwise we might get zilch. Put a field producer on it." He goes off mumbling about overtime.

ENG Coordinator moves to set up the facilities. The reporter gets on the phone to the senator's aide. Aide sounds doubtful, worried about catching heat from the competitors. Enterprising Reporter calls senator's wife. Wife says sure, and come up earlier so we can have a chat, I want to tell you more about our trip.

The gamble is on. The backup location will be installed in case the reporter has to do a live wrap around the senator's earlier remarks. But the beat in the making depends upon the success of the interview in the senator's suite.

The Team at Work

Crew, ENG Coordinator, Field Producer, and Enterprising Reporter take off. The line producer begins to restructure his program. At the hotel, Enterprising Reporter, Field Producer, technicians, and camera operator go right to the suite. Enterprising Reporter introduces them, they start the setup procedure, and the Senator's Wife tells about the trip. The double-hop microwave system works just fine; soon pictures from the suite are being received back at the station. The radio coordination circuits are working. IFB is established for the reporter. Field Producer says all systems are go.

Downstairs, the senator is running late. He shoots out the door of the meeting room, tells reporters he'll talk to them in a minute. He gets on an elevator and goes to his suite. He's a little startled to find his friend the reporter there, but says as long as they're all set up why not do it. He makes a mental note to talk to his wife about his need to keep all of the news media happy. His aide sputters a bit, but subsides.

So senator and Enterprising Reporter sit down and have a nice ten-minute interview in which he reacts to the Washington reaction and gives some more details on why he said what he said earlier. Enterprising Reporter's questions are incisive; the senator seems to enjoy fencing with her.

Back at the Shop

At the station the video and audio of the interview are logged as they flow in and editing decisions are made. A package of material including the senator's original comments and his reaction to the State Department's comments is put together. While the interview is going on News Director tells Field Producer to tell Enterprising Reporter to hustle downstairs to do a live wrap from the backup camera location outside the party room door.

There, the makings of the usual buffalo stampede are in progress. The competing TV stations are set up to go live as soon as the senator shows up. But Enterprising Reporter knows something they don't. Her story will lead the program, and the tape package is ready to go.

As usual, the senator is a little late. Reporters from the competing stations lead their program with some lame material like: "The senator hasn't arrived yet, Fred . . . but he caused quite a stir when he arrived at the airport this morning and made these comments. . . ."

Enterprising Reporter goes on the air at the same time as the others. But the package she cues into contains both the highlights of the material from the airport that morning and excerpts from her exclusive interview. She does a smooth opening and narration between the segments and signs off saying that the senator hasn't arrived yet but that she will stand by. She also says that if there is anything new to report she will come back and relay it to the audience during the program.

Perhaps there will be something new in what the senator has to say when he is confronted by all those microphones and a flurry of questions. Just to rub it in a little, the station does switch back. Enterprising Reporter does a quick wrap-up of the new things the senator said and reminds her audience that they can see more of the exclusive interview at 10 P.M.

The Results

It's a big success. Lots of factors made it so. They begin with the good relationship the reporter had cultivated with the senator and his wife over a long period of time. They include her suggestion about getting into the senator's suite and the professional way she went about it. Another factor was the solid work of the technicians and ENG crew—the use of technology to get the double-hop—and the decision by the news director to spend the time and money to do it. The rewards for the news staff are in knowing they all worked together to do a superior job—and perhaps some giggles thinking about the news staffs at the other stations watching the newscasts side by side and commenting, "Jeez, look at that!"

It was also rewarding to their audience, who got a clearer, more detailed, more carefully presented story that told the basic facts and updated the story with the latest developments. Although no one called the news staff to thank them for working so hard, many people in the audience were made aware, in an indirect way, that this station could be counted upon to give them the latest news.

A final note. The station's network called later in the evening to ask for a satellite feed of the tape of the interview. It appeared on the network's morning newscasts the next day. The reporter got network notice and exposure and made a little extra money on the side.

The Post-Mortem

Now, lest we get carried away by the euphoria of the moment, we should remember that a lot of things could have gone wrong. The setup to get the pictures and sound from the hotel suite to the news van might not have worked. Other equipment might have failed. The senator could have refused to do the interview or might have been running so late it was impossible. Cues could have been missed.

Scores of things can happen in a situation like this. But the planning and coordination by the news and technical staff was good, and they gave themselves a good chance to pull it off. It is not just a case of crossing your fingers or saying a few words to the gods of electricity. Planning is the key to success.

All of the components of the operational plan were included in this coverage.

The facilities were available. They were cleverly used to get the exclusive material and back up the coverage in case the hotel-room remote did not work out.

The staff was in place. The reporter was able to handle both ends of the live feeds. It might have been better to send another reporter to cover the party room location in case things got very tight for the reporter in the hotel suite.

The lines of responsibility were clear; each person in the chain of command knew what was expected of him or her. The news director made the important decision to set up both live locations and activated the tentative decision to have the reporter do the live wrap.

This story did not require a decision to break into regular programming for bulletins and/or special reports. It did not need continuous coverage. It did require more than average staff and facilities, but not an inordinate amount.

Editorial control was maintained. The staff might have realized earlier that it had the makings of a good story and moved to do something about it sooner. The material was carefully monitored as it came in. A field producer was sent to the scene to coordinate the visual and aural elements and to serve as liaison with the line producer, news director, and reporter so that late decisions were quickly and properly carried out.

INFORMATION CHANNELS

One of the most important needs and key ingredients for good mobile news coverage is information. In the example above, the reporter did have time to research her story so she could get the background information needed to do a professional job on the exclusive interview. And she did have an IFB so she could get the other information she needed—cues from those recording her interview, and when she was on the air at the beginning of the newscast and during the later insert. The presence of a field producer helped with the smoothness of the editing of the tape material and the program production while the reporter dashed from one location to the other.

The Spot News Information Need

When a station is covering a spot news story with mobile equipment, the need for information flowing to and from the field becomes paramount. The reporters and crews dispatched to the scene of a spot news story obviously have to work at high speed. While the crews are setting up the video equipment and microwave and getting it running as fast as possible, the reporters have to begin gathering the facts just as quickly. The information needs we are talking about here are of another kind:

1. Information needed to run and control the live broadcast
2. Information from other sources for the reporters and producers on the scene

Both kinds of information are distributed through a private two-way radio system, cellular phones, radio phones, or specially installed phones, and even computer terminals between the station control and newsrooms and the personnel at the story.

These are aptly called "co-ord circuits." Normally there are two separate systems, one for the technicians, the other for the editorial staff.

On the "tech" circuits the engineers and field technicians communicate to connect the live unit with the control rooms and monitor the technical operation. On the "news" circuits reporters, field producers, and photojournalists exchange facts, editorial decisions, and cues. It is important to separate these channels because the technicians and news people have different information needs and must be able to speak to each other at any time. These circuits are also isolated from the video and audio broadcast channels being relayed back to the station so that operational information doesn't interfere with the steady flow of news.

The major problem for a reporter at a live shot is that he or she has to be on the air and collect information at the same time. The whole point of a live spot news broadcast is to get on the air as soon as possible and stay on the air as long as it is necessary.

Often good solid facts and details are at a premium. Rumors are everywhere. Various versions of what happened are circulating. Authorities who could give information are very busy. But the reporter's job is to keep reliable information flowing, avoid rumors and speculation, and stick to the facts.

That's one half of it—the half that the audience sees and hears. The other half is the flow of information *to the field*. We tend to think of ENG as being one directional: News goes from some story location back to the station and to the audience. It must be a bidirectional system; news departments have to organize themselves during a spot news story to make it so. No matter how good the reporters and producers in the field are, the station's real news-gathering strength is in the newsroom. There the staff can get on the phone, go to other news sources, monitor radios, check the facts, dig into resource material, write scripts, prepare graphics, edit recaps, locate eyewitnesses and additional interviews, and do all the other things necessary to give shape to the story.

Also at the station are the management personnel, who can monitor what is on the air and make decisions about where the story is now, where it is headed, and what needs to be done in the next seconds, minutes, and hours to stay on top of it.

The Story Breaks

As an example, let's take a true story: the explosion of sewers in a large area of Old Town, a neighborhood of Louisville, Kentucky.

In this example, we are not going to talk about what the specific newsrooms there did with the story (although WHAS Radio and WHAS-TV won national awards for their work). We are going to look at this story to show how it exemplified the need for the bidirectional information flow.

The facts are relatively simple. Faulty equipment caused material from a local industry to flow into the sewers. This material formed a gas that exploded in the early morning hours, blowing up the streets and damaging nearby buildings like a string of bombs dropped during a bombing run.

Imagine you are on the news staff of a Lousiville station when the big blast occurred. You don't know much of anything at the beginning. Very quickly you have a strong hint that it's a big story. Several calls have come from people in the area. The police monitors have lit up, more calls are coming in by the second.

The very first thing to do is to confirm the basics: Has there been an explosion of some sort? Where is it? Is it real? Is it a hoax?

The next thing to do is to get the reporters and technicians moving, the news vans out to meet them, the helicopter in the air, and at the same time get something *on* the air. Then inform the news director and engineering supervisor. They may know something already, but don't count on it—more than one call on something like this is a thousand times better than none.

That's a lot of things to do. In doing them you have begun the information flow. You have also created a voracious monster. There's someone in the studio telling the audience the few facts so far available and both he or she, and the audience, desperately want more.

Now the system has to start churning out those facts. What are your resources?

1. The phone
2. Official sources
3. The reporters
4. The news staff
5. The mobile units
6. The helicopter

Note that the phone is the fastest thing you've got right at the beginning. You use it to (a) get more facts from those official sources, (b) relay that information to

FIGURE 9-1. WHAS-TV, Louisville, Kentucky. Reporter Jeffrey Hutter live at the scene of one of the control points established following an early-morning explosion in the city's sewers. *(Courtesy of WHAS-TV.)*

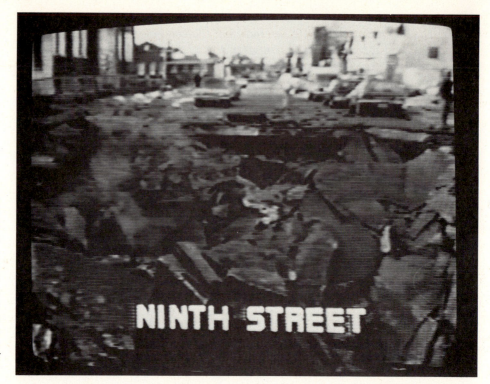

FIGURE 9-2. An off-air picture of some of the destruction caused by an explosion in the sewers in Louisville, Kentucky. Careful labeling of the various streets that were damaged was important because the blast occurred just before drive time began. *(Courtesy of WHAS-TV.)*

the on air people, and (c) summon more help. The phone and the people to use it are all-important at the beginning of a big spot news story: Those machines with all the fancy electronics in them still have to get to the story and be set up to broadcast. That's going to take some time.

So organization is all important. If your news staff is proud of its record for fast, accurate information, people will arrive quickly. Journalists instinctively head for the story or the newsroom when a big one breaks, whether they've been summoned or not. (You have to wonder about those who don't.) The important thing is to put these people to work in an organized way. It is game-plan time again: "You take the cops, you the sheriffs, you City Hall, you the power company, you the sanitary district, you the hospitals, you the eyewitnesses."

In rapping out those orders you have established a system that will begin to amass facts for the on-air broadcast. You have also established the inside half of the communications system that will sustain your flow of information even after the live units get on the air.

The Live Broadcasts Begin

The mobile units start to come on line. The helicopter is up and over the scene. One mobile unit is live from the ground. Reporters in both are describing what they see and what the audience is looking at. Another unit will come up from the police command post. A third will establish another live remote from another vantage point. Camera and reporter teams with portable videotape equipment are working other locations. Couriers are shuttling videotape tape to the mobile units—where it can be inserted into the live remotes—and back to the newsroom. Soon everyone and everything are hard at work. You have a good flow of facts and a lot of good interviews with eyewitnesses—the human side of the story—and with officials and experts who add depth to it.

The Bigger Story

So far, so good. But each of those live remotes is providing only a segment of the overall story. The reporters and photojournalists are so busy at their individual locations that they cannot get a feeling of the bigger picture, the whole story.

For instance, it has been quickly established that no one was killed and the number of injured is small. Everyone at the remotes needs to know that. It has also been learned that it was a gas explosion in the sewers; the fire department says there seems to be little danger of more explosions. Nobody knows yet why it happened. That news needs to get to the field reporters as well as the audience. Perhaps the reporters and technicians have been able to monitor the live broadcast. But don't count on it; perhaps they have been too busy to do so.

What is necessary here is editorial control. While all of the reporters have been trained not to speculate about things they don't have personal knowledge of, the broadcast will be more coherent if they get feedback through the two-way system we've been talking about. Eyewitnesses can and do tell different stories. Even though the reporters quiz them very carefully, they cannot do this well in an information vacuum.

The anchorpersons in the studio have the same problem. Their role is to provide the basic early information, to keep repeating the basic facts as more viewers tune in, and to provide continuity. The anchors are starved for information at the beginning of the broadcast but may suffer information overload as it goes on. They are so busy relaying facts, leading into the live remotes, and keeping the broadcast going that they cannot get a very good sense of the big picture, either.

Then, too, the focus of the story expands. Part of the bigger picture is the impact of the event on the metropolitan community. Here is where producers, editors, and news directors come into play. The system needs people to watch the overall broadcast. Some must check the facts, making sure that inadvertent mistakes are corrected quickly and that errors of fact are not allowed to become embedded in copy, narration, or ad-lib comments. Others need to be looking at where the story is going. If few people are dead or injured, a remote at a hospital is not going to be productive after those facts are established. If the explosion has created a massive traffic jam during the morning rush hour, that, for an hour or two, may become a major element of the story.

What about school closings? business closings? If there is no more danger of explosion, what about danger from falling walls or buildings that may collapse? What about control of people and vehicles heading toward the area? Is the sewer system still working? Is the water supply interrupted? If so, where? What other events will be canceled or postponed, and when will they be rescheduled?

Here again, the inside system is the primary mechanism for providing answers to those questions. The information it develops also enables the editors and producers to make wise decisions about where and when to move some of the reporters to new focal points of the story.

The final important decision is: When should we end the broadcast? This one lands squarely in the news director's lap. It involves a lot of considerations. Some are economic, some competitive, some editorial.

Bill McAndrew, president of NBC News in the late 1950s and early 1960s, won fame and a lot of audience appreciation for his network with a fairly simple policy: "We will go on the air *before* the other two networks, and we will go off *after* they have finished." The first part was difficult, but he spurred his troops on and they usually complied. The second part was a combination of stubbornness and machismo. Both attitudes are very competitive. The audience can develop a huge appetite for more information about a major story. Portions of that audience will stay tuned as long as there is even the hope of learning anything new.

That leads to the editorial part of the decision. As long as there is new information, or even the chance of new information, the news director who decides to quit too soon runs the risk of disappointing the audience, and missing the chance to tell them something they need to know.

Another portion of that audience becomes restless. There are, after all, other programs they may want to see. They will tune away if the broadcast becomes boring and repetitive. That's part of the economic factor in the decision. The other part is that there are faithful advertisers who sponsor other programs on the station. They deserve to have their programs shown at the scheduled times unless there are good reasons to cancel those programs.

A major news event is a good reason. News directors usually have the authority to take over programming, and they do. Over the years most news directors have acted in a very responsible way in regard to preempting regular programming to bring the audience live coverage of major important events. But it's a truism of American broadcasting that they have to take the economic factor into consideration.

ALL-OUT LIVE

When a major disaster strikes, live television news can become the ultimate channel of information for everyone. No other medium, with the possible exception of radio, can be as quick. When the full resources of television stations are focused on the major disaster they can equal the comprehensiveness of the print media. ENG, run by journalists with dedication, vision, imagination, and powerful news judgment, is what does the job. We will look now at one of those all-out efforts.

The Cloud over Dayton

WHIO-TV in Dayton, Ohio, had geared up for the 6 P.M. newscast on Tuesday, July 8, 1986, when, at about 4:30 P.M., a CSX freight train derailed and caught fire near Miamisburg, a Dayton suburb. Three live interrupts between 4:50 and 6 P.M. included shots from WHIO-TV's helicopter showing a huge and growing white cloud blowing right across the Dayton metropolitan area. The live picture of that cloud would come to be an almost permanent image on Dayton TV screens during the next thirty-two hours as WHIO-TV shifted its gears into overdrive and broadcast more than six hours of live broadcasts and special reports.

At times the cloud was fifteen hundred feet high, three miles wide, and many more miles long. Its source was a thirty- to forty-foot-high boiling fire from a ruptured tank car containing twelve thousand gallons of white phosphorus. White phosphorus is nasty stuff; it bursts into flame when it hits air, and fighting those flames with water just makes the fire hotter.

The fire itself was not the danger, since the derailment occurred in open country near the west bank of the Greater Miami River, but the cloud, "smelling like matches," everyone said, made eyes burn, noses run, and throats sore, and could cause serious problems for people with respiratory problems. Before firefighters and chemical experts got it under control, thirty-five thousand Dayton area residents would be evacuated, and hundreds would visit hospital emergency rooms.

The WHIO-TV assignment desk heard the original police traffic about the derailment and sent the company's leased Bell Ranger helicopter—"Chopper 7"—to have a look. Pilot Mark Cain and photojournalist Rick Nordstrom said they first saw the cloud when they were only a few feet off the ground. They picked up reporter Dave Freeman from a parking lot near the station and, with anchor Jim Baldridge in the studio, did three live inserts running between three and seven minutes within the next half hour.

WHIO-TV News Director Skip Hapner says that it took no longer than ten or

FIGURE 9-3. The cloud that frightened Miamisburg, Ohio. A train derailment ripped open a tank car containing twelve thousand gallons of white phosphorus, which burns when it makes contact with air. The wind carried the cloud of toxic fumes directly over Dayton, Ohio. For the next thirty-two hours, WHIO-TV, Dayton, tracked the cloud with its helicopter and transmitted many hours of live reports from it. *(Courtesy of WHIO-TV, Dayton, Ohio.)*

fifteen minutes for him and the staff to realize they had a complex story and that they were going to play a major information role for both the audience and area officials. What they didn't know was that the story would jump into an instant replay twenty-four hours later or that the staff and station resources would be tested almost to the breaking point.

"We don't have a disaster plan written down," Hapner says, "that's one of those low-priority items that you keep telling yourself you should do. But we do play 'What If?' a great deal. Even on smaller-size stories that have some sort of disaster angle to them, we often toss ideas around about what would have happened if. . . . That's helpful in deciding how you're going to react when a big one like this comes along."

Hapner also looks for people "who can react" when he hires. "I take longer than most to hire, and I spend a lot of time in personal interviews with people I'm interested in," he says. "After a while you can get a feeling for how these people will handle themselves when it comes to the all-important live coverage." He points out that reporter Dave Freeman had been with the station only about six weeks. "We put him in the chopper because he was the closest reporter available, and I thought I might have to relieve him with someone more familiar with the area. But he was tremendous, and I never thought about that again."

WHIO-TV does have a standing policy that turned out to be a key element in its coverage. The station frequently invites police and fire officials to ride in its helicopter when covering stories these authorities might become involved in.

Hapner says:

> We work very closely with police and fire authorities, always have. Some news directors will tell you they would never let a policeman or fireman ride with them . . . but my philosophy is different. I think that having them there helps the story. . . . They can use their own radio equipment to talk to those on the ground and coordinate things, and then we can interview them and pass the information on to the audience immediately. We have an official source right there with us—what could be faster than that?
>
> Furthermore, a situation like this is as much a public service broadcast as it is a news broadcast. You are fully into public service messages as you tell people about evacuation and public health procedures . . . go here . . . don't go there . . . avoid these areas because the smoke is heavy there . . . and you have the legal authority right beside you.

Another policy decision was made on the fly. "As soon as I knew the enormity of it," Hapner says, "I called my boss, Stan Mouse. I told him what we had. The first thing he said to me was: 'Okay, you make the decisions, whatever you need to do, do it. If it means canceling prime-time programs, do it. Whatever . . . you know what the situation is, and you're in charge.'"

WHIO-TV used three live mobile units for the majority of its coverage over the next two days. Chopper 7 was in the air most of the time, stopping off only for fuel. A live microwave unit with mobile editing capabilities was parked 125 yards away from the burning tank car. A third live unit moved from point to point as needed—the Miamisburg city hall, hospitals, evacuation centers, and so on. WHIO-TV also had a live production unit parked at the NCR Country Club, location of the U.S. Women's Open Golf Tournament, which was to start on Thursday. That was used to report evacuation of practicing golfers from the course.

Hapner said that the basic policy for the live broadcasts the first two days was to keep the live helicopter picture and updates from the chopper's reporting team on the air as much as possible. ''We just had to keep the information flowing . . . and since people could see the smoke cloud from almost anywhere in the area . . . we just kept that unit live as much as we could, showing where the smoke plume was headed, how big it was, how much fire there was, what was being done to try to put it out.''

WHIO-TV's other major effort was in trying to sort out the facts as to exactly how dangerous it was to breathe the toxic fumes and how and where evacuations were taking place. The pictures of the cloud were frightening and it was important to avoid panic. It was quickly established that the fumes, while toxic, were not life threatening unless someone got a heavy dose in the thick of the cloud or had respiratory problems. The major point that was made over and over again—and in as many ways as people could think to say it—was to get away from the cloud or stay indoors with the windows shut and with air conditioner vents closed so they wouldn't bring in outside air.

Regarding evacuation, WHIO-TV relied on its live units and its newsroom staff to track and relay the appropriate officials' statements and instructions and to keep in touch with the Red Cross and disaster relief authorities as the situation progressed.

WHIO-TV anchored its coverage from its news studio with anchors Jim Baldridge and Don Wayne and weatherman Bruce Asbury on the set.

The following is a digest by one of the authors of the first hour and a half of WHIO-TV's coverage of the event. (The word *window* in the column describing the pictures WHIO-TV was showing means those pictures were seen in a keyed window on the news set behind the anchors and with anchors in view. ''Live shot'' means the live remotes were seen full screen.)

Time	Words	Picture
6:00:00	Wayne, Baldridge: basic facts, location of wreck. Evacuations: Bear Creek, Orchard Hill—West	Two-shot, window: helicopter view.
6:00:46	Carollton, Jefferson Twp., Old Soldiers Home Rd., Hemple Rd., Miamisburg Rd.	Live shot: helicopter view.
6:01:05	Dave Freeman: Chopper 7: ''1,000—1,500 feet high, white phosphorus, can't	
6:01:15	put it out with water.''	Graphic: location of wreck.
6:01:20	Just letting it burn, fumes going toward Dayton, Kettering; smells like matches. ''If you	Live shot: Ground location 100 yds. from fire.

6:02:04	smell that, get or stay inside--extremely toxic.''	
6:02:06	Phosphorus used in military bombs, ''Nothing to fool around with.'' Flames above treetops 30--40 feet.	Live shot: helicopter over wreck, fire ball seen.
6:02:49	Studio: two shot: Don Wayne introduces Cheryl McHenry in Miamisburg.	Window: ground view shot, CU big boiling flames.
6:03:15	McHenry: introduces Lt. Dick Emmons, Miamisburg Fire Department. Emmons: ''Very serious,'' evacuations list, etc.	Pull back to two shot.
6:04:00	McHenry: Railroad people say smoke could be fatal if person got heavy dose close in here. In outlying areas, ''hazardous but not potentially fatal.''	
6:05:00	Emmons: concurs with that. McHenry: what's next? Emmons: not much we can do but let it burn out, command post is coordinating evacuations, we are ''settling in for the night.''	
6:07:00	Wayne, Baldridge: Wayne identifies it as C and O Train. Reviews evacuation locations. Baldridge: ''Wait for officials to come around to tell you to evacuate before you take off.''	Studio: two shot. Graphic: wreck location.
6:07:30	Wayne: practice day at NCR Country Club for Women's Open.	Window: reporter Mike Hartsock.
6:07:40	Hartsock: evacuated course late this	Live shot: Hartsock.

afternoon. All golfers
gone, several said eyes,
throats, ears burned.

6:09:20   Baldridge, Bruce Asbury,   Studio: two shot.
WHIO-TV weatherman.
Baldridge: ''The key
element is that
phosphorus match smell—if
you smell that, avoid it
and get away.''

6:10:04   Asbury: there's a   One shot:
thunderstorm coming,   ''Accuweather 7''
could affect this   set.
situation. Let's look at
the radar.

6:10:22   As storm approaches   Radar full screen.
there likely will be a
wind shift toward the SE,
which would blow cloud in
a new direction, etc.

6:11:00   Asbury, Baldridge,   Studio: three shot.
Wayne. Baldridge: wonder
whether rain is good or
bad news since water does
not put out phosphorus.
Wayne: no word yet on how
long it will take to put
the fire out.

6:11:53   Intro: Dave Freeman: Live shot:
Other cars are now on   helicopter view,
fire as it is spreading   approaching crash
along tracks, smoke   scene
moving higher in the air
now; as an oil slick   Zoom to surface of
develops on Bear Creek   Bear Creek.
where it enters Miami
River.

6:12:44   With me is Rick Melton,
Miamisburg Police, and we
are watching for any wind
shift. Melton: All   Helicopter
evacuations so far have   continues to circle
been Northeast of the   wreck scene.

FIGURE 9-4. WHIO-TV used its helicopter with a reporter and a fire captain aboard to get close to the source of this toxic chemical fire caused by a train derailment. The fire captain, an expert on such fires, was able to spot changes in the nature of the fire and cloud and relay immediate orders to firefighters and the public. *(Courtesy of WHIO-TV, Dayton, Ohio.)*

cloud, now we don't know where the next ones will come. Freeman: How will people know to evacuate? Melton: Police cruisers will go through neighborhoods using PA or door to door. Freeman: Those South of the accident, keep your ears open, and get identification if someone comes to the door.

6:14:30	We are looking at a wind shift right now. Officer Melton has radioed that to the command post. The situation may be changing.	Live shot: picture shows cloud has shifted direction.
6:15:00	Baldrige: Stay inside, keep windows closed and AC on. Check your AC to see if it is the kind	Studio: two shot.

```
              that brings in outside
              air—if you get the match
              smell you'll know. If you
              do, turn it off.
6:16:05       McHenry: intro Ed Kovar,      Live shot: ground
              exec. director, Miami         view, flames, pull
              Valley Disaster Services.     back to two shot.


6:18:00       Kovar: I want to
              activate the Emergency
              Broadcast Service at this
              time.

              People along the river to
              the East upstream from
              Miamisburg into Morraine
              should evacuate to the
              East. Those in Dayton
              should stay indoors, shut
              windows. Very toxic
              fumes. (Repeats other
              evacuation areas.)
```

Let's pause here a moment. The action by Kovar to ask the WHIO-TV reporter to activate the Emergency Broadcast Service (EBS)—system and to do so live and on camera—is an unusual event.

The Emergency Broadcast System is established all over the country to provide coordination of emergency warnings and disaster relief information on a local, state, or national basis. Although both television and radio stations are connected to the EBS system, it has to be started by a special radio broadcast by a designated station in the area. This station broadcasts a special tone which turns on warning alarms at all the other stations in the area to make sure they are alert to the emergency.

As it happened, WHIO Radio, WHIO-TV's sister station, was the area official EBS station, so it began the special process the minute Kovar's words were heard on WHIO-TV. Even so, WHIO-TV had to go back and go through the official FCC required process of making the EBS activation official.

```
  Time           Words                   Pictures
6:18:11       Formal EBS procedure     EBS logo and format.
              tone, announcement.
6:18:30       Baldridge does           Points to map
              information wrap-up       locations of evacuation
              for EBS. Wind shift       areas.
              East to Southeast.
              Stay indoors, use AC
```

only if it is
''bringing in clean
air, not air filled
with fumes.''

6:19:58	Baldridge: The air outside is full of this smoke from the fire, it is thick and we are 7–8 miles away. Lists evacuation areas. Keep pets indoors too.	Live shot: outside TV station: hazy/foggy. Graphic: wreck location, evacuation areas.
6:20:56	Dave Freeman: With Rick Melton. Union Carbide crews are on their way in a helicopter. We spotted a softball game going on in Miamisburg park. Someone should go tell them. Also: Firemen are moving closer and laying hoses. This is the closest anyone has got to the fire.	Live shot: Chopper 7 over smoke cloud and wreck. Live shot: helicopter pans and zooms to show fire trucks doing this.
6:23:04	Baldridge, Wayne, Asbury: Weather spotter in Emmon, Ohio, says smoke has reached there now.	Studio: Three shot.
6:23:38– 6:25:38	COMMERCIAL BREAK	
6:25:40	Baldridge, Wayne: recap facts to date.	Studio: two shot.
6:27:00	Mike Hartsock: interviews Tom Heine, president, Dayton Chamber of Commerce	Live shot: golf course parking lot.

	about the evacuation of the golf course.	
6:29:30	Wayne says Dan Rather and the CBS Evening News will be delayed until later.	Studio: two shot.
6:30:15	Dave Freeman/Rick Melton: How do you know you are being evacuated? Uniformed officers, or PA from squad car, or people with IDs. Wind shifting more; trucks within 100 yards of fire now; setting up to pump water from the river onto the fire.	Live shot: helicopter view. Zooming in tighter.
6:33:26	Fire diminishing some now, can see charred limbs on trees. Baldridge: (question to those in Chopper 7): How much effect would rain have?	Circling wreck.
6:33:40	McHenry: Ed Kovar says the hoses will pump directly from the river. Officials having meeting to talk about wind shift and possible evacuation of that area and locations to the South of the wreck site. ''We are just going to have to get the heck out of Dodge if those fumes shift in this direction. Kovar says a very heavy rain with lots of water	Live shot: ground location, MCU, firemen, and trucks. Pan up cloud from fire. Widen to include McHenry in frame.

would help put the
fire out, but a small
amount could
aggravate it.
Baldridge: (question
to McHenry) What
symptoms should
people look for, at
what point should
they seek treatment?
McHenry: I will get
to an expert, I've
been told a heavy
dose could be fatal.

6:36:30   Baldridge, Wayne: Studio: two shot.
Back to the golf
course for more on   Live shot:
the tournament   Golf course parking
tomorrow. Mike   lot.
Hartsock, Heine.

6:38:06–   COMMERCIAL BREAK
6:39:17

    Asbury, Baldridge,   Studio: three shot.
Wayne. Asbury: been
looking at the radar
scope, winds will
shift around as storm
comes through.

                 Radar shows storm
                 cell.
    Walks to national   Weather graphics, etc.
map and does national
weather wrap–up

6:42:15   COMMERCIAL BREAK

6:43:15   Asbury: have   Radar keyed to fill
''storm–eye radar''   background.
on 25-mile range two
cells, one nearest
storm may kick up
shifting winds. Says   Chart reads wind SE 13
wind may shift to SW   mph.
as storm moves
through and repeats

that as a correction
of the graphic.

6:44:30	Dave Freeman: At 1300 feet over West Carolton High School at I-75. Several miles away and can still see flames. Melton: Amazed to see the cloud this high and this far. Going to have to alert agencies further away.	Live shot: helicopter showing cloud all the way across the screen.
6:45:50	Baldridge, Wayne: review of basics, wind shift problem. Baldridge: ''If you are new to Dayton, etc.'' (Points to large area map on set and gives general city orientation.)	Studio: two shot. Window: graphic of wreck location.
6:46:50	McHenry: Has answers to medical questions from Ed Kovar. Fumes can cause severe respiratory problems for those with emphysema and other such conditions. Normal symptoms are burning lungs, burning eyes. Perspiration, stinging sensation. If you have those probably don't need to go to the hospital. But, if you are having trouble breathing, see a doctor right away. Also: Can't see much wind shift, officials in a meeting, stay	Live shot: ground site.

indoors and use the
AC ''if you have one
that generates its
own air.'' Baldridge
to McHenry: ''the
wind has shifted 40–
50 degrees toward you
Cheryl. We'll be
watching it and let
you know what you
need to do.''

6:49:20–   COMMERCIAL BREAK
6:50:20

Baldridge, Wayne.   Studio: two shot.
Wayne: two hours or
more now, and still
no idea when it will
end. Baldridge:
Dayton Fire Dept.
says, ''Don't use an
AC which draws air
into the house. A
sealed unit is okay,
keep the doors and
windows closed, stay
away from the toxic
fumes.''

6:51:47   Sylvia Newsome: Video tape full.
interviewing Dr. Dean
Imbogno of Miami
Valley Hospital. (1)
Danger depends on
amount breathed,
small amount not much
danger, deadly if
inhaled for a long
time. (2) Need to
stay inside, wash it
off your face, hands,
and body with water.
(3) Hospital on low-
level alert, a few
people have come in,
no one in serious
condition.

6:55:25	Baldridge/phone interview: Bill Fairmuller, Monsanto Co. chemist. White phosphorus reacts and burns in the air.	Studio: one shot holding phone.
	The cloud is P_2O_5, and becomes phosphoric acid--a weak acid like vinegar, which is why it burns in nose and throat. Rain would probably be a good thing since it would change the cloud to liquid and wash it away.	Outside studio: very smoky landscape.
7:00:00	Baldridge, Wayne, Becky Grimes: Grimes has been checking on the evacuation sites. Grimes: no new evacuations, lists previous ones; none for Kettering, none for Dayton; fire chiefs decide for each community and are monitoring it on a minute-by-minute basis. Command center is emphasizing they want to avoid a major evacuation if possible and stress you should stay in your home until told to leave.	Studio: three shot. Studio: one shot.
7:01:30	COMMERCIAL BREAK	
7:03:29	Baldridge, Wayne: Recap basics, Wayne says cloud has now moved over Dayton.	Studio: two shot. Window: helicopter view.
7:04:06	Dave Freeman: sees a	Live shot: helicopter.

softball game going
on in Shellenberger
Park right in the
middle of the smoke
cloud. Flying along
I-675, smoke along
the ground and as
high as 1,500 feet.
Officer Rick Melton:
dismayed at the smoke
going so far and
staying along the
ground.

| 7:05:34 | Baldridge, Wayne: Smoke reminds him of early morning fog in Smoky Mts. Baldridge: ''Pretty but potentially deadly. No indications that anyone has been seriously hurt. Our goal is to warn you to stay away from the cloud. One breath may not bother you, but if you begin to feel poorly, get to medical help.'' | Studio: two shot. Window: ground view. |

| 7:06:40 | McHenry: interviews Ron Parker, acting Miamisburg Public Information Officer. Lists evacuation sites, and adds parts of W. Carollton N to I-725. Declares a ''state of emergency,'' shifts of 15 firefighters putting 16,000 gallons of water per minute. ''If that doesn't work we will | Live shot: ground view, pulls back to two shot. |

	have to evacuate this area too, and let it burn itself out.''	
7:07:30	Asbury: (cross-talking to McHenry) tell him the storm is only 3—5 miles away from where you are now; winds will become more turbulent and from all directions.	McHenry listening to Asbury. Radar screen: shows storm cell right on top of wreck location.
7:09:00	Parker: I'd appreciate any wind direction you've got. A new evacuation plan is being worked on right now.	
7:10:15	Asbury: I will be on the newsroom radio circuits for Cheryl's information and will warn you about wind shifts if necessary.	Studio: three shot.
7:14:05	Dave Freeman: We may have to land because of the storm, raining pretty hard north of wreck. Still see people out by swimming pools, maybe the rain will drive them inside.	Live shot: helicopter.
7:15:20	Asbury, Baldridge, Wayne Asbury: Smoke is in our own back yard and has been drawn into the studio by our AC. Suggests holding a wet rag over nose and mouth if caught in cloud.	Studio: three shot.
7:15:30	Asbury: Storm is not very wide so it won't rain very long. No upper	Radar: shows cell over Miamisburg.

air turbulence is
indicated, but this
storm had lower air
turbulence as it moved
toward us from Indiana.

7:18:14	DUE TO TANKER TRUCK FIRE, A STATE OF EMERGENCY EXISTS. ALL AREA CITIZENS SHOULD BE ALERT FOR EVACUATION AND EMERGENCY INFORMATION.	Full screen text over landscape shot from outside studios
7:19:00	COMMERCIAL BREAK	
7:20:30	REPEATED STATE OF EMERGENCY SLIDE AND AUDIO	
7:21:00	Dave Freeman: There is now a white plume and a dark plume beneath. Dark smoke is from rail cars carrying automobiles which have caught fire too. The flames are lower, but they are still there and the rain did not put the fire out.	Live shot: Chopper 7; Freeman is in front left seat; shot is through the windshield, and Freeman points to various features as he talks.
7:25:22	Cheryl McHenry: Officials move us back about 100 yards, further away because of storm and possible wind shift. Dick Emmons: The state of emergency makes the city eligible for state and federal funds. The situation is not any more or any less dangerous than it was. We had a quick and rather heavy thunderstorm. It has stopped now.	Live shot: ground location, new venue, above railroad tracks on an overpass.

WHIO-TV interrupted its live broadcast to play a tape of the CBS Evening News with Dan Rather and to carry another kind of live broadcast—the weekly Ohio Lottery Drawing from Cleveland. But it came back again at 8 P.M. for another twenty minutes or so to recap the story again and to tell the audience that the situation seemed to have stabilized and that the total evacuations so far had reached sixteen thousand persons. This segment included live and taped reports from a hospital, a Red Cross evacuation staging center, and both the helicopter and ground locations.

By 11:00 P.M. WHIO-TV was able to bring on Cheryl McHenry and Dick Emmons to say the fire was under control, and Angela Cain, who reported from an evacuation center at Miamisburg High School that the people there didn't expect to get home before dawn. At 11:40 P.M. the station again went live to cover a news conference held by Ohio Governor Richard Celeste, who had flown back from New York City to see to the situation in Dayton.

The Aftermath

By all logic and experience the following day should have been somewhat easier for WHIO-TV's staff. The state of emergency was still in effect, and fire officials and chemical fire experts had spent the day making plans to get the slowly burning phosphorus fire to a once-and-for-all finish.

But just as WHIO-TV reporter Sam Yates was interviewing Ron Parker live from the Miamisburg Civic Center about the long-range plans, the whole thing started all over again.

Time	Words	Pictures
6:05:12	There has been another major outbreak of fire. The fire crews have run for safety. It is almost as big as yesterday. The wind is from the west, and the smoke is blowing right toward Miamisburg.	Live shot: helicopter flying toward the wreck site. A big plume of smoke is clearly rising.

For the next hour and ten minutes, the situation was very tense. Officials worried that the phosphorus and sulfur from an adjoining rail car would mix: In fact they did. About 7:11 P.M. another big belch of smoke erupted from the fire site.

Time	Words	Picture
7:12:04	Dave Freeman: Here we go again. They are moving people out. The	Live shot: more fire, more smoke.

```
flames are 15 feet in
the air, bright flames.
It has taken off again,
and there is a huge
cloud, nearly as bad as
yesterday. The wind
direction is SE, ESE. If
you are in that
direction, move out.
```

With the fire active again, civic officials started several major evacuations to the University of Dayton Arena and then to the Dayton Convention Center when it was discovered that the Arena wasn't air conditioned. Fire and police officers drove and walked through neighborhoods announcing the evacuation on bull horns.

Dayton's major shopping mall was covered by the smoke and evacuated for the second time in twenty-four hours. This caused large traffic jams and plenty of frustrated evacuees. Some people who had gone on a shopping trip in the late afternoon weren't allowed to go back to their homes until late that night. The mayor of Moraine called WHIO-TV to say there was no evacuation there, even though one had been ordered by disaster officials. In all thirty-five thousand Dayton area residents were moved out of their homes.

Through all this WHIO-TV's news crew kept the same cool heads they had the night before.

Dave Freeman called the cloud "creeping fog out of a B horror movie." Later as the fire died down again he said, "It's not the Fourth of July it was hours ago, but eerie."

Fire captain Bill Ring, looking down from the helicopter, said, "There's some heavy chemistry going on down there." Both Freeman and Ring commented on the evacuations: "A ghost town down there," they said. "Did you ever expect not to see a single car in the Dayton Mall at 8 P.M.?"

Pilot Mark Cain talked to the security officials at the Dayton Mall as the smoke cloud closed in on them. He was pleased that they (and the audience) could see people leaving as a result of their live report.

Jim Baldridge: "We'll say it again, this could be life threatening. There is cause for alarm and action, there is no cause for panic." The on-air staff struggled most with two elements of the story: how dangerous was the cloud and how to tell people what to do with their air conditioners. They were successful with the cloud. They were still struggling with the air conditioners at the end.

Bruce Asbury had another wind shift to report and again tracked it on his electronic weather maps. Asbury alerted the Accuweather Center at Penn State and got special help from them when the storms threatened to add another variable to the equation.

Cheryl McHenry reported the frustration of the fire officials: "They worked so hard to get it under control, it is disappointing. If anything could go wrong, it has."

The Post-Mortem

WHIO-TV News won the 1987 RTNDA Spot News Award for its coverage. A rating period was in effect, and they racked up a 77 share on the second night of the story. News director Hapner and others said they felt they had all the technology they needed to do the job they did. They could have used a few more hands.

Hapner said: "We used the live units so much there wasn't time to use them to ship taped material back via the microwave. We just had to drive those tapes into the station by auto. And we generated so much tape both from the roving reporter-photo crews and the live units that we were covered up with material.

"We also needed some people to stay at the evacuation centers and do more reporting from there." But Hapner was pleased, though he didn't have a chance to rest on his oars for long.

On Friday a powerful storm swept through the area, blowing down trees on the golf course where the Women's Open was in progress. On Saturday there was a small earthquake. And on Sunday a light plane crashed near the airport.

The Crash of Flight 191

In 1979, an American Airlines DC-10 crashed shortly after takeoff from Chicago's O'Hare Airport. All 279 people on board were killed. It became the worst aviation disaster in U.S. history.

WMAQ-TV covered the crash and its aftermath with a plan that news director Paul Beavers had designed from years of experience in Los Angeles with coverage of the assassination of Robert Kennedy, California earthquakes, and the Symbionese Liberation Army shootout. On those earlier events, his rule of thumb for coverage was: "Go get a lot of pictures and then figure out what to do with them." As live ENG developed his rule has changed to: "Get on the air—then support the air."

Beavers had a game plan with which to support the air. It called for putting control of the live broadcast into the hands of a small number of people with specific responsibilities.

1. *A field producer* goes to each live *remote unit*. That producer is the principal information relay to and from the station, and to the principal on-air reporter. Other reporters at each live remote site feed information to the field producer for relay to the live reporters or through the newsroom to the anchors.
2. *The assignment desk manager* handles logistics of the movement of mobile units and reporters.
3. *Producer of facts* is responsible for the intake of all facts and details; shaping the story, looking for angles, directing the in-house staff of reporters and researchers. Worries about supporting the content of the program, not the program itself.
4. *Producer for program* works in the control room with the ENG coordinators and live-program director to keep the program going.
5. *The news director* supervises it all.

WMAQ-TV, besides having Beavers' game plan in place, was lucky. A station courier was at the airport and saw the crash. A station mobile unit happened to be on the way to the airport to cover another story. The courier radioed the assignment desk about the crash. The desk ordered the crew to speed to the airport. They followed fire trucks onto the field and set up the first live link. More crews and reporters followed.

WMAQ-TV's live broadcast continued without interruption for four and one-half hours. The station was fortunate to have an articulate, very knowledgeable, extremely calm airline pilot as its weather forecaster. Much of the success of what went on the air was due to his special knowledge and the questions he asked to get the significant information needed.

But much of what went on the air was also due to the way Beavers' game plan worked. The in-house staff located eyewitnesses, checked them carefully to make sure they had real information, and then passed them on to the control room and studio set phone for the anchors to interview. The anchors were briefed about what the eyewitnesses had to say. Even the minute details were controlled; each time an eyewitness was put on the phone, that person's name was superimposed on the screen—and it was spelled correctly.

The assignment desk managed the movements of five live units and four crews with portable tape but no live capacity. The helicopter crew was told to fly over the airport immediately—not to wait until a microwave link could be established. That crew shot the videotape knowing that it would be put on the air without editing. The pictures were quite steady and remained focused on the crash scene as the helicopter circled slowly.

Beavers' system and the effort it touched off produced a mountain of raw material. On May 25, fifty-six videotape cassettes were filled with pictures and sound by the crews—that is something like thirty to thirty-five *hours* of material. In all, the WMAQ-TV crash coverage—which continued with extended news specials for two more days—produced 136 video cassettes, easily more than seventy-five hours of outside coverage. WMAQ-TV won virtually every national award for spot news coverage that year.

USES AND PROBLEMS OF LIVE COVERAGE

Producing a successful live news broadcast, as we have seen, calls for quick decisions, flexibility while maintaining careful control, and concentration. What you do is what the audience sees.

Elmer Lower, former president of ABC News and a veteran executive of all three television network news divisions, says a live broadcast is unique.

"We are," he says, "the only journalistic medium that does its reporting and editing right in front of the audience."

Lower says that at something like a national political convention, all of the editors and reporters from all the media do the same kinds of things. They get a report that something important *may* be developing. Then they go out onto the floor and into the caucuses to check it out. This is the uniqueness of live television shows. While the reporters for the newspapers and wire services are doing their checking more or less privately, the television news reporters are on the air while they are running the story down.

That has led to a number of things. A story suddenly blossoms, then wilts as the TV reporters swarm over news makers only to find that it was someone's carefully planted trial balloon that didn't fly. Other times it turns out that there really was some substance to the story. Whatever the outcome is, the TV audience is watching the *process* of journalism as well as the result.

Flashback World

When a live broadcast mixes live segments with pretaped material there is a danger that the story may move away from the linear form—beginning, middle, and end— to jumping around in time. This can cause discontinuity for the viewer—a loss of the time frame. Though the story gets to the viewer as a forward-moving sequence of scenes, the time elements don't. Here are a couple of examples.

Almost every fall the metropolitan area of Los Angeles is beset by the annual outbreak of brush fires in the parched hills which surround the city on three sides. On the network newscasts and on local newscasts elsewhere, viewers see one version of that story. Typically, it contains scenes from the fires—always more spectacular at night. They race up a hill, over the top, and down into the next valley. There are fire trucks with whirling red lights, many shots of people dazed by the sight of their burned-out homes, other shots of people trying to prevent the inevitable with a garden hose. There are lots of interviews and the victims invariably say, "We've lost everything we've got."

From television stations in Los Angeles the local audience often gets a different version in which time and place are altered by a combination of live and prerecorded scenes. One year the fires were unique in that for a time they threatened the transmitter sites of most of the Los Angeles television stations. Sometimes it was difficult to figure out who was more worried: the television people who feared they would lose their transmitters, or the viewers who feared they would lose their television programs.

Nevertheless, the stations' mobile units rushed from place to place as they fed hours of raw material back to their newsrooms. On every local newscast, and on frequent special live reports, the editors and producers selected from a tremendous volume of visual material that provided an almost continuous flow of fire stories *across* location and time.

A typical story went like this:

Scene 1:	Reporter live from some fire location.
Scene 2:	Zoom past the reporter to pick up details of whatever fire was burning near him or her.
Scene 3:	Continuation of the live camera peering around, panning slowly, zooming in on details—eyes for the audience.

| Scenes 4, 5, 6, 7, 8, etc: | On tape: scene of a fire last night, burning heavily, firefighters and fire trucks; evacuees at a YMCA; scenes of other destruction earlier that day; several different locations and time frames. |
| Scene 9: | Reporter back live at the location of Scene 1. |

The conventional wisdom is, of course, that the audience understands best those stories in which the scenes relate to each other in a linear manner—Scene 2 builds on Scene 1 and relates forward to Scene 3.

In the Los Angeles fire coverage continuity often didn't work that way. The viewer watching the example above can follow the first three scenes and is re-oriented by the final scene. But in between, time and location are uncontrolled, with flashbacks and flashforwards.

Careful attention must be given to the location and time elements in both the audio and video. Sometimes the Los Angeles reporters and producers did provide this: ''Earlier today here's what it looked like on Mulholland Drive . . . last night in Holmby Hills,'' or time and location were indicated by words superimposed on the screen. But sometimes viewers were left to figure it out for themselves.

Take another example:

Scene 1:	Reporter live at the station transmitter site. He says the fire has been reduced and *does not now* threaten the towers and equipment.
Scene 2 (live):	Firefighters in full gear walking down over the side of the mountain.
Scene 3 (on tape):	Firefighters without gear eating breakfast at their campsite.
Scene 4 (tape):	The fire last night from another point of view, bigger fire.
Scene 5 (tape):	Helicopter shots of the fire yesterday when it was a swirling mass of flames.
Scene 6 (tape):	Transmitter engineers standing around outside the building.
Scene 7 (live):	Reporter again, wrapping up, repeats the fire is *not a threat now*.

In this version both the time frame and the locations are hopscotched in a very disorderly manner. It is likely that part of the audience was confused and that the reporter's news that the fire was not a present threat was not believed.

News executives, producers, editors and all those involved along the line must make sure that the pizzazz of technology doesn't get in the way of understanding.

The File Tape Curse

An even more pernicious tinkering with the time frame of a story happens when file tape is used improperly. Videotape can be archived easily, and it is of real value when editors and reporters want to review something that happened a while ago. But when the tape from the files is mixed in with tape shot today, it is only ethical to tell the audience as quickly as possible after the file scenes appear and to label the tapes properly.

It is very important that the viewers be able to sort out what they are looking at: Is this tape of Contras in a war-games exercise *new tape* or the same tape shown last year? Are these scenes of tankers going through the Persian Gulf scenes *recorded today,* or are they the ones recorded last week? In this montage of wrecks at the same railroad crossing, why do we see snow on the ground in only some of the scenes?

Any time the video you include in a story package raises questions like these, you have distracted the viewers and have seriously hurt their ability to comprehend. The only legitimate use for file tape is to show the viewer what happened before, like an instant replay in sports. When file tape is used as "representational pictures," we are not showing the viewers what happened today; we are showing them something that happened before that looks like what happened today. The very least we can do is admit it.

Live Means Important

The audience has become accustomed to live reports on local television stations. It has also become more sophisticated and less impressed by technology.

Neil Darrough, former general manager of WCBS-TV in New York City, thinks that live news broadcasts have evolved significantly. He says:

> We've all been guilty of mistakes. Hell, I can recall at the beginning we were pleased just to get a picture. Let's shoot it, we'd say, because that will give people the impression that we are there.
>
> But the audience too quickly becomes sophisticated as to whether there's news in it or not. Our research now shows that the big word is *update*; that's the element of live news reports that makes sense. If your live operation is constantly updating a story, and you're telling the audience something they couldn't get any other way, then boy, they're with you all the way and they just plain eat it up.
>
> If you are doing it just for the sake of doing it—it's not really an important story— the audience knows, and your credibility is damaged.

The late Dick Graf, a veteran network and Boston news executive, said live is only *one way* to cover a story. For the audience, the mere fact that the story is being covered live means that it is important. He stated, "If it isn't important they are amused and angry at the same time—amused because you are going to so much trouble to cover something that isn't important, and angry because you are wasting their time."

By no means do all uses of live coverage involve spot news. Becoming popular with local stations as well as the networks is the live, on-site, "expert interview." Ted Koppel of ABC's "Nightline" pioneered the idea of using teleconferencing facilities—linking one or more experts into the program by satellite or other connections. Often experts are more willing to participate in a teleconference setup than they are to take the time and trouble to travel to the studio for a live appearance.

Live Trivia

Many stations learned the hard way. Our nationwide survey resulted in a partial list of things *not* to do live. All appeared on some TV newscast, some more than once.

2:40 on a Cub Scout talent show

A two-alarm house fire

A male go-go dancer's opening night

A senator's campaign kickoff party

A news conference that just happens to be scheduled at 6 P.M. or 11 P.M.

How to open a champagne bottle (New Year's Eve, 11 P.M. news.)

Firefighters removing a cat from a tree

Asking the pope as he passes by, "What do you think of your reception so far?"

Claiming that the question to the pope was an exclusive live interview

Covering a local convention that hasn't started yet by touring the exhibit booths with the PR respresentative

Live interview of a college professor to get his views on El Salvador

The scene of a meeting that ended two hours earlier

A courtroom where the verdict was reached in midafternoon; now only the reporter and janitor are there

The airport arrival of a movie star

Especially if her plane has not yet arrived

Interviews with sports stars who are going to speak later at a local dinner

Almost all man-on-the-street "samplings of opinion"

Any time the story is over and the reporter has to say, "We don't have much to add. . . ."

From the Interstate, where traffic is flowing normally

A live picture of the sky that purports to show what a stationary front looks like

A live weather report from a helicopter, during which the weather forecaster gets airsick

Live As a Two-Edged Sword

Another level of live reports about the trivial and ridiculous raises worries about the use of the live shot as a weapon or its intrusion into the news itself.

The arrival of local live capability brought out politicians and public relations people the way robins follow a spring rain. Earlier publicists quickly learned to release stories in time to meet morning and afternoon newspaper deadlines. Now they announced important news conferences or brought out their candidates near or at the time of major newscasts in the hopes they could lure live coverage.

A few stations got burned before they learned never to *promise* live coverage. Today they are much more likely to set up for a tape-delay operation if it looks like there may be some news in the event. That way they can study the material as it is fed in and make some news judgments as to whether any of it should be edited for later insertion in the newscast.

Yet television journalists can still get gulled. In the spring of 1983, President Reagan made one of his quick trips to the White House newsroom for a brief announcement. In the midst of it Mrs. Reagan walked in with a birthday cake and led everyone in singing "Happy Birthday." The journalists said they should have been told so that they could make decisions about whether to fire up and go live for such an event. The White House press secretary said it was a surprise to him, too.

The live shot as a weapon is another facet that requires editorial judgment. There is a line from the word game I Knew It Was a Bad Day When. . . . that goes, "I knew it was a bad day when I got up and looked out of the window and saw the TV crews on the front lawn. . . ."

It is possible to chase and corner people with a live unit in the hope they will cave in and talk. In Milwaukee the school superintendent had been hardnosed about closing the schools because of bad weather. One of the local stations had received a lot of phone calls from parents who complained that their children were being put in danger. The station tried all of the conventional ways to get the superintendent to state his views. Finally, they rolled their news van up in front of his house, turned on the cameras to show the deep snow drifts on his street, then sent a reporter with a microphone to the front door to call him out. The superintendent came out, said a few words about the weather situation, and a lot of harsher words about the station's methods and how much snow was blowing onto his front hall carpet.

When public employees were on strike in Pennsylvania, two stations owned by the same group set up a live report with the governor in Harrisburg. They put reporters with him in his office and also had reporters in their studios at both ends of the state to ask more questions. Many observers thought this setup had unfairly trapped the governor and that the reporters had become advocates for legislation to stop the strike. The stations defended their action by saying it was really a live news conference.

The Live Environment

Live television coverage can intrude on privacy and affect the way a story develops.

A Milwaukee station uncovered the fact that a local woman was the mother of a man about to be executed in the Bahamas after having been convicted of a capital crime. The mother had tried everything possible to get the sentence commuted. She was expecting a call from a United States senator who had agreed to try to help.

The station moved live equipment into the woman's home and went on the air from her living room at the time the call was supposed to come. The reporter and woman waited. The phone rang. The reporter said something like, "Here it is— let's listen." The woman proceeded to chat amiably for several seconds. The call turned out to be from a friend who wanted to tell her about a bargain at a local department store. The reporter finally had the grace to say, "I think we'd better leave."

That live report ended up with no story at all. In more significant situations the

FIGURE 9-5. WBZ-TV in Boston, Massachusetts, tries to avoid intruding into a news story by having some of its microwave vans painted a neutral color without the station's logo or other identification. After the microwave antenna goes up almost everyone will know what it is, but before that the vehicles are much less obtrusive. *(Courtesy of WBZ-TV, Boston.)*

presence of the live equipment can affect the way a story develops. Most stations try to avoid getting their staffs into the middle of breaking stories.

Don Ross, a former news director of WBZ-TV Boston and later a station group executive, said he had tried hard to make sure his staff understood the environmental impact of having live equipment too close to an event, especially in civic disorders.

> We had to rethink a lot of the splash because of tensions in the city. We painted some of our news vans a plain color, and we went out to cover an event in as low a profile as possible. Then, when the information was gathered, we'd move away, put up the antennaes and say something like, "Right down the street this happened, and here are pictures of that." Or we'd tape an interview, edit it and use that to lead into pictures of the event.

In Baltimore a news director talked about an incident in which a sniper had taken hostages. He was a mental hospital patient who had taken other patients hostage and was threatening to throw them out of a window. All of them, hostages and hostage taker, needed medication. Reporters and crews were sent to the place where the police had surrounded the sniper.

> The hostage taker demanded to go on the air to vent his grievances. We agreed, through the police, that our reporter would go in, talk to him, and then come out and tell what he had on his mind.
>
> We went live for that and the reporter did a very careful paraphrase of what the man had said. We had to be extremely careful because we knew the man was listening. It all worked out fine. . . at noon, while we were live, the man came out, thanked us . . . and the police hauled him away.
>
> After the sniper had been taken, we set up with lights and edited the video we shot during the stake out. The reporter went on the air to say that the story was over, and then rolled in the video to illustrate what had happened. You just don't go out and show puddles of blood for the hell of it.

Editorial Guidelines for Live Reports

Many stations have developed written guidelines about the proper management and handling of live reports, especially those which may involve civil disorders or situations involving hostages.

All employees at KRON-TV, San Francisco, are provided with such guidelines and are expected to adhere to them. These guidelines put the responsibility for live coverage decisions in the hands of the executive producer, the assignment editor, and the news director. The decision to go live rests on three conditions:

1. The safety of all KRON-TV personnel involved
2. The potential for inflaming the situation
3. The possibility of conflict with orders of law-enforcement agencies

If the story is about a civil disorder, the KRON-TV president or station manager must give prior approval.

These guidelines require the news director to provide operational control of the coverage and to give primary consideration to the safety of the staff and general public. They call for the station to stop coverage if it appears to inflame the situation or hamper the police.

Regarding hostages, the KRON-TV policy forbids making any telephone calls to the hostage takers and bans the start of any coverage if police forbid it. It also requires the staff to follow police orders in general. If calls are coming in from hostage takers, the staff is required to inform station officials and the police.

The rules end, ''Act as if your own children are being held hostage.''

LET'S WRAP IT UP

One prime concept weaves through the story of the senator's trip home, or the sewer blast, or the tank car fire, and all of the other live broadcasts mentioned. Virtually every one of the decisions that has to be made when a live story starts, rises to a climax, and subsides is a journalistic decision.

No machine yet invented has news judgment; no system goes out and covers the news by itself. No helicopter decides where to fly. Stories don't come in already reported. It is the planning, operation, and editorial control the journalist provides that get the job done.

Photo by Stanley Forman

PROFILE

John Premack is one of the best-known TV photojournalists in the country. Born in Minneapolis in 1944, he started his career as a part-time dispatcher with KSTP-TV, shooting 16mm black-and-white film with a single-lens Bell and Howell wind-up camera. That led to full-time work at KSTP when that station was among the national leaders in adapting color film technology to television news.

Since 1974 he has been chief cameraman for WCBV-TV, Boston, one of the first stations in the country to purchase a KU-band SNG truck. Active in the National Press Photographers Association as a faculty member of the NPPA Television News Workshop and Flying Short Course, he also lectures and leads seminars for photographers, reporters, and editors.

While his assignments take him all over the world for an average eight to ten weeks a year, John says he is happiest roaming New England in his four-wheel drive Blazer, which is equipped with every possible component of ENG. He adds, "While my duties as chief cameraman require a certain amount of paper shuffling, I've resisted every opportunity to move behind a desk."

LIVE NEWS

JOHN PREMACK
WCVB-TV, BOSTON

Nowhere has the impact of the electronic camera been more strongly noted than in the ability to report live from the scene of a news event. News film cameramen never had to contemplate the possibility. Electronic cameramen must become as adept at doing a live shot as they are at covering a news conference or a three-alarm fire.

Live shots may be the most physically demanding, boring and least creative assignments a television news cameraman is likely to encounter. Pulling cables and lumping portable microwave units into buildings or atop roofs is dirty work that often seems pointless if you realize that the same report, pre-recorded and edited, would probably look better on the air and require less time and effort as well. Nevertheless live shots have become a staple of to-day's local newscasts and deserve to be approached and executed in a smooth and professional manner.

There are three basic modes of live news broadcasts that the news cameraman is likely to encounter. First, the most common, is the reporter standup from the scene of an event. Adding variety to the usual fare of in-studio anchors and taped reports, the live standup allows conversation between the reporter in the field and the anchorperson in the studio.

The basic or "naked" standup is often relieved by the use of a "doughnut," previously recorded tape and interviews, edited with a narration track, aired in the middle of the live shot.

In the basic reporter standup, the cameraman's primary concern is to set up a shot that allows the viewer to see enough of the background to understand easily where the reporter is. This generally requires shooting at wide focal lengths and placing the reporter six to ten feet from the camera.

But selecting the shot primarily on the basis of the background—what's the point of being on location if people can't see it?—often creates the need for supplemental lighting. When the sun is out, it is rarely where you'd like it to be, and a reflector or fill light is required to prevent the reporter from suffering the indignities of harsh shadows or appearing in semi-silhouette.

Similar care must be taken after dark. With the reporter close to the camera, it's easy to place the lights too close to him or her. You should use only as much light as is absolutely necessary—too much light is the cardinal sin of shooting video at night. The cameraman must take full advantage of the light already existing in the selected background. Too much light on the reporter results in a "limbo" shot with nothing but blackness instead of the background you chose.

The second basic live shot is a variation on the first in that the reporter does the standup and also conducts an interview. This two-person, one-camera situation differs from the ordinary interview setup because of the requirement that both the reporter and the interviewee must be able to face the camera, talk to each other, and still avoid being shot in profile. This is accomplished best by putting the interviewee in a fixed position and having the reporter turn away from the camera to conduct the interview.

To do this correctly a little preplanning by the reporter and cameraman is essential. Positions are found and marked with tape if necessary. The subject should be prepositioned, standing or seated, facing the camera. Then the reporter can begin his report on a "one shot," take a few steps as the camera widens to a two shot, and then turn to the subject while the camera zooms into a one shot of the subject (changing focus to a mark preset on the lens).

Care should be taken to insure that the reporter remains nearer the camera than the subject if you are to avoid shooting the subject in profile. An easy way to guarantee that both reporter and subject stand where they should is to briefly rehearse the blocking, where each will stand, and mark the positions with a coin or piece of gaffer's tape.

It is wise to use two lavalier microphones—one for the reporter, the other for the subject—so that the reporter doesn't have to hold his hand mic in the subject's face; the cameraman also has more freedom to compose the shot. While two mics are nice, many live shots are done with a single hand mic. This is often a trade-off, swapping production values for convenience. Crews don't always have sufficient time or cable to run two audio lines, and there is no chance that the wrong mic will be turned on when only one is in use. Also, hand mics are technically superior in noisy locations.

Reporter cooperation is also essential. If the reporter doesn't understand what you'd like to do, there is the risk he or she will inadvertently block your shot while conducting the interview. It is one thing to interrupt a taped interview to reposition the reporter or subject; it is quite another when you are live. Preplanning cannot be overemphasized: When you are doing a live shot, there are no second takes.

The third and most infrequent live situation occurs when you actually have the opportunity to air a spot news event as it happens. While most live shots are done during newscasts, our ability to provide live coverage on short notice gives us the opportunity to break into programming whenever the news warrants.

The name of this game is: Get there fast, pan in the microwave, and locate the camera where it can command an uninterrupted view. Camera position is critical: It is disastrous if the studio switches to you when you aren't able to supply a look at the event. Elevation is generally required to see beyond the other crews and spectators. One common mistake in this type of situation is to compromise the camera position to allow the reporter to appear on camera. Not only do you sacrifice a vantage point of the action, you run the risk of being harassed by the news cameraman's nemeses, known locally as the hi-moms, who appear in your shot grinning and waving just as you go on the air.

There can be conflicts in deciding what the live crew is supposed to provide. If an event is big enough to require live coverage, it should be standard operating procedure to assign a second camera crew to do the tape coverage of the story. A live crew cannot do an adequate job of covering all the angles of a story if it is restricted to the end of the coaxial cable that feeds its picture to the microwave van and back to the station. One reporter might be able to swing between the fixed camera location and the portable crew, but a single crew trying to do live shots, feed tapes, interviews, and general coverage will do none well.

BREAKING NEWS

While most live shots are generally dull and routine assignments, covering a breaking story is the most challenging and potentially frustrating assignment you can have. Don't plan on a PR person to hold the action for you if you arrive late. Shots missed while changing tapes or batteries are never available again.

Breaking news events are unique because they have a momentum of their own. We have all become used to having so many of the news events we cover prescheduled, prearranged, lit, and staged for the mutual benefit of the would-be news makers and our cameras that we sometimes lose sight of the fact that we ought to be simply observers and recorders of events rather than participants in them.

It is often said that good spot news coverage depends on simply being at the right place at the right time. It is true that you have to be there, but that isn't nearly enough. Successful coverage of breaking stories requires preparation, courage, and anticipation.

Being prepared requires a lot of things. You must be as quick and as comfortable operating your camera as a carpenter is swinging a hammer. The successful news cameraman develops his own habits and routines. Charged batteries here, and dead ones there. Mike cords coiled to drop open free from tangles. Color bars laid down when the fresh tape is loaded. Equipment always put away in the same order. If your checking and double-checking become an unconscious routine, you'll never arrive at an assignment and realize that the last time you saw your tripod was when the reporter picked it up and walked away.

This devotion to your tools must extend to the creation of an unthinking intimacy with your camera and recorder. You've got to be able to set the controls by touch—without looking. If you have to look at the recorder to see if the audio level is set for auto or manual, if your hand doesn't instinctively turn the focus ring in the proper direction, if you forget to white balance for a new lighting condition, and if you are surprised when the battery warning light comes on . . . you don't know your equipment, and you aren't going to be able to give full concentration to whatever is going on around you. The camera, despite its complexity, must become an automatic extension of the photojournalist's eyes.

The other significant skill required to cover spot news is the ability to anticipate action and to get ahead of the event. The cameraman who has the camera rolling, waiting for the wall to fall or the bottles to break, is going to turn in well-framed and in-focus video, while the cameraman who tries to react to actions as they happen will miss more than he captures. Being in the right place at the right time with the camera rolling is not a matter of luck at all. It is an acquired skill that comes only from a devotion to the small details of a craft. It is a reflection of a cameraman's past experiences in similar situations and skill at selecting and positioning himself at the best possible vantage point.

There are a few basics to keep in mind when everything is going down around you. In the midst of a melee or high action of any sort, roll your recorder early, confirm that it is rolling, and don't shut it off. If your camera has two remote start buttons, press them both to prevent stopping the recorder unintentionally. Leaving the recorder on prevents lost shots and insures no problems in editing scenes that would not have had sufficient lock-up time had you been starting and stopping the recorder each time you saw something to shoot.

Once you have a few cover shots, start looking for closeups. It takes courage to isolate one element of a big event. You run the risk of not being able to hold focus and are constantly afraid that being so tight will make you miss something. That's true. You also give yourself a chance to capture some dramatic tape that can be easily edited as opposed to a series of medium and long shots that, after a while, all look the same.

Hold your shots longer than seems necessary to capture the action. Novice cameramen are often amazed to find they have most of the action, but in a series of three-second shots, once the camera movement and focus adjustments have been edited out.

Don't be afraid to stop shooting for a few seconds to look for a better vantage point. The steps of a building, the trunk of a car, or the small stepladder you carry in your own car can provide you with just enough elevation to get you over the crowd and prevent you from losing a great shot because someone got in the way. It is better to sacrifice thirty seconds shooting time than to have two minutes of unusable video as you and your camera are jostled and blocked.

If you're not wearing headphones to monitor the audio, don't forget to occasionally check the recorder's VU meter to confirm that you are recording sound. In the rush of the moment, it's possible to bump the mic volume controls or forget that the shotgun mic needs to be switched on.

It is easy to forget closeups when the action is heavy, yet the drama of an event is often best told on the faces of just a few individuals. When the action is at a distance, send someone back for the tripod. Stories where the media are kept at bay, such as hijackings and bomb-squad activity, require the longest lens you can muster and that demands a tripod. Having a 300mm lens on your shoulder is no guarantee you can make usable pictures by leaving it there.

AN ETHICAL VIEW

While the work of a television news cameraman is both technical and creative, it must be remembered that the things just mentioned are simply areas of skill required to pursue our fundamental craft—journalism. The news cameraman is a *photojournalist,* responsible for the truthfulness of the images recorded on tape and presented on television in the same way that a reporter is responsible for the script and the manner in which a story is produced and edited.

As journalists, we can neither stage nor re-create events for our convenience, nor can we allow others to stage action that would not have occurred if cameras had not been present. It is as dishonest to single out for a cutaway the only person in an audience who has fallen asleep as it is to shoot a smoky, one-alarm fire entirely in closeups. In both instances the viewer is denied the opportunity to see in fair perspective what actually occurred.

The overriding goal of a competent news cameraman should be to show someone who wasn't at an event an accurate representation of what happened, to show the person who was there what he or she missed, and to do it without allowing the presence of the camera to affect materially what was going on in the first place.

We must recognize that a television camera tends to create its own reality. Part of our job as photojournalists is to understand that our mere presence can inflame, incite, initiate, and otherwise alter events we wish to cover.

Although we don't like it, many of the events we attend are staged to some degree in order to attract news coverage. The picket line that materializes from out of nowhere when a news van turns the corner and disappears even before the camera is back in the van, the news conference, the candidate's media event, and the incumbent's "photo opportunity" are all designed to generate publicity. We as cameramen become quite used to participating in these "events." We think nothing of delaying them until we are ready, telling folks where to stand and how to pose during cutaways.

But we are photojournalists. We must not let our work habits—developed to cope with staged "news" events—extend to situations where we must be strictly uninvolved observers. Fires, riots, floods, and other stories that qualified as news before we arrived must be allowed to unfold without our assistance. We are, please remember, recorders of events. We must allow them to occur spontaneously, unimpeded by the technical restrictions of sound and light and the physical presence of the news crew.

This means giving folks a chance to get used to having us around for a few minutes instead of entering a tranquil and orderly scene with portable lights blazing. This means putting the camera in the shadows instead of under everyone's nose. This means communicating with the reporter and other crew members quietly without drawing attention from the event we are there to witness and record.

Cameramen should also remember that they represent their station to the public and dress appropriately. While the work can occasionally be strenuous or dirty, crews should not stand out like a bagel in a Chinese restaurant. While there is no need to engage reporters in a contest for sartorial splendor, denim jeans, T-shirts, and tank tops should be saved for off-duty hours.

COMMUNICATIONS

The most critical element in the successful airing of live reports is communications between the control room and the crew in the field. You can be doing a microwave relay through your helicopter overhead, a six-hop relay from two hundred miles away, or beaming across the country via satellite, and if the reporter and cameraman don't know they are on the air or can't hear instructions from the producer, the entire live shot can fall apart—on the air.

Many crews carry a portable black-and-white receiver so that the reporter can see what is on the air. That isn't nearly as critical as the need for the crew in the field to hear off-air audio *and* cues direct from the control room. Reporters and cameramen rely on a system called IFB to receive their cues and hear the newscast. IFB (Interrupted Fold Back) refers to the delivery of off-air audio which can be interrupted by the director or producer in the control room. Most stations have a two-way radio frequency assigned to this function, allowing crew members the convenience of using a walkie-talkie or other portable receiver to monitor the IFB. When the live shot originates beyond the range of a station's radio system, having the IFB is just as important. Then telephone lines are used, and the crew must be equipped with clip leads or a pick-up coil and small amplifier to feed audio from the telephone into the reporter's earpiece.

SATELLITE REPORTING

A word of caution is in order concerning the IFB fed to the reporter who is broadcasting live through the satellite. Since the report must travel over fifty thousand miles through space to reach and return from the "bird," it will take over one-third of a second for the reporter's words to reach the control room. If the incoming audio goes on the air and then is fed back via telephone to the reporter's IFB earpiece, he will hear his own words after he has spoken them. This is similar to the disorientation suffered by someone who is using the public address system in a football stadium for the first time—hearing their voice bouncing back while trying to concentrate on what is to be said next.

The solution is simple, but it must be anticipated in advance since the problem occurs only once you are actually on the air. The remote location is not fed the usual IFB mix of off-air audio and cues, but instead is supplied with what is called "mix-minus" sound. The studio audio board is set up to return all audio *except* the incoming report so that the remote crew need not be bothered at all by the built-in delay.

Another potentially embarrassing problem unique to satellite feeds is that you can't run over your scheduled time on the "bird" by even a few seconds. Satellite time is tightly scheduled and sometimes controlled automatically by a computer. That means that when your assigned time is over, the transponder on the satellite is automatically fed the next customer's program whether you're finished or not.

TROUBLESHOOTING MEANS UNTROUBLED SHOOTING

Sometimes I think it would be a good idea if cameramen could trade places with their cameras for a few days. It should go without saying that the electronic cameras and recorders we use must be treated with respect. The camera lying on its side and bouncing around in the trunk of a car, lenses that are inadvertently used to hold open a door, and tapes left lying in the sun will all deliver images far below their potential. These overt acts are bad enough, but those that result in failures from lack of attention to the needs of the equipment are worse. Recorder heads need to be cleaned regularly. Yet at some stations this simple chore is often performed as a remedy instead of as prevention. Most other equipment failures are attributable directly to broken cables and faulty batteries.

Everyone in this business needs to learn more about the insides of the cameras and recorders. Yes, I know that there are a large number of engineering managers and maintenance technicians who in various ways perpetuate the myth that no one save an anointed few may open the covers of a camera or recorder. And yes, I know that it takes only two minutes with a little green-handled screwdriver to totally negate two hours of careful adjustment and alignment. But who is going to reregister your camera at two in the morning in a motel room six hundred miles from home? Only the cameraman—if he knows how.

Most cameramen are not total idiots and with a little training and a lot of respect for the equipment can be safely trusted to operate those controls that deal with basic camera adjustments such as registration.

Everyone in this business should carry a personal kit of head-cleaning materials, small tools, spare fuses, and cables. A spare coaxial cable no more than six feet long should be permanently attached to your recorder. When the multiconductor remote cable between the camera and recorder fails a half mile from your car because you caught it on a tree stump, the spare piece of coax will keep you shooting.

The truth is that operating a camera goes far beyond locating the on/off switch and other external controls. Since it is your camera and your livelihood, you should learn how to use a waveform monitor to set levels and colorimetry. You should learn how to adjust the registration. You should be familiar enough with the layout and internal controls to troubleshoot and attempt to correct more serious problems with a maintenance technician talking you through the steps by telephone. Our job is to bring back the pictures. There are no *good* excuses.

As technology advances, the cameras and recorders will become easier to maintain and operate as well as significantly smaller and less conspicuous. Until that day comes, our goal should be to be as unobtrusive as the newspaper reporter who does his or her job competently yet quietly while seated within earshot and view of an event. We must never forget that our presence can alter the course of events. The camera tends to create its own reality. That's why there's a photojournalist operating it.

PERSONAL SURVIVAL TECHNIQUES

This essay wouldn't be complete without a brief look away from the technical and creative skills needed to be a news cameraman toward those required for personal survival—getting along. It's important to recognize that as a news cameraman, you are a small cog in a big machine. A bit of perspective is necessary to endure the job without sacrificing your individuality, curtailing your initiative, or antagonizing your co-workers.

Being a news cameraman means working under constant pressure. The next story is too far away, traffic is heavy, parking nonexistent. The assignment desk has another job waiting, and lunch turns out to be the coffee and Danish you ate at ten-thirty. Your work is, of necessity, restrained by considerations of time, equipment limitations, access restrictions, and, unfortunately, internal rivalries and personality conflicts.

You are expected to be not only a cameraman but also a technician-journalist-editor-cab-driver-field producer, and occasionally a reporter. This requirement to do many things, sometimes at the same time, can cause conflicts. When does he stop being the field producer and let the reporter take over? Who knows best how long it will take to get to the story and what is the best route? When does the cameraman stand up to the assignment editor and argue the merits of an assignment? When does he accept the assignment, whatever it is, without a fuss?

Many reporters and assignment editors would voice a preference for a cameraman who always does what he is told, never complains, and never voices his opinions. Thankfully there are also those who recognize that the cameraman can contribute more than framing, focus, and f-stop to a story. The cameraman who recognizes that he is part of a team and works at getting along is a greater asset to a news organization than the individual who defines his role strictly in terms of his skill in operating a camera. The problem for the cameraman comes in recognizing when his input and contributions facilitate the coverage of the story and when they unknowingly become negative factors.

Being "on the street" instead of in the newsroom is one of the privileges unique to being a news cameraman. Tied not to a desk or telephone but to a beeper or portable radio, the cameraman enjoys an autonomy unknown to other news staffers. He spends his work day away from the newsroom and studio, responsible only to the assignment desk and the reporter he is teamed with.

This freedom brings with it a unique problem. Working in relative isolation on only one story, the cameraman is usually unaware of what else is being covered, of the priorities and problems of the day as viewed from within the newsroom. Thus the cameraman often has a very limited perspective on how what he is doing relates to the scope of the day's overall coverage.

While it is easy to recognize a cameraman's contributions to a story, it's sometimes difficult to see that his commitment to "just one more shot" or reluctance to work a little faster or accept a change of assignment in the middle of a more interesting one can have a negative impact on the total news-gathering process.

The cameraman, of necessity, devotes himself to the assignment at hand. He usually tends to view whatever he is doing as the most important thing at any given moment. In fact there are probably at least a half-dozen stories being covered by different crews at that same moment, some of which are scheduled to run earlier in the newscast. The assignment editor must constantly reevaluate the merits of scheduled and breaking stories in response to manpower availabilities, equipment limitations, and the whims of various producers. There is a natural conflict in viewpoints and priorities between the crews in the field and the folks in the newsroom.

When the cameraman is asked to drop one story in midshot and chase across town to do an interview that could have been done two hours earlier, he must try to understand that this means that someone with an overview of the day's events is once again changing priorities.

The news cameraman must recognize that it is the final product, not simply the news-gathering phase in which he is most actively involved, that is going to determine the success or failure of his station's mission. He must recognize that time wasted on a story will be time wasted in editing, and in the time available for the other stories of the day to be shot and edited.

WORKING AS A MEMBER OF A TEAM

Ideally a news crew works in unspoken harmony. The cameraman knows what the story is about and what to expect. The reporter knows what shots have been made without asking, and the cutaways get made automatically. On the way to the story, discussion includes expectations of what will happen and what the completed spot might contain. On the way back, suggestions for opening shot, sound bites, and sequences are exchanged.

This kind of relationship doesn't occur often enough. Reporters may doubt a cameraman's enthusiasm for a story and attempt to direct everything from light and microphone placement to framing and length of individual shots. Cameraman, wary of being told to shoot everything in sight while the reporter postpones decisions that should be made then in the field—not later in the editing room—begin to develop slow reflexes. Reporters who found critical shots missing on the last story will be uptight the next time out with that particular cameraman. Meanwhile the cameraman, who begins to suspect that his shots are going to be edited by a committee, shows even less enthusiasm for the story.

Putting a story on the air requires much teamwork. The combination of skills and efforts required is not limited to the field duo of cameraman and reporter. Each story is touched in one way or another by producers, assignment editors, tape editors, and audio, program, and technical directors. Any one of these people can inadvertently cause the best efforts of the others to go down the drain. No one is entitled to give anything but his or her best effort. There are new assignments every day for the television news cameraman. You are only as good as your last story.

ENG and the Law: An Introduction

10

DWIGHT L. TEETER, JR., PH.D.
AND DAVID A. ANDERSON, J.D.

Note: As may be seen throughout this book, ENG has created both opportunities and problems for television journalists. Among the problems are those involving the law. Some relate to defamation and invasion of privacy: problems confronting any journalist in getting the job done. Others either are unique to ENG or are problems that gain new urgency because of ENG.

This chapter remains substantially intact from the first edition. Its organization—along with Richard Yoakam's pithy anecdote about the perils of a live show sans tape delay—remains. It should be noted that David Anderson, busy with other writing projects and representing clients in media law cases, did not participate in the updating of this chapter. Additions made here are the responsibility of Dwight Teeter and are listed in the notes at chapter's end. Professor Anderson's contributions remain, however, and are central to this overview.

When writing for the first edition of *ENG: Television News and the New Technology,* the authors of this chapter made use of Professor Yoakam's series of nationwide interviews with news directors. Relying on those responses, the authors tried to isolate ENG-related legal problems of most concern to these executives. Not much law has been made about ENG yet, but the news directors interviewed were concerned that new situations will develop and old problems will be exacerbated as the use of technology expands and accelerates news-gathering efforts.

From the interviews ten areas of legal concern to news directors and their staffs were spotlighted.

1. Live broadcasting presents more legal hazards than delayed broadcasts, but many people are not quite sure what they are.
2. There is a difference in the station's vulnerability between live broadcasts going directly onto the air and those that contain edited tape.
3. Live broadcasts require close editorial supervision if legal hazards are to be controlled.
4. Reporters and crews working in the field can be vulnerable unless they are knowledgeable about legal problems and sensitive to them.
5. Live interviews are more dangerous legally since they are more difficult to control.
6. Live broadcasts create more problems with defamation laws.
7. Shifting changes in courts' eddying definitions of public officials, public figures, limited-scope public figures, and private individuals may create additional problems for live broadcasts.
8. Live broadcasts create more problems with invasion of privacy, which includes *false light* (akin to libel), *intrusion* (akin to trespass), publication of *embarrassing* (or devastatingly hurtful) *private facts,* and *appropriation* (use of someone's name or likeness for advertising purposes or "commercial advantage").
9. Live broadcasts can create serious problems when defamatory or privacy-invading elements are brought up again or are reintroduced from file tape.
10. As of mid-1988, the Federal Communications Commission regulations on broadcast fairness were in flux. Although the FCC repealed its own Fairness Doctrine (not including the "personal attack" area), only two vetos by President Reagan kept Congress from fixing the Fairness Doctrine in statutory form.

Almost all of you will have been required to take a full-term course in the law of communications or broadcast regulation. If such a course is not required, you should be sure to take one anyway. This chapter is a brief overview and is not an attempt to cover the entire field.

The authors of this book have called on the expertise of two scholars in the field of communication law to refresh your memory on the basics and to deal briefly with these ten areas of concern.

Dwight L. Teeter, Jr., is a professor in the Department of Mass Communication of the University of Wisconsin-Milwaukee. He is co-author (with Professor Emeritus Harold L. Nelson of the University of Wisconsin-Madison) of *Law of Mass Communications: Freedom and Control of Print and Broadcast Media,* 5th edition (Mineola, N.Y.: Foundation Press, 1986). He was a newspaper reporter in Iowa and Wisconsin before starting his academic career.

David A. Anderson is an expert on defamation, state constitutions, and origins of First Amendment freedoms and is a frequent counsel for media clients. Professor Anderson was a reporter in Nebraska, Ohio, and Texas, and bureau chief for United Press International in Austin, Texas, before he became a teacher.

Not long ago, a radio talk-show host in a midwestern city was fielding phone calls about good places to eat and drink in that vicinity.

A caller named a bar he had visited recently and said:

Caller: I found a pubic hair in my drink.
Host: What did you say?
Caller: I found a pubic hair in my drink.
Host: You can't say that on my show!
Caller: Oh? Well, maybe it was a mouse hair.

Because the host was operating without a tape-delay mechanism, he had no way to prevent the caller's ill-considered outburst. Nonetheless, the station was potentially liable for defamation of the bar.

In New York City a few years ago, WCBS-TV reporter Lucille Rich and a camera crew arrived unannounced at a posh restaurant called Le Mistral. Over the objections of the restaurant's president, they entered the establishment with cameras rolling. The station's interest was perfectly legitimate: It was doing a series of reports on restaurants that had been cited for health-code violations. But the restaurant was private property, and the crew had no permission to enter; the restaurant sued successfully for invasion of privacy and trespass.[1]

An Ohio television station broadcast a free-lancer's film on the Great Zacchini, a "human cannonball" performing at a county fair. The fifteen-second clip showed Zacchini's two-hundred-foot trip from takeoff to touchdown. The voice-over was entirely laudatory: "It's a thriller . . . you really need to see it in person to appreciate it." But Zacchini viewed the station's unauthorized broadcast as an appropriation of his act, and the Supreme Court of the United States held that the station had no First Amendment right to broadcast the entire act.[2]

These are examples of some of the legal bear traps that await broadcasters in the age of ENG.[3] The law as it affects ENG is not new; ENG enjoys no more or less protection than conventional broadcasting, or for that matter, print media. But the new technology presents new legal problems for at least two reasons. First, ENG increases broadcasters' risks simply because it enables them to do more things. The more thoroughly and aggressively the station covers its community, the more opportunity it has to get into trouble.

Second, the new technology, with its emphasis on timeliness, has reduced the time available for decision making. In the days of film, a news director could usually expect to have an hour or so to decide whether to run a particular shot. With ENG the time is reduced to minutes, or in the case of live broadcasts, to zero.

The purpose of this chapter is to explore problems of defamation, invasion of privacy, and personal attack in the context of electronic news gathering. Congress and the FCC may or may not keep the Fairness Doctrine's personal attack rules in force or even "on the books." Even so, human decency in the form of journalistic responsibility militates in favor of both the appearance and the reality of fairness and balance. The station or journalist perceived as predatory or generally unfair is apt to draw more than its share of litigation, with all the time and expense and bad publicity litigation can entail. With an ethical concern for balance and fairness—with or without the FCC's trying to define it—virtue is not only its own reward but financial good sense as well.

Much of the discussion here must be speculative, because ENG technology is too new to have generated much law. Let's look at the existing legal principles and then attempt to apply them to the new problems created by ENG.

DEFAMATION

Defamation consists of publication of a falsehood that defames an identifiable person or corporation. Since that definition is deceptively simple, let us elaborate on each of its elements.[4]

Publication includes broadcasting. The ancient distinction between slander (oral) and libel (written) defamation has been abandoned in most broadcasting cases, and now broadcasters are generally governed by the same libel law as newspapers.[5] Publication also includes republication, which is another way of saying that the broadcaster is responsible not only for his or her own defamatory comments (the news anchor's commentary, for example) but also for those of third persons whose words are circulated by the station in its news broadcasts (allegations spoken by an interview subject, for example).[6]

In practical terms a falsehood is anything the broadcaster can't prove is true. In the 1960s and 1970s, a few cases suggested that the plaintiff—the person bringing the lawsuit—bears the burden of proving that the statement is false.[7] In 1986, the Supreme Court underlined the placing of the burden of proving falsity on the plaintiff in *Philadelphia Newspapers* v. *Hepps*.[8] The hitch there, however, is that only reports of matters deemed by the courts to be of public concern are so protected. In a 5–4 decision, the Court held that investigative stories by the *Philadelphia Enquirer* suggesting that a businessman had undue influence on state government and ties to organized crime were of *public*, not merely private, concern. In that context, the burden of proof was put on the plaintiff.[9]

Even so, "truth" may be elusive. In other words, if the plaintiff can convince a jury that the statement is false—and trial juries are often hostile to the media—then the broadcaster is apt to lose. Truth, of course, should be the goal at all times. But in practical fact, truth is relatively seldom used as a defense in defamation actions. If a media defendant can prove truth, chances are a lawsuit will not be started. Even if something *is* true, proving it in court, under rules of evidence that are labyrinthine, may not be easy. If the truth is imbedded in inadmissible evidence, or if key witnesses refuse to testify, die, or disappear, then truth becomes a purely metaphysical matter. It is sad but true for libel defendants (and plaintiffs) that the only truth that matters is the one that can be proven in a court of law.

It is important to distinguish between truth and accuracy. Suppose, for example, a reporter does a standup at City Hall, reporting that a competing contractor has accused Acme Paving Company of defrauding the city. The report may be a perfectly accurate summary of what the contractor charged, but the defense of truth is not available unless the city is prepared to prove that Acme Paving is in fact defrauding the city.[10] *Truth* means the truth of the underlying defamatory statement. The accuracy of the report may be important in giving the station the benefit of *privilege* (more about this later), but it does not establish the truth.

A statement is defamatory if it tends to damage a person's reputation. Obviously it is defamatory to accuse a person of committing a crime or of engaging in immoral or dishonest activity. But it can also be defamatory to say that he or she threw a temper tantrum, is a bigot, or is a coward.[11]

Persons are identifiable if they are named or pictured, but also if they are recognizable to their acquaintances even though they are not more specifically identified. Another example: A report that "an assistant vice president in the trust department was discharged for embezzlement" may be defamatory if there is only one assistant vice president in the trust department and that fact is known to his or her acquaintances.[12]

PRIVILEGE

Many statements are protected even if they are published about an identifiable person and are false and defamatory. They are protected because they are privileged.

Consider, for example, a live broadcast from a trial. (Some sort of photographic coverage is now allowed, with the court's permission, in a majority of states. A study by the National Center for State Courts published late in 1986 showed twenty-two states allowing cameras in trial courts, with another eight experimenting with trial or trial and appellate courts. Another eight states allowed appellate-court coverage only.)[13]

What if the witness on the stand utters a defamatory falsehood while under oath? (Assume that this statement by the witness is *not stricken* from the record by order of the judge, for if it is, it never existed in any legal sense.) The answer is *privilege*:[14] A fair and accurate report of the judicial proceeding is privileged. There are similar privileges for accurate reports of other types of public proceedings, such as candidates' forums, the official sessions of city councils, county commissions, school boards, legislatures, the United States Congress, or any committees, subcommittees, or commissions appointed by those bodies.[15]

THE FIRST AMENDMENT

Finally, broadcasters enjoy the same First Amendment protections—in libel suits, at least—as their print competitors. Thus even if a broadcast is false, defames an identifiable person, and is not privileged, it still may be protected under the Federal Constitution. If the victim is a public official, he or she cannot recover damages unless it can be shown that the broadcaster acted with actual malice, that is, knew the report was false or had serious doubts about its truth.[16]

That same rule applies to public figures, although that classification has been narrowed so much in recent years that the only persons sure to fall within it are celebrities and busybodies. Celebrities are persons so well known that their names are household words: Carol Burnett, Dolly Parton, Paul Newman. Busybodies (sometimes called "special purpose public figures" by courts) are persons who thrust themselves into public controversies with the objective of influencing their outcome.[17]

If the person defamed is neither a public official nor a public figure, the Federal

Constitution doesn't offer much protection. Such a person—a private plaintiff—need show only that the broadcaster was negligent with respect to the truth or falsity of the broadcast.[18] What negligence means in this context is not clear; a broadcaster probably could be found negligent for failing to delay the broadcast to give him or herself an opportunity to edit out defamatory matter or to investigate further. When it comes to private persons, the best advice is: When in doubt, don't.

These principles are familiar to most news directors and must be high in the consciousness of their staffs. The difficulties arise in applying them to ENG. Television news directors know there are problems in broadcasting ''live'' or ''live delayed.'' (''Live delayed'' here means using a live setup with microwave or helicopter platform links to gather videotape, to check the tape quickly in the station's control room or editing bays, and then to get it ''turned around'' and on the air as rapidly as possible.)

Some television news directors seem to feel that they are ''safer'' (or at least that they have better excuses) when their crews are sending in live reports which go on the air *immediately. Instantaneously.* They hope to be able to show that they were operating as carefully as possible, with a field producer at the scene and with producers in the control room monitoring the incoming broadcast as it proceeds onto the air. These producers are talking over the intercom system (IFB) to the on-air reporters. They can relay advice: ''Watch it! You're on thin ice; change the subject *now*!'' or ''Cut it, get off it, pan away from it.''

The defense relied upon by these news directors is something like this: ''Look, it happened. We used all the editorial control we had available, but we can't avoid blurts a hundred percent of the time.''[19]

To date the law recognizes no such defense. In court the question in most cases will be whether the broadcaster used reasonable care to determine the truth of the statements broadcast. The plaintiff will argue that broadcasting live was unreasonable for that very consideration: It gives broadcasters no opportunity to prevent defamation. It will be up to judges and juries to decide what is reasonable in each case.[20]

The best analogies provided by case law so far come from two cases involving tape delay in the context of radio talk shows. Unfortunately they point in opposite directions.

The host of a call-in show on WBOX in Bogalusa, Louisiana, was broadcasting without a tape delay when an anonymous person called in, named a doctor and a pharmacist, and connected them with drug dealing at a local pizza restaurant. The doctor, pharmacist, and manager of the restaurant all collected damages.

The court had no sympathy for the station's broadcasting live without a tape delay:

> We would have no difficulty in finding a station liable, if it received defamatory material from an anonymous source, and broadcast the report without attempting verification. The direct broadcast of such anonymous defamatory material, without the use of any monitoring or delay device, is no less reprehensible in our judgment. The publication, in either event, is done by the station, and we find that there is the same reckless disregard for the truth in either instance.
>
> Appellant placed itself in a position fraught with the imminent danger of broadcast-

ing anonymous, unverified, slanderous remarks based on sheer rumor, speculation and hearsay, and just such a result actually occurred. Such an eventuality was easily foreseeable and likely to occur, as in fact it did. In our judgment, the First Amendment does not protect a publisher against such utter recklessness.[21]

A Wyoming court viewed the tape delay matter quite differently. A caller to a talk show said falsely that a businessman, a former state official, "had been discharged as insurance commissioner for dishonesty." But the Wyoming Supreme Court held that the station's failure to use a tape delay was not proof of reckless disregard for the truth. If it were, the court said,

> broadcasters, to protect themselves from judgments for damages, would feel compelled to adopt and regularly use one of the tools of censorship, the electronic delay system. While using such a system a broadcaster would be charged with the responsibility of concluding that some comments should be edited or broadcast not at all. Furthermore, we must recognize the possibility that the possibility that the requirement for use of such equipment might, on occasion, tempt the broadcaster to screen out the comments of those with whom the broadcaster . . . did not agree. . . .[22]

The Wyoming opinion displays a far better understanding of the nature of live broadcasting than does the Louisiana case, and it contains much more thorough and persuasive analysis of the issue. But it is too early to tell which view will be followed in the rest of the states.

In the absence of any clear precedent, "delayed live" should be preferred over "live" at least when the speaker is someone over whom the station has no control or when the situation is so volatile there's a considered risk that something the station does not want to broadcast will get on the air. Where the importance of the story justifies live coverage, the reporter and the producer must be ready to change the subject instantly, to pan away, or to cut the sound when the specter of defamation rears its head.

If a defamatory blurt does occur, the station should act promptly to minimize the damage. The defamer immediately should be cut off to prevent him or her from making additional actionable remarks. The reporter on the scene or the anchor back in the studio should attempt to undo the damage that has already been done by correcting factual errors, if possible, by disassociating the station from the defamatory remarks, and by apologizing (if the circumstances make that appropriate) to the person defamed.

Though these steps need to be taken promptly, they also require careful judgment. If it is not clear whether the accusation is true or false, confessing error would be a mistake. The station might want to assert the defense of truth later in court. In such a case, the reporter, anchor, or news director merely should inform viewers that the station cannot at the moment vouch for the truth of the accusation, perhaps even suggesting that viewers keep an open mind on the matter.

In deciding whether a defamatory blurt is actionable, courts probably will take into account at least two factors. One will be the urgency of the story being covered. If the story is an important one about which the public needs immediate information (such as a riot or natural disaster), courts are likely to be more protective of the broadcaster. On the other hand, a breathless live report of a one-car rollover in which judgment is offered as to who is at fault is not likely to win much judicial sympathy.

The urgency of covering hot news has long been recognized in other contexts. For example, a generation ago the Supreme Court allowed Georgia football coach Wally Butts to recover against *The Saturday Evening Post* for implying that he had revealed helpful secrets to arch rival Bear Bryant before a Georgia-Alabama game. Justice Harlan said:

> The evidence showed that the Butts story was in no sense "hot news," and the editors of the magazine recognized the need for a thorough investigation of the serious charges.[23]

In contrast, in a companion case the court denied recovery to General Edwin Walker, whom the Associated Press described erroneously as having taken command of a violent crowd and having led a charge against federal marshals during a riot over the enrollment of the first black at the University of Mississippi. Said Justice Harlan:

> [T]he dispatch [of the AP reporter] which concerns us in *Walker* was news which required immediate dissemination. The Associated Press received the information from a correspondent who was present at scene of the events and gave every indication of being trustworthy and competent. . . . Considering the necessity for rapid dissemination, nothing in this series of events gives the slightest hint of a severe departure from accepted publishing standards.[24]

Although these cases had nothing to do with ENG or broadcasting, they show that the Supreme Court has expressed sympathy toward the problems of covering hot news under deadline pressure, but that not every sensational story can be treated as hot news.

Perhaps particular wariness is called for when stories take on the nature of a follow-up, even when there seems to be a good "news peg." In 1981, a South Carolina TV station was following a story about the unsolved murders of two teenaged stepbrothers more than a year earlier. It broadcast statements by the father of one victim that the other dead boy's father had not cooperated. It was said the other father had refused to take a truth serum, was hiding behind the Fifth Amendment, and had employed an attorney. Even though the plaintiff was not mentioned specifically in the 1981 broadcasts, the South Carolina Court of Appeals reversed the trial court's grant of summary judgment to the TV station. The appellate court found William C. Adams had been identified and that the language "was susceptible of the inference that Adams was either guilty of the murders of the teenagers or was withholding information relative to the commission of the crimes."[25]

The second factor courts are likely to evaluate is the forseeability of trouble. A broadcaster who carries a live interview with someone who is notorious for his or her venomous or intemperate remarks is more likely to lose than one who gets blind-sided while interviewing an apparently responsible person on an innocuous subject. This should come as no surprise. Broadcast journalists develop an instinct for spotting and avoiding "kooks," and many news directors expect their reporters to have some idea of what a live interview subject is likely to say. While perfect clairvoyance can't be expected, the courts will undoubtedly be unsympathethic to broadcasters who ignore obvious risks.

The broadcast journalist must remember that the courts will evaluate these factors from the point of view of the public, not the broadcaster. The news director's plea that he felt compelled to broadcast live because he feared his competitor would, or because his competitor had beaten him on the air and he was playing catch-up, or because he was under pressure to boost sagging ratings, is likely to fall on deaf ears. It is the broadcaster whose decisions are based on the publics needs and sound journalistic judgments who will succeed in the courts.

Those Sneaky Ambush Interviews

Sometimes the compulsion to get a story leads to "ambush interview" situations: the reporter pushing a microphone into an unwilling news source's face while the camera is on. The public seems to consider the ambush bad form or worse. That such behavior is disliked by nonjournalists may be seen in a jury's $1.25-million "false light" privacy judgment against reporter Arnold Diaz and WCBS-TV of New York City. While investigating dumping of chemical wastes, WCBS jumped a corporation executive with a surprise interview about chemical waste on a lot adjoining his business. The interviewee's irate reaction was later broadcast, and his tearful account of the pain caused him by the broadcast clearly impressed the jury.[26]

On appeal, however, the jury's verdict was overturned by a United States Court of Appeals, which found that the broadcast's portrayal of the unwilling man as furious and evasive was borne out by the tape of the interview.[27] The conclusion that "the TV station won" should be tempered with the warning implicit in that $1.25 million jury verdict: In a general way those jurors represent the public and its attitudes toward intrusive reporters and photographers.

WARNING LABELS FOR BROADCASTERS?

Warning labels appear on packs of cigarettes: cigarettes can be hazardous. Perhaps broadcasters should put warning labels on their own microphones and cameras. The cigarette-related defamation case of *Brown & Williamson* v. *Walter Jacobson and CBS* did not deal with ENG technology, but its fact situation contains some dos and don'ts for all journalists. To restate the obvious, *let facts shape the story, not vice versa*. There are reasons totaling $3 million for saying that: by refusing to hear this case in April 1988, the Supreme Court let stand a $3-million libel judgment against Jacobson and CBS. Libel lawyer Floyd Abrams says that's the largest media libel award to survive appeals.[28]

Brown & Williamson, manufacturers of tobacco products among other things, sued TV reporter Walter Jacobson and CBS for a "Perspective" broadcast in 1982. That program accused tobacco manufacturers of aiming their ads at America's youth in a most unwholesome fashion. Jacobson said:

Television is off-limits to [advertising of] cigarettes and so the business, the killer business, has gone to the ad business in New York for help, to the slicksters on Madison Avenue with a billion dollars a year for bigger and better ways to sell cigarettes. Go for the youth of America, go get 'em guys. . . . Hook 'em while they are young. . . . Just think how many cigarettes they'll be smoking when they grow up.[29]

Jacobson was promoted by CBS in ads for pulling no punches, for being a journalist who will "make you angry." His November 11, 1982, "Perspective" made the tobacco company angry, all right. Jacobson's broadcast included the assertion that because cigarette companies no longer can advertise on TV, they had turned "to the slicksters on Madison Avenue, with a billion dollars for bigger and better ways to sell cigarettes."

Go for the youth of America. Go get 'em, guys. Get some young women, give them some samples. Pass them out on the streets, for free, to the teenagers of America. Hook 'em while they're young. . . .[30]

Perhaps one lesson from this case is that one journalist's righteous indignation may be defamation in the eyes of a jury. Jacobson then said that cigarette manufacturers were disclaiming fault, even though children are smoking "more than ever before." He continued:

That's what Viceroy is saying. Who knows whose fault it is that children are smoking? It's not ours. Well, there is a confidential report on cigarette advertising in the files of the federal government right now, a Viceroy advertising [sic]. The Viceroy strategy for attracting young people (starters, they are called) to smoking.

For the young smoker a cigarette falls into the same category with wine, beer, shaving, or wearing a bra," says the Viceroy strategy. "A declaration of independence and striving for self-identity. Therefore, an attempt should be made," says Viceroy, "to present the cigarette as an initiation into the adult world, to present the cigarette as an illicit pleasure, a basic symbol of the growing-up maturity process. An attempt should be made," say the Viceroy slicksters, "to relate the cigarette to pot, wine, beer, and sex. Do not communicate health or health-related points."

That's the strategy of the cigarette-slicksters, the cigarette business, which is insisting in public . . . "[W]e are not selling to children."[11]

They're not slicksters. They're liars.[31]

Jacobson was commenting on a tangled fact situation, and a jury found falsity and actual malice (publication with knowing falsity or reckless disregard for the truth) in the words quoted above. The facts presented to the jury included these items:

— The advertising strategy attributed to Viceroy—even though it was written up in a report of the Federal Trade Commission—was a strategy of a market research firm hired by an ad agency working for Viceroy. The cigarette manufacturer rejected the proposed strategy and fired the ad agency, in part over displeasure with the report.[32]

— A Brown & Williamson executive told "Perspective" producer and researcher Michael Radutzky of WBBM that the strategy had not been adopted and that the report had been written six years earlier.[33]

— The ''Perspective'' report did not cite (and had not found) any Viceroy ads adopting the pot-wine-beer-sex strategy to induce children to smoke cigarettes.[34]

The Court of Appeals found that the ''most compelling evidence of actual malice submitted to the jury was the intentional destruction of critical documents by Jacobson's researcher, Michael Radutzky. . . .''[35]

Radutzky destroyed a sample script and a copy of the Federal Trade Commission report on which he had written notes. The Appeals Court wrote that Radutzky destroyed only ''the parts of the documents that would have been relevant to this litigation.'' Radutzky's explanation that he had been ''housecleaning'' was not believed; the court declared that the housecleaning was too selective.[36]

In a footnote, the Court noted—if only in passing—the Brown & Williamson contention that ratings pressures to do interesting stories during the November ''sweeps'' period might be considered ''strong proof of actual malice.''[37]

Reporters and others in the news process should take the above-listed items to heart. Journalists would be well advised to avoid behavior that asks for trouble. On air, understatement is preferable to overstatement. In the newsroom, judgmental or wise-guy notes or marginal comments are simply a bad idea. Whatever a station's policy about saving outtakes and notes—and a policy of purging such materials can be made to look suspect should a lawsuit occur—do not destroy materials once litigation is imminent or has begun.

By allowing the Seventh Circuit Court of Appeals ruling to stand, the Supreme Court left in place a ruling that the ''Perspective'' reports on the tobacco industry contained deliberate falsehoods. As the Court of Appeals said:

> Even according no deference to the jury's findings, we conclude that Brown & Williamson proved by clear and convincing evidence that the defendants either knew the Perspective was false or in fact entertained serious doubts as to its truth. *See St. Amant v. Thompson,* 390 U.S. at 732, *See also New York Times v. Sullivan,* 376 U.S. at 279–80, 84 S.Ct. 725–26.
>
> The most compelling evidence of actual malice submitted to the jury was the intentional destruction of critical documents by Jacobson's researcher. . . .[38]

PRIVACY

ENG offers the broadcaster numerous opportunities to run afoul of the law of invasion of privacy. Some of these arise, like defamation, from the broadcast of material that harms some identifiable individual. Others arise from the methods used to gather news, irrespective of what is broadcast.

Trespass or Intrusion

The case of Le Mistral restaurant, mentioned earlier, is an example of a problem arising from the *method* of news gathering. This branch of invasion of privacy is similar to trespass law, but broader. A camera crew that goes into someone's home without permission would be guilty of trespass. A camera crew that goes into someone's home with permission, but while there installs a hidden microphone, would be liable for the form of invasion of privacy called intrusion, even though there might be no trespass because the entry was made with consent. The unauthorized installation of the hidden microphone would be actionable even without trespass.[39] And in both cases there would be potential liability even if nothing were broadcast; the wrong lies in the intrusion itself, rather than in anything that may be revealed to the public. (Such revelations, as will be shown, can compound the privacy problem.)

A broadcaster's assertion that the crew was engaged in news gathering at the time of the trespass or intrusion normally provides no defense. As the courts are fond of saying, the First Amendment does not give the media a license to ignore the law in the name of news gathering.

> The First Amendment has never been construed to accord newsmen immunity from torts or crimes committed during the course of newsgathering. The First Amendment is not a license to trespass, to steal, or to intrude by electronic means into the precincts of another's home or office. It does not become such a license simply because the person subject to the intrusion is reasonably suspected of committing a crime.[40]

Thus in *Oklahoma* v. *Bernstein,* a state district court ruled that reporters were guilty of criminal trespass when they followed demonstrators onto the construction site of a nuclear power plant. Even though there was substantial government involvement with the nuclear installation, the judge held that it was still the private property of the Public Service Commission of Oklahoma, which had told the media to stay out. The judge did not doubt that the demonstrators' invasion of the plant site was a newsworthy event, but that did not excuse the reporter's trespassing.

> A weighing of respective press and government interests in the context of the total circumstances . . . indicates that the legitimate rights of the State have outweighed the arrested [person's] right of access.[41]

On the other hand, if a camera crew can see its subjects from a public place without trespass, no liability should occur. Mr. and Mrs. James Jaubert were upset when they returned from a trip to learn that a photograph of their home had been published on the front page of the Crowley, Louisiana, *Post-Signal,* with this caption: "One of Crowley's stately homes, a bit weather-worn and unkempt, stands in the shadow of a spreading oak." Although the Jauberts were awarded one thousand dollars in damages by the trial court, the Louisiana Supreme Court reversed. The court held that there was no invasion of privacy because the photo had been taken from the middle of the street in front of the house, duplicating the view available to any passer-by.[42]

The same kind of conditions apply for ENG crews shooting pictures from a public place into any kind of private area. The military frequently attempts to prevent the media from taking pictures of plane crashes, of the mobilization of equipment for the handling of civil disturbances, or of other kinds of "troop movements.'' Industry often does not want pictures of new products—such as the latest-model autos—to be made before the unveiling. But if a manufacturer is careless enough to put new models outside where anyone can see them from a public place, of if the military or police carry out their activities within public view, then they risk exposure.

The key in cases of this sort is that the camera is recording only what viewers could see if they were present. A passer-by who just happens to look into an un-curtained window commits no wrong, but the same cannot be said of a person who stands on the street peering into someone's house with binoculars. Likewise, we can expect the courts to treat the camera operator who uses a zoom or telephoto lens, or something more elaborate like a nightscope, differently from one who merely records what is visible to the unaided eye.

In general, persons in public places may be photographed with impunity, but there are limits. If the camera is used as a weapon in the service of so-called confrontation journalism, the victim may find a remedy in the precedent established by Jacqueline Kennedy Onassis against photographer Ron Galella. Galella made a career of stalking Mrs. Onassis and her children with his cameras. He was a *paparazzo,* which a federal judge described as a breed of photographers who ''make themselves as visible to the public and as obnoxious to their photographic subjects as possible to aid in the advertisement and wide sale of their works.''[43] Mrs. Onassis successfully sued for an injunction ordering Galella to stay a prescribed distance away from her and her children. Galella subsequently was held in contempt of court for violating the order.[44]

Normally, a camera crew has no right to go onto private property in pursuit of a newsworthy event without the owner's consent. Again, however, this is a generalization with many exceptions. The most important exception permits photographers to enter upon private premises at the invitation of law enforcement authorities if (a) such invitations are common local practice and (b) the owner is not present to object.

This exception arose from a newspaper case in Florida. Seventeen-year-old Cindy Fletcher burned to death in her Jacksonville, Florida home in 1972. When the fire marshal and a policeman arrived at the scene, they invited news media representatives to accompany them into the house, as was their standard practice.

The fire marshal wanted a clear picture of the silhouette on the floor of the house after removal of the body, but he had run out of film. He asked a photographer for the *Florida Times-Union* to take the picture, which became part of the official investigative records but was also published by the newspaper.

Cindy Fletcher's mother, who had been out of town, first learned of the facts involved in the death of her daughter by reading the newspaper story and seeing the photograph published there. She sued for trespass and invasion of privacy.

The Florida court ruled against her, saying that because there had been no objection to the entry and since the officials and the photographer had followed common practice, there was no trespass or actionable invasion of privacy by the newspaper.[45]

If the tenant or owner *is* present and asks that a camera crew not enter the property, a different result can be predicted. A Rochester, New York humane society investigator got a search warrant to enter a home, authorizing him to seize any animals "found to be in a confined, crowded condition or in unhealthy or unsanitary surroundings." The investigator alerted television stations about the "raid," and camera crews from WROC-TV and WOKR-TV followed the investigator into the house. The crews ignored the occupant's demand that they stay out of her home. Stories were broadcast on the stations' evening newscasts.

Based on that fact situation, a court held that the First Amendment did not protect news gathering on private premises without the consent of the homeowner, even though entry was made at the invitation of a humane society investigator.[46] The distinction apparently is that law enforcement officers may have the power to consent on the owner's or tenant's behalf when that person is absent, but not when an owner or tenant is present and objects to the entry.

Content That Invades Privacy

So far we have discussed only privacy problems that arise in the course of news gathering. Once the images and information have been obtained, there are additional hazards in the selection of material to be broadcast. One of these involves a branch of privacy law called commercial exploitation—sometimes called appropriation. This was the theory invoked by Hugo Zacchini, the "human cannonball" whose case was mentioned at the beginning of this chapter. The Zacchini case was unusual, however; not many performers have an act capable of being shown in its entirety in a fifteen-second clip.

In the normal course of news coverage, broadcasters are not likely to encounter this branch of privacy law. But they might well encounter it in their promotional efforts. If a person's name or likeness is used to promote the station or sell a product or service, the broadcaster should be sure the person had consented to that use of his or her name or picture.[47] Also, a "stay tuned" note or "bumper" promoting something to come later in a news broadcast should not contain a performer's entire act, but only a brief excerpt or highlight.

False Light

Yet another branch of privacy law comes into play if the broadcaster depicts a person in a *false light*. This can happen when file footage is used to illustrate a story with which the subject has no actual connection. For example, if videotape taken of a woman at a pregnancy clinic was used later to illustrate a story on an abortion clinic, the woman's portrayal in connection with an abortion story places her in a false light in the eyes of her friends, and colleagues.

Another example: If videotape made of people shopping in a supermarket is used in a story about the problems of shoplifting, it may give the impression that those people are shoplifters. Of special concern in this situation is what is said while the pictures are being shown. A line of narrative saying, "Shoplifters come in all shapes, sizes, and ages" that accompanies pictures of a nice little old lady taking a dress from a rack and holding it to herself to see how it fits may give the audience the idea that "This is a typical shoplifter."

The theory behind false light is similar to that behind defamation, except that the statement need not be defamatory. To say that a person favors abortion is not defamatory, but it can be embarrassing and painful to be falsely portrayed as holding those views, and the "false light" branch of privacy is the law's remedy.[48]

Sometimes, however, a broadcast can give rise to lawsuits for both defamation and false light invasion of privacy. Consider *Duncan* v. *WJLA-TV,* a case that should encourage careful editing of videotape. WJLA-TV, Washington, D.C., broadcast news reports of a new treatment for genital herpes.

In its 6 P.M. newscast on March 30, 1982, WJLA-TV presented an "on-the-street" format story by reporter Betsy Ashton. As her report began, the camera panned down K Street and focused on pedestrians standing at a corner behind Ms. Ashton. The camera focused on one pedestrian, a private citizen named Linda K. Duncan, who turned directly toward the camera and became clearly recognizable. Then, as the camera began to focus on reporter Ashton, the voiced introduction of the report began.

Ms. Duncan sued for defamation and for invasion of privacy based on the 6 P.M. report and also on that evening's 11 P.M. newscast, which was heavily edited and presented in substantially different form. In the 11 P.M. version, anchor David Schoumacher presented the story. In the later version, plaintiff Linda K. Duncan was seen turning directly toward the camera and pausing as Schoumacher said, "[f]or the twenty million Americans who have herpes, it's not a cure." The story ended as Ms. Duncan was seen turning away from the camera and walking down the street.

A U.S. District Court ruled in 1984 that the 6 P.M. broadcast was not defamatory or a false light invasion of privacy. That report was said to provide viewers with sufficient context for reporter Ashton's on-the-street report, and the audio portion did not provide information from which viewers might infer that the plaintiff was a herpes victim.

The court decided, however, that the 11 P.M. report presented a different question, which should be considered by a jury. The court said:

> Rather than using the K Street scene to place an "on-the-street" reporter in context, defendant [WJLA-TV] chose to have the anchor person read a shortened version of the report and to use the K Street film as an illustration. To facilitate its use, the film was cropped so that what remained was the segment in which the camera zoomed in on plaintiff as she turned towards it. Thus, viewers saw a closeup of plaintiff turning directly towards the camera, pausing, and then walking away. While the scene was on the screen, Mr. Schoumacher stated that "[f]or the twenty million Americans who have herpes, it's not a cure. . . ." As plaintiff turned and walked away from the camera, the film ended; viewers did not see Ms. Ashton in the foreground as they did in the six o'clock report.[49]

Thus, the court granted a summary judgment to the television station involving the 6 P.M. newscast, in effect throwing out the libel and privacy claims for that broadcast. The court, however, denied a summary judgment concerning the 11 P.M. report, saying a jury needed to consider whether the later newscast might be understood as defamatory or privacy invading.

Private Information

The final branch of privacy law that concerns broadcasters involves disclosure of purely private information. This body of law gives the individual a cause of action for the disclosure of private information that (a) would be highly offensive to a reasonable person, and (b) is of no legitimate public concern. The kinds of disclosures that most commonly fall within this definition involve medical and sexual matters. If a station should obtain and broadcast a videotape of a private person's consultation with a physician about a sexual problem, the station would probably be liable under this body of law. The same might be said of a disclosure that an individual is a homosexual or has a physical deformity.[50]

The key problem, of course, is that such disclosures are sometimes matters of perfectly legitimate public concern. Suppose, for example, that the person in the preceding examples turns out to be a presidential assassin. Can it be said that the public has no legitimate concern with his sexual problems, sexual preference, or physical deformity?[51] In a less dramatic example, suppose a city's mayor is an alcoholic, tours the bars at night, and calls for a police car to take him home in an inebriated condition. Although the mayor may claim he always gets to work on time and that his drinking is a private matter, doesn't the public have an interest in it and also in the diversion of a police car and officers from what may be more important duties?

The answer is that what is a matter of public concern depends upon the circumstances. In general, the courts have been fairly generous in determining what constitutes matters of legitimate public concern.

For example: The Iowa Supreme Court held that the name of a fifteen-year-old girl who had been sterilized involuntarily while a ward at a county home was a matter of legitimate public concern, even though the girl's lawyer had argued that the story could have been told just as well without using her name.[52] And in Illinois, a vice squad officer sued the American Broadcasting Company's Chicago station for surreptitiously filming him while he made a case for solicitation against a model in a "deluxe lingerie modeling studio." The court said: "[T]he conduct of a policeman on duty is legitimately and necessarily an area upon which public interest may and should be focused."[53]

News directors and reporters should keep in mind, however, that they are not the final arbiters of what constitutes legitimate public concern. The courts make that decision themselves, based on a case-by-case analysis of specific facts. Not everything the public is interested in is a matter of legitimate public concern.[54]

For example, although the public was undoubtedly interested in *Time* magazine's photo of a "starving glutton" who lost weight despite her insatiable appetite, the court held that the woman's privacy had been invaded.[55] The public no doubt was interested in a movie that identified a respectable California housewife as a former prostitute who had been involved in a sensational murder case eight years earlier, but a court awarded the woman damages.[56]

Hustler Magazine v. Falwell

In recent years, lawyers had found an additional cause of action to use in lawsuits against the press: "intentional infliction of emotional distress."[57] But help for the media arrived in 1988's Supreme Court decision in *Hustler Magazine* v. *Falwell*.[58]

"Intentional infliction" added up to a kind of "end run" around the more traditional and better known rules of defamation and privacy law (which vary quite wildly from state to state). Although truth can be "the glorious defense" to a libel suit, truth is irrelevant except in the "false light" category of privacy.

That was tricky enough, but lawyers were adding in intentional infliction of emotional distress as a kind of legal wild card: There could thus be liability even if the material complained of was not defamatory and did not invade privacy.[59] On its way up to the Supreme Court, the Falwell case caused considerable fright for broadcasters and publishers: The circumstances of the case were so outrageous that it seemed likely a dangerous precedent could result.

This case arose when Larry Flynt's *Hustler* magazine twice published parodies of Campari liqueur ads, with the double-entendre theme of "the first time." The amorous ambience of the couples in the actual Campari ads made it clear that "the first time" likely applied to much more than sipping Campari. *Hustler's* version, labeled in fine print "ad parody—not to be taken seriously," claimed that the first time Jerry Falwell had sex was in an outhouse, with his mother, while she was drunk.[60]

Giving a deposition before the trial, Flynt was asked if he tried to hurt Reverend Falwell's reputation. Flynt helpfully volunteered that he was trying "to assassinate it."[61] The trial jury found that Falwell had not been libeled (no one would believe the ad) and that his privacy had not been invaded. However, the jury awarded $200,000 to Falwell to compensate for intentional infliction of emotional distress.[62]

Despite Reverend Falwell's understandable anger, he actually turned the ad parody to some advantage. He used a sanitized version of the *Hustler* parody in a mailing that raised $800,000 to help him sue Flynt.[63]

The Fourth Circuit ruled that with the intentional infliction tort, all that was needed to impose liability was a jury finding of intentional or reckless misconduct.[64] The Supreme Court reversed the judgment, snatching the $200,000 away from Reverend Falwell. Writing for an 8–0 Court (newly appointed Justice Anthony Kennedy did not take part), Chief Justice Rehnquist declared that a tougher standard of proof was needed under the First Amendment: the actual malice standard from the law of defamation.[65] Where public officials or public figures are involved, liability for intentional infliction of emotional injury requires proof of publication with knowledge of falsity or with reckless disregard for the truth.

Although he expressed little tolerance for Flynt's fetid attempt at humor, the Chief Justice enunciated strong support for the sharp-edged traditions of American political satire and cartooning. The Court said that even though a showing of hostile intent might be a finding of tort liability in other areas of law, breathing space was needed for comment on public officials and figures. "Were we to hold otherwise, there can be little doubt that political cartoonists and satirists would be subjected to damage awards without any showing that their work falsely defamed its subject."[66]

File Footage

Use of old file footage poses some special problems. If the tape was defamatory or privacy-invading originally, its rebroadcast almost certainly will be actionable, too.

If the statute of limitations has expired on the original use of the tape, rebroadcast will give the subject another opportunity to sue. A tape that was unobjectionable when originally shown may become actionable through the passage of time. For example, in the California case mentioned above, accounts of the former prostitute's role undoubtedly were privileged as newsworthy at the time of the trial. Eight years later, however, the court felt that the public no longer had any legitimate interest in the matter. The limits of broadcasters' rights to dredge up the past have not been determined. About all that can be said is that matters of continuing historical interest are probably safe, while the reopening of old wounds merely for curiosity's sake is not.

Consent

In the day-to-day operation of a television station, the most important defense in all these branches of invasion of privacy is consent. Persons who admit the camera into their home, who agree to be interviewed, or who voluntarily disclose intimate facts about their lives have no cause of action because they have consented to what might otherwise have been an invasion of privacy.

The consent need not be in writing. It can be implied from circumstantial evidence, such as a tape showing the subject willingly cooperating. The key is to be sure the subject knew exactly what was being consented to; consent will be ineffective if obtained under false pretenses or if a subject did not understand how an interview was to be used.[67]

Camera crews should be warned not to exceed their authority in making representations to subjects. If an on-scene reporter, producer, or camera operator does not know how the film or tape ultimately will be used, no representations should be made on the matter. If a subject agrees to be interviewed, not knowing whether the depiction will be favorable or unfavorable, that person probably has consented even to an unfavorable treatment. But if a subject's consent is given on anyone's assurances that the treatment will be favorable—and it is not—then consent is ineffective because it was based on a misrepresentation.[68]

Because of the problem of obtaining effective consent, stories involving the mentally ill or retarded are particularly dangerous. The patients themselves often do not have the capacity to consent, and the consent of the authorities in charge of an institution may not be sufficient. The same holds true for anyone who is too ill to give consent for a picture or interview in a nonpublic place.

Delan v. *CBS, Inc.* is a case in point. In 1978, CBS News did a documentary at a state mental hospital in which David Delan was a patient. Bill Moyers and a camera crew went to Creedmoor State Hospital, photographing and videotaping a program later broadcast under the title of "Anyplace But Here."

David Delan signed a release, but the document had been cosigned by a doctor of psychology, and a court held that was not the same as having a signature from an "attending physician" as required under New York law. CBS lost this case in 1978, even though Delan's picture appeared for only four seconds in a sixty-minute news documentary. In 1983, however, an appellate court reversed, granting CBS a summary judgment on the ground that Delan's image was not used for purposes of advertising or trade under New York's narrowly drawn privacy statute.[69] Even so, the lesson should be clear: Make sure the consent you receive is broad enough to protect you.

Consent is a troublesome concept after the 1975 decision by the Ninth Circuit Court of Appeals in *Virgil* v. *Time, Inc.* Surfer Mike Virgil had been interviewed by *Sports Illustrated's* Curry Kirkpatrick about his bizarre antics, which included such varieties of showing off as eating spiders, extinguishing cigarettes in his mouth, and throwing himself down a flight of steps because "there were all these chicks around." Shortly before the article was published, another *Sports Illustrated* employee called Virgil's home to verify information. At that late point, Virgil "revoked all consent" for publication.

In words that must frighten journalists who can foresee consents being withdrawn just before a publication is made or a broadcast goes on the air, Judge Merrill said:

> Talking freely to a member of the press, knowing the listener to be a member of the press, is not then itself making public. Such communication can be said to anticipate that what is said will be made public since making public is a function of the press, and accordingly such communication can be construed as a consent to publicize. Thus if publicity results it can be said to have been consented to. However, if consent is withdrawn prior to the act of publicization, the consequent publicity is without consent.
>
> We conclude that the voluntary disclosure to Kirkpatrick did not in itself constitute a voluntary disclosure of the facts disclosed.[70]

"Public" Places

In truly public places, such as streets, parks, and public buildings, photojournalists and television crews have broad rights of access, just as members of the general public have. But another set of problems develops when these same staff members attempt to cover news in what might be termed "semipublic" places. In such places, including football stadiums, concert halls, and fairgrounds, the public has no general right of access, and neither does the press.

Admittance here is by ticket or press pass, and the photojournalist's rights may be limited by the rules under which he or she obtained access. Concert tickets, for example, often expressly forbid taping or photographing. Such restrictions are valid even though a concert or other kind of show is held in a publicly supported hall such as a civic center or memorial coliseum.

As a general rule, the photographer is bound by whatever limitations are imposed as a condition of access. If he or she accepts a press pass under rules that say it entitles him or her only to access to the press box, he or she has no right to go to the sidelines or into the spectator sections to shoot pictures. On the other hand, if a photographer is in the press box when the end zone bleachers collapse, everyone knows he or she is going to ignore the restriction and rush to the end zone to cover the story. There isn't much the stadium management can do about it. Technically a photographer who ignores the conditions under which he or she is admitted becomes a trespasser, but as a practical matter the usual sanction will be revocation of the pass rather than legal action.

In the case of professional sports and some entertainment events, the rights of radio and television crews will be determined by elaborate contractual arrangements. Here again, the restrictions normally are controlling. If the promoters have given exclusive television rights to someone else, you have no right to televise the event, no matter how newsworthy it may be. If there is nothing in the contract that says local media can have access but other outside media can't, then you are stuck with it, although you sure can and should raise a beef about it. If your station holds the contract, then your rights are whatever the contract says, and no more.

In addition to restrictions imposed by the managers of semipublic places, broadcasters also face possible invasion of privacy actions by the performers and fans. It is here that the semipublic nature of the place is most helpful. Even though the stadium or concert hall is not "public" in the sense that everyone has a right to be there, it is "public" in the sense that people who go there forfeit some—but not all—of their privacy. Unless there are specific restrictions about photographing or recording, the performers on the stage or field cannot complain when their performances are photographed or broadcast even though they may be embarrassing. If the lead guitarist falls down in a hazy stupor, if the star wide receiver drops the winning touchdown in the end zone, if the pageant queen's dress rips and exposes her anatomy, no complaints can prevail, even if it is played over and over again. Those performers have invited people to see their acts. If they are mortified so be it; the acts are newsworthy. The same is true of those who perform on the sidelines, such as cheerleaders and coaches, or the master of ceremonies, or the five-year-olds in the baton twirling corps.

But suppose a television news team is assigned to shoot a feature on drunks misbehaving at the stadium. Do drunks at games have privacy? Yes and no. If the camera catches someone vomiting onto the beehive hairdo in front of him, that's something that happened in the stands—in public. But beware of the voice-over comments; it might be difficult to prove that the incident happened because of booze and not the flu, should the person pictured decide to sue for invasion of privacy or defamation.

The judgment of on-site directors is crucial. Care should be taken in selecting shots to be broadcast from the stands. "Honey shots" of attractive women are broadcast routinely. However sexist they may be, these shots present no legal problems as long as no actionable comments are made while the women are on camera.

Even if an individual is pictured in an embarrassing way, it may not be actionable. A fan at a Pittsburgh Steelers game asked a *Sports Illustrated* photographer to take his picture; the photographer obliged. The fan was embarrassed when the picture was published because it showed his fly was open. The judge ruled that the photograph had been taken in a public place, with the fan's permission and at his urging.[71]

It is one thing, however, merely to depict what happens. It is quite another to induce someone to perform for a camera. Thomas Taggart was present at the 1969 Woodstock Festival in Bethel, New York, servicing portable latrines for the "Port-O-San" company. As Taggart performed his necessary but unpleasant task, he was interviewed by filmmakers. The result was a hilarious two-minute sequence in the film *Woodstock,* featuring Taggart talking about his job as he emptied latrines.

Taggart sued the film makers, claiming he had been drawn involuntarily into being a performer for someone else's commercial advantage. The film makers replied that Taggart had been a participant in an event of public interest. With the facts in such dispute, a United States Court of Appeals overturned the trial court's summary judgment for the film makers and sent the case back for further proceedings.[72] There is obviously a difference between a television crew's urging a group of fans to "moon" the opposing team's fans and the same crew taping "mooning" that was instigated by the fans themselves. If one of the group later found the pictures to be embarrassing, the question might be: Who started it, and for what purpose?

Halftime activities are usually fair game. Years ago, an animal trainer whose act included dogs, ponies, and monkeys performed at halftime during a Washington Redskins–New York Giants game. A portion of Arsène Gautier's act was televised, and announcers then read commercials touting a cigarette brand.

Gautier sued, claiming his name and picture were used for advertising purposes without his consent. However, the court ruled that unless there was exploitation of a name or picture in the commercial directly connected to the product being hawked, there was not "use" for advertising purposes. Therefore, Gautier's suit failed.[73] This case is, however, a reminder that, in general, no one's picture can be used in an advertisement without that person's permission.

Once the media are given access to an event, they generally have fairly broad power to depict the performances that take place. Another example from *Woodstock:* Frank Man was a professional musician who made the scene. Man climbed up onto the stage and played "mess call" on his flugelhorn for a pixilated audience of four hundred thousand. Movie cameras also were present, and Warner Bros., Inc. included Man's performance in the film *Woodstock*. Man sued, claiming his performance was included in the film without his consent. Man's contentions were unavailing, however, for a United States District Court said:

> The film depicts, without the addition of any fictional material, actual events which happened at the festival. Nothing is staged and nothing is false. . . . There an be no question that the Woodstock festival was and is a matter of public interest.[74]

The court concluded that Man, by his own choice, had put himself into the spotlight at a sensational public event, thus making himself newsworthy and depriving himself of the ability to collect for the commercial exploitation of his performance.

THE FAIRNESS DOCTRINE AND PERSONAL ATTACK

Regulations of the Federal Communications Commission are beyond the scope of this chapter. We can only urge that you be sure to know about them *if* they are in existence. Deregulation, not regulation, has been the FCC buzzword in recent years, with Commission respect for letting "market forces" do the regulating approaching zeal under the chairmanship of Mark Fowler (1981–87). Mr. Fowler was replaced by another believer in market forces, Dennis Patrick, whom Mr. Fowler said differs from Fowler only by having more hair.[75]

Tied to the FCC's recent stance as reluctant regulator is a newfound concern for the First Amendment. In August 1987, the Commission drew cheers from most broadcasters and flak from many citizens groups by announcing the end of the controversial issues part of its own thirty-eight-year-old creature, the Fairness Doctrine.[76] For the time being, personal attack and political editorializing requirements of the Fairness Doctrine were left in existence, although the FCC might in time eliminate them, too.

The Fairness Doctrine's death had been proposed to Congress by Chairman Fowler as early as 1981. His argument ran that the scarcity of broadcast frequencies had been alleviated by the increasing number of broadcast and cable voices available.

Although the Fairness Doctrine was seldom enforced in recent years, it took a 1987 United States Court of Appeals decision to embolden the FCC into actually declaring the end of a big chunk of the doctrine.[77] In the so-called TRAC Case—*Telecommunications Research Action Center (TRAC)* v. *FCC*—the court held that the FCC did have the authority to repeal its own doctrine and that a 1959 reworking of the Communications Act by Congress that made reference to the Fairness Doctrine had not placed the doctrine beyond Commission authority.

Although the controversial public-issues portion of the Fairness Doctrine has been declared dead by the FCC, that section may yet be revived. A large majoirty of members of Congress and the Senate favored legislation to codify the doctrine in statutory language, although President Reagan twice vetoed such proposals in 1987.[78]

One part of the Fairness Doctrine remaining in effect in the middle of 1988 will be mentioned, mainly because it is so closely related to the defamation and privacy torts we have been discussing. It is called the "personal attack rule" and it reads as follows:

> (a) When during the presentation of views on a controversial issue of public importance, an attack is made upon the honesty, character, integrity or like personal qualities of an identifiable person or group, the licensee shall, within a reasonable time and in no event later than one week after the attack, transmit to the person or group attacked (1) notification of the date, time and identification of the broadcast; (2) a script or tape (or accurate summary if a script or tape is not available) of the attack; and (3) an offer of a reasonable opportunity to respond over the licensee's facilities.
>
> (b) The provisions of paragraph (a) of this section shall not be applicable (1) to attacks on foreign groups or foreign public figures; (2) to personal attacks which are made by legally qualified candidates, their authorized spokesmen, or those associated with them in the campaign, on other such candidates, their authorized spokesmen, or persons associated with them in the campaign; and (3) to bona fide newscasts, bona fide news interviews, and on-the-spot coverage of a bona fide news event (including commentary or analysis contained in the foregoing programs, but the provisions of paragraph (a) of this section shall be applicable to editorials of the licensee).[79]

Because of the exception in section (b) (3), the personal attack rule normally will not apply to live news situations, but it does apply to documentaries, talk shows, and other types of public-issue programming. The distinction between editorials and commentary contained in news programs should be noted; commentary is exempt (unless the commentator has been authorized by the management to speak for the station) but editorials *are* subject to the rule.[80]

There is no personal attack unless someone's honesty, integrity, or morality is impugned. Thus, it is not a personal attack to criticize a public official's performance of his or her job, or to question a person's professional competence.[81] On the other hand, it is a personal attack to call someone a coward or to accuse him or her of undertaking a smear campaign.[82]

Although the rule speaks of an "identifiable person *or* group," the commission has declined to apply the rule to attacks on large groups. Thus, it is not a personal attack to accuse all the "men of the Roman Church" of being hypocritical and immoral, because the group is too large for identification to take place.[83]

When the personal attack rule is triggered, the station can avoid trouble with the FCC by complying promptly with the requirements stated in the rule for offering the victim an opportunity to respond. If this is done, the FCC oridinarily will take no further action.[84] The victim, of course, is still free to sue for libel or invasion of privacy, but often forthright compliance with the remedies provided by the personal attack rule will prevent private litigation as well.

SECTION 315

Just in case broadcasters needed a reminder in 1988 that Section 315 of the Federal Communications Act (providing "equal opportunity" for candidates' use of broadcast time) was still in effect, consider the case of William H. Branch. An on-air reporter for KOVR-TV, Sacramento, California, Branch petitioned the FCC in 1984 for a ruling that Section 315 was unconstitutional.[85]

Branch, it seems, wanted to run for the town council of Loomis, a municipality just northeast of Sacramento. Told by his bosses that he would have to take an unpaid leave of absence if he ran for the Loomis post, Branch then sought the ruling from the FCC. He argued not only that Section 315 was unconstitutional but also that it exempted appearances by a bona fide newscaster from the equal opportunity requirement.[86] Branch's employers calculated that his candidacy could obligate the station to provide about thirty-three hours of time to Branch's opponents if he continued to work there during the campaign period. Faced with the choice of an unpaid leave or remaining employed, Branch left the race.[87]

The FCC turned down Branch's petition and was upheld by a three-judge panel of the Court of Appeals, District of Columbia Circuit, in July 1987.[88] And in March 1988, the Supreme Court of the United States declined to review the case, leaving Section 315 in force.

CONCLUSION

Most of the problems discussed in this chapter can be avoided in two ways: first, by maintaining a heightened awareness of the problems themselves; and second, by vigilantly exercising sound journalistic judgment. Unfortunately, in the context of ENG, that awareness and judgment often must be exercised on the scene, instantaneously, and without benefit of consultation. Those circumstances obviously increase the risk of making a wrong judgment.

The legal problems raised by ENG can best be dealt with in the same way as many other problems created by the immediacy of the new technology: by careful planning.[89] Because there isn't time to devise a solution after the problem arises, contingency plans must be worked out in advance. Producers, reporters, and anchors should be given guidelines dealing with such matters as when to use delay systems, what to watch out for when viewing tape for quick turnaround, how to screen interview subjects, what to do if a speaker defames someone, and what to do when access to a news site is denied or in question.

These are matters each station should work out for itself in consultation with its own lawyers, in light of its own state law. The guidelines should address the most common situations and provide station personnel with specific answers to problems that are readily forseeable.

Such guidelines cannot cover every situation. Part of the excitement of ENG is that every situation offers its own new perils and opportunities. For that reason, each station ultimately must depend on the professional skill and good judgment of its news personnel.

NOTES

Updated materials added by Professor Teeter for this edition of *ENG: Television News and the New Technology* survey legal developments since 1985. Specific additions include the material on ambush interviews at footnotes 26 and 27; the $3 million libel verdict in *Brown & Williamson* v. *Walter Jacobson and CBS* at footnotes 29–38; material on intentional infliction of mental injury at footnotes 58–66; and information at the chapter's end on FCC regulations.

1. Le Mistral, Inc., v. CBS, Inc., 61 A.D.2d 491, 492 (1st Dept. 1978); *TV Guide*, May 3, 1980, p. 6.
2. Zacchini v. Scripps-Howard Broadcasting Co., 433 U.S. 562 (1977).
3. For a brief description of the new technology and its impact on television news, see Richard D. Yoakam, ''ENG: Electronic News Gathering in Local Television Stations,'' Research Report No. 12, School of Journalism, Indiana University (November 1981).
4. See, *e.g.*, Ralph L. Holsinger, *Media Law* (New York: Random House, 1987); Kent R. Middleton and Bill F. Chamberlin, *The Law of Public Communications* (New York: Longman, 1987); Harold L. Nelson and Dwight L. Teeter, Jr., *Law of Mass Communications,* 5th ed. (Westbury, N.Y.: Foundation Press, 1986); and Don R. Pember, *Mass Media Law*, 4th ed. (Dubuque, Iowa: Wm. C. Brown, 1987). Bruce W. Sanford's *Synopsis of the Law of Libel and the Right of Privacy* (rev. ed., 1981), published by World Almanac Publications, 200 Park Avenue, New York, N.Y. 10166, provides a useful 37-page overview of the areas of libel and privacy law.
5. See Wilson v. Scripps-Howard Broadcasting Co., 642 F.2d 371 (6th Cir.

1981), cert. den. 102 S.Ct. 984. See Annot., Defamation by Radio and Television, 50 A.L.R.3d 1311. The major exception is California, which treats broadcast defamation as slander. See Cal. Civ. Code §46, 48.5 (West, 1954).

6. See, *e.g.*, Snowden v. Pearl River Broadcasting Corp., 251 So.2d 405 (La. App. 1971).

7. Garrison v. Louisiana, 379 U.S. 64 (1964); Wilson v. Scripps-Howard Broadcasting co., supra note 5; cf. Cox Broadcasting v. Cohn, 420 U.S. 469 490 (1975).

8. 106 S.Ct. 1559 (1986).

9. Ibid., 1563.

10. See, *e.g.*, Dickey v. CBS, Inc., 583 F.2d 1221 (3rd Cir. 1978).

11. See, *e.g.*, Vitteck v. Washington Broadcasting Co., 256 Pa. Super 427, 389 A.2d 1197 (1978); Afro-American Publishing Co. v. Jaffe, 366 F.2d 649 (D.C. Cir. 1966); Ladany v. William Morrow & Co., 465 F.2d 870 (S.D.N.Y. 1978).

12. See, *e.g.*, Harwood Pharmaceutical Co. v. NBC, 9 N.Y.2d 460, 214 N.Y.S.2d 725, 174 N.E.2d 602 (1961).

13. See Nelson and Teeter, supra note 4, at 505; *Notes to Update Nelson and Teeter, 5th ed.*, p. 29 (1987).

14. See, *e.g.*, Irwin v. Ashurst, 158 Or. 61, 74 P.2d 1127 (1938).

15. *E.g.*, Holy Spirit Association for the Unification of World Christianity v. New York Times Co., 49 N.Y.2d 63, 414 N.Y.S.2d 165 (1979) (report of congressional investigation); Phoenix Newspapers v. Choisser, 82 Ariz. 271, 312 P.2d 150 (1957) (report of public candidates' forum).

16. St. Amant v. Thompson, 390 U.S. 727 (1968).

17. See, *e.g.*, Cepeda v. Cowles Broadcasting, Inc., 392 F.2d 417 (9th Cir. 1968), cert. den. 393 U.S. 840; Time, Inc. v. McLaney, 406 F.2d 565 (5th Cir. 1969), cert den. 395 U.S. 922.

18. Gertz v. Robert Welch, Inc., 418 U.S. 323 (1974).

19. Material used here was provided from the news director interviews by Professor Richard D. Yoakam as referred to in the note at the beginning of this chapter.

20. A number of states have special statutes, passed years ago at the behest of the National Association of Broadcasters, shielding stations from liability for defamatory remarks of third persons unless the plaintiff proves that the station failed to use due care to prevent the statement from being broadcast. See, *e.g.* 1 Wyo. Stat. 872; Ar. 5433a, Vernon's Ann. Tex. Stats. These statutes were enacted to protect broadcasters from strict liability rules that prevailed before the United States Supreme Court began imposing restrictions on state libel law. Whether the statutes will now be used against broadcasters, on the theory that they imply that broadcasters *are* liable for failing to keep third party defamers off the air, remains to be seen. With that last sentence's cautionary note in mind, see Robert L. Hughes's "Radio Libel Laws: Relics That May Have Answer for Reform Needed Today," *Journalism Quarterly*, Vol. 63, No. 2 (Summer 1986), pp. 288–293f.

21. Snowden v. Pearl River Broadcasting Corp., 251 So.2d 405 (La. App. 1971).

See also Holter v. WLCY-TV, 366 So.2d 440, 454 (Fla. 1978), citing Snowden v. Pearl River Broadcasting and saying that broadcasting a defamatory allegation from an anonymous source without further checking was the same as using no tape delay.

22. Adams v. Frontier Broadcasting Corp., 555 P.2d 556, 565 (Wyo. 1976). See also Pacella v. Milford Radio Corp., 462 N.E.2d 355, 360 (Mass. App. 1984), saying failure to take advantage of a seven-second tape delay was not evidence of actual malice (publication of a defamatory falsehood with knowledge of falsity or reckless disregard for the truth.)

23. Curtis Publishing Co. v. Butts, 388 U.S. 139, 157 (1967).

24. Walker v. Associated Press, 388 U.S. 130, 158, 159 (1967).

25. Adams v. Daily Telegraph Printing Co., 13 Med.L.Rptr. 2034, 2037 (S.C. Ct. of App., Dec. 8, 1986).

26. Machleder v. Diaz, 538 F. Supp. 1364 (S.D.N.Y. 1985).

27. Machleder v. Diaz, 801 F.2d 46 (2nd Cir. 1986).

28. Stuart A. Taylor, Jr., ''Justices Uphold $3 Million Libel Award on CBS,'' *The New York Times* (national ed.), April 5, 1988, p. 11. The Supreme Court was affirming Brown & Williamson v. Jacobson, 827 F.2d 1119 (7th Cir. 1987).

29. Brown & Williamson v. Jacobson, 827 F.2d 1119, 1122–1123 (7th Cir. 1987).

30. Ibid., 1123.

31. Ibid.

32. Ibid.

33. Ibid.

34. Ibid.

35. Ibid., 1134.

36. Ibid.

37. Ibid., 1137–1138.

38. Ibid., 1134.

39. *Cf.* Billings v. Atkinson, 489 S.W.2d 858 (Tex. 1973).

40. Dietemann v. Time, Inc., 449 F.2d 245, 250 (9th Cir. 1971).

41. Oklahoma v. Bernstein, 5 Med.L.Rptr. 2313, 2323–2324 (Okl. D.C. Rogers County, Jan. 21, 1980), affd. *sub nom.* Stahl v. Oklahoma, 9 Med.L.Rptr. (Okla. Ct. Crim. App. 1983).

42. Jaubert v. Crowley Post-Sentinel, 375 So.2d 1386 (La. 1979).

43. Galella v. Onassis, 487 F.2d 986 (2d Cir. 1973).

44. Galella v. Onassis, 8 Med. L. Rptr. (D.C. S.D.N.Y., March 2, 1982).

45. Florida Publishing Co. v. Fletcher, 340 So.2d 914, 915–916 (Fla. 1977).

46. Anderson v. WROC-TV, 109 Misc.2d 905, 441 N.Y.S.2d 220 (N.Y. Sup. Ct. 1981). See also Negri v. Schering Corp., 333 F. Supp. 101 (S.D.N.Y. 1971).

47. The inclusion of brief clips of newsworthy matters in station promotional materials probably is protected as long as the promotional use is merely incidental to the original newsworthy use. See Namath v. Sports Illustrated, 39 N.Y.2d 897, 386 N.Y.S.2d 397, 352 N.E.2d 584 (1976).

48. *Cf.* Raible v. Newsweek, Inc., 341 F.Supp. 804 (W.D. Pa. 1972); Arrington

v. New York Times Co., 8 Med.L.Rptr. 1351 (N.Y. 1982); Peay v. Curtis Publishing Co., 78 F. Supp. 305 (D.C.D.C. 1948).

49. Duncan v. WJLA-TV, 10 Med.L.Rptr. 1395, 1398 (D.C.D.C., Feb. 17, 1984).

50. *E.g.* Clayman v. Bernstein, 38 Pa. D&C 543 (1940); *cf.* Justice v. Belo Broadcasting Corp., 472 F. Supp. 145 (1979).

51. *Cf.* Sipple v. Chronicle Publishing Co., 82 Cal. App. 143, 147 Cal. Rptr. 59 (1978) (hero in attempt on President Ford's life identified by news media as gay; no cause of action).

52. Howard v. Des Moines Register and Tribune Co., 283 N.W.2d 289 (Iowa 1979), cert. den. 445 U.S. 904.

53. Cassidy v. ABC, 60 Ill. App.3d 831, 17 Ill. Dec. 936, 377 N.E.2d 126 (1978).

54. See, *e.g.*, Virgil v. Time, Inc., 527 F.2d 1122, 1129 (9th Cir. 1975), quoting the Restatement (Second) of Torts:
"In determining what is a matter of legitimate public interest, account must be taken of the customs and conventions of the community, and in the last analysis what is proper becomes a matter of community mores. The line is to be drawn when the publicity ceases to be the giving of information to which the public is entitled, and becomes a morbid and sensational prying into public lives for its own sake, with which a reasonable member of the public, with decent standards, would say that he had no concern. . . ."

55. See Barber v. Time, Inc., 348 Mo. 1199, 159 S.W.2d 291 (1942).

56. See Melvin v. Reid, 112 Cal. App. 285, 297 P. 91 (1931).

57. See Robert Drechsel, "Negligent Infliction of Emotional Distress: New Tort Problem for the Mass Media," 12 *Pepperdine Law Review* 989 (1985): Dworkin v. Hustler Magazine, 14 Med.L.Rptr. 1673 (U.S.D.C., C.D. Calif., 1987).

58. 14 Med.L.Rptr. 2281 (Feb. 24, 1988).

59. George Garneau, "First Amendment Victory," Editor & Publisher, Feb. 27, 1988, p. 45.

60. 14 Med.L.Rptr. at 2281 (1988).

61. David Margolick, "Some See Threat in Non-Libel Verdict of Falwell," *The New York Times,* Dec. 10, 1984, p. 6.

62. Falwell v. Flynt, 797 F.2d 1270, 13 Med.L. Rptr. 1145 (4th Cir. 1986).

63. Ibid.

64. Ibid.

65. 14 Med.L.Rptr. at 2285 (1988).

66. Ibid., at 2284.

67. Raible v. Newsweek, Inc., 341 F. Supp. 804, 806, 809 (W.D. Pa. 1972); Metzger v. Dell Publishing Co., 207 Misc.2d 182, 136 N.Y.S.2d 888 (1955); Russell v. Marboro Books, 18 Misc.2d 166, 183 N.Y.S.2d 8 (1955).

68. Cher v. Forum International, 7 Med.L. Rptr. 2593 (C.D. Cal. 1982).

69. Delan v. CBS, 7 Med.L.Rptr. 2453 (N.Y. Sup. Ct. App. Div., 2d Dept., Jan. 24, 1983).

70. Virgil v. Time, Inc., 527 F.2d 1112, 1127 (9th Cir. 1975), cert. den. 425 U.S. 998 (1976).

71. Neff v. Time, Inc., 406 F. Supp 858 (E.D. Pa. 1976). See also Harrison v. Washington Post, 391 A.2d 781 (D.C. App. 1978), which arose when a photographer—while standing on a public sidewalk—took pictures of a man being escorted by police officers. No liability was found.

72. Taggart v. Wadleigh-Maurice Ltd. & Warner Bros., 489 F.2d 435, 437 (3rd cir. 1973). When the case eventually was tried, the jury ruled against Taggart, evidently on grounds that the equipment use by film makers was so conspicuous that he must have known he was being filmed for commercial purposes.

73. Gautier v. Pro-Football, Inc., 271 App. Div. 431 (1951), affd. 107 N.E.2d 485, 304 N.Y. 354 (1952).

74. Man v. Warner Bros., Inc., 317 F. Supp. 51, 53 (D.C.N.Y. 1970). The Zacchini case, supra note 2, constitutes a very narrow exception to this rule. It merely holds that if a state wants to allow a performer to recover for the broadcast of his entire act, the First Amendment is no bar. But state law generally protects the depiction of events of public interest, as the Man case shows.

75. See, *e.g.*, "At the F.C.C., Another Man Who Loves Free Markets," *The New York Times,* Sept. 20, 1987, p. 20.

76. In re Complaint of Syracuse Peace Council Against WTVH, Syracuse, Memorandum Opinion and Order, 63 R.R.2d 5452 (1987).

77. Telecommunications Research Action Center (TRAC) v. FCC, 61 R.R.2d 330 (1987). See also Public Law 274, 86th Congress (1959), amending equal opportunities provisions of Sec. 315 of the Communications Act. Although Sec. 315 applies only to bona fide candidates for political office, with the 1959 amendment, Congress stated that broadcasters had obligations "under this Act to operate in the public interest and to afford reasonable opportunity for the discussion of conflicting views on issues of public importance." But in the TRAC case, the Court of Appeals said in effect that the 1959 amendment did not preclude the FCC from repealing the Fairness Doctrine. Adapted from Don. R. Le Duc, *Notes to Update Law of Mass Communications,* 5th ed. (Westbury, N.Y.: Foundation Press, 1988), pp. 41–42.

78. Le Duc, *op. cit.*, p. 42.

79. 47 C.F.R. §73.123.

80. See Let's Help Florida Committee, 74 F.C.C.2d 584, 46 R.R.2d 919 (1979).

81. See Mayor Henry W. Maier, 50 R.R.2d 73 (Bd. Bur. 1981); Rev. Lester Kinsolving, 67 F.C.C.2d 158 (Bd. Bur. 1977).

82. See Straus Communications, Inc., v. FCC, 530 F.2d 1001 (D.C. Cir. 1976); Red Lion Broadcasting Co. v. FCC, 395 U.S. 367 (1969).

83. Diocese of Rockville Centre, 50 F.C.C.2d 330, 32 R.R.2d 376 (1973).

84. See Anti-Defamation League of B'nai B'rith v. FCC, 403 F.2d 169 (D.C. Cir. 1968), cert. den. 394 U.S. 930.

85. Branch v. FCC, 14 Med.L.Rptr. 1465 (7th Cir. 1987).

86. Ibid., 1467, 1473, 1475.

87. Ibid., 1465–1466.

88. Ibid.

89. See Yoakam, supra note 3, at pp. 5–6.

"And Still to Come. . . ."  **11**

During any sustained period in which a new technology appears and is universally adopted, the initial effort is almost always operational—buy the machines, train the staff to use them, and put them both to work. Television news has done that with ENG. The results have been more speed, more range, and better quality in pictures and sound. Sometimes it also has brought more breadth and depth. Television news has become more important to the audience, more popular, and more widely accepted.

New tools such as helicopters, satellites, and out-of-town bureaus have also changed the mindset of local news managers who now can think about statewide, nationwide, or even worldwide horizons for their own programs.

But plenty of evidence indicates that the new technology is far ahead of the journalism. Technical competence itself has not necessarily resulted in clearer information being presented. Nor has adoption of the technology automatically led to smoother operations or wiser decisions.

Now it is time for us to look at how ENG and its related technology have changed local news focus, news management, and news department organization. If ENG is a force that controls the way we do things, what can we do to get control of it? And we need to look to the future. What's out there on the drawing boards and in the minds of the engineers and media developers that will further change the way television news is prepared and presented and the way the audience will use it?

WHERE ARE WE? WHERE ARE WE GOING?

In looking at the spread of technology in television news, you can't help but be impressed by how fast it has moved. In the span of one decade, videotape has

FIGURE 11-1. A satellite ground station. The large dish antennas can send or receive signals from geostationary satellites located about 22,300 miles above the equator. A large installation such as this one is sometimes called a satellite farm. *(Courtesy of GTE Spacenet Corporation.)*

replaced film, and electronic news gathering technology is universally accepted.

In a 1982 nationwide survey of news directors by Conrad Smith of Ohio State University,* 86 percent of them said it was not possible to be competitive without live ENG capability. Sixty-one percent said a helicopter gave them a competitive edge.

Professor Smith had the same news directors look five years ahead and found 82 percent of the large-market stations and 76 percent of the small-market stations expected to have satellite uplinks by 1987.

In 1987, Stephen Lacy, Tony Atwater, and Angela Powers at Michigan State did a similar survey.† And they found that the predictions that came out of Smith's survey weren't too far off.

Seventy-four percent of all the stations surveyed in 1987—including independent, non–network-affiliated stations—said they used satellite news networks and SNG equipment. Ninety percent of those news networks were those connected with ABC, CBS, and NBC. Forty-three percent of the stations subscribed to an additional, non–network-based satellite news service.

*For further details of Smith's study see *The RTNDA Communicator,* December 1982, and *Journal of Broadcasting,* Vol. 28, No. 1, Winter 1984, pp. 99–102.
†Stephen Lacy, Tony Atwater, and Angela Powers, "Uses of Satellite Technology in Television News," *Journalism Quarterly,* vol. 65, no. 4 (Winter 1988).

The spread of mobile uplinks—SNG trucks—has not been as great. About 16½ percent of the stations, mostly in the larger markets, reported that they had access to an SNG vehicle. Another 10 percent said they planned to buy a truck within the year.

What about the impact of these electronic news gathering methods on newscast content?

Smith's 1982 study showed news directors were worried. Eighty-six percent said the emphasis on ENG had influenced news content, and by a four-to-one margin they thought the influence had been a negative one. They said they felt the ability to go live too often was a reason for doing a story in the first place. They worried that the speed of ENG in getting things on the air led to a sacrifice of depth. And they said the live coverage sometimes suppressed another strength of ENG: the ability to verify information right up to air time and polish the story through editing.

The Michigan State trio didn't ask parallel questions in this area, but they did find SNG had a powerful influence on news directors' attitudes toward quality. Almost 83 percent of them said they felt satellite news networks had greatly or at least somewhat improved the quality of their local newscasts.

The news directors were evenly split on the question of whether satellite news networks had increased the amount of out-of-state news in their newscasts. But once again, when they were asked whether having an SNG vehicle improved the quality of the news coverage in their **ADI** (area of dominant influence) and in their state, they were extremely positive. Seventy-five percent of all the news directors said ADI coverage quality had improved greatly or somewhat. Ninety percent said their coverage of state news was improved.

"WHAT WE NEED IS A LONGER ARM. . . ."

It is quite clear then that the spread of cable TV in the last decade caused a parallel spread of the area news directors had to cover. In earlier days stations considered that their coverage area included only those viewers who could receive the station's signal over the air. But cable service is now in more than 50 percent of American television homes. In Los Angeles, for example, the local news programs of Los Angeles stations are seen, via cable, in virtually the whole southern third of the state of California.

And the largest ADI in the United States is Salt Lake City, where the station must try to cover news in Montana, Idaho, Wyoming, Colorado, and Nevada as well as Utah, because viewers out there depend on them.

The answer to providing coverage of events involving more distant audiences has come in three ways: purchase or lease of a helicopter, the establishment of news bureaus staffed by station personnel, and the purchase of an SNG vehicle.

Bureaus and Birds

Of all the things the new technology has brought to local news, the arrival of the helicopter—"Skycam," "Skyeye," "Flycam,"—has brought controversy, booming promotion, and a whole set of costs, opportunities, and worries to the television newsroom staff.

Radio news reporters have used the helicopter for years to cover traffic during rush hour. With ENG and portable microwave equipment, suddenly television news reporters discovered they and the helicopter were made for each other. Certainly WHIO-TV made the best use of one in Dayton, Ohio, as we have already seen in Chapter 9.

This awkward-looking aircraft can fly slowly and at low altitudes; it can even hover in midair or back up. It takes off and lands vertically, so it can be used to deliver reporters and crews to a news event and return them to the station with their visual material. It can fly to and from a distant news story at 130 miles an hour, and can land at almost any convenient location.

Equipped with elaborate radio communication systems and a microwave receiver and transmitter, it can be used as a platform in the sky that can deliver live pictures and sound. Or it can relay pictures and sound from the news story on the ground back to the station's receiving antennas. A fully equipped helicopter can cost a half million dollars or more. It provides room for a pilot and a photojournalist—for as many as four persons in larger models—along with all of the high-technology transmitting and receiving antennas. Helicopter pilots are also expensive: The average salary is $25,000 or more a year. They require special training and licenses, and they operate under stringent rules regarding health and safety requirements. And by necessity they are more concerned with the flying rules enforced by the Federal Aviation Authority than they are about the broadcasting rules enforced by the Federal Communications Commission. With the aircraft and the pilots, as one news director put it, "We are running a small airline as well as a news service."

When helicopters first came into use, stations got a lot of glamour and promotability—and even perhaps a ratings edge—out of being the first on the block to have one. A lot of that hoopla was generated by the stations' own promotion departments.

"Now," they said, "Skycam 11. . . . the new world of TV News Coverage. Skycam 11 can go where no one else can, get news no one else can get. . . . Look for Skycam 11 in the sky—then watch our news."

Problems with Helicopters Choppers have good uses and bad uses. The cost is stiff; at a Louisville station, the helicopter budget allocation for six months was spent in the first six weeks of use. Most stations learned quickly that the worst use of a helicopter is to send it up in the morning looking for some news. The "it's-a-dull-day-maybe-the-eye-in-the-sky-will-find-something" syndrome faded rapidly as the bills came in.

Beyond that, the helicopter can't fly in bad weather any more than a small plane can. It can't fly just anywhere you want; flight paths are regulated around airports and in controlled airspace. Even though the bird is tethered to a landing pad on the roof of the station or in the backyard, a flight plan and permission from air traffic control is required.

An example: When the World Unlimited Hydroplane boat race was held in San Diego harbor, a local station made extensive plans to use its helicopter for both live shots and taped coverage. So did a lot of other stations, including those from Los

Angeles, 127 miles away. That meant five or six TV news helicopters in the air at the same time, plus the police, fire, coast guard, marine rescue, and ambulance choppers.

So the FAA held a coordination meeting. What the choppers could and could not do was carefully—and firmly—spelled out. Lower-altitude hover points were designated where closeup pictures of the race could be made. No more than one helicopter at a time could be at any one hover point. Most important of all, no hovering was allowed over the actual race course because the down drafts from the helicopter blades would make dangerous turbulence on the water for the jet boats to run through.

When important people or big crowds are on the ground, no helicopter is allowed to fly directly overhead. The Secret Service does not allow helicopters to twirl down for a closeup when the president is in a parade; local authorities kept strict control of overhead flights when the pope visited the United States.

San Francisco harbor authorities accused a San Francisco station's chopper crew of causing the Coast Guard difficulty in recovering the body of a woman who had jumped from the Bay Bridge. The Coast Guard said the wash from the helicopter blades forced the body under the surface just as a crewman was about to retrieve it with a grappling pole. The station's manager denied the charge, adding coldly that a review of the tape showed the woman was dead anyway.

Then there is the danger inherent in flying the ship. Helicopters are more dangerous than other kinds of aircraft. A number of stations, police departments, and other civilian users have had fatal accidents. Others have had injuries. If the engine fails the helicopter is supposed to ''spiral down'' like a maple seed, but if it is too low in the first place, the landing is much more like a crash than what is called an ''auto-rotate descent.''

Over densely populated areas or crowds, such a crash could be disastrous. Add to ownership cost huge insurance policy premiums. Many stations carry five-million- to ten-million-dollar liability coverage at a cost of thirty-five to forty thousand dollars per year and not only hope for, but demand, extreme caution.

Some station personnel don't adapt well to flying. One station, planning to put its weatherman up in the air to do the forecast live from the helicopter, found that the weatherman suffered from extreme vertigo problems. On his first—and presumably last—night up, he turned green and mumbled weakly about ''Fine weather tomorrow, and now back to you, Ken.'' Other stations have found that some older reporters, and many who are married, simply refuse to go up at all. Helicopter assignments have become a very sensitive issue in union contract negotiations.

Shooting pictures from a helicopter is not easy. Even with stabilizing gyroscopes, there is some vibration from the helicopter blades. It is relatively easy to get stable wide shots but it is quite difficult to get good closeups with the zoom lens fully extended because the vibration is magnified along with the rest of the picture. Even wide shots present problems. A lot of moving wide shots, with the major point of interest disappearing under the ship, or even slow circles that change the aspect of the scene as the ship moves around, do not provide a good visual reference point for the viewer. Such scenes also do not provide the closeups and details that make a story visually interesting.

Some aerial scenes may not even be relevant. A Baltimore station covered the opening day of a sensational rape trial by shooting scenes of the street corner where the rape occurred from its helicopter. It was a bright, sunny day. The rape occurred at night. And six months earlier.

Some Answers   All of that having been said, the helicopter does represent a tool for news coverage that many news directors say they cannot do without.

Let's look at some ways choppers have been used effectively. They are, of course, perfect for covering widespread disasters. Floods, forest fires, train wrecks, air crashes, big city fires, traffic jams, and wind damage give the station a chance to take the audience to the scene and to provide a perspective of it that can be achieved in no other way. The pictures are dramatic and worth looking at. The helicopter can get reporters and photojournalists to the news almost as it occurs.

If the pilot is very good and very brave, it is possible to do such a valuable service as that performed by an Atlanta station. There the helicopter tracked a tornado while flying near it and thus gave the audience precise advance warning of where the storm was headed.

In the summer of 1986, photojournalist Tom Emprey and pilot Max Messmer of KARE-TV heard a pilot talking about a tornado just after they took off to shoot some aerial scenes of Minneapolis's Acquatennial celebration. They spotted the tornado over Brooklyn Park, a northern suburb, and for the next ninety minutes made some of the most spectacular videotape ever seen of a tornado at work.

Messmer kept about one-half to three-quarters of a mile away as the twister

FIGURE 11-2. The tornado that everyone saw. Station KARE-TV's helicopter flew around this tornado in northern Minneapolis for more than an hour, feeding live shots of the twister as it developed, ripped through a manufacturing and storage complex, and dissipated in a suburban forest. *(Courtesy of KARE-TV, Minneapolis, Minnesota.)*

threw huge rocks in the air and uprooted fifty-foot trees. Emprey used a camera with a fourteen-thousand-dollar gyro lens to make extremely steady pictures as Messmer circled the funnel cloud. Their work was broadcast live by KARE-TV with meteorologist Paul Douglas alternately telling people to take cover and pleading with Messmer and Emprey not to get too close.

When thirteen inches of rain fell in one hour on Little Rock, Arkansas, station KARK-TV's helicopter covered the flooding as it occurred. Residents were able to get out of the way and emergency crews into position by watching the station's news specials and live coverage.

In Denver, KBTV's helicopter got over a reservoir break in North Central Colorado to broadcast immediate warning reports that allowed farmers to move livestock out of the way of the rushing water and get themselves to higher ground.

In Phoenix, Arizona, Jerry Foster of KPNX-TV is a reporter-photographer-pilot all rolled into one. At an RTNDA conference Foster explained to a breath-holding audience of news directors how to fly a helicopter (by putting the control stick between your knees) and shoot pictures (by holding the camera in one hand) at the same time.

Foster showed tape of a police chase and capture of a man wanted in a shooting. It was worthy of any prime-time police series. Foster flew sideways and backward and hovered over the scene to keep photographer Howard Shepard pointed at the action as the chase wound through residential streets, over lawns, down alleys, and onto a freeway where the escapee's van crashed into a truck. Because Foster had kept his newsroom informed of exact locations at all times, another crew was able to be there when the police arrested the man and led him away.

Helicopter reporters have known for a long time that they can help direct traffic. A Chicago traffic reporter said it gave him a feeling of super-power:

> There I am up there and if there's a jam-up on the freeway . . . I can tell people where to turn off to avoid it. Then all of a sudden I see them following my orders . . . I have dreams about a mad traffic-copter reporter bringing the whole city to its knees by orchestrating the world's largest traffic jam.

A Boston station used a camera in a flying helicopter and another camera in a news van on the ground to explain the precise effects and costs of a toll road fare increase. The chopper flew various routes alongside the road. The news van drove the road and through tunnels and toll gates. Character-generated words showing costs and distances were flashed on the screen as the chopper shots were edited together with those made in the news van. The viewers got an exact map and a preview of what it was going to cost them on their favorite route to and from work.

A New York station investigating the environmental impact of new tidal control measures on Long Island Sound was able to show its audience new shoreline erosion caused by the control measures even though the Port Authority denied it was taking place.

"Our Man In. . . ." Helicopters are a good means of transportation. Many news directors say they use their helicopters about half of the time for the more simple but crucial task of getting the crews, and pictures and sound they collect, to

and from news events faster than can be done with ground-based transportation. They also use them to reach out to cover distant stories and audiences. If the reporters are running late, they can feed sound bites and B-Roll back for editing and then do their live wraps from the chopper as they fly home.

Columbus, Ohio, is almost exactly in the center of the state. Station WBNS-TV sees its helicopter as an "outreach machine."

"Take Akron and the auto and tire industry there," said the news director. "Things that happen there impact on the auto parts industry in Columbus. We can make and show those connections a lot better by flying up there and back."

He also said that many stories about how other cities are coping with things like environmental issues and urban management can show Columbus viewers what may happen locally before it happens.

"If we can show how others have handled such problems," he said, "then maybe our city council won't have to invent the wheel all over again each time a new problem develops here."

In Cincinnati, Indianapolis, Miami, Little Rock, Denver, and Houston, helicopters are used almost every day to get out of town and cover stories of significance to the local audience.

In Boston a news director wants his audience to think of his station as a New England station.

> Boston is a community that relates to a number of states. Before we had our helicopter I wanted to go to Maine to cover a story about forest areas being sprayed with an insecticide that was making pregnant women ill. It would have taken two days to get there and back by conventional transportation; we could have done it on the same day the story broke if we had the chopper.
>
> Likewise, I wanted and got heavy coverage of a train wreck in Canada that spilled dangerous chemicals. Why is this interesting to our audience in Boston? Because a lot of people from here vacation in that area and they are familiar with it.
>
> If we can get it into the viewers' minds that we will go anywhere in New England to cover stories of interest to Bostonians, boy, that can mean a lot to you in terms of audience loyalty and ratings.

Our innovative news director from New Orleans said that while his staff is adjusting the video systems they often use the helicopter as a "phone booth in the sky," broadcasting live *audio* reports through the plane's two-way radio link even before the pictures are ready to go.

"Now, from Our Bureau. . . ."

Another way to provide the longer arm needed to reach out for wider coverage is to establish news bureaus in other cities that have significant and important news for the local audience. These bureaus are permanently staffed with station personnel and equipment. On a daily basis those staff members feed news from that area into the regular news programs.

Station KRON-TV in San Francisco was among the first to go deeply into regional bureau development. Its philosophy grew out of some hard thinking about the role of local TV news in a metropolitan area, about the implications of urban growth, and about the topography of the San Francisco area. It is a model that can be useful elsewhere.

First, the philosophy: Metropolitan areas, the thinking went, are really a group of smaller units—cities within cities—that are entities in themselves. San Francisco is like that, only more so.

Now, the topography: San Francisco's metropolitan area is a circle of contiguous cities around the bay. The city of San Francisco itself is on a hilly peninsula. The Pacific Ocean is to the west, and the San Leandro mountain range is to the east.

As for urban growth, the San Francisco metropolitan area was squeezed into a series of ribbon cities that grew northward and southward at accelerated rates between 1950 and 1970. Then, the suburban growth moved over the mountains and spread out into the San Joaquin Valley to the southeast and the Sacramento Valley to the northeast.

Population growth was tremendous. Marin County to the north of San Francisco had 146,820 residents in 1960. By 1976 that had grown to 219,600. Contra Costa County boomed from 409,030 in 1960 to almost 600,000 by 1976.

All of these people received their newscasts from the San Francisco stations. But for years it was very difficult for the San Francisco stations to provide much visual coverage from these areas of huge population growth. Ground transportation was squeezed onto the freeways and bridges; it was a long, time-consuming drive from the South Bay area to the downtown San Francisco station headquarters.

Enter the new technology. The famous San Francisco hills caused serious interference problems for ground-level microwave systems. But those mountains were to the east. Microwave towers were built on the mountains. Soon KRON-TV was able to broadcast live from almost any location around the bay by beaming the signals from the ground to the mountain towers and then back to the station's antennas.

Yet the ground transportation problems remained; sending out the crews from the downtown headquarters to the scene of the news events took just as long. So why not establish bureaus in the cities to the south, east, and north and link them up with microwave? And why not use the microwave to go over the tops of the mountains and down into the newly populated cities in the valleys to the north, east, and south?

It was very imaginative thinking at the forefront of adaptation of the new technology. Bureaus were established in five suburban cities and in the state capital at Sacramento. Some were made live capable. Some had their own mobile news van equipment assigned to them. Personnel were assigned who lived and worked right in the suburb. They planned local coverage of their community and coordinated this with the editors in the downtown newsrooms.

What developed from the establishment of this electronic system was a much broader view in the minds of the news editors as to what was news for the station's audience on any given day. The reports would contain, they said, local news from a number of cities *including San Francisco*. The test would be whether that story was important to the local residents wherever they were.

Jean Harper, former News Director of KRON-TV, said the location of the story didn't matter.

People are interested in news. What we want to convey to them is that if something happens where they live we will be there and cover it. We want them to believe that, and that if they are looking at a local story from another city, we'll get to the interesting one from their city in a few moments. We are putting the emphasis on local, local, local kinds of stories rather than worrying about making the story universally interesting to everyone in the Bay Area.

Some metropolitan newspaper editors have been working with the same idea. Many big-city newspapers contain sections in each edition that deal with the news of suburban and regional cities as well as the central city news. They've done this to combat the growth of suburban newspapers and television.

But there's a big difference. The local news in newspapers with zoned editions is divided up. Readers in one suburb do not get the local news section aimed at another suburb. KRON-TV was "publishing" and delivering all of the sections at one time.

There have been some modifications. Some of KRON-TV's bureaus have been closed. They were neither financially nor editorially successful. But the philosophy of news behind this combination of technology and editorial planning continues.

A less successful experiment with the bureau concept occurred in Detroit. In 1977, WWJ-TV (now WDIV-TV) took the new technology and designed a bureau organization to cover Detroit and its metropolitan area. Bureaus with full-time staff and mobile remote equipment were established to the southwest, northwest, and northeast. Because the station operated on Channel 4, it was decided that the downtown newsroom itself would become the Downtown Bureau. This decision seems to have been made solely so that the station could dub its news "News 4, Plus 4."

With much promotion of that catchy phrase the system took off—and crashed. Each night an anchor person in the studio would introduce a suburban bureau chief, who would then recount a major story from that part of the metropolitan area. Sometimes the bureau chief would switch to a live report from the specific location of the story. Then back to the studio, and another switch to another bureau for another story—and so on around the horn.

The format had a lot of problems. The production elements called for words like "Stand by, Northeast Bureau" to appear on a screen next to the studio anchor as he was introducing a story. Just before the switch to the bureau, the face of the bureau chief would appear on that screen. If a live report or a tape package was in the report from the bureau, the bureau chief would sometimes have to introduce the reporter before the viewer got to see him or her. Therefore, frequently a story was introduced three times: once by the anchor, once by the bureau chief, and finally by the reporter, before the audience got any details.

The staff didn't really get the feel of it. Bureaus competed to get their stories on first. Someone suggested that a fifth bureau was needed. Incredulously a news executive asked, "Do you mean 'News 4, Plus 5'?" The weatherman frequently joked about the effects of the weather on the bureaus. And because the Downtown Bureau chief was actually seated at a separate desk in the same studio, the weatherman would raise his voice so, he said, the Downtown Bureau chief could hear him.

It was clearly a case of technology and format dictating both content and production, and it didn't last long.

A Baltimore station tried to use a bureau arrangement to combat competition for the news audience between it and the local stations in Washington, D.C. The focus for the Baltimore station was on two areas—Howard County, which is located almost exactly halfway between Washington and Baltimore, and in the Maryland state capital in Annapolis. The population of Howard County increased 90 percent between 1970 and 1980. The people who live there commute to work in both cities, so the battle for viewers in that county is a serious one for all concerned.

A broadcast group vice president, who was a reporter for another Baltimore station at the time, watched the Howard County and Annapolis bureau development with amusement.

> It was terrible, boring. They'd take a thirty-second copy story and turn it into a bureau report, giving it more emphasis than it really deserved. I lived there and I tried to cover the news from Columbia, Maryland, and the truth is there just wasn't much news there.

The Annapolis bureau worked somewhat better because it was in the state capital and there was enough news of state government—and, at the time, state executive shenanigans—to make it worth the effort and expense. But the bureau idea did not change the audience size for the station that tried it.

Other applications of the bureau concept are being tried. Five group-owned stations in Kansas—KARD-TV in Wichita, WCKT-TV in Great Bend, KGLD-TV in Garden City, KOMC-TV in Oberlin, KTSB-TV in Topeka, and KTVJ-TV in Joplin, Missouri—call themselves the Kansas State Network. They are all linked by microwave so they can share news with each other. They also opened a state capital bureau in Topeka so they all can have direct microwave coverage each night live from the legislative chambers.

What becomes clear from these examples, and others, is that a bureau operation must be thought of as a part of the news-gathering system, not as a way to isolate target audiences or to force a "total news concept" out of a series of individual reports that do not have a common denominator of interest across the audience.

It is generally agreed that bureaus can and do allow local television news to reach out into the fringe and related cable-serviced areas to provide more coverage. It is also agreed among many news directors that the news covered in those fringe areas must have some kind of universality of interest or relate to the viewers in the central coverage areas.

Jim Snyder, a former news director at WDIV-TV who cancelled the "News 4, Plus 4" experiment when he arrived there, comes down on the side of universality. He says:

> If you are running any news operation, but especially those in large metropolitan areas, and you are getting involved in the neighborhood stuff, you find yourself covering a lot of stories that would run on page 42 of the newspaper. There are stories you have to cover, even though they don't have universality, because they are important and it is your duty to serve the public.

But you cannot do anything without news judgment. If you let your bureaus warp your news judgment, they aren't going to do what they can do best. That is, they must stay on top of and give coverage to stories that are important or interesting because they involve something that a lot of people relate to.

"Why Don't We Do It by Satellite?"

That question was not heard in local television newsrooms at the beginning of the 1980s. Today it is a perfectly normal question asked in many newsrooms on a daily basis. If ENG moved quickly into the electronic news scene, satellite news gathering swept in like a hurricane.

A satellite news gathering system is the space-age equivalent of a ground-based microwave system. Twenty-two thousand, three hundred miles above the earth's equator is a parking lot for geostationary communications satellites. They were put there by spacecraft from the United States and a number of other nations and later by the American space-shuttle program.

These satellites come in various shapes and sizes. Some look like giant helicopter blades. Others are spherical—about the same size as a big above-ground outdoor swimming pool—with a fan-shaped antenna on top. All are covered with solar power cells. All are draped with other antennas of all kinds.

On the ground is a sending-receiving unit. Simple ones are receive only, like the backyard units in rural areas and those used by motels that get a movie service. More powerful units that can both send and receive are larger. But one of the most significant developments in electronic journalism has been the development of send-receive units small enough to mount on a medium-size truck or large van. These satellite news vehicles (SNV) can be moved to any point the truck can reach and can send pictures and sound from that location to any other point in the United States.

Let's define a few terms:

Geostationary satellite. This is a satellite that is placed into orbit about 22,300 miles above the earth's equator. It flies in the same direction as the earth turns and at a speed that, at that altitude, is the same as that of the earth's rotation. Therefore in effect it stands still.

Communications satellite. This satellite contains receiver-transmitters that can receive signals transmitted from the ground and retransmit the signals back to the ground. It is powered by batteries charged by solar cells.

Uplink. A transmitter on the ground that sends signals to the satellite.

Downlink. A receiver on the ground that receives signals from a satellite.

Transponder. The receiver-transmitter in the satellite that receives the signals from the uplink and retransmits them on the downlink.

C-band. That part of the electromagnetic spectrum between 3.7 and 4.2 gigahertz assigned for United States satellite use.

Ku-band. That part of the electromagnetic spectrum between 11.7 and 12.7 gigahertz assigned for United States satellite use.

Footprint. The area on the ground covered by the satellite downlink transmission.

The satellite is, therefore, an electronic backboard in space. Because it is in space it can be used to "bounce" radio frequencies between two points that are a great distance apart at ground level. In the United States, most of the satellites used for SNG have a footprint large enough to cover the entire continental United States. As with ground-based microwave systems, the super-high-frequency signals do not bend, so the antennas must be aimed carefully and must have line of sight between the earth station and the satellite in space.

In 1965 just one geostationary satellite, called Early Bird, flew above the Atlantic Ocean. It provided 240 telephone circuits and one quite fuzzy black-and-white television channel between Europe and the United States. By 1969 a global system operated by the International Telecommunications Satellite Organization—Intelsat for short—was in place. Today Intelsat is a 110-nation consortium that supervises a globe-girdling system of twelve satellites providing two-thirds of the international telephone and data traffic and a majority of all international television exchanges. Forty nations use Intelsat for domestic telecommunications. Other systems are INTERSPUTNIK (a Soviet consortium); INMARSAT (used to link land-based telephone and Telex with ships at sea); a raft of regional satellite systems with names

FIGURE 11-3. An artist's conception of a geostationary satellite in orbit receiving and sending an SNG transmission. All such satellites can receive and retransmit a number of signals at the same time. SNG trucks on the ground lease time on these satellites to send and receive pictures and sound of news reports and special live broadcasts, and to exchange news stories. The small light area on the globe illustrates the sending point, the large light area illustrates the footprint of the satellite. (*Courtesy of Western Union.*)

like EUTELSAT (for Europe), ARABSAT (for the Arab League countries); and domestic systems that serve the Soviet Union, China, Australia, Brazil, Mexico, Canada, India, Indonesia, and Japan. With twenty-seven satellites in orbit, the United States has the most.

The C-band domestic satellites came first. PBS, not the commercial networks, was the first to deliver all its programs to its affiliates by satellite. CNN, the Cable News Network, went heavily in C-band satellites to set up its twenty-four-hour news network and is the granddaddy of the satellite news systems. Using the Turner Broadcasting Service antenna farm in Atlanta, CNN has simultaneous access to as many as eleven satellites, including both C- and Ku-bands.

C-band was reliable and sturdy, and overcame interference from storms. For a while C-band was all that was available. Its disadvantage was that the satellites shared frequencies with ground-based microwave systems. The FCC required anyone setting up a C-band ground station to make an exhaustive survey to be sure its transmissions would not interfere with others in the same area. It was hard to come sweeping up on a spot news story with such restrictions and with antenna dishes as big as 9.1 meters across.

Ku-band offered the answer for news operations. It did not share frequencies with anything else. Therefore higher-power amplifiers and smaller dishes (1 meter) could be used to uplink to the satellites from any location, and the satellite's antenna could concentrate its return signal into a narrower beam; thus smaller antennas were needed on the receiving end. That all meant the systems could be made transportable.

For quite a while engineers were cool to Ku-band because it was subject to a lot of interference by heavy rain. RCA did the experimentation, and NBC led a gamble that broke through. The RCA engineers realized that most of the tests of Ku had been along the ground, that is, along the horizontal axis of most rain storms. They theorized that using Ku for satellite transmission would mean shooting upward through weather a much shorter distance to clear skies. That, and application of more power, proved to be true. NBC switched to Ku-band for all its program distribution. When it launched its SATCOM K2 satellite, RCA Americom gave away hundreds of Ku-band receivers, and cash to defray the cost of hooking them up, to television stations. NBC also began a program to share the cost of sixty-one transportable earth stations with its affiliates around the country. Both CONUS and Independent News Network (INN) also use SATCOM K2 for their news transmissions and exchanges.

The other major satellite news systems operate on Ku-band from GTE's GSTAR and SPACENET satellites. These include CBS and ABC, CNN Newsbeam, and the Florida News Network. ABC and CBS were slower to get into satellite news distribution with their network affiliates, but by 1987 all three networks had two-way satellite communications with its members' newsrooms, daily news feeds, and cost-sharing programs to help affiliates afford the high start-up costs of SNG.

A Satellite Culture

In the beginning the daily use of satellites to deliver raw videotape, story packages, and live broadcasts was thought of as a ''network'' kind of activity. ABC, CBS, and NBC had the facilities and the world-wide news coverage organizations. They used satellites to cover world news and to ship material back to their New York headquarters. Then CNN came along and built its cable news services with satellites as the basic foundation.

It is possible to fix a single date when the use of satellites for news gathering by local stations made a deep and lasting impression on these stations and their audiences. That was Tuesday, January 20, 1981, the day President Ronald Reagan was inaugurated. That was also the day Iran released the fifty-two Americans who had been held hostage in Iran for 444 days.

Never before had communication satellites been so important. In place were the networks' inaugural coverage plans. More stations than ever before would cover the local angles of the ceremonies with their own reporters in Washington.

During the weekend before the inauguration a break in the hostage story had been strongly indicated. The networks' long-standing contingency plans for covering the hostage return went into high gear. These included not only coverage from the Middle East and Europe but also coverage of the hostages' families in their home towns all over the country. Elaborate plans to dispatch network correspondents to "stake out" the hostage families were made. Sometimes that wasn't so easy; many small towns were difficult to reach and had no satellite facilities, let alone land lines that could be used to transmit videotape of family reactions. A number of hostage families didn't want the publicity. The mother of one hostage retreated to the family summer home in a remote mountain location and told a nosy network correspondent she wouldn't come down until she heard something official.

As the hostage story got hotter so did the interest of local stations. It became even more important that they have their own people in the nation's capital. On January 19, Iran announced it had reached an agreement through Algerian diplomats to release the hostages in return for U.S. concessions. By the time of the inaugu-

FIGURE 11-4. The Americans held hostage in Iran on their return to the United States. On the day the hostages were released and President Reagan was inaugurated, and on the days that followed, satellite use by American networks and individual stations was at the highest level in history. (AP/Wide World Photos.)

ration the next day—noon in Washington—almost everyone was sure both things would happen at the same time. They almost did except for one final irony: The Iranians waited to let the hostages' plane take off from Tehran until just a few minutes after Jimmy Carter stepped down and handed the leadership over to President Reagan.

That evening the whole world watched as the Algerian airliner carrying the hostages landed in Algeria. Network correspondents in the United States, one of whom had spent weeks memorizing the faces of the hostages from still picture files, did a flawless play-by-play narration as live pictures of the hostages coming down the plane's steps flowed in, by satellite, from Algerian television. For the first time we knew that all fifty-two had been released. They were counted, live, as everyone watched. A few moments later Assistant Secretary of State Warren Christopher took charge, and United States military planes flew the hostages to Frankfurt, Germany, on their way home at last.

American television and its viewers were thankful the Algerians had the satellite connection on January 20, 1981. One top network television executive suggested that RTA, the Algerian television network, should get an Emmy for its coverage of a major world news story.

The hostage return story didn't remain a "network story" for very long, if it ever had been one. Scores of local TV stations sent crews to Frankfurt to get the first interviews with hostages from their areas. Hundreds were on hand when the hostages landed at West Point and later when they arrived in Washington.

From that day on the local television stations around the nation looked at satellites in another way—as local reporting tools and ways to deliver information.

Satellite downlinks are being used as delivery systems. Both American wire services use satellites to deliver their services. Both CNN and CNN II are delivered by satellite to cable systems and to stations that are affiliated with them. PBS and NPR deliver all of their programs by satellite. Group-owned stations have combined to share satellite costs so that they can get same-day and/or live news feeds from their Washington bureaus.

Satellites are being used to share news on an informal basis and to form new networks. Those stations that have both downlink and uplink facilities have the world at their fingertips. By having the ability to send and receive, stations can make permanent or temporary arrangements with other stations in other parts of the country to get news of local interest.

Satellites are being used for special coverage by the station's own anchors, reporters, and photojournalists. We are not talking here about the once-every-few-years trip to Washington to interview a state senator or to a national political convention where a state politician is a candidate for high office. Nor are we talking about the occasional coverage of a national story with strong local ties, like the return of the American hostages from Iran in 1981. We are talking about how satellite technology has changed the definition of what local news is.

Dean Mell of Spokane, Washington, a former president of RTNDA, spotted the trend early. In 1982 he said, "We are going to have to expand our psychological perimeters. It is not just the satellites, it is the whole new array of news sources they give us. The strongest thing a station has to sell is its local identity; that begins with a strong news department. The ability of a station's reporters to cover events outside of their local markets will bolster that identity."

Mell's remarks at that time reflected the awakening of local stations to the utility of satellites. Sure, some stations had used them before to cover major national stories like political conventions. These efforts were usually accompanied by a lot of flash and splash from the station's promotion department, and often what came back was a pale version of what the network correspondents did on a daily basis.

Have Dish, Will Travel. . . .

But with experience came more serious attempts to show how something that happened far away had an impact on the local community. And many of the earlier uses were far away. Distance seemed to be paired with the word *satellite* in the minds of many editors.

Salvadoran refugees, fleeing to Honduras, began showing up in Houston, Texas. So KPRC-TV sent its crews to El Salvador to look more deeply into the problems there. WDAF-TV in Kansas City followed Senator Nancy Kassebaum to El Salvador when she and other members of Congress went there to monitor the country's election.

WTVD of Durham, North Carolina, used a satellite and its Washington bureau to give its audience live, daily coverage of debate on the farm bill, particularly regarding the tobacco-growing industry.

KBTV in Denver has purchased a mobile satellite uplink and thus is able to cover news stories in towns and cities around the state that cannot be reached by existing ground-based microwave equipment . . . and on the same day they happen.

WCSC-TV in Charlotte, North Carolina, went to Cairo for the funeral of Anwar Sadat because a South Carolina teenager had been a pen pal of Sadat's. Its competitor, WSOC-TV, went with hometown native Billy Graham to Russia and used the Soviet satellite network to get its live stories back to the local viewers. Many stations sent their anchors to Barbados and Grenada following the U.S. invasion.

When the Catholic bishop of Phoenix died, KPNX-TV joined the newly appointed bishop and a large group of local Catholic laity going to Rome for his consecration.

Chicago has the largest Polish-American population in the nation. So WGN-TV sent a reporter to Vienna to interview some of the first Polish refugees coming out of Poland and sent those interviews back to Chicago for immediate use.

IT'S NOT JUST A TRUCK ANYMORE. . . .

Another big change for local stations thinking about satellites came with the development of the Ku-band technology and the satellite ground station on wheels. Station news operations were familiar with an ENG van; it was their basic tool and the way to get to the news within forty or fifty miles of the station. Now here was another vehicle, usually a medium-size truck, that could go virtually anywhere and send back live pictures and sound by satellite within fifteen minutes after it got there.

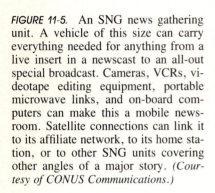

FIGURE 11-5. An SNG news gathering unit. A vehicle of this size can carry everything needed for anything from a live insert in a newscast to an all-out special broadcast. Cameras, VCRs, videotape editing equipment, portable microwave links, and on-board computers can make this a mobile newsroom. Satellite connections can link it to its affiliate network, to its home station, or to other SNG units covering other angles of a major story. *(Courtesy of CONUS Communications.)*

Although the concept is startling, the application of satellite technology to this kind of a setup is not really very complex. The truck carries a dish antenna that unfolds and can be rotated horizontally and tilted vertically by motors. The dish antenna, which ranges in size from 1.8 to 4.5 meters, is driven by a traveling wave tube amplifier system so that it sends a television signal containing pictures and sound to a specific transponder on a specific satellite over the equator.

The truck bed also houses the other transmission and receiving equipment and a place for the crew to work. This can be simple or elaborate, but most carry the controls to line up the dish antenna and power up the transmitter, technical monitoring racks, power generators, levers and handles to put down feet to make the truck level and stable, videotape recording and editing equipment, and an extensive telephone system to provide communications. On top of all that, some trucks are equipped with portable computer terminals, modems, and terrestrial microwave receiving and transmitting equipment.

If that sounds fairly ponderous, it is. One reporter, watching an SNV get ready, said it looked like a giant upright freezer box with a dish antenna that unfolded like a Venus flytrap. But technology is always in transition, and some SNVs are as small as an RV, with equipment in them that can be quickly removed and packed into a twin-engine executive airplane to be reassembled on the ground on arrival.

A satellite live shot is much like a microwave live shot. While the reporter and photojournalist chase the news, technicians get the truck ready to go and line up the signals. Transponder time is sold by the companies that own the satellites. Most news operations using SNG belong to a consortium or network that contracts for transponder time and sells it to the news operations in appropriate time blocks. Or a station can contract for time directly with a satellite time vendor. It is perhaps the least expensive element of SNG operations. Whereas C-band transponder time might have cost eight hundred dollars for a minimum thirty minutes, Ku transponder

FIGURE 11-6. Inside an SNG van. SNG coordinators can receive and send satellite signals, take in video and audio from a number of sources, edit videotape, originate a live broadcast, or feed back on-the-spot material within minutes of arriving at a news story. Communications to coordinate such activities are often just as important as the satellite link itself, so the vans are packed with telephones, two-way radios, and mobile and cellular phones, along with the more exotic satellite gear. *(Courtesy of Centro Corporation.)*

time is sold for seventy-five dollars for five minutes and sometime for as little as eight dollars a minute.

All SNVs must operate through a satellite control center. The engineers, like a ship's captain, first get out their navigation compasses, then maneuver the truck so the dish is facing the equator. The dish is tilted and panned until it is aimed at the specific satellite to be used. A small amount of power is then applied to the antenna, and the SNV operator talks to the satellite control center to complete technical adjustments and full powering procedures. This is the tricky part and engineers are very careful about it. If things aren't done properly, an SNV could hit the wrong transponder and knock someone else—like the entire NBC television network—off the air.

FIGURE 11-7. A smaller version of an SNG van. Getting to the news can be difficult for large semi-trailer–type SNG vehicles. So some stations are equipping themselves with smaller units like this for what they call a "first-strike capability." Some stations also have "flyaway" satellite links that can be dismounted, folded up, and fitted into a small airplane for even faster spot news origination at distant points in their coverage areas. *(Courtesy of Centro Corporation.)*

When the uplink connection is made with the satellite that also establishes the downlink transmission from the satellite. Since the footprint is very wide, that downlink signal is being seen by both the satellite control center and the SNV's home station.

Two-way voice communication between the truck and its station is established either as a signal carried on the band edge of a video transponder or with the use of another transponder dedicated solely to voice circuits. Technical matters completed, the broadcast of pictures and sound from the SNV to the station can begin.

Okay, We're Saturated. . . .

That's what the SNV engineer says to the reporter when he or she's ready to begin a satellite feed. The office cynic might be heard to mumble, "Boy, we sure are. Oh, for the old days."

Not all stations can afford a satellite truck; probably some never will buy one. Yet some predict that between two hundred and two hundred fifty SNVs will be in use by the 1990s, and others think those figures are conservative.

SNVs are expensive. One with all the special communications gear, on-board computers, and other electronic gadgets, can cost close to five hundred thousand dollars. It costs from seventy-five to one hundred thousand dollars a year to maintain it. They are trucks, and all but the smallest ones need ICC licensing. The driver must have a chauffeur's license and follow over-the-road regulations. SNVs don't travel as fast as an ENG van, nor can they go into rough terrain. Repairs of delicate equipment that breaks from being bounced over a corduroy road can run in tens of thousands of dollars. Time on transponders can run from thirty-six to seventy thousand dollars a year or more.

Yet once the initial expense is amortized, most SNG owners say buying a vehicle is a sound investment and that they cannot do without them in a competitive local market. At least one major-market station now has two SNVs. Several stations gave up their helicopters to get SNVs.

It Depends on What You Do With It. . . .

Almost unanimously news directors whose stations own SNVs said they used them to put their newscasts on the road when they first got them. This was akin to the kind of promotional showmanship that accompanied ENG. But most say it didn't last as long, and many felt that there were real benefits to moving their newscasts out of the studio and to the scene of major news from time to time. Many said they continue to use their SNVs to produce live stories about the scenery, culture, and unique areas of their states.

Most everyone agrees that SNV's primary use should be to cover spot news. A Texas news director: "I don't worry so much if the truck sits out back for a day or two, but I do get worried if it gets too far away from the station. We would never hear the end of it if we had another plane crash in Dallas, and the truck was in Amarillo."

In Baton Rouge: "The live truck on the scene is worth everything. Our market research shows that when the big story hits, people turn to us. We had five hurricanes within ninety days of buying that truck, and we covered them all . . . live. . . . The governor was put on trial twice in New Orleans eighty miles away. . . . We covered teachers striking—not here, in the same old place, but in places we'd never have gone to before.''

In Phoenix: ''Spot news is more accessible now; you can focus attention on the place and the story in a more concentrated, attention-getting manner. And you can stay with a story longer, be less hit-and-run, making second-day angles and 'why it happened' a lot clearer.''

In Pittsburgh: ''It has saved us a number of times on spot news stories. Our terrain is hilly. The farther East we get, the more mountainous it becomes and the less effective the microwave [ENG] becomes.''

Using It Well Means Everything. . . .

Perhaps the most intriguing thing about a satellite news system is its power as a production tool. This factor covers the entire spectrum of stories—major spot news, major issue-oriented stories, features, and even minor news events.

Greg James of KSL, Salt Lake City: ''It's in the planning of it. . . . Here's a way to use the truck to do something that would have been very hard for us to do, or impossible for us to do. . . . That's the key factor.''

Baton Rouge news director John Spain says using the satellite system to its full potential is part of a mindset: ''Producers need to think about how it can be used to do things we haven't been able to do before. Like say, the oil economy is bad. Why don't we think about calling our friends and partners, affiliates in Oklahoma, Alaska, and Texas, and see if we can't get the experts or the governors to interact. In the old days, we would say that takes long-range planning, or let a network do it; now we could do that next week.''

Item: A group of CONUS members worked together on a series about the impact of devaluation of the Mexican peso on Sun Belt states. One station went to Mexico City, others to border cities, others covered banking, industry, and commerce in their own area. All fed material to each other. The segments were anchored locally, but the local anchors and reporters were also included in the programs as they appeared elsewhere. From concept to air, the project took about two days.

Item: During the 1986–87 holiday season, a station in Phoenix was faced with Penn State versus Miami in the Fiesta Bowl in Phoenix and Arizona State in the Rose Bowl in Pasadena. So they moved about half of their newscast personnel to California, and did some of their regular newscasts from two locations. During the winter the station exchanged meteorologists with a Minneapolis station because so many Minnesotans go to Arizona during the bad weather.

Item: An Indianapolis station parked its SNV outside the Detroit headquarters where General Motors and Delco union workers were negotiating a new contract— and left it there with a reporter on duty for several days. When a settlement came near newscast deadline, the station had a full live report for its Delco-worker–viewers in a number of Indiana cities.

Item: A Dallas station sent its SNV four hundred miles away to Abilene,

Texas, to cover a high school senior prom. Not a big story? It was the first senior prom in history for Anson High School of Anson, Texas, a town where dancing had never been allowed.

PROBLEMS WITH SNG

Controlling Costs

If there is an SNV owner who doesn't worry about the cost factors in owning one, he or she hasn't been found. Yet it is not so much the initial expense or even the operational costs that matter. As is true of other elements of news coverage, logistics can damage the budget the most.

Transportation, housing, and feeding of staff costs more than transponder time. Special combinations of satellite hookups, ground-based microwave and communications packages can run the bill off the graph. Nobody sends the truck out in the hope it will find some news. Most say they think twice before sending a crew off to Paris because a local person was wounded in a terrorist incident. All agree that except when a disaster strikes, editors and assignment desk personnel must be cost conscious in dealing with SNVs.

But another cost cannot be measured in dollars. SNG use by local stations has raised viewer expectations the same way ENG did. Once the audience learns that a station can use SNG, it assumes this will be done from now on. Nobody wants to figure the cost in station prestige and, ultimately, lost viewers if their expectations for news coverage are not met.

Network-Local Relations

A major impact of SNG has been on the traditional relationships between the commercial networks and their affiliates. In the last few years, it has been popular to talk and write about the ''Death of Network News''

While only the doomsayers think this will happen, things have changed. No longer does the local affiliate have to jump when the network makes demands. Independent SNG systems, such as CONUS, Group W NEWSFEED, CNN, and group co-ops, give the local stations many new avenues and partners to work with. ''Old-boy networks,'' influenced by geography or composed of news directors and managers who know each other from previous jobs, journalism schools, or other professional contacts, have sprung up throughout the country and operate on a daily basis.

This has led to something that almost never happened before satellites: an ABC affiliate sharing material with an NBC member, or a CBS station borrowing something from CNN. Not in the same city, mind you—not that much fraternizing! But the informal networks, the groups, and the independent SNG systems have ABC affiliates in Denver sharing videotape with CBS affiliates in Pittsburgh—or any other kind of cross-affiliation intercourse that you can imagine. And none of those involved are apologizing to anyone, except when, through a mistake or a slip in communication, something someone shipped out to a friend shows up on a rival station in the same market.

All these new venues demand loyalties that siphon off the power of ABC, CBS, and NBC to make their affiliates toe the line. In fact the affiliates have made the demands in the last few years, and the networks have made moves to appease them. The current elaborate satellite-delivered news feeds, network cost sharing on the purchase of SNVs, and increased transponder time availability for affiliates followed heavy pressure from the networks' members.

Some observers of the changing network/local scene think there will be even more changes. They say the affiliates will demand more flexibility by the networks in making transponder time available and less attention to news feeds and other network program services. However it turns out, the networks have begun to see that the SNG arrangements with their affiliates may be the glue that holds the network together.

The Local Look

Greg James thinks that SNG is only the latest development in the electronic news era. And he says it has grown from local stations' willingness to adopt new technology and to experiment with it. Furthermore he says it is a part of what has become ''the local look'' for television news. He says, ''I think the local people have learned a lot from the networks, and the networks have learned from us.'' But ''they have yet to learn something of the flavor of how to do a local newscast.''

James thinks that flavor comes from live coverage, and he credits local news operators with willingness to take risks and perfect their skills so that live coverage is routine. ''The networks are paralyzed by the thought that a live shot will fail, and perhaps the price of failure at the network level is so high it is unthinkable,'' James says. He claims that SNG has simply opened up more possibilities for live shots. It is not unusual to have five to eight live shots in a local dinner-hour newscast any day of the week.

''We don't like to lose a live shot either,'' James says, ''but people watching a breaking story are pretty forgiving if you have a good reputation and are giving it your best try. Your first job is to get the information out. . . . We can worry about making it prettier the next time.''

A regional trend may also be developing in local television news. At least a lot more regional news is becoming available to network affiliates through the satellite-delivered news feeds.

Bob Crawford of WXIA-TV in Atlanta says SNG is helping this trend. ''Atlanta is the Mecca of the South,'' he says. ''It is where Southerners come to make it. So there are a lot of former Mississippians, and Tennesseans, and people from the Carolinas who watch us. And since they are interested in what's going on where they came from, we pay some attention to that.''

Crawford also thinks that the word *South* is an operant word for Atlanta news editors. ''If it happened in the South, or to people who live in the South, then it's more important. That's crowding out coverage of the easy-to-get 'inside baseball' at City Hall or 'pictures of the fat old men in the three-piece suits in the legislature.'''

Crowding on Interstate Skyways

SNG via the Ku technology sprang up very quickly—in about two years beginning in 1984. As the number of SNVs grew and more material was flashing along the uplinks and downlinks, some operational glitches began to develop.

Although a Ku truck can operate independently, it must observe some electronic manners. Satellites are lined up along the equator at 2-degree intervals. Therefore the truck's electronics must be able to operate within that 2-degree spacing. This calls for precision and careful maintenance to keep that precision. The trucks are also supposed to identify themselves in the material they are beaming up. The FCC may take a hand in this and make such requirements a regulation.

A more difficult issue is piracy. Nothing except signal scrambling prevents anyone from grabbing anything out of the air as it comes back down from a satellite. Entertainment channels such as HBO have resorted to scrambling. News people don't really support such scrambling. Yet everyone involved in SNG has a war story about material they developed that showed up on someone else's feed. There is no question that copyright and content-ownership laws apply. Yet the ease the systems bring means it's also easier for some to conduct themselves illegally or unethically.

An SNG Crunch

As the number of SNVs increases, transponder use goes up. Although plenty of transponder space was available most of the time during the mid-1980s, now everyone wants to use the satellites for live feeds during the dinner hour and late news. And if it's a major breaking story, everyone wants to lead with it.

That sometimes means that the users get together to decide a priority order. It often means a great deal of scrambling by assignment desks to book satellite time—most of the vendors sell on a first-come first-served basis—so woe to the station or network that is slow to make a reservation. This also puts a premium on producers to make decisions and satellite coordinators to know how to get the signals from there to here the quickest way possible. Furthermore if a producer can't get a "window" at the top of the program, the story must be produced so that live material can be worked in whenever the window becomes available.

Reporters have had to learn to be even more careful about timing. When the satellite window opens, the reporter has got to be ready; when the window closes, it does so with the finality of a bank vault.

Watch Out for the News Drought

One element of SNG's great flexibility and outreach is frightening: the crunch that can develop almost instantly when even a fairly good story breaks on a slow news day. The stations in the market jump quickly to begin their coverage. And almost as quickly the phone starts to ring with calls from out-of-town stations wanting some coverage.

In the days before SNG, a station could spend a lot of precious time making dubs of videotaped material and getting it to the airport. Now that's been made easier. Stations can simply put their live coverage up on a satellite transponder and let everyone interested know where it is. Or they can edit a package of material and send it up at a certain time.

But the problems multiply when out-of-town stations want to send their own crews and use the local station's SNV to uplink. Or the out-of-town stations want the local station's already stretched-out staff to do feeds, including especially tailored throws to and from the out-of-town anchors.

Finally, we are already seeing indications that news judgments get twisted simply because a live satellite shot is possible. Many SNG news operations report that stories can almost take on a life of their own with SNG. Because the SNV is on the scene, a report will be filed, and another, and another. Pretty soon the truck—not the event it went to cover—is the story, and the technology is running the journalism.

A NEWS FLOOD

A major part of the impact of SNG is the flood of national, international, and regional video stories that flows toward a station affiliated with any of the networks' SNG news-feed services. Each of the three commercial networks offers an extensive daily schedule of feeds beginning in the late morning. ABC calls its service News One (30 member SNVs and projecting 50); NBC, SkyCom (46 affiliate-owned SNVs); and CBS, NewsNet (31 affiliates). The Cable News Network (CNN) also maintains slightly more informal affiliate relationships with a number of stations to exchange stories on a daily basis.

Each of these systems uses satellite uplinks and downlinks to move the material along electronic highways connecting the stations with the satellite control centers and the videotape delivery hubs. ABC, CBS, and NBC provide a national feed, which everyone can get, and as many as four regional feeds, which affiliates can tap into depending on their interests and needs. The station affiliates pay a prorated share of the costs.

A lot of material is involved. A one-day sample of just one of the network SNG news feeds showed that 110 individual stories moved on the national regional feeds between 4 and 7:30 P.M. In addition there were twenty-six special feeds—unilateral exchanges—between two stations. And the network fed all affiliates eleven still graphics (photos and drawings) relevant to that day's news that could be keyed into local newscast productions. It also sent ten weather graphics that showed the east, west, national, and Pacific satellite weather maps, plus national maps showing the temperature highs and lows, tomorrow's A.M. and P.M. outlooks, and the path of the jet stream.

The 110 stories contained a wide variety of material. Twenty-six of them involved national and international items: politics from Geneva, South Africa, Japan, and Spain. From Washington: General Maxwell Taylor's funeral, sound bites from congressional hearings, network reporters' packages on Salt II, and the GNP and economic trends. Also included were features about a British couple who had a baby who is a twin to her eighteen-month-old sister because of an in vitro egg implant, and an orangutan foster mother in the L.A. Zoo. The five sports items included baseball action roundups for the American and National leagues, Cards-Cubs action, a hockey roundup, and a tape segment from an Oakland As game in which two As outfielders collided while trying to field a fly ball.

One breaking story came from Bridgeport, Connecticut, where a building being constructed by the "lift slab" technique collapsed, killing a number of workers and injuring many more. The network moved two early stories on this in a regional feed and extended its national feed time to provide seven items totaling more than thirteen minutes' duration, including four live reports from New York City affiliate reporters on the scene—all in time to make it into the 6 P.M. or 7 P.M. local newscasts.

This was just a trickle compared to the regional feeds. The network's affiliate northeast feed provided eleven stories from members in Boston, Philadelphia, Washington, New York, and Buffalo. The midwest feed—coming from St. Louis, Columbus, Cleveland, and Chicago—contained twenty-one stories from network members in those cities and from others in Milwaukee, Eau Claire, and Madison, Wisconsin, Louisville, Kentucky; and Indianapolis, Indiana.

Twenty stories came from the southeast. Like the midwest feed, the southeast feed switched to various locations to deliver the items. Though directed from the network's bureau in Atlanta, the southeast feed also switched to Raleigh to pick up five items from Charlottesville and Durham, North Carolina, and to Birmingham, Alabama, for two stories from the affiliate there. In all, the southeast feed stories came from North and South Carolina, Virginia, Tennessee, Alabama, Georgia, and Florida. A story about the bombing of a van owned by a civil rights activist in Tennessee was picked up by the national feed.

The southwest feed contained sixteen stories, coming from Houston, Dallas, Corpus Christi, Austin, and San Antonio in Texas; Oklahoma City; Little Rock, Arkansas, and Baton Rouge, Louisiana. Some file footage of Dallas Cowboy Larry Bethea, who had committed suicide, was also picked up by the national feed.

Although this satellite news delivery system provided all stations with the Bridgeport building collapse and two other stories from the regional feeds, the overwhelming impression is that the regional feeds are truly regional. They provide area stations with a large number of visual stories that were not available before SNG made it so easy to deliver almost any story to almost anywhere the same day it happens.

Of even more interest were the special feeds—one station to another through the satellite network—and items of special interest. A Charlotte, North Carolina, station used the system to get pictures of the front pages of the *Minneapolis Star-Tribune, Miami Herald,* and *Orlando Sentinel,* apparently to help illustrate a story about new National Basketball Association franchises in Minneapolis, Miami, Orlando, and Charlotte that were announced that day. In fact, that was the most actively pursued story, as an Atlanta station fed reactions of the Atlanta Hawks to the new franchises to a station in Miami, and that Miami station and another in Orlando fed reactions in those cities to a station in Philadelphia.

A number of stations also used the special feed setup to move stories developed by its own staff. The Charlotte station had a reporter in New York looking into basketball franchise angles there. A Lynchburg, Virginia, station got a package from its reporter in Washington, D.C., involving U.S. Senator John Warner and a

Virginia energy project. A west Texas station got its reporter's package from Austin on a bill of special interest to that part of the state. A Philadelphia station got file tape of the Declaration of Independence and Constitution in their display cases at the National Archives. A Kansas station took in file tape of a shooting in an Illinois high school, and a Texas station got tape of a New York miniskirt fashion show. A Casper, Wyoming, station apparently missed the weather graphics the first time they were sent, so they were fed again.

In many instances the news feeds tailor the material to fit the stations' needs. Much of the material is fed as a natural-sound-on-tape or "clean-feed" version. That is, the voice-over of the reporter who originally covered the story is removed, and only the natural (ambient) sound plus the sound from the sound bites and interviews moves along with the pictures. This gives each station a chance to do some editing and write its own narration. On the national feed, many of the world or Washington stories are fed both ways—natural-sound version and with network reporter narration included. All sports action is fed with an instant replay of the key action included in the package.

State by State

Even more localized news exchanges are being tried on a statewide basis. The Carolina News network started in 1983 with microwave interconnection of stations in Charlotte, Greensboro, and Raleigh. That expanded to Wilmington and to Spartansburg, South Carolina.

In Florida at least three satellite-connected news networks have sprouted at one time or another. The Florida News Network, which claims to be the first in the world to use mobile SNG equipment as the basis of its networking, now has eight stations and offers a daily feed plus special events coverage of all kinds.

Mel Martin, news director at WJXT-TV in Jacksonville, one of the Florida News Network's founding stations, says that the geography of Florida—the capital in Tallahassee and its largest metropolitan area of Miami some five hundred miles away—may have helped with the success of the cooperative effort.

In the beginning, stations in Miami, Jacksonville, Orlando, and Tallahassee founded the system by using their SNG Ku-band vans to interconnect for an exchange of video stories. Then they opened and staffed a bureau at the state capital so that the Tallahassee station wouldn't have to do all the state government coverage.

Stations along Florida's west and east coasts joined up so that the network is capable of covering virtually the entire state and doing cooperative special-events coverage of things like hurricanes, statewide elections, and events at Cape Canaveral.

It is also cost effective. The stations pay a prorated share of the costs, again depending on market size. The network buys satellite time in bulk through GTE SkyNet. And it uses it for the daily feed and in increments as small as five minutes. Thus a reporter from a Tampa station covering a story in Miami can send a story for the station's noon news for fifteen dollars. In more expensive time slots later in the day, a five-minute window would cost perhaps fifty dollars. But if the story went to seven stations, the cost breaks down to about seven dollars apiece. And that is cheaper than sending a videocassette by express mail.

The development of such a statewide cooperative effort in a highly competitive atmosphere even has a philosophical angle. Martin believes that having a network of eight stations that exchange local news from each community gives the word *local* a new meaning. Martin says his producers have new judgment criteria: "Is it important, is it different, is it local—meaning now, within Florida. . . . Does it relate to a story here . . . is it of value to the viewer to know beyond just the fact that it happened somewhere in Florida? . . . Is there a follow-up here on that particular story?"

Florida News Network director Mike Hurt says Florida cities have a lot of common interest: "In Jacksonville there were problems with harbor development. Tampa had been through the same situation and solved it. Another city was involved with land fill problems. The same kind of problems had cropped up elsewhere. Through the news network, the stations were able to get coverage from each other that gave a much better picture of how others have solved similar problems."

Martin thinks the Florida News Network allows its members to have access to more expert reporters than if each member tried to cover each story alone. Martin says:

> Take the shuttle disaster. WFTV in Orlando has a reporter, Katherine Smith, who knows everything about it, since she covers the cape full-time. She knows where to go, who to call, and had sources among the engineers that nobody else had. So we got excellent coverage, and we were doing it exactly the opposite of the way the national networks and CONUS do it. Instead of sending an inexperienced reporter down there to front the story from somebody else's SNG truck or relying on a network reporter who also was not covering it daily . . . we had the experienced people. The Florida News Network moved three trucks in and we cooperatively generated twenty or thirty stories out of there.

And Martin says the way SNG Ku-band equipment can reach out can add breadth and depth to a major story like the shuttle explosion for a local station.

> We got together with WBRZ-TV in Baton Rouge, which has great contacts at Martin Marietta, and KSL-TV in Salt Lake City with Morton Thiokol, and WBRC-TV in Huntsville, Alabama, and KTRK-TV in Houston . . . and that same day . . . that afternoon we had many more angles to the story than anyone, including the networks, had ever had before. We all shared each other's expertise. . . . That's vastly different than "Let's all send our anchors to all these places and make it look like we know what's going on."

Most of the time the Florida News Network stations churn away on daily coverage, sharing local stories with each other or using the network to deliver unilateral stories or story angles from one point to another. Again the volume is great. The average exchange on one test week showed about eleven stories a day, sixty-one in a five-day week.

Coopting the Traditional News Systems

Another person who experimented with Ku-band satellite systems was Stanley S.
Hubbard II of St. Paul–Minneapolis Minnesota, owner of KSTP-TV and other communications interests. In June of 1984, Hubbard formed CONUS Communications
and got a group of television stations in other cities to join him in a "confederation"
that would use trucks equipped with Ku-band satellite uplinks and CONUS Master
Control in St. Paul to coordinate live television coverage of news from virtually
anywhere in the United States.

It is a giant commercial microwave system, using satellite transmissions to
do for the whole nation what microwave transmission systems can do for a metropolitan area. To the broadcasters Hubbard's setup looked like an idea whose
time had come. Hubbard put up 85 million dollars to own or lease transponders
on two Ku-band satellites. He also set up the Master Control and a subsidiary
company that manufactured the trucks and equipped them with the satellite
uplinks and TV news production equipment so they became newsrooms on
wheels.

Hubbard even brokered the news product. The functional idea was simplicity
itself. A station bought into the CONUS Co-op and became a limited partner. It
bought a truck—although that is not a requirement for entrée to the club—and
started covering news anywhere it wanted to go. When the station wanted to send
that news back to its home studio, the crew in the truck fired up its satellite uplink
and called CONUS in St. Paul. There CONUS set up time on the transponders,
helped the truck fine-tune its uplink (it takes about thirty seconds), and then sent
the story by way of another transponder back to the home station. If a live report
was wanted, a specific time on the transponders was set, and the reporter did it on
cue, just as if he or she were down at city hall.

Since CONUS was a cooperative and not connected to a commercial network,
all members could share news or have access to any other member's news simply
by recording it or taking it live as it was returned to earth on the downlink. The
independence from network affiliation meant that stations dealt with each other
through CONUS, not through the affiliate relations setup of the network in New
York.

Networks traditionally, and by contract, demanded loyalty from their affiliates.
They were to broadcast the networks' news programs and provide coverage and
facilities in their area if asked. In return the networks provided a news feed of
national and international stories once or twice a day.

CONUS was in business only because it had members, and so a new loyalty
developed—to CONUS first and then perhaps the network. And stations could deal
with anyone they wanted to deal with in another city.

The opportunity to share satellite facilities was intriguing to the CONUS group.
A station in one city could send a reporter to link up with a CONUS member's
truck in another city. A station could ask another member for file tape or to provide
some coverage of an angle to a story the first station was working on. And on a
major story like Hurricane Elena, CONUS members could literally line the shore of
the Gulf of Mexico to share with their viewers pictures of the hurricane as it roared

FIGURE 11-8. The CONUS nerve center. In Minneapolis CONUS employees coordinate satellite feeds from their members all over the country. Coordinators here are the essential link between the SNG van at the news story site and the home station. They help the van operators line up and lock in with the satellite and the home station to get the pictures and sound on time. This control center can handle many stations at one time, but the dinner hour is usually the busiest as stations line up for live shots into their early newscasts. *(Courtesy of CONUS Communications.)*

along and put their meteorologists on the air to talk to each other and to Hurricane Center Director Neil Frank.

Since it started CONUS had grown to nearly eighty station members by the summer of 1988, and Hubbard predicts it will have one hundred stations in the not-too-distant future.

From the beginning it provided a daily news feed made up of stories covered by its members, cooperative stories contributed by ad hoc groups formed to cover regional stories, and from other sources such as WTN, an international coverage service. It has taken a leadership role in developing regional interest. For example, CONUS members cooperated on the series covering the economic impact of the devaluation of the peso. CONUS is quick to jump on a live story and to hook into a member station's live coverage to provide it for all members via satellite. And it routinely provides the facilities for the delivery of thousands of live individual stories—fourteen thousand live shots in the first eighteen months—seven days a week back to the members' home bases.

It is not cheap to be a CONUS member. Stations might pay several thousand dollars a month, depending on market size and how much service they want. And the SNVs are expensive to buy and to maintain. But like the networks and CNN, CONUS is able to buy large blocks of satellite time at discount. Those savings are signficant: CONUS charges about seventy-five dollars for five minutes of satellite time for a regular story feed.

Today CONUS, Tomorrow the World?

As it has grown, CONUS has taken on larger aspirations that reflect the ambitions and inspirations of its owner and the impact of satellite news gathering technology. It has created TV Direct, an additional service, in cooperation with the Associated Press. AP reporters and editors from the wire's broadcast services provide the staff of TV Direct. CONUS provides a full-time truck to deliver stories of general and special interest from Washington. TV Direct also provides live coverage of presidential news conferences; White House, State Department, and Pentagon briefings; and computer-enhanced "videographs." These come from the AP's world-wide still-picture service and include maps, graphs, and concept graphics customized for TV use.

In March of 1987, Conus announced that NHK (Japan Broadcasting Corporation), which owns more than fifty stations in that country, will participate in CONUS. NHK will take the three CONUS daily United States news feeds; live satellite transmissions between CONUS and NHK in Japan will be uplinked and downlinked from a number of American locations.

In the summer of 1987, CONUS announced it had gotten together with a subsidiary of the *Christian Science Monitor* to provide what it called an "international TV news insert service for sale to local stations." The setup will provide excerpts from the "Christian Science Monitor Reports" program, an arrangement whereby local TV reporters and anchors could interview *Christian Science Monitor* correspondents around the world on major stories. The whole thing is delivered by CONUS's satellite system.

Hubbard is evangelistic about his satellite news cooperative. He says his business gives individual stations independence from their network and lets them cover breaking news anywhere in the country. "It has," he says, "returned to local station management the ability to decide how a national story should be covered in order to be most meaningful for the viewers in the local market."

Hubbard likes to talk tough to the commercial networks. He points out that CONUS members now cover more than 50 percent of the national TV audience.

Charles Dutcher III, vice president and general manager of CONUS, takes it even further:

> What the networks used to have was that they were central controller of the wires . . . and everything had to go through those wires. That's absolutely meaningless today. Right now, the way we are hooked up, we have a larger news organization than a network . . . and we have a "network correspondent" in more than fifty cities. Now we can do shots from anywhere in the U.S. and all over the world.

Dutcher's analogy of what organizations like CONUS can do for local television stations must send chills up the spines of network news executives:

> The analogy is the U.S. newspaper. You get all of the news from your local paper: local, state, regional, national, world. Everyday the editors fill up the newspaper with news from all over that they get from their reporters, wire services, special services. That's something that is cost effective and possible to do.

> Suddenly video is going to be just as available as the words and pictures the newspaper editors receive. Television news editors are going to have dishes on their roofs and be able to get video news from anywhere . . . syndicated news services that they can choose from.

Dutcher doesn't think that the local television station is going to get into the national and international news business exclusively. He says:

> The local station is going to keep its main focus on local, but its also going to be able to handle everything that's national or international that is of true significance to the station's marketplace, just like the newspaper does.
>
> If the networks continue with their present programming, they've got twenty-two minutes; the local broadcaster has three, four, five hours a day. He's got the space. . . . It's the same principle as the newspaper. . . . They've got the space.

Group Organizations

Another set of players in the SNG game are group-owned stations. These consist of stations with a common ownership located in markets around the country. One of the most organized is the group of stations owned by the Gannett Company.

This big newspaper chain was very aggressive in the 1980s in developing its broadcast division. It owns stations in Washington, D.C., Minneapolis–St. Paul, Oklahoma City, Denver, Atlanta, Boston, Jacksonville, Greensboro, Austin, and Phoenix. It has established its own Washington-based broadcast bureau and a policy of group loyalty among its station news operations.

Here again, sharing facilities and coverage works as a multiplier. Gannett newspapers have long supported the Gannett News Service (GNS) to cover major stories for its papers and to share stories among its papers. It also has established a broadcast arm of GNS in Washington, D.C., to provide coverage for its stations. That service has expanded to include a number of reporter-photojournalist crews that cover the federal government on a regular basis and that are on call for special assignments. And it includes a flying squad that is ready to go anywhere in the world to provide coverage for the group.

Each of the Gannett-owned stations has an SNV, and since the policy is to share, the group can mount a major effort on a story in a hurry. Some examples:

> On a Jerry Falwell news conference regarding the PTL Club in the spring of 1987, Gannett's Atlanta station provided the SNV and sent its own crew. The group's Washington station sent its own crew, and GNS sent a reporter-cameraperson-producer team to cover for the other six Gannett stations.

> On a massacre at the Edmond, Oklahoma, post office, Gannett's stations in Oklahoma City and Atlanta booked the only C-band uplink available, thus denying satellite service to all three commercial networks until the Gannett station group was finished feeding its material.

> On a plane crash at Milwaukee, quick-moving Gannett desk editors bought up time on the available uplinks and serviced the group members first.

Traditional network affiliate loyalty has been superseded by a loyalty to a closer and more dominant influence: the company that issues the paychecks. But it is also clear that the Gannett stations see their horizons being broadened by satellite technology and the ability to work together on stories of national as well as local interest.

Such group activity blossomed wildly at the 1988 national political conventions in Atlanta and New Orleans. More than 330 television stations sent some of their own staff to cover the convention local angles. Of that number, more than 300 were members of a permanent group, or ad hoc groups formed to share the cost of facilities. And pooling resources was the order of the day. Gannett, Cox Broadcasting, Gillett, and Group W all put together pools of personnel and equipment to service their own stations and added other stations that joined on just for the conventions.

Some interesting and creative pairings resulted. Midwest Communications (whose stations are on Central Time) and King Broadcasting (on Pacific Time) comfortably shared a broadcast booth and a Ku uplink, since their major coverage for their stations back home used windows that came at different times.

Potomac Television, an independent television news, programming, and production company from Washington, D.C., organized what it called the biggest non–network news gathering effort of all time. Stations owned by Scripps-Howard, LIN, Multimedia, Lee, Nationwide, and Hallmark Univision signed up with Potomac to use their production and uplink facilities. Potomac reserved 150 hours of satellite time in advance of the Democratic convention.

AN SNG WATERSHED: THE POPE'S 1987 AMERICAN VISIT

Just as the release of the American hostages held in Iran marks a significant date in the history of ENG, the trip of Pope John Paul II to the United States in the fall of 1987 marks a watershed event in the history of SNG.

For the first time on such a large scale, local television news operations took over from the commercial networks the primary responsibility for continuing coverage of a major running story as the pope moved through nine cities in ten days. While the networks covered the story for their own news programs and provided aid and counsel through their affiliate satellite news systems—NewsNet, Absat, and SkyCom—the major coverage was planned and carried out by local stations and local pools. For the first time it really didn't matter how the national networks covered the story. ENG/SNG technology, network affiliate exchange systems, syndicate co-ops, such as CONUS, and ad-hoc networks made extensive live coverage possible. Satellite transmission of the stories from station reporters and pool pictures from each city made hours of material on the story available to anyone with a downlink. Even if a station was not involved in any of these, the Catholic Church picked up the pool signals and made them available by satellite to anyone who wanted them, free of charge.

Long-Range Planning

It would be expected that the TV stations in the cities the pope was going to visit would plan and carry out extensive coverage. They've done so each time the pontiff has visited the United States. They did it again this time. In Miami, the Carolinas, New Orleans, San Antonio, Phoenix, Los Angeles, Monterey, San Francisco, and Detroit, planning began six and even eight months in advance, usually with the local Catholic diocese.

Stations in Miami, New Orleans, and Los Angeles, which compete intensely every year to provide the "best-most-widest-longest" coverage of football bowl festivals, had blueprints and plans they could dust off and adapt. Yet local pools and production and technical committees worked for months to set up the coverage. The Florida News Network provided SNG vans and personnel. Some Miami stations broadcast as many as sixteen hours of programs about the pope's stay there. WSVN-TV says it produced the most extensive single-story coverage in its history. It used six microwave links and ten live cameras for its own coverage. At one point just staying on the air was a problem as a wild thunderstorm over Miami forced the pope to stop an open-air Mass, and several technicians were slightly injured by a lightning strike.

The New Orleans and Los Angeles stations did fourteen-hour stints, and at the end of the trip, a Detroit station stayed on the air throughout the night the pope stayed in suburban Hamtramck.

For WIS-TV in Columbia, South Carolina, the six hours the pope spent there called for a maximum effort that brought in WBTV, Charlotte, North Carolina, WYFF-TV, Greenville, South Carolina, and WCSC-TV, Charleston, South Carolina to pool people and equipment. The result was live coverage at each local papal stop.

Sharing was the name of the game at most locations. Some of it got pretty complicated: WYOU-TV, Scranton, Pennsylvania, is a CBS affiliate and a member

FIGURE 11-9. When the pope travels, the media are close by. The pontiff travels in a special van dubbed the "Popemobile," which not only provides security and visibility, but also is a mobile studio. It can generate a close-up TV picture of the pope, which is microwaved so that it can be inserted into local broadcasts. *(Reuters/ Bettmann Newsphotos.)*

of CBS's NewsNet. WYOU's satellite truck went to Columbia to serve as the NewsNet facility there. WYOU's anchor, Russ Spencer, went to Miami for the pope's arrival; weekend anchor Beth Powers went to Columbia. Spencer's and Powers' reports with interviews of Scrantonites who were meeting the pope ran live and back-to-back in the station's major newscasts—all accomplished by the satellite set-ups in three different cities.

Other examples:

WOTV (TV) Grand Rapids, Michigan, used its membership in the Michigan News Exchange Cooperative to get help from WDIV-TV Detroit, set up a motor home at the Pontiac Silverdome as an editing base, and used the Group W Satellite truck to get its stories from the papal Mass at the Silverdome back to Grand Rapids.

KIRO-TV, Seattle, Washington, used its network satellite links and cooperative friends in Los Angeles to cover both Masses the pope celebrated while he was in Los Angeles.

Many stations from large, medium, and even small markets sent reporters to cover some or all of the pope's stops. At each point these reporters usually lined up with their network affiliate services to use editing equipment or plug in their own, and to uplink their reports back to the stations. Most affiliates had high praise for the help provided by their networks. CONUS established a special extra-cost papal trip unit, feeding very frequent update reports during most days and providing extra windows for members' coverage and virtually round-the-clock uplinking of the various pool pictures.

Coverage Closeups

WBRZ-TV, Baton Rouge, Louisiana, was a part of the New Orleans pool; it ran more than ten hours of its own broadcasts and fed the ABC-TV and affiliate satellite network all at the same time. It accomplished this with a simple but subtle plan that should be instructive because—despite heavy security around the pope—it used all the advantages of a large high-tech facilities pool while allowing the station to maintain its own identity.

In New Orleans the ground rules worked out by the pool forbade the building of anchor sets along the parade routes and also ruled out microwave or satellite transmissions from any of the event sites. Therefore the pool provided video coverage from ten event locations, while open coverage was allowed from just four spots.

WBRZ-TV set up its satellite truck and cameras across the street from the New Orleans cathedral and then moved to another location for the next day's parades and events. Using an anchor team in the home studio in Baton Rouge, the incoming pool signal, roving camera/reporter teams, and the satellite truck as a remote broadcast point at New Orleans' Jackson Square, the station was able to mix its own coverage with the pool and anchor the whole thing with its own personnel.

Skip Haley, WBRZ-TV's assistant news director, says that it is important to highlight the station's presence in a broadcast that contains a lot of pool material and runs for many hours. He said, ''We concentrated on the people who were there, not so much on the ceremonies that were going on—'Why are you standing here for four hours to see this man who you'll never see again?' We also carried ten hours of the events. It is important that you provide the whole thing, but put your own reportorial stamp on it.''

And they used the station's computer system to manage the coverage. They carved a video editing room from a suite of hotel rooms and wired the computer system back to the station and to the satellite truck. That enabled them to see all scripts from any location, to create scripts and other ''on-air words'' for all on-air staff, and to manage the flow of dozens of videotape packages they created.

Haley says that the broadcast could have been done without SNG, but that it would have been much more expensive, and the station would have been much more limited and inflexible in its coverage. He said: ''The truck probably cost two thousand dollars for a thing like that; hard-wiring the circuits through the telephone company instead of using the satellite would have run it up to between eight and ten thousand dollars just for the lines. And, of course, the pool and our own roving camera/reporter teams gave us a huge amount of interesting program material to choose from.''

In Phoenix, where among other events the pope met with Indian tribal leaders, a lot of advance planning and a history of cooperation among broadcasters seem to have been crucial to what one news director called ''an incredible amount of work, incredibly expensive, and incredibly fun television.''

David Howell, news director of KTSP-TV, said the event was the biggest challenge that any of the local stations had ever faced: ''We couldn't have done it without the pool—we each could not have covered all the elements of the story—and so the pool gave us a chance to go all out together.''

Behind it, however, is an interesting connection to another issue in broadcast news—coverage of courtrooms. Howell explains: ''Arizona is one of the states that has pioneered cameras in the courtroom, so there's this pattern of pooling together to get one camera in a courtroom and share the video.''

Unlike the New Orleans situation, the local arrangements in Phoenix allowed for anchor locations to be established and built along parade routes, and the stations made good use of the press box at Sun Devil Stadium to cover a papal Mass.

Touchdown to Take-off

In Detroit, the pope's last stop, WDIV-TV provided all-out coverage of the visit along with an advance build-up to it that began months before. This included trips by a WDIV-TV documentary team to cover the pope's spring trip to Poland and to the Vatican in Rome to gather other material.

The WDIV-TV executive producer of news specials, Terry Oprea, developed a plan that is unique in its scope, depth, and creativity; it is an excellent example of the way local special-events producers can use satellite technology to expand and innovate elements for a local station broadcast that only networks would have attempted in the past.

''Without the satellites,'' Oprea says, ''we would not have done it. Without satellites we would have had to piggyback on some of the network feeds, and that wouldn't have carried it through. The way we worked—signing up with a bunch of

Group W stations for satellite time—we could get the time at a reasonable cost and when we needed it.''

Oprea also felt the need to work up to the pope's visit over a period of time. He did this for two reasons. First, the audience needed to know much more about the pope; second, the news staff needed to become more familiar with the technology before it launched into heavy use under pressure.

''It was incremental,'' Oprea says. First a trip to the Vatican with eight satellite feeds through NBC's facilities in four days. Then we went to Poland, gathered material for the documentary, and covered the hard news as the pope braced the Polish government over human rights. We were the only crew there when a demonstration became somewhat violent.''

As the pope traveled across the country, a five-person WDIV-TV reporting team followed him. That team fed or went live by satellite fifty-four times in those nine days, providing fresh material for each major newscast and much of the content for nightly fifteen- to thirty-minute news specials that followed the 11 P.M. news. The hour-long documentary, ''The Polish Pope,'' played in prime time three days before the pope's arrival.

Preparations for WDIV-TV's broadcasts while the pope was in Detroit were just as extensive. Other reporter/camera/producer teams prepared more than forty packages for use during that time. Because that included Saturday morning, WDIV-TV even produced a series of packages about the pope that were prepared by children and aimed at the child audience on Saturday morning.

It's safe to say that both WDIV-TV and its audience were ready for the pope. Oprea then hauled out his final touch—the station would stay on all night while the pope slept in Hamtramck, a heavily Catholic suburb. WDIV-TV reporters gave live reports throughout the night as the station repeated some of its earlier coverage of the pope's arrival and its documentary.

The next day the pope met with the people of Hamtramck and with Catholic leaders and lay people, made a speech in Hart Plaza in downtown Detroit, said Mass in the Pontiac Silverdome, and left the United States in mid-evening.

The Detroit pool setup was elaborate. Thirty-five cameras were set up in thirteen different live locations. WDIV-TV helped out in the pool and in addition had six of its own live locations plus a roving ENG van to supplement the live pool coverage and prepackaged material.

Was it a success? Was it wise to devote that much time and so many resources to such an event? Oprea says yes:

> We proved a number of things. First: You can budget for such a series of events; our budget was in six figures, and we came quite close to those numbers.
>
> Second: The audience will be with you and will grow with the extension of your coverage. The ratings showed that at times we doubled the combined ratings of the other stations. The public reaction, based on the mail, was very large and very positive.
>
> Third: We had about two hundred of the WDIV-TV staff of two hundred forty involved in this thing. A lot of our people who don't normally have much contact with the news department—advertising, public relations, promotion, community relations, administrators—were called in to help out with various parts of the preparations. They got caught up in it. . . . There was a very warm feeling throughout the station in the days that followed.

Fourth: Sometimes I think we news people need to think about our own demographics. . . . A number of times I heard, ''People don't care about the pope,'' but 28 percent of the Detroit population is Catholic. . . . And it's clear they care about the pope, and that the non-Catholics in the audience will follow it as a story if you make it interesting and understandable to everyone.

JOHN PREMACK'S GUIDE TO SURVIVAL IN THE SNV JUNGLE

Authors' Note: John Premack's essay on ENG and the photojournalist's work appears earlier in this book. Now technological change has brought SNG into his life. In his world now it is not unusual for a dozen or more SNG vans to be on the scene of a major story. He says: ''These trucks guarantee that no news story is more than a plane ride away. . . . If you're in Boston and the event is in Baltimore, chances are your satellite uplink will be in place before you even pick up the keys to your rental car.'' So we asked him to tell us more about it. Here is ''On the Road with SNG.''

It is one thing to jump in the car and head for an out-of-town assignment at nine o'clock in the morning, secure in the knowledge that your own private uplink and editing suite will also be driven to the story and waiting for you on site no later than two o'clock in the afternoon. Your biggest problem might be deciding where to have lunch and canceling that evening's plans, since your drive home won't begin until after the obligatory live shot.

However, it's something entirely different to arrive at the scene of a major news event in another city and discover that the satellite facilities your station arranged to *borrow* are also being *loaned* to four other stations. The excitement of covering a big story quickly fades when you learn you are scheduled to have only forty minutes to edit your spot, and the meter is already running. And that's just one of the problems you're likely to encounter when you hit the road with a satellite news vehicle (SNV).

The key to successfully dealing with SNVs can be summed up with the two words that are burned into the memory of every kid who ever joined the Boy Scouts: Be prepared! On the basis of personal experience and observations made while working with the second satellite news vehicle in the entire country and covering the pope's 1987 trip around the United States, I can offer a few hints and suggestions to help you earn your merit badge.

There are actually three areas of difficulty that you (and every other itinerant news crew) are likely to experience: communications, editing, and actual transmission.

Communication

When you're on the road out of two-way radio range, it is impossible to stay in touch with your newsroom without a phone. It's hard to work a story without one, too. Fortunately many news operations are beginning to realize that the telephone (especially the cellular telephone) is as important a news gathering tool as the camera and the videotape recorder.

Most SNVs are equipped with at least one *cellphone*. This is fine as long as the story you are covering is located near a population center big enough to support cellular service. Many SNVs also have telephone service by way of their satellite system.

Unfortunately these phones are unfailingly located in the tiny cabin that also houses the editing and transmission systems, which is convenient when there's only one person in the truck. This frequent oversight can create mayhem when six people want to make calls, edit tape, and uplink live shots from the same twenty square feet of floor space.

Even when phones are available, they may be in heavy demand. Don't count on using the only phone in the truck for one of those long story conferences with the producers back home, especially when three other stations are waiting to feed tapes. If you want unlimited access to a telephone, bring your own. A portable cellular phone makes life easier for everyone.

And it doesn't hurt to toss an inexpensive one-piece telephone in your road kit either. With so little room and so much going on in an SNV, visitors may be denied access to one of the phones installed in the cabin simply because it would interfere with an editing or recording session. Connecting your own instrument across the phone line where it connects to the SNV on the outside of the truck allows for unrestrained telephone access.

Editing Problems

While communications problems can usually be resolved, difficulties with editing a video story can seriously imperil the quality of your report. There never seems to be enough time to turn out an elaborate piece when you're on the road, even when you aren't sharing an SNV's editing station.

There is rarely a traffic manager supervising and scheduling the editing sessions in a satellite news vehicle. Visitors have to line up and are at the mercy of the host station.

Since editing in an SNV is so often an act of desperation instead of creativity, one of the first ''Rules of the Road'' is: Don't overshoot. Shooting too much videotape wastes time twice; once when you shoot it and again when you edit it. Keep your interviews brief and to the point. Try to shoot the story in sequence. Keep a running log as you shoot the story so you won't waste time later searching for a particular shot. Every minute saved while editing pays major dividends in improving the quality of your edited spot.

You can get a big head start on editing if you carry a tiny battery-operated monitor, like a Sony Watchman. Most portable video recorders can play back in the field. You'll save a lot of time if you plug an earpiece into the recorder's headphone jack and use the Watchman to screen your tapes before you begin to edit.

Another time saver is recording narration tracks in advance. The well-upholstered interior of an automobile is an excellent place for a reporter to find the isolation and relative silence needed to cut audio tracks. Remember to use a separate videotape for this function so you won't have to shuttle back and forth as you switch between the reporter's voice-over and sound bites from the event.

Remember, too, that many SNVs are staffed by a transmission engineer whose duties do not include editing. You must be prepared to do the editing yourself, possibly on machines that are unlike the ones you are most familiar with. If you want to do more than bang a few sound bites together, you should be prepared to edit early. When time is short, sitting down to an editing session with too much tape, too little preparation, and jumbled, skimpy, unreadable logs is an invitation to disaster.

Being prepared also means packing a few tapes ready for use as edit masters. It's always easier to grab a tape prerecorded with control track than it is to hook up your camera and make one in the field. Always edit onto a twenty-minute cassette instead of the hour-long tape that you use at home. There's a good chance that you'll be expected to feed your edited tape from the portable field recorder. While the smaller cassette can fit into any machine, no one has ever played back a full-size Umatic cassette from the field recorder.

It is important to create a perfect sound mix as you edit. You may be used to riding levels during playback at your station, but satellite time limitations can thwart any chance to refeed a spot just because the sound mix was bad. Feed time can be precious. Make sure it is right the first time.

Another potential problem grows out of the way satellite time is scheduled. Because of cost considerations and limitations on the number of satellite uplinks and transponders available, most stations book satellite time in five-minute increments. These bookings aren't always available at exactly the time you'd like to feed tape or go live. They're often made hours in advance as producers try to anticipate the requirements of the crew in the field and where the story is likely to play in the newscast. Sometimes these preemptory bookings turn out to be strokes of genius, guaranteeing the precious "top of the hour" position for a breaking story. At other times they serve to lock you into a time slot that doesn't coincide with the latest revision of the newscast lineup, or one that requires feeding your editing story earlier than you'd like.

Most stations book two "windows," one for the live shot and an earlier one to feed the edited tape report in advance. While this allows maximum flexibility, some cost conscious stations avoid the prefeed and roll the cut spot from the SNV while on the air. This technique has the added benefit of allowing editing to continue up to the last minute but carries the major risk that if something goes wrong, nothing will get on the air.

One of the tricks to avoiding total disaster when confronted with feed times that don't mesh with your schedule is to feed a back-up open or close which can be edited into your report if it looks like your window is going to slip out of sync with either the beginning or end of the live portion of the report.

Another technique that is helpful when you're editing down to the wire is to edit both picture and audio tracks as the spot is built. Many reporters and editors are more comfortable with the *cut-and-cover* editing technique—laying down the reporter narration and other sound on blank tape and then covering the blank spots with appropriate video B-roll. While this technique assures that the story can be reassembled without major problems before too much time is invested, it doesn't consider the possibility that an editing session could be terminated before the spot is completed. Editing both audio and video as you go guarantees that an editing session that is terminated before the spot is fully edited will at least produce a partially edited story, one that will be airable even if it's incomplete. Stories edited with the cut-and-cover technique will always contain color bars or black holes until the last minute and thus cannot be aired uncompleted.

Transmission Problems

By the time you are ready to do the actual live shot, most of your problems should be behind you. Live broadcasts are actually the easiest part of working with an SNV. Short of technical malfunction, the only thing that is likely to give you trouble is the IFB, the system that delivers cues and off-air audio from your station's control room.

There is nothing more embarrassing than watching an anchor introduce a live report only to have the reporter stand there like a vegetable because he or she has not received a cue and doesn't know if he or she is on the air.

There are two things you can do to avoid this imbroglio if you hit your window and haven't heard word one from the folks back home. The reporter should turn his or her back to the camera while the photographer or field producer tries to reach the control room by phone. (Here's where your cellphone or hand set comes in mighty handy.) Few directors will punch up a shot of a reporter's back, and still fewer will fail to understand the message you are trying to convey. You can try to make a little sign and hold it up to explain the problem—but who has a marking pen and paper when they are needed most?

While some stations will insist on using satellite news vehicles to do the weather forecast from remote locations, the trend is to use SNVs for expanded news coverage—like the pope's trip—both locally and across the nation. Whether you are working out of your own truck one hundred miles from the studio or another station's SNV three times zones away from home, you're more and more likely to be covering an important story.

The responsibility of the crew in the field, photographer and reporter, is to recognize the satellite news vehicle for what it is—a tool, an expensive, high-tech tool—and to use it efficiently and effectively. A little bit of planning and anticipation can go a long way toward mastering this latest approach to electronic news gathering.

MANAGING THE NEW TECHNOLOGY

From the very beginning of this book we have emphasized the need for the human mind, intelligence, judgment, and creativity to be brought to bear on the technology. Nothing in the future of television news is more important than that.

Let's turn then to a discussion of how that can be done from operational, organizational, and philosophical points of view. The first step is to get the operational matters of the daily news function under tighter control.

Computers in the Newsroom

More and more television newsrooms are switching to computerized operations, and it is a certainty that computers will take over many news-management functions in the very near future. It has already happened in the newspaper, magazine, and book publishing fields. Computers are used to create and edit material, set type, lay out pages, and control printing presses. In the print media, computers have resulted in true cost effectiveness. It remains to be seen whether television newsroom computers will have as dramatic a cost-saving impact. Experts say there is no reason they won't. However, the first impact will be to make possible more efficiency and tighter control in the news operation.

The Tale of Two Newsrooms   There is a big difference in the size of newsroom staffs in large and small markets. That is because of overall station budgets and revenues—the cost of operation versus profit bottom line.

At WSET-TV, Lynchburg, Virginia, Rog Wellman is the news director. His Lynchburg staff includes fourteen persons:

1 assignment editor

1 producer, who also is one of the two anchors

1 sports director

1 meteorologist

4 reporters

1 chief photographer

2 photographers

1 part-time photo editor

The station has five full-time stringers, two of whom come in on Sunday night to present the weather and sports segments for those programs.

In addition, WSET-TV has a full-time bureau in Roanoke. That includes a bureau chief, a reporter, and a photojournalist.

This is a total of twenty-three persons to keep track of. The table of organization is direct:

		News Director		
Assignment Editor	Producer	Bureau Chiefs	Chief Photographer	Anchors
Assignments Reporters Interns Trainees	Writing, producing the news	All bureau matters	Equipment, photographers	Air work

It is an easily understood setup that can handle the job of presenting the several thirty-minute WSET-TV daily broadcasts. The work to be done and the number of people to do it are manageable. As in Ann Compton's early experience, a lot of responsibility falls on everyone because everyone is required to do several parts of the news gathering and producing job.

Contrast that with KRON-TV in San Francisco. The KRON staff includes a news director, four associate news directors, a news editor, two ENG/SNG supervisors, seven people who work on the assignment desk, producers for each of the station's newscasts, and two coordinating producers. Other staff members are:

16 editors
8 writers
23 ENG crews totaling 27 persons
An SNG technical crew and vehicle supervisors
32 reporters

In the station's bureaus:

San Jose Bureau: 3 reporters, 4 crews, 1 producer
Sacramento Bureau: 1 reporter, 5 photojournalists, 2 producers
East Bay Bureau: 2 reporters, 1 photojournalist, 1 editor
Washington Bureau: 2 reporters, 3 crews, a bureau chief (two other stations share this bureau)

Including support personnel, four field producers who are assigned full time to the station's "Target 4" investigative unit, and five or six part-time employees, that makes more than 130 people to keep track of.

KRON-TV produces nearly four hours of news daily, and hours of other news-related programs each week. This is by no means the largest television news staff in the country. In even larger cities like Los Angeles and Chicago, let alone New York City, the staff size and work volume are bigger. By their own testimony the KRON-TV news executives found they could not really manage with the more traditional organization and operation that serves Rog Wellman so well.

The most obvious answer is a computer system. It has come to KRON-TV and others, and applications of it are rapidly coming down the line all over the country. No matter what the size and scope of a computer system, all have some basic concepts in common. Learn these and you will no longer be what one producer calls a "techno-peasant."

1. Computers store information
2. Computers recall information
3. Computers can change stored information
4. Computers work quickly and consistently

FIGURE 11-10. Computer terminals have replaced typewriters in the newsroom of WBNS-TV, Columbus, Ohio. This scene is being repeated almost every day around the nation as TV stations adopt another new technology for coverage management, gathering research information from data bases, script writing, and program production management. (*Courtesy of WBNS-TV, Columbus, Ohio.*)

Add one other thing to that list: Computers are run by people. Now you've got all the basics except the difference between "hardware" and "software."

Hardware is the machine itself; software is the computer program that tells the machine what to do. Again, people design and build the machines and write the software programs that run them.

What can computers do for television news operations?

First, computers are a library system that can store and retrieve anything put into them. Further, they can index and organize that material in any way desired.

The Computer As Archive

TV newsrooms have always had serious problems trying to store and then find news material produced earlier. Searching through file drawers full of old scripts and rooms full of videotape is time consuming and frustrating even though that material is carefully indexed. Someone removed the precise script you want and forgot to put it back. The video cassette you want was last seen leaning next to the spare coffeemaker on the top shelf in the control room.

Computer memories and files containing stories indexed by category, date, reporter, and source can spit them back out in seconds. Files of video cassette logs can be used to locate visual material just as quickly. Further, the computers can merge those files and organize them chronologically by subcategories, by key words, or by any other method asked for. Consider the computer, then, as a big file drawer from which things cannot be lost.

Take the library function a step further. Computers can be linked up to bigger computers containing huge databases. They become a source of background information for almost any kind of story at the touch of a few buttons. TV reporters now have a vast new tool for researching needed facts about stories they've been assigned to cover. And the information collected from big databases can be stored in the newsroom computer for reuse.

The Computer As Operations Tool

Using a computer to help the newsroom operate is another application that promises great benefits for content control.

Computers can store all of the wire service high-speed wires for several days. Handling wire copy is a tedious chore. Someone has to read it all. The Teletype machines keep spewing it out. Finding the latest version of a story takes more time. Others need copies of certain stories—sometimes several people at the same time. Stories can get lost or misplaced.

Consider the traditional task of the early morning assignment editor in Montgomery, Alabama, who has to read all of the wire copy from overnight while getting the day's news coverage activity started—laborious and time consuming at a time when time is important.

With a computer, the assignment editor can tell the computer to show him or her every story that has the word *Alabama* in it. The computer searches through the whole wire file in a second or two and presents an index of all those stories on its screen. That list may show that there are two breaking news stories worth covering immediately. The reporters and crews are on their way.

As the work progresses the computer continues to store the wires. Updates can be called up immediately. All of the stories on a given important subject can be routed to another file. That flood of news is now controllable.

Computers can be used to organize and carry out the news coverage plans. The assignment editor can get from the computer the overnight editor's report, the log of what the competition had on its 11 P.M. news, messages about who is available to work, and what equipment is in the repair shop. Before computers appeared, those notes were on pieces of paper that could get lost or buried under a mound of other pieces of paper. Now that information is permanently stored in the computer.

The assignment editor gets to work at his or her terminal. Stories are assigned to reporters and crews with times, locations, and deadlines. More important, the focus of the story, notes on background, expectations, and particular problems can be added. The whole assignment is printed out so there is less confusion about what needs to be done.

There is other information that involves other people in the operation. Will the coverage require a satellite, a microwave setup from a bureau, a live report? All that goes into the computer and can be called up by the technicians who order facilities. Then, they can indicate the technical plans that have been or still have to be made.

These plans can be updated instantly. So the computer serves as a checklist and status report. The computer is also a great bulletin board. Messages can be "mailed" to anyone on the staff who can just ask the terminal for any messages and up they come. The computer doesn't forget to tell someone something important when he or she gets back from lunch.

The Computer As Writing Tool

The computer is a wonderful writing and

text-editing system. Those who have used computers for text writing and editing say that the computer can help us write cleaner copy and write faster.

Take a late-breaking wire story from the AP newspaper wire. If it is going to get on the air it has to be rewritten and put in TV script form. Under pressure it is easy to make a lot of typographical errors on a typewriter. With a computer the cleanly typed words of the basic wire story can be trimmed and rearranged quickly.

Most TV newsroom computers are programmed to show the length of the story in minutes and seconds when it is first called up. Since newspaper wire style calls for the story to be structured in an inverted pyramid—the important points at the beginning, less important details later—the story can be trimmed from the bottom up. Then when it has been cut to about the right size, sentences and paragraphs can be rearranged to make the story clearer to the viewer and easier for the anchor to read. If certain words need emphasis, they can be highlighted on the screen. The computer will underline those words when the script is printed out.

If a sound bite goes with the story, the audio cues can be entered right into the wire copy. If a graphic is needed—say, a lower-third super—the video cue for when that is wanted also goes right in the copy. At the touch of a button the computer will rearrange the story into TV script form. Touching another button prints it out. More time to write and polish could have produced a better story, but the computer has served to "pencil edit" and "cut and paste" the story into usable form.

Many believe that a computer can improve news writing. There is something inhibiting about having to pull a sheet of paper out of a typewriter and start over

FIGURE 11-11. A writer uses a computer terminal to script the introduction to a story. The computer automatically puts the script into the TV format, times the story as it is written, and saves the story for later editing and printout. With the touch of a few keys, insertions, rewordings, and corrections can be made quickly and entire sentences and paragraphs rearranged. *(Courtesy of WBNS-TV, Columbus, Ohio.)*

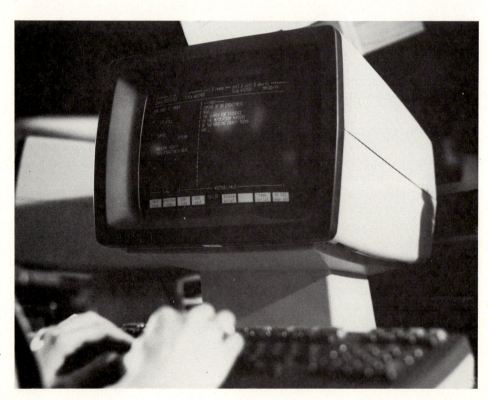

again. Those crumpled-up sheets that miss the wastebasket cause murmurs from your colleagues and frowns from the bosses. Too many times a writer tries to force the words and sentences to have meaning whether they do or not. The result is often a bunch of run-on sentences, fuzzy phrases, and tortured syntax.

With a computer keyboard and terminal a writer can experiment with language, try out structure, work with words. If it doesn't come off the first time, just back up and type right over what you had. The bad stuff goes away, the good stuff is still there. If the structure is wrong, a few key strokes allow you to move words, phrases, paragraphs, and entire copy blocks to a more appropriate place in the story. Unless you miss a typographical error, the copy comes out perfectly clean with no crossed-out words or copy editing symbols to confuse the anchor.

The computer can't make dumb people smart or lazy people work harder. It won't turn you into a Hemingway overnight. On some computer terminals the key you touch when you want to start writing says "create." That should give you a little challenge. Maybe you will even write better.

The Computer As Editor

The computer also works at the other end of the writing effort. It is a superb text editor, something that is badly needed in every newsroom.

Using a typewriter and script forms that are stuck together in four- to six-copy "books," even a story of modest length can run three or four pages. It is a cumbersome pile of paper. Performing major editorial surgery on it results in a lot of scribbles and copy editing marks. Then the whole thing has to be retyped. As deadlines get closer a writer is under strong pressure just to let the problems go and hope the audience can understand what has been written.

With a computer, the stored draft of a story can be called up from the memory so that editors can work it over. A few key strokes pull a buried lead up to where it belongs. Labored sentences can be clarified. New information can be inserted. Facts and figures can be checked and updated without having to retype the whole story.

Sometimes a story is led in a certain way so that it will relate to other stories within a program segment. If the segment is rearranged, that lead may no longer be relevant or provide the planned transition. The offending lead can be changed quickly while the rest of the story remains the same.

Editors no longer wear green eyeshades or work with soft-lead pencils. They do their work looking at a screen and can do it faster and with greater precision.

The Computer As Production Tool

Computers are tireless, unconfusable helpers in the program production process. In the hands of a producer the computer almost becomes an assistant producer.

The producer's rundown—that roadmap used to lay out the order of content for a program—has always been a physical problem. When the producer changes the rundown, copies of the new one must be distributed to all who need to know. But typed or handwritten rundowns never get distributed soon enough, resulting in constant confusion as to which version of the rundown is the current one.

A computerized rundown format lets the producer be flexible and precise at the same time. The rundown in the computer is always the latest one. As the producer changes story order, the computer makes a new rundown. It also automatically moves all of the other production elements such as video cues and graphics. ENG coordinators, directors, and technicians can call up the rundown on their own terminals and instantly determine the effect of the changes on their functions. The computer also serves as a stopwatch, since it automatically times program segments and adjusts the totals as changes are made.

When the time comes to put the script together the producer's rundown serves as a template. The producer simply dumps the rundown into the computer, which sorts the script into its proper order. That action also sends the script to the Tele-PrompTer™ in the studio and the videotape playback order and graphics rundown to the control room.

When the program gets on the air there should be far fewer production errors. Chances are much smaller that last-minute changes that affected the order of the script, videotape playback, or graphic and production effects did not get to the people who needed to know. Misunderstood telephone messages or lost pieces of paper are eliminated.

In the future the computer will be employed to do many more things. The graphics frames contained in the frame storer can be indexed into the computer. This will provide an up-to-the-second list of what graphic frames are available. It will also make it possible to program this list so that any graphic frame can be called up and inserted into a program on cue. Linked to the station's satellite communication system, the computer can communicate printed information to and from the field—times, cues, scripting. It can also be used to provide TelePrompTer™ service at a remote location. In the satellite van, the reporters and field producers can have a terminal just like the one they have back at the newsroom. It will do the same things: link to databases and wires; create scripts, rundowns, and cut sheets; and deliver electronic mail.

Sometime in the future we will probably switch to a digital video system. Instead of electronic signals on videotape, the pictures and sound will be translated into digital information and stored in a minicomputer housed in the camera. When reporters and editors want to look at and edit the raw material gathered at a news event, they will plug the camera computer into the digital editing machines and the digital information will be converted back into pictures and sound. If the pictures and sound are digitized, computer technology could be used to create complete logs and shot lists. Cut sheets could be entered instantly. Editing could be done by telling the computer to edit the raw material according to the cut sheet. The edited version is ready in an instant. Then logs, shot lists, cut sheets, raw material, and edited version could be stored in the memory for later retrieval.

There is also no reason why the computer cannot be used to drive the control-room switcher and all effects. Thus, the director could preprogram all of the camera shots, video and audio commands, and graphics and effects. This would allow more creativity and control for the director and error-free production at airtime.

Finally, the computer serves as an excellent way to review the entire newsgathering and production effort. The assignments can be studied, the script reviewed, the program rundown critiqued.

It is often difficult to pin down just what caused a production or content error. There are too many pieces of paper, starting with the assignment itself and continuing on through the news-gathering, production, and on-air process. Perhaps the trouble started with missing or wrong information in the assignment. Perhaps it came in the writing and editing. Perhaps necessary information was missing in the program and production rundowns.

A computer can't solve problems by itself, but it can quickly bring all of the necessary information together so that the problem can be identified and steps taken to see that it doesn't happen that way again. When the computer is told what those remedial steps are, it can "sense" them and warn its users that they are about to repeat the error.

All of this sounds like a recommendation to turn things over to another technology. In one way it is; in another it is not. ENG and its related technology have pushed the horizon for television journalism much farther away from the newsroom door.

ENG has also made operational things more complex, thus distracting journalists' minds from journalism. Computer technology can help greatly in managing ENG and newsroom operations. That, in turn, should help journalists concentrate on the things they do best: news enterprise, news judgments, and news content that informs, clarifies, and illuminates. Plenty of evidence shows that the audience will respond to that. That's cost effective.

THE STATION AND THE NEWSROOM

Most broadcast stations today are organized about the same way they were fifteen to twenty years ago. They are not very much different from any corporation established to produce and sell a product or service at a profit. They have a production facility and a staff divided into groups by skills. Technicians run and maintain the equipment (as much automation as the unions will allow), and supervisors and managers see that the product is turned out, sold, and delivered on time. Various departments deal with personnel, sales, promotion, buyers of products from other manufacturers (syndicated programming) to fill out the product line, public relations, community relations, and billing and accounting. Add to that a relationship with a network that provides most of the regular programming and a legal department to deal with contracts and federal regulation. Supervising all this is a management structure whose central focus is on making a profit in a very competitive arena.

If that sounds like your average maker of Framistans, wait. A couple of things are different: a government license to operate and journalism—the news and the department that produces it.

These last two elements are related. The station exists only as long as it holds its license from the Federal Communications Commission. The law that provides for licensing of broadcast stations in the United States calls for them to operate "in the public interest, convenience, and necessity." All of those words mean news and information; they add up to the station's reason for being.

Beyond that, local news and information are the only things most stations do every day that distinguishes them from their competitors, other stations, cable, pay cable, and anything else the future may bring.

Yet the economics of broadcasting has unique features. They are different from regular manufacturing economics and different from broadcasters' cousins, newspapers and magazines.

The print media that exist today are confronted with the high costs of the raw materials used in producing newspapers and magazines and very difficult and vastly inflated distribution and delivery costs. So they think as much about controlling their circulation and tailoring it for more specific audiences as they do about expanding it. Each additional copy of their publication created by circulation expansion may cost more, not less, to produce and deliver.

Such unit-cost economics does not apply as fully to broadcasting. Like the newspapers, the news department produces a totally new product built from scratch each day and viable for only a few hours. And the news department is very labor intensive. Putting it another way: The basic costs are just about the same when there is little news as they are when there is a great deal of news.

But, unlike that of newspapers, the distribution system costs the same no matter what you are broadcasting. Light news day, heavy news day, big audience or small, it costs just as much to produce and deliver a news program (or any program) that everybody watches as it does to produce a newscast that nobody watches. And as you improve your unique, short-lived product—the news program—by the use of new technology and more creative work, you will attract a larger audience and sell more advertising at higher prices. Economy of scale tells us that you can then expand the amount of air time devoted to news to earn even more money.

New Newsroom Organizational Ideas

It is time to look at the newsroom organization to see how it can be improved to bring about product improvement while bringing greater control to the technology that improves it. We have already made it clear that ENG/SNG has had a big impact on the news and the people who produce it. The organizational changes in newsroom operational structure needed to cope with that impact have been slower to appear.

TV newsrooms historically have been understaffed at the news management level. Old-time news directors often tried to run things alone. They dealt mostly with the news-gathering and producing end of the effort rather than the budgeting, personnel, organization, and policy end. The assignment desk was a one-man band. The reporters and crews were pretty much on their own after receiving an assignment and promising to keep in touch in the field. When the news gathering was finished, the same small group got it into shape for the broadcasts.

The easy answer is to hire more people. But where and to do what? More reporters and crews certainly are needed to cover the bigger menu of news opportunities, but the parallel need to bring more people into the management command chain is just as crucial. Seasoned professionals have come up with some ideas about that. These, in turn, should prompt beginners to study how the changes can become career opportunities. Among the new careers are, or will be:

More Assistant News Directors   Ten years ago if a station had one assistant news director you asked about featherbedding. Now often several persons have these jobs, each with specific duties.

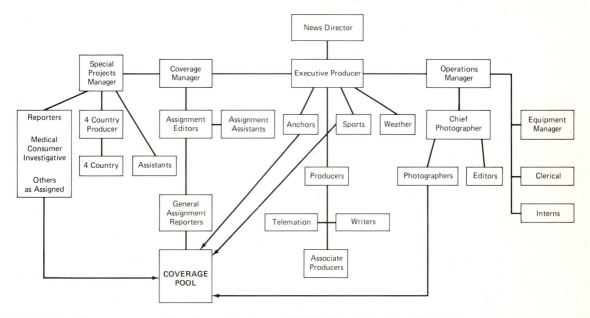

FIGURE 11-12. The newsroom table of organization at KDFW-TV, Dallas–Fort Worth, Texas. News Director Bill Wilson designed this structure to provide a clearer chain of command, better technology management, and better management of the wide variety of news and public affairs programs the station produces. *(Courtesy of KDFW-TV.)*

One may be a business manager and budget supervisor. Another may handle such things as close contact with the newsroom staff, carrying out and enforcing editorial and operational policy. A third may deal solely with liaison with the technical staff. Another may be in charge of the increasingly important nonregular-news production. However the jobs are parceled out, someone near the top-management level is the in-house technical guru. Since there is so much technology to manage it requires people with special technical expertise and a feeling for the journalism to become the systems management leaders Tom Wolzien talked about earlier in this book.

Director of News Operations   Besides assistant news directors, another management staff member may be in charge of the logistics and coordination of the technical functions and the news-gathering functions. That person probably commands the ENG/SNG coordinators and video producers who supervise the minute-by-minute use of technology to bring in and digest news stories.

A news director who developed this system says, "The director of news operations handles before the fact, the producers and editors handle the facts, and the business manager handles after the fact."

Coproducers with Stepped Seniority   This structure is fairly common. One producer is "senior," the other is "associate." The associate producer handles all of the video, scripts, teasers, and bumpers, and also supervises the writing. The senior producer is in charge of the program order, reads the script carefully, edits it, changes it, times it, and makes sure the program gets on and off the air on time.

With these responsibilities clear, the executive producer now has the time to supervise all of this activity. He or she circulates, reads, makes suggestions, talks, cajoles, and orders things done with the focus on quality control and getting everyone to work as a team.

Since the news gathering of most TV stations is only as good as its (1) advance planning and (2) ability to react to a breaking story, there has been much tinkering with assignment-desk operation. Most of this tinkering is aimed at a sharper division of responsibilities.

An Assignment Manager

This person is in charge of day-to-day coverage. Ideas for stories are funneled to him or her from all directions: executives, producers, reporters, and crews. The tactical operations that produce this coverage are the duty of the assignment manager—assigning and placing crews and reporters, moving them to meet new developments, and setting up technical support.

Assignment Editors

Note the word *editors*. It has significance because these people work on both immediate and future coverage, and their thoughts and actions have to be more journalistic than in the past.

Those working on immediate items keep coverage going and get support and information to the reporters and crews in the field. They locate and identify additional sources or new angles and provide close liaison with the technical coordinators.

Those who work on future planning are downstream in the news flow. They identify, consider, and evaluate stories for the following day or days and plan special coverage. As they do this, they identify both tactical and logistical problems—how to cover a story, and who and what to cover it with. They serve as an "early warning system" to identify news that should be covered and how best to do it.

A Los Angeles news director reflected on the importance of assignment planning and coordination in his newsroom:

> In the old days the assignment desk got everyone working as early as possible, and then drove them to get the visual material shot as early as possible.
>
> A lot of assignment desk guys ran it as if they were taxi dispatchers; get everyone where they were supposed to be, and then nag them to go faster.
>
> Now the technology allows you to work later, get later angles and use it to get the material back quickly or go live into the program. That takes a more journalistic person in the slot, and more planning behind it.

News executives say they are fighting a mindset that the traditional assignment system itself seems to generate. A former Los Angeles news director, now in Chicago, says a tyranny is built into the traditional assignment desk operation.

> In Los Angeles we would start out the day with thirty-five to forty-five stories assigned. Up on the wall was a big chart filled with the slug of each story, the crews and reporters assigned, and the time they started to work. Imagine, thirty-five to forty-five stories— because we had a three-hour dinnertime news program to fill.
>
> Well if you take that list seriously you've got yourself on a wheel. It's turning and you can't get off. The hardest thing to do is to break out of that locked-up schedule and

meet the breaking news head on. The list on the wall becomes a work ethic; there are so many chores to perform and they all must get done.

A Boston executive producer called the assignment list ''a security blanket.''

You have to plan to cover the obligatory news—the things that are important that you know are going to happen. You can't just come in in the morning with a happy face and say, ''Gee, I wonder what's going to happen today.'' But we've got to find better ways to break loose from the routine and follow a story to its conclusion. Too many times I hear our desk personnel saying things like ''Yeah, that would be fine, but I've got three other things for you to do then.''

Beefing up the personnel on the assignment desk and setting short-term and long-term responsibilities for them will go a long way toward strengthening their essential function.

Reporter-Writer-Editor Teams In most local TV newsrooms, reporters write the scripts for the stories they cover. Many times they edit them, too, or work with a technician to edit them. Because of the speed and volume of material ENG provides, local news executives are recognizing the need for more journalistic attention to what is said and shown, more editorial control.

Some news operations have reacted by installing writer-editors to work with the reporters on the material they have collected. Writer-editors may be in charge of the actual editing of the material, with the reporter on hand as a team member helping to shape the story into its final form. They often are called on to edit the story from notes dictated by the reporter still in the field. They serve as another pair of journalistic eyes on the production of the story. They ask about missing facts, unclear meaning, or the appropriateness of the visual material and the words that go with it. They help bring focus to the story. They provide another angle of thinking about the news judgment of the reporter, who was there and saw the story develop, and the news judgment of the producers, who have their own notions about how the story should be put together.

Quality Control Most of these organizational changes are aimed at solving the news director's chief editorial concern: content quality control. News directors say that it is the editorial control of the words and pictures that suffers the most and is the biggest problem at a time of day when they have precious little time to make more reasoned judgments.

The producers, who are responsible for the entire program, want to come up with that mix of hard news, features, services, revelations, and illuminations that will be the most appealing and valuable to the audience. They want production elements, a high story count, and a sense of completeness. In Milwaukee, a TV managing editor says:

The system is almost too easy to use, and we've developed some people who are more interested in the TV side of it—the pictures—than they are about the facts, carefully and properly put into perspective. A major problem, because of the speed with which we can work, is that things get on the air before they have been looked at. We often have available more relevant pictures and facts. But we don't have a system that makes sure that someone takes a hard look at how the words and pictures go together and what their combined meaning is.

In Columbus, Ohio, a news director says he is *really* worried about the words. He says:

We've got an awful lot of pretty newscasts in this country, and we have fewer that are informative. I didn't anticipate that when we went into ENG.

He thinks pictures can be addictive.

The staff spends all of its time looking at the pictures—"Let's see what the video has to offer"—and then they start worrying about writing the story. That slows down the whole process . . . and my problem is that I'm afraid we have left out the information in a lot of cases.

My producers keep telling me that we must be competitive with the production smoothness and visual impact of entertainment programs. But I'm worried about what we're saying, not what we're showing. If slickness and flash are the only way to bring the audience to your channel, it isn't going to last. Once you get the viewers there, you've got to make sure they understand it. If you don't, you're not going to keep them very long.

Toward an Information Department

Many competitors and potential competitors fight for television stations' news audiences. Two all-news cable channels are operating twenty-four hours a day. They operate on a rotating schedule that provides for frequent repetition of major news stories. They emphasize spot news and will break into their regular pattern to go live at almost any time. They keep on top of breaking sports stories, the markets, and the weather. They have regional bureaus. To cover other regional stories they have made reciprocal arrangements with stations around the country to provide some of their coverage for the cable service.

Although the all-news cable services are aimed primarily to compete with the national televison networks, local cable channels also carry local news services. Local cable systems are presenting their own highly local news coverage on a daily basis in Jefferson Parish, Louisiana (near New Orleans); Denton, Texas (near Dallas); Naples, Florida; Fort Lee, New Jersey (near New York City and in an area that historically had no local television stations); Fall River, Massachusetts; and other suburban areas. These programs are, like suburban newspapers, aimed at covering the news the big "downtown" media are not covering. In other parts of the country, less formal news programs and special events are presented frequently. Some cable systems that now carry the all-news services will soon start putting local news inserts into special time blocks programmed into the all-news services.

These current developments have come against a background of speculation about the relationship between local television stations and the networks with which they are affiliated. The "worst case" scenarios have it that the traditional American network—with its national and international news, prime-time, and daytime enter-tainment programming—will disappear. People will get their television programs and news through home video centers—from cable, direct home satellite recep-tion—and entertainment from home video recorders and videotapes and disks they will buy or rent.

If the networks did disappear, it would have a very serious effect on the network affiliates. These local stations are, after all, the networks' distribution system and get the majority of their programs from those networks.

The scenario writers say that perhaps someday the only thing a local TV station will broadcast is the local news. The whole station would become one big news-room. Local news then would be almost continuous, or as lengthy as it had to be to cover the news. Or the news would go on whenever there was something to report. Or multiple newscasts and information programs would be aimed at different parts of the station's signal area, and others produced to be fed by cable and satellite to regional areas outside the station's normal range.

News directors and station managers are watching cable and satellite-to-home systems the way the eagles watch the fish from the bird sanctuaries along the Mis-sissippi River and in southern Florida. They have seen some new directions in the way news and informational programming has grown in their own stations.

It is not unusual for major regional stations to produce twenty to twenty-five hours of regular news programs per week. In addition some similar size stations are producing twenty-five to thirty hours a week of informational programming outside of their regular newscast schedule. This may include regular programs aimed at farmers and people living in rural areas. The stations also produce consumer infor-mation, "gripeline" material, public affairs, a magazine program, and sports. A producer from one of these stations said:

> Five years ago we wouldn't have dreamed of doing that much, but ENG (and now satellite news gathering) can help you do it, and do it relatively easily. There is an enormous amount of material out there that needs to be reported on. . . . Some cries for the hard news approach. . . . Other events are not so easy to pin down because you can't put a "this happened today" label on them. Some of it calls for longer, more sensitive treatment; some of it even falls into the soft entertainment sort of thing, but it is all informational.
>
> What we have to do is to begin to erase some of the traditional boundary lines in station organization and to revise our philosophy about what is news, what is entertain-ment, and what is public affairs. Our present organization has different units spread all over the building. . . . Some are in news, some in sports, some in production. All use the same equipment and all produce programs that are news related.

He referred to public affairs as an example. Broadcasters have always had a difficult time defining just what public-affairs programming is and how it differs from news. The broadcasters do know they should do some of it and are happy to brag about it when license-renewal time comes around.

> For years now public affairs has been in the closet. They produced the Saturday after-noon panel show with the minister, the rabbi, the priest, and the black leader sitting around a table in the studio. That was about it.

But ENG has taken public affairs out of the closet and into the neighborhoods and streets where it always should have been.

With ENG they can do about anything they want to do, but it sure looks like more news, and it uses the same technology and resources.

Sports programming has also expanded.

Sports is all over the place. It used to be just the reports in the regular newscasts, or the games, and they had to fight for a camera crew to do interviews. Now they're all over the lot—at the stadium with live reports during the news, or producing specials about games and athletes from the area. They have much more flexibility, and that means more programs, more time, and more people.

What we need to do is form an information department that will stimulate, coordinate, and think of new things to do to meet new audience needs. This department would have overall responsibility for all information and would make sure that this unit and that unit were working in the same general direction.

Such a reorganization would, he said, do two important things. It would be more cost effective. And, it would tear down the walls now preventing creative people from thinking about the broader implications of, and needs for, information and using ENG to provide it.

THE LAST WORDS

. . . Let's thirteen it back to the truck, and two-gig it via Diablo for turnaround and wrap. The Washington site and wrap will be on K-2, Transponder 21.

Translation: Send it to the mobile van using a 13-gigahertz portable microwave transmitter and send it from the truck using the 2-gigahertz "dish" on top of the truck by way of the microwave receiver-transmitter on top of Diablo Mountain to the studio, where it will be edited into a package for the live reporter to include as part of his live report. The material from Washington bureau will be on Transponder 21 of the K-2 satellite.

That's the way news people talk these days in local television newsrooms all over the country as they use ENG and all of its related marvels to gather and report the news. Everyday use of the new technology for local news gathering and broadcast is routine. It makes it possible to reach out farther and think bigger. The helicopter and the regional bureau lengthen the technological arm. The satellite makes the reach even longer.

As broadcast journalists ponder what has happened, one central question stays at the top: How can we use the new technology to do a better job?

Content Power

It is time to begin believing in the power of the content of the news. Television broadcasting is a very trendy business. News appetites get dull, then some development or dramatic event comes along and the audience turns back to the news.

People come along with new formats, new production gimmicks, new "research" about air personalities. "Action News," "Eyewitness News," "Happy Talk" became all the rage because someone tried new formats and had new rating success. So a big part of the industry goes racing off in this or that direction—until someone discovers another idea that gives them quick response in the all-important fall and spring "books."

But we are in a craft that can broadcast live from the moon, replay repeatedly in slow motion the Super Bowl winning touchdown, freeze a face at the moment of victory or defeat, show the exact split second a bullet enters the president's chest. We can use a satellite to follow a story with a local angle anywhere in the world. We can show the audience that there are enough rings around Saturn to name one for each living astronomer. We can show, in color and with fantastic clarity, the shelling of Beirut, or the horror of a bomb blast in a Marine compound, or the ugly dome of a mine bobbing in the Persian Gulf. We can create and animate graphics and effects that can be of real help in explaining even the most complicated concepts.

Clearer policy standards are needed to ensure higher quality of content. The components of content quality are simple:

> the right pictures
> with the right words
> and the right sounds
> at the right time

Then those elements have to be organized—edited, if you will—for the audience so that it can receive the information accurately and clearly. Unless this is done, the most complex and wonderful technology cannot possibly hide the fact that content is disorganized or missing. In fact, sometimes it even emphasizes this.

John Corporon of Independent Television News, a veteran news executive, says that if these standards are not set, he fears bad news will drive out good.

> I mean lesser news, news of less significance and importance—news that may be of less interest, by the way.
>
> When you see a producer trying to lure in more viewers by playing the lesser story over the more significant story—a more interesting story, he thinks, simply because it happened later or has stronger visual values—you can see the problem clearly.
>
> There are some things that are of overriding importance, and it doesn't matter at what time they occur or what raw material you have to work with. If you are trying to give people a rounded picture of what happened in their world today, you can trivialize the whole thing if you ride the technology too far.
>
> It's very slick, it's very late. But where's the analysis on the economy and where are the earlier angles that gave insight, and where's the piece you did about the long-range impact of X?
>
> It's just like your favorite dinner. You've got to have the turkey and the potatoes. You add the piquant touches later. But don't replace the turkey with the sauce.

So let's establish the standards needed to assure that the power of the content will come through as the strongest element of the news program no matter what other elements are included:

Reporting   Reporters, writers, editors, and producers must accept the idea that complete stories are wanted, structured so that the words and pictures work together quickly for the highest possible level of audience understanding.

Editing   Strong editorial control of the processing of raw material must be maintained in order to have coherent stories that contain the right mix of words, pictures, and sounds that in the briefest possible time will present a clear and complete story.

Production   The purpose of the use of production elements is to make the news easier to understand. Rely on production values less for entertainment and more for focusing and highlighting content.

Operation   Operational standards must be aimed at more advance planning of news coverage, supervising it as it takes place and is processed. Most important, more eyes must be focused on and more time spent reviewing and evaluating the quality of the content of the coverage.

We are not talking here just about the times when exhaustive planning, extreme skill, and superb luck have brought the cameras and the people to the epicenter of a major news story. We are talking about a dedication to the idea that the quality of the content of local television news is *the* key factor for success in whatever goals the television newsroom sets for itself.

Appendix A

CODE OF BROADCAST NEWS ETHICS
RADIO-TELEVISION NEWS DIRECTORS ASSOCIATION

The responsibility of radio and television journalists is to gather and report information of importance and interest to the public accurately, honestly and impartially.

The members of the Radio-Television News Directors Association accept these standards and will:

1. Strive to present the source or nature of broadcast news material in a way that is balanced, accurate and fair.
   A. They will evaluate information solely on its merits as news, rejecting sensationalism or misleading emphasis in any form.
   B. They will guard against using audio or video material in a way that deceives the audience.
   C. They will not mislead the public by presenting as spontaneous news any material which is staged or rehearsed.
   D. They will identify people by race, creed, nationality or prior status only when it is relevant.
   E. They will clearly label opinion and commentary.
   F. They will promptly acknowledge and correct errors.
2. Strive to conduct themselves in a manner that protects them from conflicts of interest, real or perceived. They will decline gifts or favors which would influence or appear to influence their judgments.
3. Respect the dignity, privacy and well-being of people with whom they deal.
4. Recognize the need to protect confidential sources. They will promise confidentiality only with the intention of keeping that promise.
5. Respect everyone's right to a fair trial.
6. Broadcast the private transmissions of other broadcasters only with permission.
7. Actively encourage observance of this Code by all journalists, whether members of the Radio-Television News Directors Association or not.

Appendix B

CODE OF ETHICS
NATIONAL PRESS PHOTOGRAPHERS ASSOCIATION

The National Press Photographers Association, a professional society dedicated to the advancement of photojournalism, acknowledges concern and respect for the public's natural-law right to freedom in searching for the truth and the right to be informed truthfully and completely about public events and the world in which we live.

We believe that no report can be complete if it is not possible to enhance and clarify the meaning of words. We believe that pictures, whether used to depict news events as they actually happen, illustrate news that has happened or to help explain anything of public interest, are an indispensable means of keeping people accurately informed; that they help all people, young and old, to better understand any subject in the public domain.

Believing the foregoing we recognize and acknowledge that photojournalists should at all times maintain the highest standards of ethical conduct in serving the public interest. To that end the National Press Photographers Association sets forth the following Code of Ethics which is subscribed to by all of its members:

1. The practice of photojournalism, both as a science and art, is worthy of the very best thought and effort of those who enter into it as a profession.
2. Photojournalism affords an opportunity to serve the public that is equalled by few other vocations and all members of the profession should strive by example and influence to maintain high standards of ethical conduct free of mercenary considerations of any kind.
3. It is the individual responsibility of every photojournalist at all times to strive for pictures that report truthfully, honestly and objectively.
4. Business promotion in its many forms is essential, but untrue statements of any nature are not worthy of a professional photojournalist and we severely condemn any such practice.
5. It is our duty to encourage and assist all members of our profession, individually and collectively, so that the quality of photojournalism may constantly be raised to higher standards.
6. It is the duty of every photojournalist to work to preserve all freedom-of-the-press rights recognized by law and to work to protect and expand freedom-of-access to all sources of news and visual information.
7. Our standards of business dealings, ambitions and relations shall have in them a note of sympathy for our common humanity and shall always require us to take into consideration our highest duties as members of society. In every situation in our business life, in every responsibility that comes before us, our chief thought shall be to fulfill that responsibility and discharge that duty so that when each of us is finished we shall have endeavored to lift the level of human ideals and achievement higher than we found it.
8. No Code of Ethics can prejudge every situation, thus common sense and good judgment are required in applying ethical principles.

Glossary

Acronyms

AAE automatic assemble editing
ABC American Broadcasting Company
AC alternating current
ACEJMC Accrediting Council on Education in Journalism and Mass Communications
ADI Area of Dominant Influence
AEJMC Association for Education in Journalism and Mass Communications
AFTRA American Federation of Television and Radio Artists
AGC automatic gain control
AM amplitude modulation
AP Associated Press
ATR audio tape recorder
AUTO Automatic
AWRT American Women in Radio and Television

BBC British Broadcasting Corporation
BEA Broadcast Education Association
BG background

CART cartridge
CATV Community Antenna Television
CAV component analog video
CBC Canadian Broadcasting Corporation
CBS Columbia Broadcasting System
CCD charge-coupled device
CCTV closed circuit television
CCU camera control unit
CE computer editing
CG character generator
CH channel
CNN Cable News Network
COAX coaxial
COMSAT Communications Satellite Corporation
CPB Corporation for Public Broadcasting
CRT cathode ray tube
C-SPAN Cable-Satellite Public Affairs Network
CT cartridge tape
CU closeup
CVE component video effects

DB decibel
DBS direct broadcast satellite
DVTR digital videotape recorder

ECU extreme closeup. See *XCU*.
EFP electronic field production
EJ electronic journalism
ELS extreme long shot. See *XLS*.
EM electronic mail
ENG electronic news gathering
ENP electronic news processing
ESPN Entertainment and Sports Programming Network
ETV Educational Television
EVF electronic viewfinder

FAA Federal Aviation Authority
FCC Federal Communications Commission
FF fast forward
FM frequency modulation

gHz gigahertz

HDTV high definition television
Hz hertz

IBEW International Brotherhood of Electrical Workers
IFB interrupted foldback; interrupted feedback
INN Independent Network News
INTELSAT International Telecommunications Satellite Organization
INTRO introductory
IPS inches per second
ITNA Independent Television News Association
ITV instructional television

JOB Journal of Broadcasting
JQ Journalism Quarterly

K Kelvin
KHz kilohertz

LAV lavalier
LCD liquid crystal display
LED light-emitting diode
LO local origination
LPTV low-power television
LV laser video
LS long shot

MAN manual
MBS Mutual Broadcasting System
MCU medium closeup
MDS multipoint distribution service
MHz megahertz
MIC microphone
MS medium shot
MSO multiple systems owner (operator)

NAB National Association of Broadcasters
NAEB National Association of Educational Broadcasters
NATSOT natural sound on tape
NBC National Broadcasting Company
NewsNet The daily electronic feeds of syndicated newstape from CBS to its affiliates
NewsOne The daily electronic feeds of syndicated newstape from ABC to its affiliates
NPPA National Press Photographers Association
NPR National Public Radio
NTSC National Television Systems Committee, the U.S. television broadcast standard

OC on camera

PAL phase alternation line, television broadcast standard widely used in Europe
PBS Public Broadcasting Service
PIC still picture
PREAMP preamplifier
PSA public service announcement
PTV Public Television
PUP portable uplink

REC record (verb)
REPRO reproduce
REW rewind
RF radio frequency
RPM revolutions per minute
RTNDA Radio-Television News Directors Association
RTNDF Radio-Television News Directors Foundation

SECAM *sequential couleur à mémoire*, television broadcast standard used in Europe and other parts of the world
SECS seconds
SEG special effects generator
SkyCom The daily electronic feeds of syndicated newstape from NBC to its affiliates
SMATV satellite master antenna television
SMPTE Society of Motion Picture and Television Engineers
SNG satellite newsgathering
SOT sound on tape
SPJ, SDX Society of Professional Journalists, Sigma Delta Chi
STV subscription television
SUPER superimpose

TBC time base corrector
TVRO television receive-only

UHF ultrahigh frequency
UPI United Press International

VCR video cassette recorder
VG videographics
VHF very high frequency
VHS video home system
VO voice-over
VOA Voice of America
VTR videotape recorder
VU volume unit

WB white balance
XCU extreme closeup. See *ECU*.
XLS extreme long shot. See *ELS*.

Terms

A-Roll A separately recorded videocassette containing some of the material (frequently sync-sound portions) to be used when editing various recorded elements into the final (air) version of the story. Also the main edited story, usually containing lip-sync shots.

actuality The voice and remarks of a newsmaker or eyewitness recorded as part of the coverage of a news event. See *sound bite*.

alignment The correct electronic balance of a unit or units of equipment.

ambient sound Sound that surrounds and encompasses the environment of a news scene. Also called "natural sound," "indigenous sound," "background sound," or "wild sound."

amplifier An electronic component to increase a signal's power, current, or voltage without drawing power from the signal.

analog Refers to the direct physical transfer of variables, for example, electrical voltages or shaft rotations. See *digital*.

anchor A major air personality in television newscast.

angle A viewpoint; in videotape recording, it is the location of the camera relative to what is being recorded.

aperture The size of the opening controlling the amount of light passing through a lens and expressed numerically as an f-stop. See *iris*.

artificial light Light produced by artificial sources such as incandescent, quartz, fluorescent bulbs, etc. Opposite of sunlight, moonlight.

assemble editing The assembling of video and/or audio and including control track onto a blank videocassette.

assignment editor A person who assigns personnel to news coverage, monitors the progress of the coverage, and directs shifting of assignments as a response to the ebb and flow of news events.

audio Sound.

audio mixer A unit for receiving sounds from various sources so that they can be combined and blended into a unified whole.

audio track Those portions of the videotape that store the sound recordings.

automatic gain control An electronic device that automatically regulates the levels of audio and video intensities within prescribed limits.

available light The amount of existing light without additional illumination.

B-Roll Separately recorded video containing some of the material (frequently motion-picture sequences that illustrate sound portions) to be used when editing the various recorded elements into the final (air) version of the story. Also called ''cover material.'' See *A-Roll*.

back light Illumination from behind the object of interest.

background sound See *ambient sound*.

backtiming The precise timing of the final two or three items of a newscast, designed to help the production crew and talent end the newscast on time.

barn door Hinged flaps attached to the housing lighting instrument, allowing some control over where the light will fall.

bearding See *overdeviation*.

beta Home video system; video camera-recording system.

bite See *sound bite*.

blanking The interval during which the electronic scanning beam of the television camera or receiver tube is turned off for return to begin the next scan.

bridge A transition; usually refers to audio material.

bumper A piece of visual material (slide, still frame, etc.), sometimes with accompanying bumper music, inserted at the end of one newscast segment to allow for a smooth transition to another segment or commercial break.

burst A portion of the synchronizing signal that includes a timing reference for the color sub carrier. The color sub carrier is that portion of the video signal which carries the color information. It is called a burst because it occurs for only a short amount of time as it is inserted at the beginning of each TV line.

capstan An electrically driven roller that rotates and transports the videotape moving past it at a precise and fixed speed.

capstan servo A videotape editing deck feature that automatically controls tape transport speed.

cassette An enclosed container with two reels, one holding a supply of audio tape or videotape and the other acting as a takeup. The container is designed to be inserted directly into a record or playback machine, thus eliminating the need for hand threading.

C-band A section of the electromagnetic spectrum between 3.7 and 4.2 gigahertz assigned for United States satellite use.

cellular telephone A mobile radio-telephone service. Also called *cellphone*.

character generator An electronic device to create words or graphics that may then be electronically inserted into a television picture.

chroma The purity of a color, determined by its degree of freedom from white or gray.

Chromakey™ The electronic combining of two video sources into a composite picture, creating the illusion that the two sources are physically together. A matting technique whereby all of a primary color (usually blue or green so as to not affect flesh tones) is removed from the foreground scene and a background scene substituted. **Key** utilizes black in the same way that Chromakey uses a primary color.

closeup A picture showing the object of interest in detail, with little or no setting surrounding the object.

cold Refers to a presentation without the benefit of rehearsal or preparation.

communication satellite A satellite containing receiver-transmitters that can receive signals from the earth and then retransmit them back to earth.

compression Electronic reduction of audio and video signal levels to prevent distortion.

condenser microphone A very high quality but also extremely delicate microphone; it uses its own battery power supply.

contrast ratio A comparison of the difference between the brightest and the darkest areas of a scene.

control track That portion of the videotape containing the electromagnetic information required for synchronization of elements in playback.

copy A piece of paper on which a news story is typed.

cover shot Sometimes referred to as a ''protection'' shot, meaning an extra shot recorded by the photographer just in case it wasn't done right the first time. The term ''cover'' is also used by some people as a synonym for establishing shot. See *establishing shot*.

crosstalk Unwanted signal interference; leakage of one signal into another. Also used by some to indicate questions and answers between an anchor and a reporter in the field.

cue Notification to take (or cease) action; an alerting mechanism for smooth collaboration in production.

cut sheet A list of those scenes selected from videotaped material that will be edited into the final (air) version of the story.

cutaway A shot that looks away from the central action being shown and into the periphery or immediate vicinity of the action. See *reaction shot*.

cut-in A shot that looks in (tightly) to the central action being shown, to show fine detail and exclude everything else surrounding that detail. See *insert*.

decibel A unit of measurement of the loudness of a sound.

definition The clarity of the detail of a television picture.

depth of field The distance (from near to far) within which all objects are in focus. The smaller the lens opening, the greater the size of the depth of field. The shorter the focal length, the longer the depth of field.

dichroic filter A filter that allows only certain light wavelengths to pass through it.

digital Refers to transfer of variables—such as electrical voltages—into discrete numerical units, which allows for the electronic processing of that information with fidelity. See *analog*.

direct narrative A voice-over scripting technique in which the text is related directly to the pictures. See also *keying* and *indirect narrative*.

directional microphone A microphone which picks up sound from only one direction or area.

director The person who commands the studio and control room personnel during the airing of the newscast.

dissolve The coordinated fading out of one picture from the screen and the fading in of another picture.

dope sheet When prepared by the assignment editor, it is background information on the assignment; when prepared by the photographer or reporter, it is information from the assignment or about the coverage.

down time A period of time when equipment is not in use, usually meant to refer to broken or malfunctioning equipment on the "to be repaired" list.

downlink A ground receiver that receives signals transmitted from a satellite.

dropout Loss of picture signal.

drum servo The part of a videotape recorder that automatically controls the speed of rotation of the head drums.

dub A duplicate copy of a videotape; also, to add audio track to the videotape by editing.

dynamic microphone Of somewhat lower quality than the condenser type, but considerably more rugged and durable; it is a widely used general-purpose microphone in television news work.

editing The process of selecting portions of picture and sound recordings, including their timing and sequence, and the piecing together of these elements into a finished news story.

establishing shot A segment designed to orient the viewer by showing the story's location or time, or the surroundings within which the story happened or is happening. See *cover shot*.

eyewash File (library) videotape of generic shots, pictures that can be used to cover a current news story, as for example, supermarket aisles (to go with a food costs story), grain being stored at an elevator, loaded at dockside (to go with a commodities exports story), etc.

fade A graduated change in picture or sound; or a gradual fade-out or fade-in at the beginning or end of a scene, segment, or program.

field The scanning lines in one-half of one video frame. These scanning lines create the video picture in that frame by converting light values into electronic values one line at a time. In the U.S. video system (NTSC) there are 525 scanning lines in each frame. Each of the two fields in that frame creates 262.5 of those scanning lines. In videotape recording, each of the two recording heads on the head drum lays down one field alternately across the frame to create a picture meeting the 525 line standard.

fill light Additional illumination to soften shadows.

filler Extra programming material, for example, news copy, used for flexibility in timing; if time permits, the copy is presented; if time is short it is not. Also called "pad copy."

flat angle Refers to a shot made head on at eye level.

flood light General or overall illumination.

floor director The person in charge of television studio floor activity who is linked by headset to the director in the control room and who executes the director's orders. In smaller television station operations the duties may be performed by a studio camera operator.

fluorescent light A tubular electronic discharge lamp in which light is produced by the glowing of the phosphorus coating the inside of the tube.

footprint That portion of the earth's surface covered by the retransmitted signal from a communications satellite.

format A term used widely in broadcasting to indicate some sort of constant. "Program format" refers to the production's framework as distinct from its content; a videotape recorder's "format" refers to the size of the videotape it uses, for example, quarter-inch, half-inch, etc. "Format" can also refer to an electronic system, e.g., beta, VHS, M, etc.

frame The smallest unit of videotape picture measurement.

from the top Refers to doing something over from the beginning.

futures book A file of upcoming news events.

gaffer An electrician.

gaffer tape A heavy-duty press-apply adhesive tape used to hold lighting and other electrical gear in place temporarily.

gain In audio, the amplification (apparent loudness); in video, the contrast ratio.

generation The number of duplications (dubs) away from an original videotape recording. The "first generation" is the original; a "second generation" is a duplicate of the original; a "third generation" is a duplicate of the second generation, etc. Some signal quality is lost with each succeeding generation.

geostationary satellite A satellite in orbit about 22,300 miles above earth, positioned along earth's equator, moving in the direction of and at the same speed as the earth's rotation; in effect, the satellite remains stationary relative to the earth.

glitch Technically, a kind of picture distortion, but also used casually to indicate something that went wrong with the production.

happy talk Banter between or among anchors during a newscast.

hard copy Typewritten copy printed on paper. Also, the original copy in a multi-copy set.

helical scan A term to describe a process of recording visual information on a videotape. As the videotape moves horizontally, the recording head crosses it diagonally. Signal information is recorded in these parallel, slanted lines, the three-dimensional effect of which would be a helixlike spiral.

hertz Unit measure of cycles per second.

hi mom Photographer's reference to people who, when aware that the camera is aimed at them, wave energetically or make rude gestures.

high angle Refers to a shot looking down on the action below.

hot Refers to an area with too much light. Also used to describe something that is turned on, as in "hot mike." See *live*.

incandescent light A lamp that emits light due to the glowing of a heated material as a filament.

indigenous sound See *ambient sound*.

indirect narrative A voice-over scripting technique in which the text is not directly related to the pictures being watched while the narration is being delivered. See *direct narrative*.

insert A synonym for *cut-in*.

insert editing The inserting of new video and/or audio onto a videotape that already has control track recorded on it.

into frame, out-of-frame With tape rolling and camera stationary, subject of interest (a) enters picture and is centered to become the visual center of attention, or (b) moves from the visual center and departs the frame.

iris The adjustable component of a camera lens system that allows for the control of the amount of light passing through the lens.

jitter Picture instability in VTR playback.

jump cut Adjoining scenes of the same size and angle that do not match; the jump cut occurs at the point where the scenes join and shows an unnatural jump in the action, thus interrupting the flow of the visual story line.

Kelvin A unit of the measurement of the color temperature of a lighting source.

key See *Chromakey*.

key light A focused light aimed directly at the object of interest; the main source of illumination.

keying A voice-over scripting technique in which text is correlated with the visual so that certain words or phrases are delivered at key locations in the picture story, for example, a name identification delivered at about the time the face of the person appears on the screen. See *direct narrative*.

Ku-band Similar to C-band, but in the 11.7–12.7 gHz portion of the electromagnetic spectrum.

lavalier microphone A small, unobtrusive microphone; may be worn around the neck with a neckstrap much like a necklace; smaller and miniature models may be clipped to a lapel or similar part of a garment in the chest area, with good pick-up results.

lead (pronounced LEED) Normally considered to be the first sentence or paragraph of a news story.

lead-in That part of the story text that introduces a sound bite.

library Filed footage from prior news coverage.

line-up A listing in chronological order of each item in a newscast and including various pieces of production information; also, variously, the "rundown."

lip flap Occurs when a speaker's lips are shown moving but out of synchronization with the sound track. In videotape the speaker's lips move but no sound is heard.

lip sync The situation in which lip movement matches the sound track of the words being spoken.

live A broadcasting term that is used with a variety of meanings. A camera or microphone that is turned on is said to be "live." Programming that is not recorded is "live." The term may also be used to describe the acoustical properties of a studio.

long shot A shot taken from a distance that is sufficient to show the object of interest and at least some of its setting.

low angle Refers to a shot looking up to the action above.

lower thirds Graphics that use the bottom portion of the television picture to add information to the picture, for example, captions, identifications, etc.

medium shot A shot showing a view of the object of interest that is somewhere between a long shot and a closeup; a "medium medium" is thought of by some photographers as a top-to-bottom shot, for example, a building framed from ground level to the roof or a person shown head to foot.

minicam A video camera much smaller than a studio model, thus much lighter and portable; used for news gathering in the field.

montage An editing technique in which a number of scenes of very short duration (a second or less) are edited together for a "rapid-succession" visual effect.

mooz Describes the action of zooming out from a closeup view to a medium- or long-shot view. See *zoom*.

natural light Sunlight, moonlight, or light filtered by overcast.

neutral density filter A filter that cuts down the amount of light passing through the camera lens without altering any of the other qualities of that light.

nickel-cadmium (Ni-Cad) battery A heavy-duty, multipurpose, portable, rechargeable battery used in the field to power a videotape camera-recorder ensemble.

noise Random, unwanted sound or picture interference; heavy picture noise is called "snow."

outtakes Shots that are edited out of the final (air) videotape of a news story; discarded, unused video scenes.

overdeviation A black fringing effect in an overly bright picture or overly saturated color, caused by an excess of chroma or video level that is too high for the tape to handle. Also called *bearding*.

package A self-contained field report of a news event, complete with its own introduction and conclusion. All the studio anchor has to do is introduce it.

panning The horizontal movement of the camera, left to right, right to left, or both.

parroting Scripting a lead-in to a sound bite in which the lead-in text uses the exact words of the opening of the sound bite; also called "echo effect."

preroll The number of frames between the cue point and the edit point, essential to the synchronization of the VTRs.

producer The person in overall command and with overall responsibility for all elements of an entire newscast.

protection shot See *cover shot.*

pull focus An on-air focusing adjustment technique involving the foreground and background of the scene whereby sharp focus is shifted from one to the other.

quadruplex A videotape recording technique that uses four recording heads.

quick study In theatre, a performer who memorizes lines quickly and effortlessly.

reaction shot A shot showing the facial expression or other actions of a person or persons witnessing a news event. See *cutaway.*

real time Actual elapsed time.

reel-to-reel Refers to a recorder whose supply reel and takeup reel must be inserted and threaded manually.

reproduce To play back recorded material.

reverse shot A shot taken from exactly opposite the previous one; the reverse angle shows a scene "from the other side."

ringing The secondary edge or ghost edge, usually on the right side of objects in the picture, caused by excessive enhancement.

rundown See *line-up.*

running time The interval of time (either estimated or actual) that it takes for material being timed to be completed.

safe area In picture composition, the boundaries set up as a guide so that important action or titles will not be lost in the transmission process.

scene See *shot.*

scene count See *shot list.*

scrim A lighting accessory mounted to reduce the amount of light coming from the unit. A gauze material may be used with a scrim to diffuse the light.

sequence A group of shots in series.

servo system Those components of a videotape editing system that use tracking and sync pulse to regulate tape speed and head drum rotation.

shooting ratio The amount of videotape actually used expressed as a percentage of the amount recorded.

shot The amount of videotape recorded from the instant the camera is triggered to run to the instant it is triggered to stop. Used interchangeably with the terms "scene," "take." Several shots make a sequence.

shot list A chronological list of each shot of raw videotape together with notations of its content, and running time.

shotgun microphone A highly directional microphone that can be aimed directly at a sound source, thus picking up the desired sound at a fairly good distance (up to several hundred feet) while excluding surrounding extraneous noise.

side bar An offshoot of the main story, an oddity, something offbeat, a story within a story.

signal-to-noise ratio The amount of noise as a percentage of the transmission. See *noise.*

slant track Another term for helical scan.

slug One or two words for quick identification of individual news stories; also, more broadly, identifying information put on each news story, such as the date, the newscast the story is for, the writer's name or initials, and the like.

solid-state Refers to electronic equipment in which vacuum tubes are replaced by transistors. For instance, CCDs— silicon chips—are solid-state elements that are replacing picture tubes in ENG cameras.

sound bed Background sound that is loud enough to be barely audible but not so loud as to intrude on the main sound.

sound bite A sound-on-tape statement by a person in the news.

split edit A type of edit whereby either the audio or video of the source is delayed from being edited for a given amount of time.

spot A commercial.

spotlight A lighting unit capable of being focused.

squeeze frame An electronic video effect that begins with a full frame of picture and squeezes it until it occupies only a portion of the screen, with the rest of the screen space being given to other visual material.

standup A reporting technique in which the reporter on the news scene delivers a monologue while facing the camera, either as an opener, or a transition, or a closer, or some combination of these. Also called "standupper."

A variation is the walking standup, in which the reporter walks (usually toward the camera, less frequently away from it) as he or she delivers the monologue; or the reporter may walk at right angles to the camera while the camera moves with the reporter in a trucking movement.

Super Motion A Sony Corporation slow-motion technique achieved by increasing the field rate of the picture from 60 per second to 180.

sync The synchronizing portion of the video signal. It provides a timing system that synchronizes the scanning of all related equipment such as cameras and video monitors.

take See *shot*.

talent Those people who appear before the camera. See *anchor*.

tally light An indicator light, usually red, giving visual confirmation that a camera is "on." The light at the front of the camera alerts the talent, and the light behind the camera (for example, within the viewfinder) alerts the camera operator.

teaser A headline or other brief reference to an upcoming news story, purposely vague and designed to arouse viewer interest and anticipation.

tight shot See *closeup*.

tilt Camera movement in the vertical plane.

transponder The receiver-transmitter device in the satellite that receives signals from the uplink and retransmits them on the downlink.

truck Camera movement that is lateral, at right angles to the scene being shot.

two shot A videotaped scene in which two subjects or objects appear in a closeup together, i.e., two people sitting together, two differently styled clocks arranged side by side on a table, etc.

update New information about a previously reported story.

uplink A ground transmitter that sends signals to a satellite.

voice-over Narration delivered in conjunction with visuals, in which the person delivering the narration is not seen in the picture.

walking standup See *standup*.

wash light A floodlight or spotlight placed so that its light falls on a background to provide separation of the subject from that background.

whisper line A partial line of text.

white balance The adjustment of a camera so that it will reproduce colors accurately in a given lighting condition. Each time the lighting condition changes, the camera must be white balanced again.

wild sound See *ambient sound*.

wind screen A protective foam covering on a microphone to reduce or eliminate the sound of wind rushing over the microphone.

wireless microphone A microphone with a built-in miniature transmitter that can transmit sound to a distant (up to several hundred feet) receiver. (In some models the transmitter is an accompanying unit.)

wrap To end.

wraparound Material such as narration preceding and following an audio or video segment, the former to introduce the segment, the latter to finish it.

zoom Describes the action of moving in from a long-shot view to a closeup view.

Bibliography

This bibliography is designed to be illustrative and thus is indicative only. It is certainly not meant to be either prescriptive or exhaustive. Many of the references are current, but several are historical rather than contemporary. Some references contain material that cuts across the categories used to group the books. The assignment of a book to a given category is in some cases arbitrary. We have purposely excluded material from the periodical literature as well as unpublished works.

General

ABRAMSON, ALBERT. *The History of Television, 1880–1941*. Jefferson, N.C.: McFarland, 1987.

ARCHER, GLEASON L. *History of Radio to 1926*. New York: American Historical Society, 1938. Reprint. New York: Arno Press, 1971.

ARLEN, MICHAEL J. *The Camera Age: Essays on Television*. New York: Farrar Straus & Giroux, 1981.

BARNOUW, ERIK A. *A Tower in Babel: A History of Broadcasting in the United States*. Vol. 1, To 1933. New York: Oxford University Press, 1966.

_____. *The Golden Web: A History of Broadcasting in the United States*. Vol. 2, 1933–53. New York: Oxford University Press, 1970.

_____. *The Image Empire: A History of Broadcasting in the United States*. Vol. 3, 1953–. New York: Oxford University Press, 1970.

_____. *Tube of Plenty: The Evolution of American Television*. New York: Oxford University Press, 1975.

BEVILLE, HUGH MALCOM, JR. *Audience Ratings: Radio, Television and Cable*. Hillsdale, N.J.: Lawrence Erlbaum, 1985.

BLUM, ELEANOR. *Basic Books in the Mass Media*. 2d ed. Urbana: University of Illinois Press, 1980.

BROADCASTING MAGAZINE. *The First Fifty Years of Broadcasting: The Running Story of the Fifth Estate*. Washington, D.C.: Broadcasting Publications, 1982.

_____. *Broadcasting-Cable Yearbook*. Washington, D.C.: Broadcasting Publications (annual).

BROWN, LES. *Les Brown's Encyclopedia of Television*. New York: Zoetrope, 1982.

CHESTER, GIRAUD, et al. *Television and Radio*. 5th ed. Englewood Cliffs, N.J.: Prentice-Hall, 1978.

CROSBY, JOHN. *Out of the Blue*. New York: Simon and Schuster, 1952.

HEAD, SYDNEY W., and STERLING, CHRISTOPHER. *Broadcasting in America: A Survey of Electronic Media*. 5th ed. Boston: Houghton Mifflin, 1986.

HILLIARD, ROBERT L, ed. *Television Broadcasting: An Introduction*. New York: Hastings House, 1978.

LICHTY, LAWRENCE W., and TOPPING, MALACHI C., compilers. *American Broadcasting: A Source Book on the History of Radio and Television*. New York: Hastings House, 1975.

METZ, ROBERT. *CBS: Reflections in a Bloodshot Eye*. New York: Signet, 1976.

NATIONAL ASSOCIATION OF BROADCASTERS. *Broadcasting Bibliography: A Guide to the Literature of Radio and Television*. 2d ed. Washington, D.C.: National Association of Broadcasters, 1984.

PALEY, WILLIAM. *As It Happened: A Memoir*. New York: Doubleday, 1979.

PAPER, LEWIS J. *Empire: William S. Paley and the Making of CBS*. New York: St. Martin's, 1987.

QUINLAN, STERLING. *Inside ABC*. New York: Hastings House, 1979.

SMITH, F. LESLIE. *Perspectives on Radio and Television: Telecommunications in the United States*. 2d ed. New York: Harper & Row, 1985.

STERLING, CHRISTOPHER H., and KITTROSS, JOHN M. *Stay Tuned: A Concise History of American Broadcasting*. Belmont, Calif.: Wadsworth, 1978.

STERLING, CHRISTOPHER. *A Guide to Trends in Broadcasting and Newer Technologies 1920–1983*. New York: Praeger, 1984.

STEVENS, JOHN, and PORTER, WILLIAM. *The Rest of the Elephant: Perspectives on the Mass Media*. Englewood Cliffs, N.J.: Prentice-Hall, 1973.

Media Law

ASHLEY, PAUL. *Say It Safely: Legal Limits in Publishing, Radio and Television*. 5th ed. Seattle: University of Washington Press, 1976.

ASHMORE, HARRY S. *Fear in the Air: Broadcasting and the First Amendment, The Anatomy of Constitutional Crisis*. New York: Norton, 1973.

BERGER, FRED R. *Freedom of Expression*. Belmont, Calif.: Wadsworth, 1980.

BITTNER, JOHN R. *Broadcast Law and Regulation*. Englewood Cliffs, N.J.: Prentice-Hall, 1982.

BROADCASTING MAGAZINE. *The Decline and Fall of the Fairness Doctrine*. Washington, D.C.: Broadcasting Publications, 1987.

COLE, BARRY, and OETTINGER, MAL. *Reluctant Regulators: The FCC and the Broadcast Audience*. Rev. ed. Reading, Mass.: Addison-Wesley, 1978.

COOPER, LOUIS F., and EMERITZ, ROBERT E., preparers. *Desk Guide to the Fairness Doctrine*. Bethesda, Md.: Pike & Fisher, 1985.

COWAN, GEOFFREY. *See No Evil: The Backstage Battle Over Sex and Violence in Television*. New York: Simon and Schuster, 1979.

CULLEN, MAURICE R., JR. *Mass Media and the First Amendment: An Introduction to the Issues, Problems, and Practices*. Dubuque, Iowa: William C. Brown, 1981.

DEVOL, KENNETH S., ed. *Mass Media and the Supreme Court: The Legacy of the Warren Years*. 2d ed. New York: Hastings House, 1976.

FRANÇOIS, WILLIAM C. *Mass Media Law and Regulation*. 4th ed. New York: Wiley, 1986.

FRANKLIN, MARC A. *Cases and Materials on Mass Media Law*. 3rd ed. Mineola, N.Y.: Foundation Press, 1986.

FRIENDLY, FRED W. *The Good Guys, the Bad Guys and the First Amendment: Free Speech vs. Fairness in Broadcasting*. New York: Random House, 1981.

_____. *Minnesota Rag: The Dramatic Story of the Landmark Supreme Court Case That Gave New Meaning to Freedom of the Press*. New York: Random House, 1981.

GILLMOR, DONALD M., and BARRON, JEROME A. *Mass Communication Law: Cases and Comment*. 4th ed. St. Paul, Minn.: West, 1984.

GINSBURG, DOUGLAS H., and DIRECTOR, MARK D. *Regulation of Broadcasting: 1983 Supplement*. St. Paul, Minn.: West, 1983.

HEMMER, JOSEPH J., JR. *The Supreme Court and the First Amendment*. New York: Praeger, 1986.

HOLSINGER, RALPH L. *Media Law*. New York: Random House, 1987.

JONES, WILLIAM K. *Cases and Materials on Electronic Mass Media: Radio, Television, and Cable*. 2d ed. Mineola, N.Y.: Foundation Press, 1979.

KAHN, FRANK J., ed. *Documents of American Broadcasting*. 4th ed. Englewood Cliffs, N.J.: Prentice-Hall, 1984.

KRASNOW, ERWIN G., LONGLEY, LAWRENCE D., and TERRY, HERBERT A. *The Politics of Broadcast Regulation*. 3rd ed. New York: St. Martin's, 1982.

_____, and QUALE, JOHN C. *A Candidate's Guide to the Law of Political Broadcasting*. Washington, D.C.: National Association of Broadcasters, 1980.

LAWRENCE, JOHN SHELTON, and TIMBERG, BERNARD. *Fair Use and Free Inquiry: Copyright Law and the News Media*. Norwood, N.J.: Ablex, 1980.

MINOW, NEWTON N. *Equal Time: The Private Broadcaster and the Public Interest*. New York: Atheneum, 1964.

_____, and SLOAN, CLIFFORD M. *For Great Debates: A New Plan for Future Presidential TV Debates*. Twentieth Century Fund Paper. Priority Press, 1987.

MURRAY, JOHN. *The Media Law Dictionary*. Washington, D.C.: University Press of America, 1978.

NELSON, HAROLD L., and TEETER, DWIGHT L., JR. *Law of Mass Communications: Freedom and Control of Print and Broadcast Media*. 5th ed. Mineola, N.Y.: Foundation Press, 1985.

OVERBECK, WAYNE, and PULLEN, RICK D. *Major Principles of Media Law*. 2d ed. New York: Holt, Rinehart and Winston, 1985.

PEMBER, DON R. *Mass Media Law*. 4th ed. Dubuque, Iowa: William C. Brown, 1987.

PERRY, LARRY, et al. *Perry's Broadcast News Handbook*. Oak Ridge, Tenn.: Perry, 1982.

ROWAN, FORD. *Broadcast Fairness: Doctrine, Practice, Prospects*. New York: Longman, 1984.

SANFORD, BRUCE W. *Synopsis of the Law of Libel and the Right of Privacy*. Rev. ed. New York: Newspaper Enterprise, 1986.

SIEBERT, FREDERICK S. *The Rights and Privileges of the Press*. New York: Appleton-Century, 1934.

SIMMONS, STEVEN J. *The Fairness Doctrine and the Media*. Berkeley: University of California Press, 1978.

ZUCKMAN, HARVEY L., and GAYNES, MARTIN J. *Mass Communications Law in a Nutshell*. 2d ed. St. Paul, Minn.: West, 1983.

Journalism Commentary, Analysis, and Method

ALTHIDE, DAVID L. *Creating Reality: How TV News Distorts Events*. Beverly Hills: Sage, 1976.

BARRETT, MARVIN, ed. *The Alfred I. duPont/Columbia University Survey of Broadcast Journalism 1968–69*. New York: Grosset & Dunlap, 1969.

_____, ed. *Year of Challenge, Year of Crisis: The Alfred I. duPont/Columbia. University Survey of Broadcast Journalism, 1969–70*. New York: Grosset & Dunlap, 1970.

_____, ed. *Stage of Siege: The Alfred I. duPont/Columbia University Survey of Broadcast Journalism 1970–71*. New York: Grosset & Dunlap, 1971.

_____, ed. *The Politics of Broadcasting: The Fourth Alfred I. duPont/Columbia University Survey of Broadcast Journalism*. New York: Thomas Y. Crowell, 1973.

_____, ed. *Moments of Truth? The Fifth Alfred I. duPont/Columbia University Survey of Broadcast Journalism*. New York: Thomas Y. Crowell, 1975.

_____, ed. *Rich News, Poor News: The Sixth Alfred I. duPont/Columbia University Survey of Broadcast Journalism*. New York: Thomas Y. Crowell, 1978.

_____, and ZACHARLY SKLAR. *The Eye of the Storm: The Seventh Alfred I. duPont/Columbia University Survey of Broadcast Journalism*. New York: Lippincott & Crowell, 1980.

_____, *Broadcast Journalism, 1979–81: The Eighth Alfred I duPont/Columbia University Survey*. New York: Everett House, Dodd Publishing, 1982.

BOYER, PETER. *Who Killed CBS: The Undoing of America's Number One News Network*. New York: Random House, 1988.

BRINKLEY, DAVID. *Washington Goes to War*. New York: Knopf, 1988.

CRAFT, CHRISTINE. *An Anchorwoman's Story*. Santa Barbara, Calif.: Capra, 1986.

CHANCELLOR, JOHN, and MEARS, WALTER R. *The News Business*. New York: Harper & Row, 1983.

DIAMOND, EDWIN. *Good News, Bad News*. Boston: MIT Press, 1978.

_____. *The Tin Kazoo: TV, Politics, and the News*. Boston: MIT Press, 1975.

DONALDSON, SAM. *Hold On, Mr. President!* New York: Random House, 1987.

EDWARDS, FRANK. *My First 10,000,000 Sponsors*. New York: Ballantine, 1957.

ELLERBEE, LINDA. *And So It Goes: Adventures in Television*. New York: G.P. Putnam, 1986.

EPSTEIN, EDWARD JAY. *News From Nowhere: Television and the News*. New York: Random House, 1974.

FRIENDLY, FRED W. *Due to Circumstances Beyond Our Control*. New York: Random House, 1967.

GANS, HERBERT J. *Deciding What's News*. New York: Pantheon, 1979.

GATES, GARY PAUL. *Air Time: The Inside Story of CBS News*. New York: Harper & Row, 1978.

GELFMAN, JUDITH. *Women in Television News*. New York: Columbia University Press, 1976.

HEWITT, DON. *Minute by Minute*. New York: Random House, 1985.

JOYCE, ED. *Prime Times, Bad Times: A Personal Drama of Network Television*. New York: Doubleday, 1988.

KENDRICK, ALEXANDER. *Prime Time: The Life of Edward R. Murrow*. Boston: Little, Brown, 1979.

KURALT, CHARLES. *On the Road with Charles Kuralt*. New York: G.P. Putnam, 1985.

LEONARD, BILL. *In the Storm of the Eye: A Lifetime at CBS*. New York: G.P. Putnam, 1987.

LOWER, ELMER. *Broadcasting and the 1984 Presidential Election*. Syracuse: Newhouse School, Syracuse University, 1984.

MACNEIL, ROBERT. *The Right Place at the Right Time*. Boston: Little, Brown, 1982.

MADSEN, AXEL. *Sixty Minutes: The Power and the Politics*. New York: Dodd, Mead, 1984.

MATUSOW, BARBARA. *The Evening Stars: The Rise of Network News Anchors*. Boston: Houghton Mifflin, 1983.

McCABE, PETER. *Bad News at Black Rock: The Sell-Out of CBS News*. New York: Arbor House, 1987.

NELSON, LINDSEY. *Hello Everybody, I'm Lindsey Nelson*. New York: William Morrow, 1985.

NEWMAN, EDWIN. *Strictly Speaking*. New York: Warner, 1975.

_____, *A Civil Tongue*. Indianapolis: Bobbs-Merrill, 1976.

PEARCE, ALAN. *NBC News Division and the Economics of Prime Time Access*. New York: Arno, 1979.

POSTMAN, NEIL. *Crazy Talk, Stupid Talk*. New York: Delacorte, 1976.

POWERS, RON. *The Newscasters*. New York: Nordon, 1978.

RATHER, DAN, and HERSKOWITZ, MICKEY. *The Camera Never Blinks*. New York: William Morrow, 1977.

REASONER, HARRY. *Before the Colors Fade*. New York: Knopf, 1981.

ROBINSON, JOHN P., and LEVY, MARK R., with DAVIS, DENNIS K. *The Main Source: Learning from Television News*. Beverly Hills, Calif.: Sage, 1986.

ROONEY, ANDREW A. *Pieces of My Mind*. New York: Atheneum, 1984.

SAVITCH, JESSICA. *Anchor Woman,* New York: G.P. Putnam, 1982.

SCHORR, DANIEL. *Clearing the Air*. Boston: Houghton Mifflin, 1977.

SKORNIA, HARRY J. *Television and the News: A Critical Appraisal*. Palo Alto, Calif.: Pacific, 1968.

SMALL, WILLIAM. *To Kill a Messenger: Television News and the Real World*. New York: Hastings House, 1970.

SPERBER, A.M. *Murrow: His Life and Times*. New York: Bantam, 1987.

STAMBERG, SUSAN. *Every Night at Five*. New York: Pantheon, 1982.

TUCHMAN, GAYE. *Making News: A Study in the Construction of Reality*. New York: Free Press, 1978.

WALLACE, MIKE, and GATES, GARY PAUL. *Close Encounters*. New York: William Morrow, 1984.

WALTERS, BARBARA. *How to Talk with Practically Anybody About Practically Anything*. 2d ed. New York: Doubleday, 1970.

WESTIN, AV. *Newswatch: How TV Decides the News*. New York: Simon and Schuster, 1982.

WOLF, WARNER, and TAAFFE, WILLIAM. *Gimme a Break*. New York: McGraw-Hill, 1983.

WOODRUFF, JUDY, and MAXA, KATHY. *This Is Judy Woodruff at the White House*. Reading, Mass.: Addison-Wesley, 1982.

ZOUSMER, STEVEN. *TV News Off-Camera*. Ann Arbor: The University of Michigan Press, 1987.

Reporting, Writing, Editing, and Interviewing

BIAGI, SHIRLEY. *Interviews That Work: A Practical Guide for Journalists*. Belmont, Calif.: Wadsworth, 1985.

BLISS, EDWARD, JR., and PATTERSON, JOHN M. *Writing for News Broadcast*. 2d ed. New York: Columbia University Press, 1978.

BLOCK, MERVIN. *Writing Broadcast News*. Chicago: Bonus Books, 1987.

BLUEM, A. WILLIAM. *Documentary in American Television: Form, Function, and Method*. New York: Hastings House, 1965.

BRADY, JOHN. *The Craft of Interviewing*. Cincinnati: Writer's Digest, 1976.

BROUSSARD, E. JOSEPH, and HOLGATE, JACK F. *Writing and Reporting Broadcast News*. New York: Macmillan, 1982.

BROWN, DONALD E., and JONES, JOHN P. *Radio and Television News*. New York: Rinehart, 1954.

COLUMBIA BROADCASTING SYSTEM, INC.-CBS NEWS. *Television News Reporting*. New York: McGraw-Hill, 1958.

CHARNLEY, MITCHELL V. *News by Radio*. New York: Macmillan, 1948.

DARY, DAVID. *Television News Handbook*. Blue Ridge Summit, Pa.: TAB, 1971.

FANG, IRVING. *Television News, Radio News*. 4th ed. St. Paul, Minn.: Rada, 1985.

HALL, MARK W. *Broadcast Journalism: An Introduction to News Writing*. 2d ed. New York: Hastings House, 1978.

HOOD, JAMES R., and KALBFELD, BRAD, compilers and editors. *The Associated Press Broadcast News Handbook*. New York: Associated Press, 1982.

HUNTER, JULIUS K., and LYNNE S. GROSS. *Broadcast News: The Inside Out*. St. Louis: Mosby, 1980.

KEIRSTEAD, PHILLIP. *Modern Public Affairs Programming*. Blue Ridge Summit, Pa.: TAB, 1979.

———. ed. *The Complete Guide to Newsroom Computers*. Prairie Village, Kan.: Broadcast Communications Magazine. Globecom Publishing, 1982 (2d ed., 1984).

LEWIS, CAROLYN D. *Reporting for Television*. New York: Columbia University Press, 1984.

MACDONALD, R.H. *A Broadcast News Manual of Style*. White Plains, N.Y.: Longman, 1987.

MAYEUX, PETER E. *Writing for the Broadcast Media*. Boston: Allyn & Bacon, 1985.

MENCHER, MELVIN. *News Reporting and Writing*. 4th ed. Dubuque, Iowa: William C. Broan, 1987.

MERTON, ROBERT K., et al. *The Focused Interview*. Glencoe, Ill.: Free Press, 1956.

RADIO-TELEVISION NEWS DIRECTORS ASSOCIATION and TIME-LIFE. *The Newsroom and the Newscast*. New York: Time-Life Books, 1966.

RIVERS, WILLIAM L. *News Editing in the '80s: Text and Exercises*. Belmont, Calif.: Wadsworth, 1983.

SHERWOOD, HUGH C. *The Journalistic Interview*. 2d ed. New York: Harper & Row, 1978.

SHETTER, MICHAEL D. *Videotape Editing: Communicating with Pictures and Sound*. Elk Grove Village, Ill.: Swiderski Electronics.

SHOOK, FREDERICK, and LATTIMORE, DAN. *The Broadcast News Process*. 3rd ed. Englewood, Conn.: Morton, 1987.

SILLER, ROBERT, WHITE, THEODORE, and TERKEL, HAL. *Television and Radio News*. New York: Macmillan, 1960.

SILLER, ROBERT C. *Guide to Professional Radio and TV Newscasting*. New York: Macmillan, 1972.

SMEYAK, G. PAUL. *Broadcast News Writing*. 2d ed. Columbus, Ohio: Grid, 1983.

STEPHENS, MITCHELL. *Broadcast News* 2d ed. New York: Holt, Rinehart and Winston, 1986.

STRUNK, WILLIAM, and WHITE, E.B. *The Elements of Style*. 3rd ed. New York: Macmillan, 1979.

UPI. *The UPI Broadcast Stylebook: A Handbook for Writing and Preparing Broadcast News*. New York: United Press International, 1979.

WARREN, CARL. *Radio Newswriting and Editing*. New York: Harper Publishing, 1947.

WHITE, PAUL W. *News on the Air*. New York: Harcourt, Brace, 1947.

WHITE, THEODORE, MEPPEN, ADRIAN J, and YOUNG, STEVE. *Broadcast News Writing., Reporting, and Production*. New York: Macmillan, 1984.

WIMER, AUTHUR, and BRIX, DALE. *Workbook for Radio and TV News Editing and Writing*. 5th ed. Dubuque, Iowa, William C. Brown, 1980.

WULFEMEYER, K. TIM. *Beginning Broadcast Newswriting: A Self-instructional Learning Experience*. 2d ed. Ames: Iowa State University Press, 1987.

YOAKAM, RICHARD D. *ENG: Electronic Newsgathering in Local Television*. Research Report No. 12. Bloomington: Indiana University School of Journalism, 1981.

YORKE, IVOR. *The Technique of Television News*. 2d ed. Stoneham, Mass.: Focal Press, 1987.

Motion Pictures

BUDDELEY, WALTER HUGH. *The Technique of Documentary Film Production*. 2d ed. New York: Hastings House, 1969.

CLEMENTS, BEN, and ROSENFELD, DAVID. *Photographic Composition*. Englewood Cliffs, N.J.: Prentice-Hall, 1974.

DONDIS, DONIS A. *A Primer of Visual Literacy*. Boston: MIT Press, 1973.

GASKILL, ARTHUR L., and ENGLANDER, DAVID A. *How to Shoot a Movie and Video Story: The Technique of Pictorial Continuity*. Dobbs Ferry, N.Y.: Morgan & Morgan, 1985.

RADIO-TELEVISION NEWS DIRECTORS ASSOCIATION. *Television Newsfilm Standards Manual*. New York: Time-Life Broadcast, 1964.

———. *Television Newsfilm Content*. New York: Time-Life Broadcast, 1965.

SAMUELSON, DAVID W. *Motion Picture Camera Techniques*. 2d ed. Boston (or Stoneham): Focal Press, 1984.

STONE, VERNON, and HINSON, BRUCE. *Television Newsfilm Techniques*. New York: Hastings House, 1974.

WILLETTE, LEO. *So You're Gonna Shoot Newsfilm*. Ashville, N.C.: Inland Press, 1960.

ZAKIA, RICHARD. *Perception and Photography*. Rochester, N.Y.: Light Impressions, 1979.

Index

About the Authors

Richard D. Yoakam is Professor of Journalism and Telecommunications at Indiana University. He received his B.A. and M.A. in Journalism from the University of Iowa. He began his career in broadcast journalism as a reporter, editor, newscaster, and sports announcer at WHO, Des Moines, Iowa. He was news director at KCRG, KCRG-TV, Cedar Rapids, Iowa. He has been a newscaster, writer, and editor for NBC in Washington and New York City. For twelve years he served as NBC Indiana election manager for primary and general election research and coverage planning. He has also been a news editorial consultant for ABC News.

Professor Yoakam has served as faculty chairman of the National Press Photographers TV News Workshop, and chairman of the NPPA International Flying Shortcourses to Asia and Europe. He is a former chairman of the Accreditation Committee of the American Council for Education in Journalism and Mass Communications.

Professor Yoakam's research on the production of the 1960 Nixon-Kennedy, and 1976 Ford-Carter presidential debates, on broadcast editorializing, and on the news distribution and production practices of European television networks has been published in several books and journals in the United States and abroad.

Charles F. Cremer is Associate Dean and Professor of Journalism, and head of the broadcast news division at West Virginia University. He received his Ph.D. in Mass Communications from the University of Iowa, his M.S. in Journalism from the University of Illinois, and his B.A. in English from Loras College.

Professor Cremer began his journalism career as news editor at WILL, Champaign-Urbana, Illinois. He was news director at WREX-TV, Rockford, Illinois, and WSUI Radio, Iowa City, Iowa. He was later Administrator of News and Public Affairs at WTHI-radio and TV, Terre Haute, Indiana, and has also worked as general assignment reporter for the *Terre Haute Tribune*.

Professor Cremer is a former president of the Wabash Valley Press Club, the Radio-Television Journalism Division of the Association for Education in Journalism and Mass Communications, and a former secretary of the Iowa Broadcast News Association. He also served as an ex-officio member of the RTNDA Board of Directors, and is currently a member of the Board of Trustees of the Radio-Television News Directors Foundation.